Thursday's Lotus

Thursday's Lotus

The Life and Work of Fuengsin Trafford

Paul Trafford

Thursday's Lotus: The Life and Work of Fuengsin Trafford

© Paul Trafford 2016
ptworld.net

Cover design: Chanaphan Rassameepiyarak

ISBN-10: 1523935189
ISBN-13: 978-1523935185

Typeset in Gentium Plus and TH Sarabun New

Printed by CreateSpace

British Library Cataloguing in Publication Data.
A catalogue record for this book is available
from the British Library.

Dedicated to Phramongkolthepmuni (Sodh Candasaro), the late Abbot of
Wat Paknam, who rediscovered the Middle Way meditation
and Vijja Dhammakaya.

Thursday's child has far to go.

Anon. (traditional)

Contents

List of Illustrations

Preface

Whenever Fuengsin met anyone she would have got to know them very quickly — even, perhaps, in the time it takes you to read these opening paragraphs. It would not matter what their background, within a few minutes she would have a fair idea about them as a person, the strength of their character, and what made them tick. Those who knew her were soon left with strong and very distinct impressions, a unique person whose approach to life naturally encompassed East and West, the sacred and the secular. A modern pioneer in many respects, yet deeply rooted in ancient traditions, this was not a person to throw out the baby with the bath water.

So I, as her son, thought it might be of value to write about her life and work, to tell the story of my mother so that others may likewise be inspired by it. This is just a first attempt, an invitation to a multi-threaded journey, where we can learn through one individual how heritage, education, culture, and life's purpose can gel. It is the art of spirituality. All being well, as a reader of this biography you will be able to reflect on *your* family and its special qualities. For Fuengsin would be keen to stress how precious human life is; how each one has potential for Enlightenment, a truly happy state of being.

The nature of the material may be unfamiliar in places, so just a few notes of preparation. This book will weave in some background about Thai people and their land going back centuries, qualities that Fuengsin embodied, which we shall later see echoed in her life. History is marked by dates (those who take the British citizenship exam can testify to this!). Most dates have been given according to the Common Era — CE (or AD) — convention. However, a few are given according to the Thai system, where dates are commonly based on the Buddhist Era (BE), which starts from the Buddha's Enlightenment, traditionally reckoned to be 543 BC. Hence, for example, the year 2501 BE is equivalent to 1958 CE.

One particular issue I've had is how to refer to people as I'm writing this book for audiences with a variety of cultural backgrounds and levels of formality. In the West, modern biographies often adopt consistent use of first name terms, whereas that is considered too familiar in Oriental circles. As a kind of compromise, I try to use the names that befit people at that particular stage in their life — so the reference to someone as a child might be by their given name, whilst later on I would prefix this with their title. I trust this is appropriate. Also, there is quite a lot of terminology relating to Thai culture and Buddhist practice, so I've included a glossary after the chapters.

Acknowledgements

My first acknowledgement is to Fuengsin herself, for her life as a mother and spiritual teacher, generously leading by example in bestowing tangible and intangible legacies. Fuengsin herself would pay tribute to her many teachers, especially in dhammakaya meditation: Luang Phor Sodh Candasaro (Chao Khun Phramongkolthepmuni), Khun Yay Maharattana Upasika Chan Khonnokyoong, Ajahn Gaew Potikanok and Luang Na San Tippasanto. For spiritual guidance in this work I wish to pay tribute to the present day luminaries of this meditation tradition, especially Luang Phor Dhammachayo (Phrathepyanmahamuni), the Abbot of Wat Phra Dhammakaya and Luang Phor Dattajeevo (Phrabhavanaviriyakhun), the Vice-Abbot.

Reflecting the very many people who knew Fuengsin, the list of people to be acknowledged in the preparation and writing of this biography is long and I apologise to anyone who has helped but is not mentioned here. I would like to start by thanking Fuengsin's husband and my father, Tony Trafford, for his patience and forbearance as I probed him with many questions about the past. He has contributed many recollections and been meticulous in checking and correcting historical accounts, helping to improve their accuracy. I would also like to thank other relatives for their support, with contributions from Sean Trafford, Liz and Patrick Baker-Jones and Christopher Thomas, who reassured me that Fuengsin's life was worthy of being told in the West.

In Thailand there are many relatives who have contributed recollections in interviews and informal conversation. Fuengsin's sister, Umpai Sarayutpitag, was instructive as to Fuengsin's early life in Thonburi. Fuengsin's niece, Kumutnart Hormchaem, one of the first relatives to join Fuengsin in meditation at Wat Paknam, has shared some memories and assisted in reading and translating passages from her diary. Worradol Posanacharearn, Fuengsin's nephew, who also went to meditate at Wat Paknam and took temporary ordination there, has shared many insights relating to his practice and the family traditions coming from his assistance of Khun Yay Somboon. I would also like to thank Khun Chaiwat and Yui Peumpoon for their contributions and many other relatives for their kind hospitality whilst I gradually explored my mother's background.

I was fortunate to receive valuable assistance from the Potikanok family, coordinated by Ajahn Gaew's daughter, Khun Darunee; and Khun Goo, who was a monk for several years at Wat Paknam, provided valuable materials relating to his father's work supporting the temple in the 1950s. As Fuengsin's friend since childhood and through university days, Assoc. Prof. Tewee Bodhiphala has shared valuable memories. With regards to Fuengsin's time particularly as a university student, Vasana Kamkoon has made many contributions with further anecdotes from her husband, Khun Jamras.

For translations and especially the more scholarly analysis, I wish to highlight especially the considerable contribution of Mananya Pattamasoontorn, who has enabled so many details to come to light, particularly materials relating to Fuengsin's meditation practice as well as Thai history and culture. I am also grateful to Dr Chanida Jantrasrisalai, who helped identify the contents of the audio recordings with Luang Na San; to Kruawan Sookcharoen, for aspects relating to meditation; and to Dr Wilaiporn Sucharittammakul and Vorakan Thangsurbkul, for additional assistance in my research. I would also like to thank Assistant Prof. Dr Pornapit Darasawang, particularly for her kind assistance regarding the history of KMUTT.

Among Fuengsin's friends who knew her over an extended period in the UK, I offer my respects to Sangha members who supported Fuengsin and offered their recollections, particularly the Venerable (henceforth abbreviated as 'Ven.') Dr Rewata Dhamma, Phra Ajahn Khemadhammo OBE, and Ven. Bodhidhamma. I would also like to acknowledge other teachers and sources of inspiration. I would especially like to thank Jane Browne, who has maintained her unstinting support for the development of Theravada Buddhism in the UK and contributed recollections going back to the mid-1960s. In Birmingham Vajira Bailey and Yann Lovelock took time to share their valuable memories also.

From Fuengsin's career, for recollections at the Institute of Education, I am grateful to Prof. David Bridges and Judith Weyland (nee Powell), who provided a great deal of information about people and events at the Institute and at the wedding (and also for some excellent photographs). Many of Fuengsin's former colleagues from the Birmingham area have shared experiences including Peter Tyler, Douglas Bennett and Ramona Kauth, who discovered at the eleventh hour the manuscript of her MUFRU interview with Fuengsin in 1986. Canon Dr Andrew Wingate and Prof. Aasulv Lande have been very supportive of the whole family and given encouragement and advice, conveying vividly the work at Selly Oak Colleges; Friedericke Rice shared many insights about the pioneering work of the Multi-Faith Resources Unit (later Multi-Faith Centre). Still further contributions came from friends in Hagley, including Alfred and Elsie Crabtree, Francesca and Yolanda Stone, to name but a few.

I have spent many years writing, often at a snail's pace, so encouragement in such circumstances was much appreciated from practitioners in the UK, particularly Ven. Thanissaro (Luang Phi Nicholas), who has recognised the contribution Fuengsin has made in spreading the Dhammakaya method. I am also grateful for the support from friends and colleagues in Oxford: Sandy Bharat, Leah Offer, Hugh Poulton, Peggy Morgan, Dr Silke Ackermann, Lucy Blaxland and Nick Welsh, who suggested the T.S. Eliot quote. In Qatar, with the long summers, I had more time but it was not always easy to find motivation, so for helping to keep me enthused I am grateful to Mohammad Jumah, Burhan Wazir and Carole Thompson, who also reminded me of library and cataloguing standards.

As the process of writing reached some maturity, Sue Mumford-Smith kindly cast an editorial eye over an early draft and Jane Struthers offered important pointers to get the manuscript in shape for publication. Robert Bullard subsequently carried out copy-editing, Robert Papini compiled the index and, finally, Sue and Adrian Mumford-Smith assisted in proof-reading. Thanks also to Paul Godfrey for technical advice in computing and publishing and to Junying Kirk for her encouragement and advice as an emerging author.

1

Breaking New Ground

After one or two holidays in Thailand, what impressions might visitors get? They may be struck by the tropical climate, ornate temples, coconut palms and beach resorts, a relaxed and tolerant people, offering exquisite food and fine hospitality, all of which testify to its reputation as 'the land of smiles'. Some who have spent longer there discover that it too has its foibles and problems — ranging from chaotic traffic and inane TV adverts to more chronic issues such as poor urban planning and less than salubrious lifestyles fuelled by a mixture of poverty and greed.

Thailand leaves many tastes and it is the Thai people who have created the essence of these tastes, but their origins are seldom related and in the midst of all the development much of significance is being forgotten, allowing superficial things to float to the surface. Relatives, friends and associates who got to know Fuengsin learned that there are other facets to discover, a much more rewarding encounter than a picture postcard or urban smog. The basis of this was Fuengsin's character, which was honourable, strong and deeply rooted in Thai traditions and lifestyle that had been instilled in her through her family, especially by her parents. So to get to know Fuengsin better we should explore her parents' background and her childhood.

However, tracing Thai family history is more challenging than for a European or North American. In most cases, unless the family has royal blood, historical archives are likely to be few for there is no equivalent of parish records, surnames were only formally introduced in the early twentieth century and the tropical climate will tend to ravage official documentation, photographs, letters, or any other paper-based materials. Anything from before the reign of King Bhumibol (from 1946), say, would be considered rare.

It is quite fortunate then that there is some substantial material for Fuengsin's family — whilst they are not large in quantity, they are concentrated, evocative in their details and the recollections around them remain redolent in the family today. Whilst the materials we have don't cover a period much beyond 100 years ago, the personal qualities and family traditions that they convey are considerably older. Indeed visitors to the family — now in Wong-WienYai — are often struck by the old customs and practices still retained in the family, the buildings, the style of dress and so on. So describing the family members themselves is like exploring old history books.

Among them, the most durable is in the form of a *nangsu anuson ngansop* (cremation volume) for Fuengsin's father, Capt. Luang Sarayutpitag. This is a record of the deceased's life and career, a memorial highlighting their virtuous conduct, copies of which are distributed at their cremation. It is a tradition that is apparently unique to Thailand, having originated in the royal courts around the time that the first printing presses were arriving in the country. According to some analysts it had a quite specific purpose of counteracting missionary propaganda, but it was then popularised by becoming broader in outlook.[1]

This particular book is in US legal size with a fuchsia and black cover, a colour combination that was apparently in vogue. However, its content, which is comprised mainly of text with a few photographs, is in a long-standing format: after an exhaustive list of career details, there follow tributes (*kham wai-alai*) including anecdotes, essays and many Buddhist teachings. Whilst the structure of these volumes is quite formulaic, the qualities of the individual personality emerge strongly in what and how he or she is presented. There is a natural curiosity about why someone passed away, the karmic causes, the sequence of events that happened. Details may be provided together not only about the medical condition but, where knowledge is available in the family, also about possible cures. It generally depends upon whether or not the circumstances cast the deceased in a positive light — the wish to help them in transition is very strong and it is believed that recollection of all the positive virtues can illuminate their onward path — and the tributes themselves often encourage everyone to participate like this.

The volume is unusual in the breadth and erudition of its contributions. The topics cover religion, history and archaeology (one of his nephews was a professional archaeologist). Whilst ostensibly biographical, what makes this volume particularly unusual is an extended essay by Fuengsin describing her experiences in the UK together with articles in English about how Buddhism was emerging there in the 1960s. It is thus a work of historical cross-cultural significance, with the added benefit of having been produced to a high standard, printed at the Department of Military Communications.[2]

The other main source is a just a single photograph that provides the key to Fuengsin's mother, Somboon Sarayutpitag. It dates to the beginning of the 20th century and has very significant provenance; it soon became a source of pride in her life. As it was dearly cherished it was protected and then became a surprising vehicle for cultural transmission. We shall delve into both the cremation volume and the photograph as our text unfolds.

* * *

Fuengsin's genealogy is not extensively documented. According to one of her sisters, Umpai, her parents and ancestors originated from 'up country', i.e. north of Bangkok. It is recorded that her father was born in the central province of Angthong ('Golden Bowl', thought to have been named after the colour of the rice grown there), which borders Ayutthaya, the former provincial capital. His date of birth is given as 28 August 1893. He was an only child of Mr Wai and Mrs Chun and given the name Feun, which means 'recovery' or 'renaissance'. He was sent to Bangkok for his secondary education at Wat Thepsirin School. (*Wats* are monasteries or temples and are everywhere in Thailand, even in small villages.) In his parents' days there was no established national education system; monasteries were still responsible for the mainstay of formal education and only boys could attend temple schools.

Feun entered military service as a regular, and undertook further studies at an officer school, also in Bangkok, subsequently becoming a light armaments officer in an infantry division. It was probably during this period that he met Miss Somboon Rukyati,[3] the daughter of Mr Choei and Mrs Phiw, and they were subsequently married. As she had already a surname this was probably shortly after 1913, the year in which the Thai Surnames Act was introduced under King Rama VI (before this it was the norm to have only single names, albeit qualified by other means such as location).

Miss Somboon was born in 1895, when important changes were starting to ripple through the education system. At the turn of the century it was still the case that girls from affluent backgrounds tended to stay at home or went to join the ladies of the Court to learn culture, cooking, general domestic work and manners. The main purpose was to train them to be good wives and mothers and to act like ladies if they were to marry middle- or upper-class men. If they were less affluent, they would be helping on farms, in orchards or on plantations, having to work to assist their husbands. However, schools started to become available to provide primary education and they charged modest fees, so even poor families would try to send their children there for a short while to receive some benefit.

Miss Somboon was thus one of the first to receive an education in Bangkok and that is almost all that we might have learnt about her life before marriage if it were not for the following photograph:

Fig. 1: Group photograph at Satriwithaya School, 9 March 1908.[4]

Satriwithaya School, located in the heart of Bangkok, was one of the country's first girls' schools. It was originally founded as a private school at the end of the nineteenth century, opening its doors in 1900 for a few children at pre-preparatory level. Government (state) education started to be introduced in the following year and it subsequently became state run. The young Miss Somboon moved to Satriwithaya School with a cohort of pupils from Wat Anongkaram School — a traditional temple school, where monks did much of the teaching.[5] The pupils were mainly boys, but there were growing number of girls; it was starting to get full. So the chief governor of the school looked for a ^ new site, especially for the girls, and hence identified Satriwithaya School and brought it into the new state system. After expanding into the preparatory level, it later became secondary only.

When the photo was taken King Chulalongkorn (Rama V) was coming to the end of his long reign, in which he had encouraged the process of Western-style modernisation, though it was still to permeate fully. This is reflected in the school uniform which comprises the Thai traditional *jong kraben*, which is a piece of cloth wrapped around the waist to look like loose-fitting trousers, combined with European-style socks and shoes. A few years later, *jong kraben* became uncommon as the clothing became further westernised under King Vajiravudh (Rama VI).

The Western influences in this school ran deeper than mere uniform. It is known that the founder and head teacher of the school was Lucy Dunlap (or, as she would have been known to her pupils, 'Ma'am See') and that she was 'Thai-American'. A rare account about her life is recorded in a short biography by Margaret McCord, who had met her in Thailand. This relates that Miss Dunlap was actually an ethnic Thai adopted by an American missionary couple, Dr and Mrs Dunlap, and hence was given their surname. Her mother had been in prison, but was released at the request of the Dunlaps so that she could be cared for in childbirth. They then adopted the baby and gave her the name Lucy, taking her with them to the United States at the age of nine, where she was brought up as a Protestant Christian. She remained there until the early 1890s, when she returned to Thailand to spread her faith, which she tried to do by establishing the school and giving it a Christian ethos.[6]

Miss Somboon would have been unaware of all the missionary intentions, but she did pick up the ethos of education, its intrinsic value in helping towards a better life, and the growing opportunities for all. This would have been instilled in her by her parents, who could only afford to pay for her to stay at this school for a limited period — reckoned by one family member to have been just a month. Yet the timing was opportune as she was the eldest pupil when this photograph was taken and had the privilege of receiving a copy. No wonder then that she treasured the memento and kept it on display as best as she could; later, when she had her own household, she placed it prominently, high up in her room for all to see — especially her children and grandchildren.

The photograph became cherished even more because of another pupil, Miss Sangwal, who was standing in the row behind her, third from the left. She was later to become Her Royal Highness the Princess Mother, Somdet Phra Srinagarindra Boromarajajonani, the late mother of His Majesty King Bhumibol Adulyadej, known generally by her colloquial title of Somdet Ya. She was originally a commoner, like the others at the school, and became much loved by Thai people as she was known to be very caring and approachable. The school now has a museum dedicated to her memory, the Srinagarindra [Somdet Ya] museum, and it features in its boardroom an enlargement of the photograph above, with the following description in its online catalogue:

> A prominent feature of the Srinagarindra [Somdet Ya] museum is the royal source of some valuable old pictures of the Princess Mother. One part comes from the collections of alumni and former teachers, whilst another has been requested from the Bureau of the Royal House. One exceedingly valuable picture

is a group photograph of first year pre-elementary students (now equivalent to kindergarten) taken on the 9th of March R.E. (Ratanakosin Era) 127 (B.E. 2451). The Princess Mother [can be seen] at the time when she was still a girl, Miss Sangwal; Her Royal Highness is residing in the central row, 3rd from the left. As an original picture it is extremely faded to the extent that it is not possible to read the writing on the plate mounted on the board behind; it is necessary to use the description that the owner has attached on the back of the picture. This picture was received with the assistance of the descendants of Mrs Somboon Sarayutpitag. In the picture Miss Somboon is in the front row, 6th from the left.

Miss Sangwal subsequently went on to study nursing at Siriraj Hospital and thence went on to further studies in the United States, where she was to meet her future husband, Prince Mahidol. Miss Somboon, who had a teacher in common, did well and could also have had the opportunity to study at the hospital; it was thought that she wanted to become a doctor, but her parents could not afford to support her. However, it seems the poverty was embarrassing so her original intention was covered up, and later accounts had it that she refused through fear of ghosts. Yet she held on to the photograph and its provenance came to have a marked influence on the whole family — it captured educational aspiration, to be instilled in every family member, especially Fuengsin.

The schooling for Fuengsin's father had no such distinction; at least it is not mentioned in his cremation volume. So we have only his career and family life to narrate. In 1913 Feun was stationed in Ayutthaya province; in 1918 he moved to Roi Et. During this period, which was in the reign of King Rama VI (1910-1925), he received his surname, Wayam'ra, which was a name chosen by His Majesty and is recorded in a book of names given by the King.[7] The entry reads: '2nd Lieutenant Feun Wayam'ra, an officer in the light artillery, 10th division, father's name Wai.' According to the cremation volume, he attained to that rank in 1915.

Meanwhile Mr and Mrs Wayam'ra started to have family, with the birth of a daughter, Wijit, in Ayutthaya. The family moved to Roi Et, where three daughters were born: Wilai, Umpai and Umpun. At that time Thailand was largely agricultural, before any national health service was available, so childbirth was at home and health care was based on self-reliance and using local wisdom. These were not always effective: according to some family accounts there were several cases of infants not making it into childhood. Indeed the relatively scarce data that is available indicate that outside of Bangkok registered infant mortality rates were more than 3 in 10, which was common for many developing countries before they became industrialised and introduced modern health care for the general public.[8]

Fig. 2: Thai Army Officers: Feun Wayam'ra standing on the left (c.1920s).

Feun Wayam'ra gradually progressed through the ranks, accumulating 15 years' service by 1926, an occasion marked by the receipt of a Chakra Mala medal. He stayed in Roi Et until 1927, when a significant opening became available in Bangkok and the family moved there. The young officer was promoted to the rank of Captain (*Roi Ek*, with 3 stars). But at this stage he started to steer another path: he became more involved in administration, joined the Procurement Department of the Armaments Division and started to teach himself accountancy until he was professionally qualified. We cannot be sure why, but it may have been through conscience. He was a devout Buddhist who didn't drink at all and nor did he go out very much, preferring to stay at home, where he kept a large collection of books on Dharma and related topics. However, at the same time he had to do his duty according to the expectations of society. When reflecting on his early career in the military, he said, 'That was my living and I had no choice.' Many men had to fight for their country and even if he did not want to kill, it was his job, so he had to accept it.

The family then settled in Rajadamnoen in the heart of Bangkok and continued to grow, with the birth of a son, Surapan, on 5 December 1927. He was the only son to survive into adulthood and happened to be born on the same day as Bhumibol Adulyadej, the future king of Thailand; the astrologers noted however that their times of birth were different and hence so would be their fortunes — Surapan was not to enjoy the same luxury or longevity as His Majesty. There were now five children together with some relatives and servants. The modest army pay of 135 baht per month (equivalent then to around £12 sterling, i.e. roughly £700 today[9]) meant the household was near its limit in terms of numbers and required tight budgeting.

As was traditional for Thai women, Somboon Wayam'ra was responsible for the household, including the land, together with associated crafts — in effect Thai women are the real owners of their land and by extension their villages; a husband is merely a guest in their wife's home. She was very thorough in the way she ran the household and also in carrying on the tradition of supporting the temples and monks. She would provide food and requisites, helping to raise the money for repairs of the buildings and encouraging the whole family to participate in various ceremonies and rituals. In addition, due to economic necessity, she sought employment opportunities in Bangkok, which were available as the city had been growing steadily and now had a population of up to half a million.

Khun Somboon cannily applied her business instincts in view of this potentially large customer base: after honing her culinary skills, she developed her own brand of curry paste, keeping her recipes secret. The curries were particularly difficult to reproduce as a key factor was the tasting — written instructions were not sufficient by themselves. Only her long-serving maid, Na (Aunt) Shu, whom she personally taught, and one other friend were able to deliver curries of the same quality. Khun Somboon had many friends and enjoyed conversation, inviting many people to come for lunch. She solved the problem of catering for crowds by devising a mass production process to generate large quantities so that even when receiving large numbers of guests, all of them could take back home some surplus dishes. Furthermore, with copious supplies she was able to set up a stall to sell the product in Sanam Luang, outside the Grand Palace. It was just as well since she started this initiative as Thailand went into a period of economic stagnation, which descended still further when the global depression really started to bite.

A year after arriving in Bangkok, Capt. Feun was sent back to the North East to Nakhon Ratchasima, and a couple of years later, in April 1930, he was stationed to the west in Nakhon Sawan. His service was recognised on 3 June when he was awarded the title of Luang Sarayutpitag, a mid-ranking title in the centuries-old system of nobility.[10] Like other names of royal origin, this surname has its roots in Pali, an early Indian language of Buddhist texts, to lend it a sense of authority. In practice it makes it quite difficult for Thais not only to interpret, but even to spell correctly.[11]

During that period he consolidated his role in administration and in April 1932 became chief accountant of the 7th infantry regiment, still in Nakhon Sawan. However, all this was achieved against an unsettled backdrop. That year was a momentous one in Thai history as it was marked on 24 June by the 'Siamese Revolution of 1932', a coup d'état that brought to an end 700 years of absolute monarchy. Hatched in meetings in Paris it was not a straightforward transition — whilst the takeover itself was bloodless and had been long in the making, for most Thais the monarchy remained indispensable.[12] The complete abandonment of the king was out of the question, so it was replaced with a constitutional monarchy where the newly formed Khana Ratsadon (the People's Party) came into government. Key to the ongoing success of any government was the support of the armed forces or, at least, most of the armed forces. They were sewn into the political fabric from the outset with control being effectively two-pronged: through ministers (the civil faction) and the military, with fluid movement (and sometimes rivalry) between them.

In the midst of these momentous changes, particularly for the armed forces, Capt. Luang Sarayutpitag was drawn close to all the commotion when at the end of 1932 he became chief accountant of His Majesty's 1st artillery battalion.[13] The Royal Guard, with members from various regiments, is particularly close to the king. Circulating in and around Bangkok he would have inevitably been in contact with the politics and anyone in active service would have been on a state of high alert. Not surprisingly, there was some resistance. In 1933, Prince Boworadej initiated a royalist rebellion, marching on Bangkok from the north. However, the nascent government was able to command sufficient loyalties of various regiments such as the one in Nakhon Sawan, which helped to drive back the rebels in mid-October. Capt. Luang Sarayutpitag was not long gone from that regiment and probably retained connections. In any case the following year he received a medal for 'Saving the Constitution', which was awarded to those on the winning side of that battle.

Whilst Luang Sarayutpitag's deliberations in the midst of these political changes are not recorded, we do know about his character from relatives and friends. Descriptions of him consistently indicate a highly ordered mind, someone refined in manners, and a long-time philanthropist. A trait that emerges very strongly from the tributes in his memorial book is his preference for peace and quiet. Phra Chinwongsawatee, the monk who later presided over his cremation ceremony, remarked:

He didn't study only to be merely well-versed, but also applied the Dhamma he knew to his conduct. We can see that Uncle was a person who loved tranquillity. He was tranquil in body, speech and mind.

Fig. 3: Capt. Luang Sarayutpitag in uniform, late 1930s.
The medal in the centre is the Companion (Fourth Class) of Most Exalted
Order of the White Elephant; far right is Safeguarding the Constitution.

However, a new constitution that incorporated increased influence of the army in politics, amidst ongoing tensions with royalty, was unlikely to have been conducive to such an outlook. He would have been mindful of ramifications for members of his family, who would have known about the uncertainties in the political arena even if they were protected from exposure to the details. It may well have been such reflections that persuaded him to change his career. On 1 June 1934 he transferred to the Ministry of the Interior and became a Civil Servant in the Department of Corrections (Prison services), serving in the Phra Nakhon district of central Bangkok. The new working environment seemed to suit him as he quickly established himself in accounts, becoming within a few years Head of the Accounts Section, Benefits Division. It was an occupation where he could develop further his administrative and organisational skills.

Fig. 4: Luang Sarayutpitag at the Ministry of the Interior, Bangkok.[14]
Luang Sarayutpitag is in the front row on the right, wearing a black armband
because his mother had recently passed away.

It also allowed him to spend more time, at least initially, with the Sarayut-pitag household, which extended across several generations. One of the relatives who joined the family was Luang Sarayutpitag's nephew, Chalerm Suttirak, who studied at an officer school (for lieutenants) over a period of five years from 1935 through to 1939. He had been placed in the care of the Sarayutpitag family by his father, Feun's elder brother. When they were small, the elder brother would often take care of his young sibling, carrying him on his back as he travelled around, even into his teenage years. When Luang Sarayutpitag was travelling around for work, he continued to visit him.

So now the younger brother repaid this care to his brother's son, which Chalerm was mindful to recollect: 'Neither Uncle Luang nor Aunty in any way refrained from giving loving kindness and support. They were concerned about every aspect of my education, eating, and sleeping, as well as health and sanitation.' Furthermore, Chalerm had a younger brother, Nikom, who de-scribed how he was similarly cared for from school days, through university and graduation.

It was into this large family that the diminutive frame of Fuengsin emerged on Thursday 24 December 1936. She was a somewhat unexpected arrival as both of her parents were in their forties and she was 9 years younger than her nearest sibling. Her name was actually Fuengsilapa, which means 'she who flourishes in the liberal arts'. The name had been chosen by a monk.

* * *

Whilst a new addition to the Sarayutpitag family was welcome, even auspicious, it did pose a further financial burden. The natural inclination would have been to stay put, but the family needed to consider other options out of economic necessity. Fortunately, these were already becoming apparent as the 1930s also saw developments on the other side of the venerable Chao Phraya river, in Thonburi — 'Chao Phraya' is itself a title, the highest of the venerable ranks in Thai nobility issued until 1932. For a few years, in the late eighteenth century, this town had been an interim capital when King Taksin and his army had regrouped following the Burmese ransacking of the previous capital, Ayutthaya. Now in the twentieth century it was the site of a new and ambitious construction project: a major network of 11 roads with Wongwien Yai as its hub and a memorial to King Taksin at its centre. As the name suggests, this was a large roundabout, and it offered connections on all sides, including a road straight to the Memorial Bridge (Phra Phutta Yodfa Bridge), which had been recently completed on 6 April 1932, to commemorate the 150th anniversary of the Chakri Dynasty and Bangkok City.[15] Thonburi's growing status was confirmed when in November 1936, just a few weeks before Fuengsin's birth, an announcement in the Royal Gazette declared both Thonburi and Bangkok city municipalities.[16]

Another of these roads was named after the king — the Somdet Phrajao Taksin Road, which ran south. It was a main artery along that side and started attracting interest from across the river. Among the interested parties was Somboon Sarayutpitag, who had taken on the responsibility for finding somewhere more affordable and convenient to live. Despite all the honours, the family was still poor and she was struggling to manage on a limited budget; several of the children were already being schooled in Thonburi and after they returned home they had do their homework by street light. So it was desirable to move nearby, especially as the land in Thonburi was quite plentiful, offering the prospect of more space.

When Khun Somboon first went looking for a new plot of a few hundred square wah (1 wah = 2 metres), Taksin Road was still being built, but land besides the road was already comparatively expensive — she was offered it at

Fig. 5: Faded memory of three generations of an extended family.
Capt Luang and Mrs Sarayutpitag, her father, their four daughters and one
son, together with a few other relatives on both sides, mid-1930s.

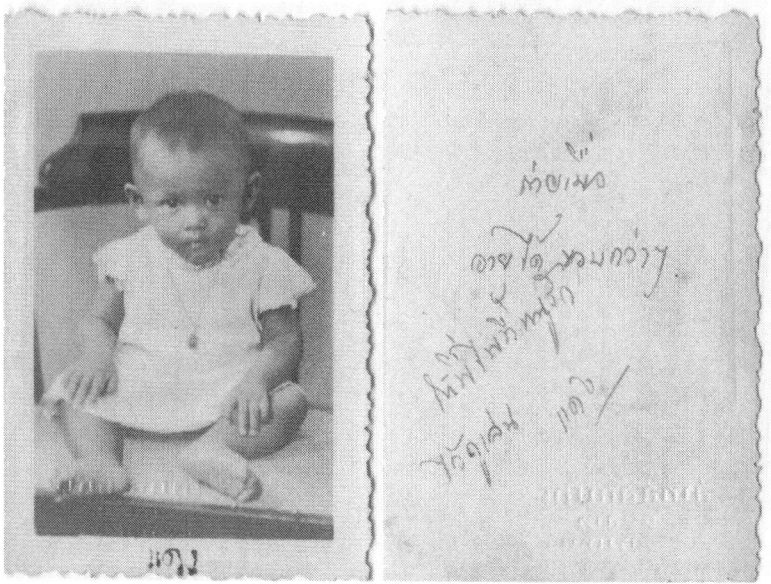

Fig. 6: Baby Fuengsin, just over a year old.
The message on the back says that she gives this to her sister, Umpai.

20 baht per sq. wah, a price the family couldn't afford. On the other hand, land in the fields away from the road was only 6 baht per sq. wah. At that time her husband was earning 240 baht per month, so even the cheaper rate meant an investment amounting to almost a year's salary.

The deal was finally made and the family prepared to move; but what were they moving to? All that had been purchased was some land in the middle of fields, with each field having a private owner; but there were no houses in the fields and no means of access. This meant that when the family went to the land they had to pull up their trousers and sarongs to reach their plot, circumnavigating other plots to get there, walking around edges, tracing a zigzag route, etc. This topography was to have a lasting effect leading to narrow lanes that to this day prevent all but small vehicles from reaching the property.

The plot itself already had quite a mature orchard and was covered in trees and irrigation canals, so it would be a huge effort to establish a large household there. First they had to cut down some of the trees and fill in a few of the canals, whilst diverting others, to make room for a house and road access. Once the land had been cleared a house needed to be built. The responsibility fell on the shoulders of Da Hoy, a relative who was a professional architect and builder, who specialised in wooden houses. He proceeded to coordinate the dismantling of the old house, its transportation across the river and along the canals, and then its reassembly at the new site, with some alterations and improvements in design.

There were no formal plans for the house; advice was sought from local wats, and this led to a house being designed on traditional lines; Khun Somboon stayed nearby to ensure everything was in order whilst it was being constructed. It was made of teak wood, with stilts about two metres high — not only for flood protection, but to prevent creepy-crawlies and other wildlife from encroaching. However, it was also quite innovative; unusually it had two storeys and instead of one or two large rooms partitioned into individual spaces, this was a house with quite a few rooms separated by walls. The first room was the shrine room, which features in most Thai houses as a focus for dedicating life to the ideals and practices of Buddhism. In this house it was placed upstairs, on the second floor. Then there were the bedrooms; the parents especially wanted each of their children to have their own space. Da Hoy also built an annexe, where he stayed on the 1st floor. Underneath was a kitchen, containing on one side huge pots where the curry paste was made to be sold every week outside Sanam Luang — the production facility was soon re-established! Da Hoy continued to stay with the family for many years, eventually moving to another home that he helped build for one of the children, next door to the main house.[17]

It is not known exactly when the family moved, though it is generally accepted as being before the start of the Second World War and probably at the end of the 1930s, around the time the country's formal designation of Siam was changed to Prathet Thai, giving it a modern nationalist tweak. According to the land registry document, which was first issued in the reign of King Rama V and is signed by the Registrar of the area, Capt. Luang and Mrs Somboon Sarayutpitag became owners on 13 November 1939. When they did move some roads were not complete and parts were still barely navigable — it was necessary to walk.

Within a few years they were joined by further relatives and close friends who became neighbours — Khun Yai Nuan and Khun Pon (later to become Admiral Bodhiphala). A soi become established with a few narrow lanes following the borders of the orchard plots. As the population grew around the narrow lanes, another friend, Khun Brahman, established a school to respond to the increasing demand. For many families, the move improved access to schooling along the canals: one canal ran adjacent to their plot of land and carried on through the heart of that area in Thonburi, to Wat Anongkaram and beyond.

Khun Somboon continued to preside over domestic affairs and with her greater maturity she became Khun Yay.[18] Two daughters got married locally and subsequently each had their own house built on the land — since Khun Yay was so fierce, her eldest daughter, Wijit, chose to situate her house at the edge of the plot, near the neighbours (the Bodhiphala family), leaving the next daughter, Wilai, obliged to have her home opposite and very close by the main house. As educational opportunities continued to advance, the younger daughters were encouraged to pursue higher education. Thus the third daughter, Umpai, became a teacher, and Umpun completed a degree in accountancy at Thammasat University, following the example of her father. In 1941 he became Chief Accountant, Collection Services Section, responsible for collecting land rent, also becoming Inspector-General for prison tax affairs in the provinces. The promotion of education was progressive and would have been very unlikely in the provinces as parents there still thought that girls were destined to get married and not to use their academic knowledge. Furthermore whereas primary and secondary school fees were quite modest, higher education remained expensive with few grants available, so the sacrifice that the family made was considerable.

Notes

These notes and the notes from other chapters include hyperlinks, which may be tedious to type out and are likely to become out of date. So a list with all these links is available online at:
http://fuengsin.org/lotus/notes/

1. Cremation volumes belong to a genre of literature known as *nangsu anuson ngansop* (lit. 'book of cremation remembrance'). See e.g. Grant A. Olson, 1992. *Thai Cremation Volumes: A Brief History of a Unique Genre of Literature*, Asian Folklore Studies, Volume 51, pp. 279-294
http://nirc.nanzan-u.ac.jp/nfile/1734

2. The cremation volume for Capt. Luang Sarayutpitag was published in 1969 by the Department of Military Communications at their press in Phra Nakorn (Bangkok), Thailand. There is a copy in the reference section of the Pridi Banomyong library at Thammasat University, call number CRE 1969 42900.
http://koha.library.tu.ac.th/cgi-bin/koha/opac-detail.pl?biblionumber=42900

3. Miss Somboon *Rukyat[i]*. In Thai the surname literally means 'loves relations', which proved to be very apt.

4. The 1908 group photograph from Satiwithaya School has been the focus of considerable historical interest. The account here is based partly on the recollection by Napadol Posanacharoern, one of Khun Yay Somboon's grandsons, who donated the photograph through the Satriwithaya School Alumni Association.
http://www.sac.or.th/databases/museumdatabase/review_inside_ByMember_Detail.php?id=166&CID=4642

   The image shown is actually a partial view that was sourced from Wikipedia:
http://en.wikipedia.org/wiki/File:Sangwal_in_Satri_Wittaya_School.JPG

   The photo has featured in an article by Weena Noppakunthong, entitled, 'A school good enough for the Princess Mother', published in the Bangkok Post, August 14, 2007. Furthermore, it has facilitated the enquiries of Princess Kalyani, the elder sister of King Bhumibol, who became interested in the history of education and the Royal Family. Somboon Sarayutpitag's grandson, Mr. Napakadol Posanacharoen, had received many recollections from his grandmother and was able to share these with her Royal Highness.

5. The detail about Wat Anongkaram School is partially corroborated by a memorial sign in Somdet Ya Park, as reproduced on a personal blog:
http://myunseenthailand.blogspot.com/2008_07_01_archive.html

6. Further research by the author has uncovered a 12-page potted biography by Margaret McCord. *The Story of Lucy Dunlap*, August 1945, Margaret and Kenneth Landon papers, Wheaton College Archives:
http://archon.wheaton.edu/index.php?p=collections/findingaid&id=24&q=&rootcontentid=61305

   Margaret McCord herself was a Presbyterian missionary, which may explain how her work has found itself in the collections of Margaret and Kenneth Landon, who also belonged to the same organisation. Margaret Landon is probably most widely known for her novel, *Anna and the King of Siam*, concerning Anna Leonowens, who had been governess in the Court of Rama IV for the purposes of educating his family members in English and Western scientific knowledge. Generations of Thais have felt strongly that what ensued through her and those who wrote about her subsequently are largely a misinterpretation of the king and Thai society. Yet this may have been given an impetus for greater rapprochement between East and West so that deeper understanding may be cultivated.

7. A copy of the book of names given by King Rama VI was kept by a daughter, Umpai Sarayutpitag.

8. Varavarn, H.S.H. Prince Sakol, 1930. *Public health and medical service*. In *Siam in 1930, General and medical features*, Executive committee of the Eighth Congress of the Far Eastern Association of Tropical Medicine, Bangkok Times Press, pp. 185–244. Re-printed by White Lotus Press, Bangkok, 2000.

9. An echange rate of 11 baht per one pound sterling was established in January 1923: see e.g. page 161 of James C. Ingram, 1971. *Economic Change in Thailand: 1850-1970*, Stanford University Press. The estimated current value (as at 2015) is determined by the Bank of England's online Inflation Calculator, which uses figures for the composite price index supplied by the Office for National Statistics.
    http://www.bankofengland.co.uk/education/Pages/resources/inflationtools/calcul ator/index1.aspx

10. The Thai system of royal titles, which some historians refer to as a form of feudal-ism, existed for at least several centuries until ending with dissolution of the abso-lute monarchy. Accounts from various expeditions dating back to the 17th century, including Iranian and French, were all curious to know about the hierarchy of the nobility and noted the various ranks — *Luang* is roughly in the middle.
    https://en.wikipedia.org/wiki/Thai_royal_and_noble_titles#Titles_of_Peerage_of_Ci vil_and_Military
    (but the comparison with UK titles should be taken with a drop of fish sauce!)

11. On Thai spelling (from the author's learner perspective). The Thai language was formalised with the intention of preserving original spellings from Pali and Sanskrit. This has resulted in its alphabet containing multiple letters that sound the same; furthermore as these languages made distinctions between aspirated and unaspirated sounds, there can sometimes be letters that nowadays sound the same. So if you hear a Thai name for the first time it may be difficult to know the spelling, especially if it is unfamiliar; for the surname Sarayutpitag, the first letter is already a challenge as more than one letter produces an 's' sound; here it is ศ ('so sala') and not ส ('so suea'). Then there is the matter of how to spell what sounds like 'yuth'. Some research indicates it should be spelt in Thai ยุทธ, which has two aspirated 't' sounds, hence หลวงศรายุทธพิทักษ์, but to most Thais the extra 't' sound seems redundant so usually the ท has been omitted. All this complicates the process of finding out about the family. By comparison Anglo Saxon surnames seem very straightforward.

12. The most detailed English-language reference for these events is: Judith A. Stowe, *Siam Becomes Thailand: A Story of Intrigue*, 1991, University of Hawai'i Press. It was

published in the UK by C. Hurst & Co., also in 1991, a preview being available from Google Books:
https://books.google.co.uk/books?id=YTgJ8aRwZkAC

13. A page (in Thai) about this Royal Artillery Battalion is at:
http://th.wikipedia.org/wiki/กรมทหารปืนใหญ่ที่_1_รักษาพระองค์

14. The main building and even the trees remain largely the same today.

15. Wongwien Yai was completed in the 1930s, but the statue of the king on horseback was completed later, in 1954, with an official opening ceremony on 17th April.

16. The declaration that both Thonburi and Bangkok were city municipalities was announced in an article in the Royal Gazette in November 1936, illustrated by a plan showing the navigation routes, including canals and the main roads. The name was slightly revised a couple of weeks after the initial announcement, demonstrating a trait that is not untypical among Thais.

17. Thai architecture. Since long ago, Thai houses were designed as separable units that could be taken down, moved and reassembled. Traditionally, houses had no nails. Further, the front of the house would be south facing to receive the refreshing breezes and maintain the house at a comfortable temperature. There are still builders who work using traditional methods and designs: some may be found in the Bang Pahan area, in Ayutthaya province, and some also in Angthong.

18. *Khun Yay* is a term of respect that means 'Grandmother'. The degree of respect with which Khun Yay Somboon was regarded persisted into her final years: when the soi became heavily built up, it developed a reputation for being an area where bandits roamed. Some knew Khun Yay and even as her frail form went out for lunch in her early 90s, they would just say a cheerful 'Sawasdee khrub!' as she walked past.

2

Fuengsin's Childhood:
From Wartime to Roaming Free

nai nam mi pla,
nai na mi khao
In the water there is fish!
In the field there is rice!
From King Ramkhamhaeng's inscription, 13C[1]

Fuengsin's infancy was spent in Ratchadamnoen before moving with her family as a toddler to Thonburi.[2] With five siblings and relatives from both sides of the family, she had few material possessions solely for her own use — as a young child she had to make do with only a rag doll as a toy to call her own. She was also quite isolated as her brother and sisters were considerably older, so it would be many years before she could relate to them as someone of the same generation. Yet there was always plenty for Fuengsin to observe in her family and the orchards provided a picture postcard setting for her childhood; for a youngster their plot of land near Wongwien Yai seemed vast. Initially it was an idyllic setting with the freedom to roam in a land rich with vegetation, but the sense of the care-free was soon to be disrupted.

From the end of 1941 Thailand, which had never been colonised, came under Japanese occupation. The country was used as a launch pad for offensives against the Western powers, especially in Malaysia and Burma. The local population had no choice but to accommodate the presence of many Japanese military personnel, who gained access to the Thai infrastructure, especially strategic transport routes. As the Thai government had signed an agreement with the Japanese and was drawn into siding with the Axis powers, the British and Americans responded with bombing raids, particularly targeting central Bangkok. The area was populated, so civilian lives were at risk from these aerial attacks. One of Fuengsin's early childhood memories was hearing these bombs dropping from the British planes and exploding. Her sister, Umpai, had a far closer and more painful encounter: whilst fleeing across the Memorial Bridge as it was being bombarded, she was struck in the head by shrapnel; she survived, but one of her friends who was with her lost her life.[3] It was an uncomfortable situation and some Thais fought against their Oriental occupants. Among them was Fuengsin's cousin, Chalerm Suttirak; after his graduation, he became involved in the Free Thai Movement, an underground organisation where he was trained to resist the Japanese incursions, helping to pass on intelligence to the Allies. The experience was a significant entry point into a career in military communications.

The harsh realities of war were spreading across the world and pervaded Fuengsin's small life just like so many others, even if kept mainly in the background. Yet, being somewhat insulated as a young child, the stories might have even fuelled Fuengsin's curiosity and sense of adventure. She pursued this with fellow adventurers next door, two daughters of a Chinese family nicknamed 'Big pigtail' and 'Little pigtail'. Together they were like three young musketeers and all they needed was intrepid spirit and imagination![4]

Fig. 7: Ploen and Dtoi, childhood friends.
A note in Fuengsin's handwriting on the back reads:
"Taken with Ploen and Dtoi", who were nicknamed
'Little pigtail' and 'Big pigtail' respectively.

Fuengsin enjoyed her friends' company very much, which was made more memorable by the taste of food, as she later admitted:

One day when I was supposed to stay at home, I sneaked off and went next door to play with them. We had a lovely time — and ate a delicious soup with fish and ginger. Their house was on the bank of the canal and a big rowing boat came by as we sat there eating the soup. Who was on it but my mother! I quickly hid and stayed hidden until the boat went by.

Her friends' father was a vegetable farmer. 'He would go into his garden every day and collect two baskets of vegetables, which he would attach onto the ends of a pole before hoisting it onto his shoulders, keeping the baskets in balance. He then went off to sell the vegetables in the market, returning in the evening, usually with hot fried noodles for his children.' Fuengsin sometimes received an invitation to join them and would accept with alacrity. The New Year brought additional treats in the form of special Chinese cakes that were met with much approval.

Much of the children's daily play revolved around food — its cultivation, appreciation and consumption; they comprise many of Fuengsin's earliest recollections as related here, with the main source being a series of tales that she wrote for *The Taste of Thailand*, a cookery book. For instance, Fuengsin relates that the mango season in Thailand tends to start in April, which is a generally hot and dry period that lasts until June, when the monsoon rains come. At this time of the year Fuengsin used to stay with relatives outside Bangkok, not so far away, in the central provinces. In the evening she would watch the storms come and blow down the mangoes. 'We went out to pick them up and put them in big baskets ready to be stored, cooked or preserved by cooking with sugar and then spread thinly on banana leaves and then dried in the sun.' It was easier like this even though fruit could get bruised, as she explained: 'The problem with picking mangoes is that red ants live on the mango trees. So we pick them using a pole with a little basket on the end. But you have to get to them before the squirrels do.'

One year she was in central Thailand during the monsoon floods. They had to go everywhere on water by boat so they decided to take their boat to a high covered platform and settled down to have a picnic. When the rains abated they could gaze across and admire the beautiful scene: 'There were lotus plants everywhere as far as the eye could see. We picked some and offered them to the Buddha. We also brought some home because they are edible — the stem would be fried with some prawns and we also made soup with coconut cream.'

Most of the memories that Fuengsin retained were from outdoors, but there was one other episode that left an impression in Fuengsin's early memory and it came inside the house and had nothing to do with food. One day she was in her parents' bedroom and saw a note attached to the wardrobe. She went over to read the note and discovered that it was a prediction about her: it foretold the birth of a daughter (her birth), and also that of a son to this daughter, 'whom she would miss for a long time'.

* * *

With many offspring and other adopted members, it was an extended family with children of all sorts of ages. Very much the baby daughter of the family, Fuengsin was closer in age to her cousins, nephews and nieces, as can be seen in the following photograph.

Fig. 8: Fuengsin surrounded by nephews and nieces.

Taken when she was about 12 years old, here she stands alongside four children of Wijit, her elder sister: flanking Fuengsin on the back row are Ad and Od, with Yui and Ead on the front row either side of Diu, who was a distant relative, another adopted family member from Angthong.

As Fuengsin hints in the quote above, where she hid from her mother, her parents were strict, keen to instil discipline and good conduct. They laid down some ground rules to keep things in order, but they were sometimes completely disregarded by one or two individuals in the pursuit of their hobbies:

> My father forbade everyone from catching fish in the pond in front of our house. When he was on a trip for the civil service, my brother emptied all of the fish out of the pond into buckets. He was really fond of fish! Once during the monsoon season, there was such a big flood that the water rose up the stilts which supported our house. My brother stuck a fishing rod out the side window and caught a big fish.

The children found this regime difficult; life wasn't easy-going, and they were often testing their parents' boundaries. Yet the lasting impression on subsequent generations — on the grandchildren especially — was very positive as they were later to express profound appreciation.

In keeping with his preference for peace and quiet, after retirement Luang Sarayutpitag's daily routine was often spent living with trees and books. He enjoyed cultivating just about any kind of tree and would normally get up very early to spend some time looking after the trees he had planted. Later in the morning, he would come into the house for a meal and then withdraw to his own room to attend to his affairs or read a newspaper — he didn't like to be idle. He was also a stickler for punctuality, perhaps because of his training in the Civil Service: lunch was to be served at midday precisely and dinner at 6pm. He presented a formidable presence, yet even when he was working full time he was always willing to give advice and when his nephew, Chalerm Suttirak, returned home from his officer's training at the weekend he would wait so as to join him for a meal, no matter how late. The trainee officer summed up his character:

> Usually Uncle Luang was a person who upheld rules strictly regardless of whether they concerned official matters, uniform, or any kind of business activities. He spoke few words, but listened a lot. His expressions were inclined to be concise, but principled and given deep thought. For this reason then he was somebody who was loved and respected among all relatives together with his friends and subordinates.

He went on to describe how his uncle would skilfully dispense advice:

In any instruction he often did not speak directly, but talked about life and all kinds of experiences that he went through including great hardships with only himself to serve as an example. He thus advised the listener, leading them to think it through, just like this — thoroughly and comprehensively.

Fuengsin herself would often spend time with her father, seeking his wise counsel. He in turn appreciated her company and was pleased to support her in her studies as far as she could take them, and would keep encouraging her when obstacles arose.

The Sarayutpitags taught their children to have perseverance in their endeavours, to be strong and to know self-sufficiency. They each had different characters, but all manifested this self-sufficiency in some way or another. For instance, Khun Umpai, the recipient of Fuengsin's infant photograph, retained much of her father's personality, saying little, but being to the point; she always took care of herself, seeking little from others, remaining a spinster all her life. Her friends were mainly fellow teachers from the local school and they kept in touch long after they had retired. Apart from the relatives in the compound, her only other company were cats, usually rescued from around the soi, even those that were blind.

Khun Umpan followed her father's career — around the time Fuengsin was playing with her nephews and nieces, she was completing studies in business administration at Thammasat University and with his encouragement she went on to qualify in accountancy. She subsequently married a telecoms engineer, Khun Ophas, who trained abroad, specialising in topics such as wide area networks. Following Thai tradition, her husband came to join her wife's extended family and they lived initially in one room of the main house until a new house was built next door into which they moved in the mid-70s, and this has remained their family home ever since.

As we have seen Somboon Sarayutpitag was likewise supportive of her children's education, but her personality was radically different, complementary to that of her husband. Whereas he spoke little and in a restrained manner, she was gregarious and voluble, not afraid to speak her mind; whereas he was content to be in a room by himself, she sought company and would invite many friends over and they had animated conversations. It was well-known that she was very particular, which was one of the qualities that enabled her become an exceptional cook, but she made life tough for her servants who were helping her. Her temperament could be ferocious and many were afraid of her, but she was fair and to those who persevered she would share all her knowledge and they too became very good cooks, better than some of her daughters.

Khun Somboon was also very pragmatic and lived a healthy lifestyle; on a blackboard that she used over the decades she had a transcription of a Pali chant for health and long life, with a specific recommendation to eat cumin leaf when it's young. Cumin seeds featured in one of her most popular dishes: Massaman curry, which was originally from the South (its name is a reference to Muslims). Among its other ingredients were peanuts and coconut, which are more usual in curry made by the Malays. Furthermore the coconut was extracted using a new and improved coconut grater that she had herself devised: it could extract the flesh very efficiently once the shell had been opened. Whilst being very traditional in her customs she exemplified the Thai trait of adaptability — at home she would only eat with her hands except for juice or soup, where she used a spoon. However, when in company, she would use cutlery.

* * *

Integral to Fuengsin's instruction and upbringing was support for the Buddhist way of life through the threefold practice of *dana* (generosity), *sila* (moral virtue) and *samadhi* (meditation practice) — these terms, like many in the Thai language, are drawn from Pali. The conventional view was that everyone could practice *dana* and *sila*, particularly the observation of the Five Precepts, which is an undertaking to refrain from: taking life, taking that which is not given, sexual misconduct, false speech and taking intoxicants. However, usually only the monks and nuns meditated. Fuengsin's family was typical with no-one practising meditation, but their faith in the Buddha's teachings was very strong: Fuengsin's father possessed a large collection of books on Buddhist topics and quite a few male relatives had become bhikkhus (monks).

It was central to their daily life to support the bhikkhus by providing *Sanghadana*, which are various requisites, including food, offered to monks on their morning alms rounds. Fuengsin was encouraged to show her respect by taking her turn in making offerings and she willingly agreed, sometimes volunteering because she liked to talk to the monks. These activities could also be viewed as a means of perfection, providing the best quality food that they could produce and prepare.

As devout Buddhists they believed that carrying out such meritorious deeds was a means to spiritual advancement. Their strict observance also helped them to become respected members of society and become a focal point for communal activities. On occasions like these the Sarayutpitags welcomed many relatives and neighbours to join in the acts of giving so as to share in the merit that would be for their future welfare. Their style of offering was quite distinctive as it involved placing the rice in the monks' bowls, which most likely was a practice they brought from Angthong province.

Fig. 9: Alms offering at the Sarayutpitag household.
(Capt. Luang Sarayutpitag and Mrs Somboon Sarayutpitag in the centre.)

Led by Khun Somboon, the family became well known donors, with a wooden bench in their yard ready each day for several bhikkhus to sit and receive the offerings. Throughout their married life, Fuengsin's parents had monks to come to the house for meals every day. They were so reliable that for a number of years they signed a contract with the local temple that guaranteed morning alms for two or three monks. In fact the welcome became widely known and also attracted monks on *thudong* — wandering monks, who camped for a while in their garden before moving on without settling anywhere. Sometimes there were as many as 15 to 20 novices and monks, who were free to pop in any time, and they knew that there would be food and shelter for them.

So Fuengsin was expected to observe a moral code of conduct, to be honest and respectful. She was also required to carry out basic chanting every day in the morning and evening, paying homage to the Triple Gem (Buddha, Dhamma and Sangha). She would commence by offering fresh flowers, perhaps arranged in a garland, then light candles and finally transfer a flame to three incense sticks, a symbolic illumination: to the Buddha, the one who founded the path to the end of suffering; to the Dhamma, which were the teachings that the Buddha realised through his own efforts; and to the Sangha, the community of his disciples. Fuengsin also practiced this observance, which is universal in

Thailand, in temples as she joined her parents on visits to perform ceremonies, where she was encouraged to listen to the sermons. But at this stage her conduct was largely a matter of routine and she found it of limited help in addressing personal issues. Nevertheless, the continued presence of these monks and the encouragement in Dhamma study of her father naturally had an enduring effect on Fuengsin and her siblings.

Notwithstanding her domestic and filial duties, Fuengsin readily had opportunities for fun and games. The house was surrounded by an orchard full of coconut trees; during the day children used the branches and leaves to swing 'like Tarzan' between canal banks, whilst in the evening they could admire from the top of the house a beautiful scene at sunset. Fuengsin's brother was in charge of collecting coconuts, especially when they were fresh and green; he used a ring to climb to the top of the tree where he could then reach them and pick them with his hand. Fuengsin quipped: 'In the south of Thailand and in parts of Malaysia, monkeys are trained to climb the tree and collect the coconuts, but my brother made a very good monkey.' There also used to be many wet areas where Chinese watercress would grow, and there were plenty of freshwater ponds where fish and prawns were abundant. The family took full advantage of the flourishing natural resources around them. Indeed much of the family life revolved around production and cultivation (as well as consumption).

For many centuries the staple diet of Thais has been rice; noodles were a more recent addition, one that was very welcome by gastronomic consumers: 'Many of the noodle pedlars were poor Chinese people. Some of them had just arrived from China. They brought with them the gift of cooking really tasty noodles right on the spot. There were two Chinese noodle pedlars who came to my house often. When they came, they stayed a long time because we needed 15 bowls of noodles to feed the whole household!' The visitors were scrutinised by the youngsters and given purely descriptive but not-so-flattering names such as 'the chap with the rolled up eyes'. They weren't all poor for Fuengsin recalled a very wealthy Chinese lady who was hyperactive — unable to relax at home and lead a comfortable life, she became a pedlar and sold Thai puddings, which received much acclaim.

If they fancied some other culinary dish, then they didn't have to walk far to find a different lunch or snack: stepping out onto the lane in front of the family house, the voices of pedlars could be heard continually echoing in the soi, advertising their produce. Nearby there was also a canal in which Fuengsin used to swim with friends and neighbours. The canal was a busy thoroughfare with many boats passing by, selling all sorts of food to the households on the banks of the canal. They plied their trades all day and even late into the night. The coffee boats in particular sounded their horns. Competition was fierce, with the traders jostling with each other, rowing and shouting at the same time to gain position and attention. It was useful training: some noodle boat traders became famous and went on to start successful restaurants. Fuengsin recalled that even His Majesty, the King of Thailand, was known to have a Chinese pedlar come and feed everyone in the palace. The pedlar took advantage of the royal patronage and started a restaurant called 'The Royal Noodle Trader', something equivalent to 'Under Royal Appointment to Her Majesty the Queen' in Britain.

One outlet that lingered in Fuengsin's memory was a Chinese noodle shop located in a remote and beautiful orchard in Bangkok. The food was out of this world and drew as its clientele the wealthy and educated; the establishment was regarded especially by the younger crowd as upmarket because it had a stereo, a very rare and major status symbol at that time. As to why the food was so good remained a bit of a mystery, but it had to do with the noodle stock which had a very unusual taste. This drew the suspicion of the police, who investigated the stock to see if it contained heroin, but it didn't. The owner's reputation was protected and he went on to become very famous.

Yet there was really no need to go an upmarket restaurant to excite the taste buds, as Fuengsin recalled: 'Most of the noodle restaurants are found in back lanes and in gaps between shops and the cinema. They are nothing much to look at. One of the best places — it was cheap and the noodles contained lots of tender beef and pork — just had a piece of canvas for a roof. Every time it rained, people had to put up with a bit of dripping on their head! But the noodles were better in these shops than they were in the posh restaurants.'

Trading took place wherever space became available. Wongwien Yai acts as a railway terminus with a line that goes to Mahachai, at the mouth of the Chao Phraya, which was then just a village. In Fuengsin's childhood steam trains would puff up and down, blowing their horns to move traders off the rail track, but as soon as they had passed by the traders would resume their positions and continue trading. The whole place smelled of fish as lots of seafood were shipped by train into Bangkok and taken to Wongwien Yai. Today diesel units have replaced the coal-powered engines and traders content themselves with their stalls; the fish smells may have abated, but there is plenty of other more varied smells in their place.

The tropical climate also enabled trade throughout the waking hours and beyond. In the evening many people would frequent the markets, which remained open until late at night, to buy cooked food to take away. Rows of sweet stalls would stretch as far as the eye could see; and some of the female traders (*Mae Kha*) were young and attractive, wearing beautiful clothes and exotic cosmetics, as a way to try to stand out from many others. In front of them were colourful trays filled with a great variety of nuts. Fuengsin observed quite a number of male customers coming round to chat them up, with occasional outbreaks of fighting if the Mae Kha were especially pretty.

There were also regional choices available from particular locations. Fuengsin commented: 'Thais from the Northeast like to eat their food very hot and spicy, especially papaya salad, which is one of their most famous dishes. An area near Bangkok's boxing stadium contained many restaurants and stalls that specialised in papaya salad, chicken and glutinous rice. All sorts of people came and congregated there, including rickshaw men, taxi drivers and builders from the Northeast, many coming for a taste of home.'

There is a general theory as to why Thai food tastes so good and is readily available. It's attributed to the fact that they have for centuries been offering the finest food to the monastic community, thereby earning merit that literally bears sweet fruit. Certainly the Sarayutpitag household believed this and contributed whole-heartedly in this vein. Even travelling provided opportunities to take care of the monastics: fried rice has always been served on trains in Thailand — a popular delicacy is a large plate of well-cooked rice with a fried egg accompanied by sliced cucumbers, spring onions and a lemon slice — and Fuengsin's mother always bought some whenever she saw a monk travelling in the same carriage.

With a professional kitchen in regular operation and so many options for dining out Fuengsin did not have many cooking duties. The Bodhiphala family next door had a daughter, Tewee, who was slightly younger than Fuengsin. They often spent time together, swimming in canals, climbing trees and playing badminton (Tewee's family had a court). They would also *play* at cooking under a tree because they didn't have to do any in practice: Fuengsin had older siblings and servants to take care of it all. But lest she become lazy, it was expected that she use her free time wisely, especially for study.

There were a few occasions, though, when she was called on for assistance. Her mother was exceedingly industrious and occasionally bought numerous baskets of fresh fish. She recruited all the members of the family to help her clean and cook the fish; she usually cooked them in fresh sugar cane and salt so as to preserve them for a long time. Sometimes the salted fish were laid out on the veranda to dry, but only after chasing away all the cats.

Cooperation was also needed on festival days. The 13 April marks the Thai lunar New Year, called *Songkran*. On that day Fuengsin's mother would rise at 4:30 a.m. and call the whole household to get up and help her to prepare special nut cakes to offer to the monks, friends and neighbours. These delicious cakes along with other special treats were not made at any other time of the year. On this occasion offerings would be made to monks not only on their alms round or at temples, but also in designated areas in the parks where they gathered and stood in long rows, waiting to receive food.

The temple attendants came along behind the monks with containers to take food back to the monasteries, so as to ensure surplus was properly used. Later, the lay community would follow on and attend further festivities at the temple, where they could participate in the procession of a statue of the Buddha. In a carnival-like atmosphere, the image was sprinkled with perfume and covered in flowers, whilst people splashed each other with water. They would also visit their elders, and bathed them with soap and water as a sign of respect and gratitude — water symbolised purification and blessing.

It wasn't just human beings who were party to the celebrations. Thais generally believe in many realms of existence, seen and unseen; near many Thai houses there is a 'spirit house' with a statue of the spirit inside, surrounded by an entourage of servants. Flowers, incense and candles would be offered to the spirit and when food was offered to the monks, it was offered afterwards to the spirit as well. The spirits were not just regarded as cohabitants, but also as protectors: when people in the house became ill, they sometimes would ask the spirit's favour to help them to get well again; if the wish was granted, food would be offered. Similarly if money or valuables had become lost and were later found following a request for help then an offering would be made. Likewise, when someone in the house won the state lottery, passed exams or was lucky in some other way, special food would be cooked and offered to the spirit along with the classic threefold combination of incense, candles and flowers, especially jasmine garlands. Any claims of being superstitious might be brushed off, especially as it was quite likely that the site in Wongwien Yai had been host to a camp of King Taksin's army and it was believed that the spirit of some soldiers still roamed around. . . .

And as for the phrase 'kick the bucket', Thais have a completely different take on it. Thais have a sweet tooth, which means extra sugar in items such as bread. There are different sources of sugar in common use, including coconut sugar, which is brown and normally stored in a big square tin. It is also called *namdarn peeb* — *namdarn* means 'sugar' and *peeb* means 'square bucket', usually used for containing water. An old man who can make a lot of noise when he kicks a *peeb* is considered to be still full of life, rather than just passed away!

Food was also very much a feature at the workplace — at least in Fuengsin's recollection. She also noted about her father: 'Quite a few of the men who worked under him were very good cooks and loved showing their skills at weddings.' She evidently took advantage of certain opportunities to gain an appetite for fine living: 'The aristocratic ladies at court are all highly trained cooks. My father's boss's wife had been a member of the court of King Rama the Fifth. I spent hours and hours listening to her stories of the magnificent food that was served at court and of the beautiful ladies of the court. She still remembered how to make that wonderful food. At big celebrations she offered big trays of food to all the neighbours.'

However, the Thai desire for aesthetics sometimes has unexpected nutritional side effects: white is regarded as the colour of purity and thus to be cultivated, even if it means soaking away all the food's innate goodness. Thus Fuengsin also noted that misbehaving prisoners were denied white rice and fed instead on much healthier wholegrain rice.

* * *

Fuengsin's formal schooling began in the early 1940s, at a time when the state education system for children had already become well established nationwide. It offered a considerable advancement on what was available to her mother and comprised 4 compulsory years — *Prathom* (primary) and eight optional years, *Mathayom* (secondary or high school). The naming of the years is based on the first letter of these respective stages followed by a number; hence for *Mathayom* Thais say '*Mor*' followed by a number *n* to indicate the nth year in secondary school, with Mor 7 and Mor 8 considered preparatory years for Higher Education (university).[5] In addition many schools, like the one founded in the soi by Khun Brahman, were privately owned and as such could change hands. They were often not-for-profit ventures set up by charities, particularly Christian organisations, whose legacy continued from the early pioneering efforts instigated by King Rama IV.

Fuengsin's parents sought the best full-time education for their children, keen that they spend as much time learning as they could. They were prepared to undergo sacrifice to have some of them privately educated, but it was a difficult decision for it meant having to make economies elsewhere on an already meagre budget. When it came to choosing the first school for Fuengsin, like many parents they wanted her to go to a Christian school since the standard of education there was very high. Accordingly, they identified Santa Cruz School, which belonged to the Portuguese Mission. Centuries earlier the Portuguese had travelled to the Far East and got on very well with the Thais, so some settled in Thonburi and lived there as a community, establishing a Portuguese village. They maintained their Roman Catholic faith and educational systems which continued among their descendants living in the area. Santa Cruz School was regarded particularly highly for its teaching of English language and generally had a very good reputation, superior to that of most state schools. All schools charged some level of fees, but those at Santa Cruz were quite high; at that time they could only afford to send Fuengsin to a state-run school. Fortunately, there was a good one nearby, Suksanari, which was a quite famous primary school located near Wat Anongkaram, but it was less diverse for there was only one girl who was Roman Catholic and she later moved St Joseph's, an expensive Roman Catholic school.

The national curriculum included Buddhist theory in the form of teachings in the Theravada tradition and a little practice — every day the pupils had to perform some chanting to recollect the virtues of the Buddha, the Dhamma and the Sangha, similar to her practice at home. There were also weekly classes concerned with Buddhist doctrine and monks came occasionally to teach, especially about basic morality.

Fuengsin then proceeded to Wattana Suksa School, a private school that was at that time also close by in Wongwien Yai, facing the statue of King Thaksin, on the east side.[6]

Fig. 10: Wattana Suksa School classmates, 20 November 1950.
With friends Asavin, Yui and others.

Every day, the pupils would go round the roundabout and proceed through a narrow entrance. On arrival they would line up at 8 a.m. outside in front of the flag pole, *wai* (salute) the Thai flag and sing the national anthem. Then they'd proceed to lessons. As this happened at every school, primary and secondary, the country would have been resounding with the anthem everywhere!

There were further classes on Phra Buddha Sasana (the Buddha's teachings). Fuengsin was thus introduced to the basic and very deep foundations, including the Four Noble Truths, which are perhaps the most widely-cited teachings in introductory courses around the world. These teachings state that life is *dukkha*, full of unsatisfactoriness and mental suffering; that there is a root cause of *dukkha* (craving rooted in ignorance); that there is cessation of *dukkha*, so there is a way out; and that the cessation is achieved by following a certain path of practice, which the Buddha expounded as the Eightfold Noble Path. They are very deep teachings and hard to explain, so Fuengsin may have found them a bit of a chore, yet she may already have related to them with a keen sense of dukkha as she found her family life restrictive.

Other teachings were more accessible. She learnt about the life of the Buddha, which is depicted throughout Thailand on temple murals along with Jataka stories. These illustrate the effects of *karma* (intentional actions) and their *vipaka* (results) during his many previous lives as a Bodhisattva, in which he was perfecting his mental qualities on the path to Enlightenment. She also learnt the four Brahmaviharas (Sublime states), the Buddhist expression of love — loving kindness, compassion, sympathetic joy and equanimity.

On a particularly practical level the pupils were taught with reference to the suttas, recorded teachings that the Buddha gave to people from all walks of life, not just his monastic disciples. Prominent among them was the *Mangala Sutta* (the *38 Blessings of Life*), a very popular sutta in Southeast Asia, in which students are taught how to be a good member of society. The blessings are expressed in brief phrases, which include, for example, the advice not to mix with bad people, but to have good company. They are graded, and the final ones relate to the highest states of achievement. One manifestation was the respect accorded to schoolteachers, which was highlighted every year with Teacher's Day, a tradition that is still maintained today, where children offer presents and other tokens of their appreciation.

Fig. 11: *Wai Kru longrien* (Teachers' Day)
with Khun Jongkala, Wattana Suksa School.

Thai schoolchildren would participate in many commemorative occasions, and with the constitutional monarchy still less than 20 years old, many of these were for the preservation of tradition and reinforcement of cultural identity. Whatever the sociological perspectives, they were certainly occasions that were colourful and required pupils to be neat, orderly and well presented.

One such occasion is celebrated on 23 October every year for the commemoration of the day that King Rama V, King Chulalongkorn, passed away. It takes place near Chulalongkorn University.

Fig. 12: Wattana Suksa School commemorates King Rama V.
Flowers prepared in a wreath.

Every school would prepare flowers to offer, normally in a form of a wreath. Groups of students, some coming from afar, would then personally venerate the Rama V monument by offering the flowers and paying respects to him. The monument depicts the king on the back of his horse, and at this time of the year is — as shown on the following page — festooned with garlands, wreaths and other decorations, with flowers as part of the ceremony. The writing is very difficult to read, but it mentions helping, probably to prepare the wreath or the laying of the wreath. It may be that they are looking for a wreath that is already donated; perhaps it was contributed as part of a group and laid on their behalf. The text relates how Bangmod School laid the wreath; also discernible in the photo is an arrow, which points to a crest near to the King on his steed, possibly connected with the school.

Fig. 13: Monument to King Rama V (King Chulalongkorn)
with floral tributes.[7]

There are quite a number of school group photos in which Fuengsin is included; they show her as a diminutive figure, usually the smallest in her class, with the physique befitting a child two or three years younger. Most of them show everyone standing so the disparity is obvious and Fuengsin was very aware of this difference and was not comfortable with it. This may have been partly why few such photos show her with signs of being at all happy — in some there is a certain kind of inscrutability, sometimes a serious expression, or else a far-away look that simply ignores the photographer. As well as the outgoing explorer, there was a quieter, reflective and sometimes pensive side to Fuengsin. Looking back many years later she related that as far back as the age of seven years old she would sit under a tree and contemplate, but she didn't explain how or why. Even so, she struggled with internal sensitivities, conscious of being small and dark, a self-perception that was reinforced in school plays when she would usually be cast as a beggar.

But there were other activities she enjoyed, such as physical education, especially running and hurdling; and there was always the prospect of lunch: for their school meal children often had a fried egg on rice wrapped in a banana leaf or placed in a tin. Moreover whilst Fuengsin's physical frame was of limited stature, she distinguished herself at school through her mind; she was generally bright, especially in reading and writing, where she was advanced in years and making rapid progress.

There was still the problem, though, of an internal lack of fulfilment, and she used literature to search for solutions. As she progressed towards adulthood, she became more emotionally aware and felt an increasing sense of frustration, whilst retaining the naivety of a young child. One day she placed a poetic advertisement in a lonely hearts column, writing with a mature style that belied her youth. She received a response and a meeting was arranged. Fuengsin, seemingly oblivious to the implications, went along and met the young man who was looking for romance. But when he saw her he was immediately shocked: he was 20 years old and this young lady who had composed these sweet lines was only 12, and looked considerably younger. In a mixture of embarrassment and consternation he told her off and explained the inappropriateness and dangers of her action. The message was duly taken on board, but the sense of longing for fulfilment inside continued.

Gradually over the years Fuengsin did find some inner fulfilment through her poetry compositions. Her talents were recognised by the teachers, with invitations to read the poetry in front of the class; and she developed her literary sense with a healthy dose of everyday earthiness that permeated her later writings. In her cookery book she noted, 'Thai people like literature very much and often they put food and literature together. For instance, when the street traders announce what they are selling they put it in a rhyme which is like the list of characters in a book. In English it might be a bit like this:'

Our play on offer today is the tragedy of Hamlet. Hamlet, the hero, is played by the delicious fish curry and Ophelia is played by some crisp, tender bean sprouts. Hamlet's uncle, the villainous king, is played by some powerful dried chillies and Hamlet's mother by some very slippery noodles.

Fuengsin's taste in literature was wide-ranging, covering many genres; food was interwoven easily with folk:

A long time ago a folk drama called 'Likay' was very popular with the majority of the Thai population. Many Thai women were infatuated with an actor called

'Pho Wek', a Likay hero who was a real heartthrob. There was a story about one of his lady fans who went to a sweet stall and said to the trader, 'Two parcels of Pho Wek, please'. (Pho means 'father' or an affectionate term for a man or boy).[8]

School was also a chance for her to make more friends, whom she occasionally invited to the home, but sometimes with reluctance because she feared her mother and the domestic rules she imposed. This compounded some of her struggles and she sought to escape to other people's homes; but most of the time she was forbidden — she was effectively grounded by her parents who were exceedingly strict, considerably stricter than many families.

Fig. 14: Fuengsin's friend Supatra (nickname Dim).
Taken when she came for the first time to visit
Fuengsin at her home in 1950.

On the other hand, she enjoyed the company of her father, the family's shady tree. He was now a senior figure in the prison services department and had been promoted to Ka Luang (Governor) of a couple of prisons, latterly for the province of Ratchaburi between 1948 and 1949.[9] Although he continued to travel extensively, particularly when he became a Governor-inspector (auditor) of accounts across the country, he always tried to make himself available to his family, whether in open groups or individually in private. He was a steadying influence for his youngest daughter, who regarded him as far-sighted and very gentle in manners. Fuengsin's temperament was more like her mother than her father, in that she had a tendency to be fiery — as her nickname of Daeng ('red') indicated. Her father's presence would remind her of the benefit of *jai yen*, a cool mind (and head).

Fuengsin's enquiries weren't confined to studies in the classroom or to associations with her formal teachers or peers. One of her friends, who became an adopted aunt and was well liked by everyone, was Na Ing, a lady who had an unusual pastime: since the 1930s she had been making scrapbooks from newspaper and magazine cuttings, eventually amassing a collection of 800 books, which she subsequently donated to a library. She came from Samut Songkhram, to the south-west of Bangkok, where she lived in a house of traditional design, near a wat. Fuengsin was introduced to this world in the 1950s and proceeded to develop her interest over three decades, making copious use of photojournalism with articles from around the world. This widened her horizons and motivated her to continue her studies. It may also have whetted her appetite for international travel.

Yet despite the solid grounding in moral virtue she received at home and at school, her growing literary aptitude and the encouragement from family friends, Fuengsin continued to feel unsettled and frustrated. Problems started to mount in her teenage years and she had no means of solving them; her knowledge of Buddhist teachings was more theoretical than practical. It was at this stage that help appeared in the form of one of the wandering monks who came to the house. He was a relative on her father's side. When he visited, many people rushed to him because he was full of compassion.

Fuengsin observed his serene countenance and decided to approach and put her trust in him. She started to gain some direction and allowed him to have a moderating effect on her behaviour. Before she did anything wrong he would spot it and say, 'You seem to have lost your respect for your parents. That is why you are confused!' So he instructed her, 'Take some flowers, candles and incense and ask your mother's forgiveness.' The monk knew that Fuengsin held her mother in contempt because she didn't let her roam freely. Fuengsin believed him because he was a good teacher and very kind; he was quite an influence on her so she followed his advice. She became more reasoned and shrewd, so that from time to time she would think about her bad karma, especially why she was imprisoned and not let out anywhere without her parents' consent, besides school. Yearning for her freedom, Fuengsin then developed a plan of action. She often went to the market to buy fish — live fish — so that she could free them. Before releasing them into the river, she would say to the fish:

Now may all this good karma enable me to be free; in future, may I be free like you, may I be let out of the house. I hope one day I will go away and never come back to this house!

Notes

1. The quotation about nature's abundance is from King Ramkhamhaeng's inscription as described in *Folk Crafts in Thailand*, MOENet Thailand Service, Ministry of Education,
   http://www.moe.go.th/index-cratf/intro.htm
   King Ramkhamhaeng is traditionally attributed with formalising the (written) Thai alphabet.

2. The site of the family's former home at Ratchadamnoen is now occupied by the National Lottery Commission(!).

3. The Memorial Bridge was a constant British target; it was rebuilt and damaged several times.

4. Many of Fuengsin's childhood recollections were first recorded in *The Taste of Thailand* by Pranee Sunasavenonta and Fuengsin Trafford (ed. Margaret Breiner; unpublished manuscript, c. 1988).

5. The main reference used here concerning the development of Thailand's education system is: *History of Thai Education*, Ministry of Education:
   http://www.moe.go.th/main2/article/e-hist01.htm

6. Wattana Suksa School. Its name literally means 'a school for progress/development in studies'. The school subsequently changed hands and was renamed to Chaloipon. The area is presently used mainly for markets, with the Chalermkiat theatre located on the land it once occupied. The school eventually closed down due to economic circumstances.

7. King Chulalongkorn statue. The original photo was not good because it omits the king's head so a montage has been created with a contemporary photo to provide the essential missing details.

8. 'Pho Wek' is quite a well-known anecdote and even gets a mention in academic articles — Virulrak, S. (1980) *Likay: A popular theatre in Thailand.* — PhD Thesis, University of Hawaii. This in turn is quoted in *Theatre and Seduction: the Politics of Aesthetic Judgements in Thailand* by Dundi Mitchell, The Asia Pacific Journal of Anthropology, Volume 9, Issue 3, September 2008, pages 219–230. (However such academic treatments would not be popular with many Thais.)

9. Capt. Luang Sarayutpitag as Governor of Rajburi Prison. According to a list of Commanders of Ratchaburi Central Prison, he was the second Prison Commander, serving for a year:
   http://www.correct.go.th/copratc/commander.html

3

University Days and a Carefree Life

F uengsin's family also valued education as a career: by the time Fuengsin was in her teenage years, her sister Umpai was a schoolteacher, special-ising in English grammar.[1] Fuengsin started to develop interests in this field. She left Wattana Suksa on completing Mor 6 and went on to Triam Udom Suksa, which was established in 1938 as a preparatory school for Chulalong-korn University (commonly abbreviated as *Chula*).[2] Its founder was Mom Luang Pin Malakul, who spent a long and varied career in education, and had *inter alia* a prolific literary output. Somewhat like Sixth Form in the UK, students spent two years preparing for entry into higher education; at Triam Udom this meant specifically the Chula entrance examination. Now the blouse ribbons were dispensed with, a sign of growing independence. Furthermore, the school was mixed, and had in fact been the first co-educational school in the country.[3]

Fig. 15: Triam Udom School, Mor 7, 16 August 1952
(Fuengsin bottom row, far right).

Fig. 16: First Year (Mor 7), Triam Udom School, 22 August 1952.
(Fuengsin is in the 2nd row from back, 5th from right.)

As she posed for these obligatory photographs, which may have been taken towards the end of the first term, Fuengsin could now sense that opportunities were growing, but she still struggled with her personal circumstances. One day she had to confront a disappointment about life and became very down-hearted. She went to the same monk who had given her advice previously. He listened to her account and realised that the time had come for her to meditate, and to practice 'not merely conventional Buddhism'. He said: 'Go and see the Abbot of Wat Santidharma[ram],' which was just up the road from Fueng-sin's home in Tambol Samre. 'Tell him that I sent you there and he will look after you.'

Fuengsin believed him and went to see the Abbot. It turned out he held a title, Luang, the same as her father; his name was Phra Luang Pichit Chaloton. He had been an admiral in the navy and become quite prosperous, but was then moved to renounce the world and devote his energies to spiritual mat-ters, especially to meditation. He ordained and was asked to set up a temple on a ruined site, which used to be a residence of the sangha a long time ago. To begin with it wasn't established properly as a temple, not least because the land was located in a Roman Catholic area and owned by a local Catholic. How-ever, through his exemplary practice, he gained sufficient trust to gradually buy up the land from the Roman Catholics and a proper temple could then be built. Later, the Chinese Buddhist society went to help him and in subsequent years the temple became prosperous.

Phra Luang Pichit also became a very good teacher of meditation. His knowledge was very broad for he was well-versed in astrology and also taught Abhidhamma, the higher Dhamma that explains in detail mental processes and how they operate concurrently. Since Thonburi was the capital immediately before Bangkok it had become a repository of knowledge of teachings salvaged from Ayutthaya when the Burmese ransacked the city in the late eighteenth century. That was how these venerable Ajahns were transmitting knowledge via their disciples through many generations, going back centuries.

Luang Pichit earned considerable respect from the teachings he gave to residents of the monastery and also to interested members of the public. Fuengsin attended every Sunday and joined in the various activities, particularly the meditation practice, which she would refer to as 'Vipassana', insight practice. She spent many weekends learning there, sometimes practising in one of the huts which belonged to a *maechi*, a Buddhist white-robed nun. Fuengsin found the nuns agreeable company and began to chat frequently with them until it became a regular activity. They took care of her, feeding her, and she felt better; life was becoming less burdensome and she began to sit in meditation at home.

Fuengsin now had a solid grounding, an orientation that respected and cherished the Buddhist way of life. She was no longer satisfied with merit-making and being an upstanding citizen; an inner longing was starting to exert itself as she sought to find out answers to questions of life. It was the beginning of her journey to explore Dhamma, spiritual truth and reality, and would give her more stability as she made her way as a very privileged student — for she had passed the entrance exam into Chula.

Chulalongkorn University was founded by King Vajiravudh and named in honour of his father. It was the first Western-style university in Thailand, with a number of faculties specialising in a range of subjects covering the arts and sciences. It had grown out of a college that was originally set up to educate members of the royal court and the gentry. Fuengsin entered the Faculty of Arts and Education, the subjects brought together in recognition of the need for those formally trained in theory to apply their knowledge in practice.[4] During this time the Faculty consisted of four divisions: Thai and Oriental Languages, Foreign Languages, Geography and History, and Education. Fuengsin enrolled in 1954 at the age of 17 for the four-year Bachelor's degree in Arts.[5] The university was still relatively young, with the separation of the Arts and Science faculties having been made just a few years earlier; and new structures were still being introduced, with a Division of Library Science established within the Faculty of Arts in 1955.

Fuengsin was the first member of her family to enter Chula, so it was a significant achievement and an opportunity for everyone to celebrate, particularly for her father who had just retired the previous year. Fuengsin would be their representative, whilst other family members, especially her nieces, would accompany her there, curious to see where their aunt was studying and what it was like.

Fig. 17: Fuengsin at home, in Chulalongkorn University uniform
(as a 'freshie', indicated by the white shoes and socks).

This photo was taken at the house, by what was then the back gate (it is now near the main entrance into the soi). Immediately behind Fuengsin is a walkway over a small irrigation canal for the plants. The bench, as already mentioned, was used for offering food to the monks. In the foreground on the right is a *chompoo salek* (genus Eugenia, rose apple or Surinam cherry), a tree popular for its fruit that gives it name to a shade of pink, though the ones bought at the market are green!

Fig. 18: Fuengsin with University study materials.
Location unknown, but reckoned to be somewhere in Thonburi suburbs.

Fig. 19: Fuengsin at Phra Pathom Chedi, Nakhon Pathom.

For the first time, Fuengsin can be seen smiling broadly in many of her photos, evidently delighted and proud to have made it to Chula, where she enjoyed her new-found freedom. The soi had further cause for celebration as her next door neighbour, Tewee, was also successful, being accepted to read science. As Wongwien Yai was within a few miles of the university, they were both able to live at home, but students from other provinces would be placed in various accommodation — both within University grounds and outside; at that time most male students would stay at temples and assist the monastics in various duties, thereby learning other life skills. Halls of residence were not so common, whereas today it has become the norm, following the Western model.

Fuengsin and Tewee were enrolled in different subjects with different time-tables, so they would only meet occasionally, mainly during weekends and when there were major holidays. So it meant Fuengsin had to make some new friends. The transition from a small school to a university was huge, for there were many more students of high ability, who came from far and wide, and subjects were studied to a greater depth. The degree course was grounded in subjects specific to Thai culture, but was strongly influenced by Western European programmes and syllabi. This international flavour of learning was in those days quite rare; Chula occupied a uniquely privileged position in the Thai educational landscape.

There were more than 100 students in the same cohort (year of entrance). In the first two years classrooms would often fill up as students came together for compulsory subjects, including Thai, History and English. Later they would separate according to their choice of specialisation: Thai or Pali; English, French or German; Geography or History. In the 1950s it was still the case that arts subjects were largely the domain of women (perhaps only 10 out of 100 would be men), whilst such ratios were reversed for the sciences.

The European flavour was reflected in the teaching staff, of whom we have a remarkably vivid record. In 2004, alumni from the Faculty of Arts cohort of 1954 decided to celebrate the fiftieth anniversary of their entry into Chulalongkorn's Faculty of Arts by the publication of an anniversary book covering their undergraduate years, 1954–58.[6] The book contains many memories and tributes in a chunky volume of several hundred pages, containing text, photographs and drawings. Among these is a page of photographs of 'Ajahns Farangs' (European teachers) taken within the grounds of the University. They have been gleaned from formal sittings, including graduation ceremonies, and also more informal occasions.

อาจารย์ ปีเตอร์ เจ. บี   อาจารย์ โรเบิร์ต สะวอนน์   อาจารย์ จอร์น โบลเฟลด์

าตาจารย์ ดี.เจ. เอนไรท์   อาจารย์ อี.ซี. แมคกาแฮน   อาจารย์ฟรังซัวส์ เกรกัวร์

อาจารย์บาทหลวงอัลเฟรด บอนแนง   อาจารย์ นิโคล เดอ โบเวส์

Fig. 20: 'Ajahns Farangs' at Chula.

Along the top row, from left to right, are Ajahn Peter, J.B., Ajahn Robert Swann and Ajahn John Blofeld. Underneath are Professor D.J. Enright, Ajahn E. C. McGann and Ajahn François Grégoire. In the third row are Ajahn Father Alfred Bonninque and Ajahn Nicole de Beauvais. These were educational pioneers, many of whom had distinguished careers in and beyond academia. For example, Robert Swann, who came to Thailand to work for the Foreign Office and, in the 1970s and 1980s, became a prominent figure in developing relations between Arabs and non-Arabs; Prof. Enright was a noted man of letters; whilst Ajahn Father Alfred Bonninque was a Jesuit priest who became committed to Thai social welfare, helping to establish the first credit union in Thailand in the mid-1960s. Most of them had a radical outlook — just to be in Thailand at that time was not something for 'the man on the Clapham Omnibus'.[7]

The undergraduates generally regarded the Ajahns with affection and respect, especially those with European connections. However, the figure that was — unbeknownst at the time — to prefigure somewhat and influence Fuengsin later in her life was John Blofeld, who lived and remained in Thailand from the late 1940s until his death in 1987. Little is actually recorded about his years in Thailand since he had already developed a strong affinity for dynastic China, which he had studied intensively for twenty years. Perhaps only his close friends knew about it at that time (Fuengsin certainly didn't), but many years later most of the biographical details he related paid homage to that period; the rest he largely disregarded. Yet Thailand was the country where he spent more years than any other and provided the mainstay of his subsistence with a decade of teaching at Chula from 1951 to 1961; he was there throughout Fuengsin's study period.

Ajahn Blofeld was appreciated as a benign and encouraging presence by his students, as exemplified by a poem which he addressed to newcomers. Entitled, 'The Four Years', he produced verses of the simple 4-line rhyme scheme, describing the challenges and delights of life as a student at Chula. There was one verse per year plus a further verse for the final year. It ended:

> The last exam is much abhorred,
> But this is followed by a day
> When names are posted on the board —
> "Nai Dum and Nangsao Dang, B.A." !!!
>   John Blofeld.[8]

'Nangsao Dang' was an appellation that could apply to Fuengsin and the verse expressed an outcome to which she doubtless aspired. However, she was not a model student. The book also includes a page-long tribute to Fuengsin, who by way of reminder to her former classmates is introduced as 'our diminutive friend with a dark skin, very nimble and agile'. She is described as full of mischief, earning from her close friends the nickname of 'Fuengfoi', which literally means 'she who flourishes in bragging' as she was very chatty and talkative, always pushing boundaries. To illustrate her character, an episode is recounted where she had observed that Ajahn Grégoire, their French teacher, was actually an engineer by background and he would arrive in a rush from teaching in the engineering department. The class had become bogged down, struggling with the subject matter. So Fuengsin cheekily suggested that he would be better off staying with the engineers rather than coming over and bothering the class of Arts students.

Fuengsin grew in confidence as she found much to enjoy at Chula, so much so that one friend remarked that it was as though she owned the place! Her liveliness and clever choice of words made her attractive so that despite her mischief, she was regarded as having a charming and amusing personality, enabling her to get on well with many people. She was also known for being helpful in unconventional ways, making friends relax even if they were in serious difficulties close to the exams. Over the course of four years she would encourage others in her group to study informally together in the lobby of the Faculty of Arts building, where they would tease and joke with each other, pull each other's leg, and engage in eloquent debate, with everyone cheering on. She was in her element in this environment and made learning fun.

Fig. 21: Auditorium, Chulalongkorn University examinations venue
(October 2010).

Fuengsin readily admitted to being a crammer, preferring to make the most of student life in a very broad sense — she was living it up and enjoyed perhaps a bit too much the many opportunities for socialising. Yet, despite her apparent rebelliousness, she had an exceptionally perceptive and retentive mind and acted as a coach for other students. This was the case with European literature, especially plays, whose meaning many students found hard to fathom; but Fuengsin could grasp and explain the meaning, including the plays of Shakespeare.

Ivory towers offered sublime delights, but were no deterrent to Fuengsin's continued pursuit of earthly tastes, particularly lunch. She recalled:

> When I was a student at Chulalongkorn University . . . When the bell rang for lunch, everyone used to make a mad dash . . . I used to sit at the back of the lecture room as close to the door as possible so that I would get there first!

And especially if it meant meeting unusual people:

> I became friendly with a dark, muscular female boxer. At lunch time she was one of the traders who gathered near the university canteen. . . . After I had eaten my noodles, I went over to where my friend was selling banana fritters to the students. Because she liked chatting with me she gave me free bananas every day.

Fuengsin took the opportunity to seek some pugilistic advice and learnt a few moves, including a one-two combination, '*Dhow lukoy, doy lukang!*', being a blow to the body, and then the chin, which she would later demonstrate with her 'bony fists' — fortunately in slow motion. In an effort to strengthen her physical body she also used to practise with dumbbells.

Food was a vehicle for getting to know many friends, including one who gave her rice and assorted food every day. Her name was Vasana and her family lived not so far away from Fuengsin's in Banglampoo. They would often go out together and visit each other's homes. Despite Fuengsin's scrounging, Vasana became one of Fuengsin's closest friends for the remainder of her life, someone who shared a deep interest in education, but who was of different character and acted as a stabilising influence. She was also very tolerant and may have allowed for this scrounging knowing that Fuengsin's family was relatively poor with a limited budget, though Fuengsin would have still been well fed.

Fig. 22: An opening gala to welcome Freshies.
Attending as 3rd Year students, (round the table, l to r)
Vasana, Orasa, Natsawang, and Fuengsin.

Fig. 23: Fuengsin (top left) with some classmates and Ajahn;
in this case aided by a cheeky wave.

Fuengsin enjoyed socialising and exploring what life had to offer, in both the urban and rural environment. Bangkok was an exciting place for these students, offering opportunities to sample films, art, 1950s fashions, and so on, driven strongly by influences from the United States, which had really come to the fore. The visual image was especially gaining in prominence. Like many of her contemporaries in Triam Udom School, Fuengsin joined a craze for black and white portrait photography, taking lots of snaps and signing them with various intimate messages for close friends, and adopting the hairstyles and poses of Hollywood film stars.

The photos were more varied at Chula, but many of them remained sentimental, requesting to be remembered, especially when far apart. Quite a few were shared with humorous messages that were perceptive about each other's character. One photograph from a junior student read: 'To Sister Fuengsin to remember that you have a good heart, more than I can describe, more than I can count . . . look at this photo and remember me — especially when you are angry . . . Just joking!' Her fiery temperament was well known. Another joker instructed Fuengsin to pay homage to her photo before going to bed and no doubt Fuengsin had a suitable riposte.

A few others would tease her about her dark complexion: among a set of wedding photos was one taken at the reception of a formal dinner. Surrounding the bride and groom were civilians and officers formally dressed in suits, one with ceremonial sword. They were all wearing white. On the back of the photo the message addressed to Fuengsin read: 'When feeling fed up take a look at this photo. If you look very often at this photo your skin colour will become lighter, and you will become fair!'

Fuengsin built up quite a large collection as she associated more widely than just the Faculty where she studied; she would also wander over to the Faculty of Political Science and retained photos that bore the Faculty stamp. She was keen to explore widely different views of the world, especially if they were dynamic and challenging. Although she didn't herself engage actively in politics, some of her friends did, a few leaning strongly to the left. She extended her circle further, beyond Chula, particularly to Silapakorn University, where she would often hang out with friends in fine arts. She enjoyed their creativity and alternative perspective on life, no doubt offering further radical views.

There were many group trips to other provinces near and far, with students from different years travelling together, mainly organised by senior members. Some were day trips, whilst others lasted three, four or even five days; sometimes this was for training, when accommodation was arranged in places such as a teacher's college, and then they'd go out in the evening.

Quite a number of trips were 'up country', towards Northeast Thailand, including one to Nakorn Rajasima, where Vasana's brother was the guide as he was at that time stationed in the army there.

Fig. 24: Phra Prang Sam Yod, Lopburi.

The journeys took in some famous architectural sites, including Phra Prang Sam Yod (Three Holy Prangs [or Towers]) in Lopburi. This site is probably Khmer, twelfth or thirteenth century, and on examination of some of its decoration is thought to have previously been a Hindu temple with the three prangs symbolising Vishnu, Shiva and Brahma. It was converted to a Buddhist shrine later on. With the benefit of their classical education, the students could reflect in an informed way, though how much they did only the students would know. They may have preferred just to enjoy each other's company and chatting.

The students took full advantage of Thailand's wonderful natural environment with outings that included rural idylls of caves and waterfalls, grassy meadows and hillside brooks.

Fig. 25: Chequered designs were *in* for that rustic look in the 1950s.
Fuengsin is third from the left.

Fig. 26: Fuengsin with friends in a cave.

Fig. 27: A delightful picnic.

On another occasion, in the 3rd Year of study in the Faculty of Arts, a group went to visit a Thai Royal Air Fleet in Korat. It was where Khun Vasana met her future husband, Khun Jamras Kamkoon, who was at that time a pilot instructor.

Fig. 28: Group photo at Air Fleet, Korat.

Other friends could come along who weren't necessarily students at Chula; in Korat they were joined by Songsee (shown in the photo, fourth from left), a childhood friend of Vasana whom Fuengsin came to know well also. They were welcome to join the trips, some of which headed towards the coast, including Chonburi, where they would pop across to Koh Samet, taking a boat from the shore to the island; and further east, to Ban Phe in Rayong. Fuengsin enjoyed these outings immensely — and revelled in various poses for the camera, free to wear casual clothes, here as a 'tom boy' complete with cap. This was in complete contrast to her days in school uniform.

Fig. 29: Group atop a rocky outcrop along the shore.

Fig. 30: Fuengsin by a fishing boat, Silacha

Life off campus was a beach, a forest, a field, all in the company of many friends. She had so much fun that however good her potential, it took a long while for Fuengsin to master personal discipline; when she wrote the following it may well have been from experience:

> In April when mangoes are young and green, people sit under their mango trees and eat them raw with fish sauce, onion, chili and sugar. If you eat too many, you will get a painful stomach. April is also the time of the year when students are writing their final exams. Often times they are tempted by the green mangoes and end up writing their exams in terrible agony.

Fuengsin didn't achieve the marks she was capable of, but she did manage to pass, so she could duly take her place among the other successful candidates and participate in the graduation ceremony in the auditorium. In those days the graduates had the great honour of receiving their awards from the King of Thailand, His Majesty, King Bhumibol Adulyadej, who in his lifetime has presented approximately 500,000 certificates.

Many photos were taken on this happy occasion, both individual and in various groups, particularly with the Ajahns.

Fig. 31: Portrait photo of Fuengsin in her graduation gown[9].
(Bachelor of Arts, Chulalongkorn University.)

Fig. 32: Chula Graduates besides the *nagas*.

A popular spot was on the steps besides the *nagas* (dragon-like beings act-ing as protectors) in front of the auditorium.

Fig. 33 (left): Fuengsin alongside Ajahn Robert Swann, Lecturer in English.

Fig. 34 (right): With Prof. Dr Kitkasem Sriboonrearn (French, phonetics) and two fellow students, both of whom later became professors.

Fig. 35: Graduation: group photograph with Prof D. J. Enright.
(Fuengsin standing, fifth from the left.)

Fuengsin performed sufficiently well to have the opportunity for further study, which she subsequently chose to undertake. Gradually her temperament became more restrained, and in their tribute her Chula friends tells us that the wildness that characterised her BA years was to diminish some time later when she went to further her studies in the Faculty of Education.

Notes

1. Khun Umpai retained her formal correctness in English conversation right through until old age, correcting her younger relatives if they made any obvious mistakes.

2. Fuengsin could choose from only a handful of universities in Thailand: the first for lay people and most prestigious was Chulalongkorn University (1917), followed by Thammasat University (1934) and then Kasetsart University, Mahidol University, and Silapakorn University (1943), and Srinakharinwirot University (1949). The earliest universities were monastic institutions.

3. Triam Udom. The Wikipedia article about the school (now a Sixth Form college) talks about teacher training being extended to High School.
   http://en.wikipedia.org/wiki/Triam_Udom_Suksa_School

4. Faculty of Arts and Education. Until 1948, the Faculty had simply been called the Faculty of Arts.
   http://www.arts.chula.ac.th/06about/history1-en.html

5. Summer in Thailand (the hot season) is from April to June, so current terms are June to October and mid-November to mid-March.

6. *Faculty of Arts 50th Anniversary Book: 2497-2501* Thai title: เพื่อนสนิทมิตรสหาย ณ เทวาลัย อักษร ศาสตร์ จุฬาลงกรณมหา วิทยาลัย 2497-2501

7. The careers of some of the European Ajahns are given in the following references.

    Robert Swann Obituary, The Guardian, 24 August 2001:
    http://www.guardian.co.uk/news/2001/aug/24/guardianobituaries.richardeyre

    D.J. Enright, Poet and Novelist, Dies at 82, New York Times, 12 January 2003:
    http://www.nytimes.com/2003/01/12/obituaries/12ENRI.html

    Ajahn Father Alfred Bonninque: See e.g. a profile on the Thai Cooperative website,
    http://www.coopthai.com/kmj/Fathercultthai.html

    and the Credit Union League of Thailand page,
    http://www.gdrc.org/icm/cult-thai.html

    John Blofeld. See especially his autobiography, *My Journey in Mystic China: Old Pu's Travel Diary* translated from the Chinese by Daniel Reid.

8. John Blofeld. *Timeless words for New Members, 2500*. From the Chula Faculty of Arts Alumni 50 Years anniversary volume, p.237.

9. The background of this photo has been touched up to be closer to the original — with apologies to the purist who would leave all photos untouched.

4

Professional Life:
Teaching and Meditation

It was little more than a decade after the end of the Second World War. Thailand was witnessing a period of growing industrialisation, with considerable attention being given to education to help run a modernising economy. Despite her sporadic application as a student, Fuengsin had shown an ability to teach and decided to pursue a professional career in this field. In doing so she was joining an expanding subject area.

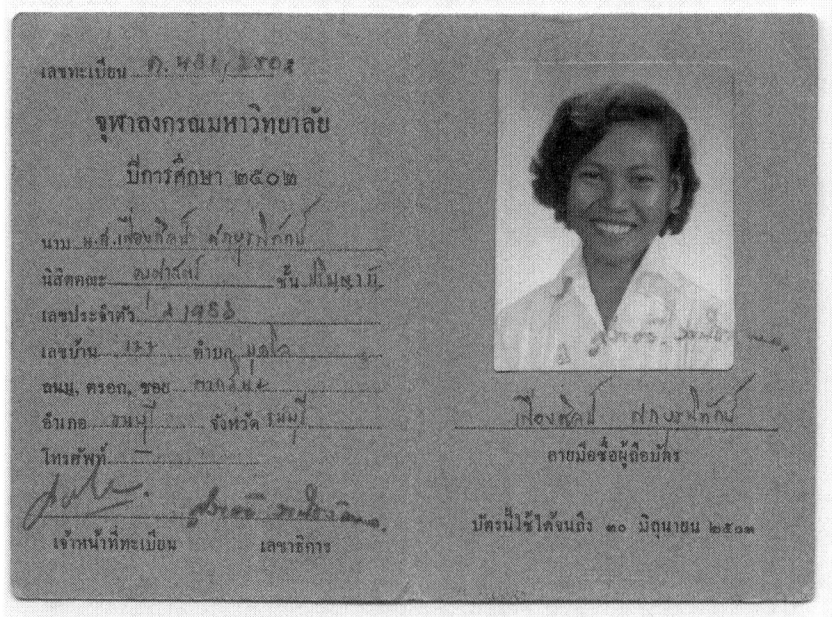

Fig. 36: Fuengsin's ID card at the Faculty of Education, Chulalongkorn University, 1959.

On completion of her BA, in 1958, Fuengsin enrolled on a two-year post-graduate Bachelor of Education, which was a year after the Division of Education was promoted to become the Faculty of Education.[1] The degree required gaining practical experience of teaching — its preparation and delivery — and all students in the Faculty were required to apply their training to the various subjects they themselves had studied, including English and History.

Fuengsin thus acquired useful administrative skills and gained an appreciation for orderliness and steady application. It was no longer the case that she could get by with doing things at the last minute, especially as she was conscious of the need to take care of her students. Occupying the other side of the fence, as it were, made her realise greater responsibility.

Fig. 37: Fuengsin preparing for lessons on a Remington typewriter.

Fig. 38: Fuengsin comments on herself:
'In this picture I look *choie laek* ('out of date')'.[2]

Fig. 39: With a Mathayom student during teacher training.

Fuengsin duly completed the BEd, graduating in 1960. In customary style she followed a precise ritual: as she had done for her BA, she went up to the

King, who was seated, knelt before him, and then revealed that her hand was empty, before reaching out to collect her degree.[3] The ritual to show that nothing is concealed in the right hand is an echo of the country's sometimes turbulent history, and therefore a way of showing that somebody is trustworthy.

Fig. 40: Fuengsin Sarayutpitag receiving her BEd degree from
H.M. King Bhumibol Adulyadej, 21 April 1960.[4]

Fuengsin's first job was teaching English as a foreign language at the new Thonburi Technical College in Bangmod (*bang* means 'district', and *mod* means 'ant'), an area a few miles to the south. The college had been formally established by the Ministry of Education on 4 February 1960. It came under the Office for Technical Colleges, Department of Vocational Education, and received high school graduates in science.[5]

Compared with the celestial environment of Chula, which occupied a prime location in central Bangkok, this college was basic in its design and quite out of the way. On arrival at the site, there were no Thai architectural gems to marvel at and no mature gardens through which to wander at leisure. It was completely utilitarian and fit for purpose: the College occupied a vacant building that already had mains electricity, water on tap and telephone lines, which meant that the property could be used immediately. In fact, it had been in use as a teaching facility for a few years previously. Fuengsin kept in her possession a New Year card from that time.

Fig. 41: New Year Card, showing a college building in 1954,
before it became home to Thonburi College of Technology.

This New Year card had the following message on the back:

On the occasion of the New Year, I wish that you obtain the following blessings:
1. May you pass the examinations with highest marks
2. May you be top in every course of study — get top grades
3. May you be beloved to the teacher.

Fuengsin joined in summer 1960 and started her first post as an Ajahn. When she arrived the College still occupied just the single building on two floors. It contained 14 classrooms, housing for the faculty, and a small cafeteria. More capacity was needed and construction work was already on the way. To address the country's recognised skill shortages, developments were now accelerating across many fronts. In May 1961, the Ministry of Education approved a new curriculum in engineering consisting of four subject areas: civil engineering, electrical engineering, mechanical engineering and metallurgy. A year later the college started to make use of an entrance exam alongside universities, run by the National Education Council.

Fig. 42: Fuengsin and other Ajahns at Thonburi Technical College,
where the site was being developed (underneath some scaffolding).

Fig. 43: Ajahn Fuengsin Sarayutpitag comes for an English Department
examination as heavy rains fall.[6]

Not everything was plain sailing. Thailand's monsoon season brought particularly heavy rains in 1962. In those days the road network was still basic and liable to flooding, with roads becoming boggy. According to accounts of King Mongkut's University of Technology Thonburi, it meant teachers and students would walk for five kilometres, trying to avoid the mud. Many students missed class, but the Ajahns had to make every effort, including Ajahn Fuengsin, especially when there was an examination.

The academic environment was also rather different from Chula, in terms of students, their abilities and their interests. Instead of abstract discussions about European literature, Fuengsin was required to ensure that the engineers could understand technical information in English and make themselves understood. Of course, it would not have escaped anyone's attention that Fuengsin was one of the few female academics. However, the diminutive Ajahn had no problem controlling the class; the students respected her and dutifully tried their best in a subject that many found very challenging.

There were also group activities, though this time Ajahn Fuengsin refrained from the exhibitionism that characterised her appearances in some of her student photos. Formally attired, her former wildness was now subdued, at least on the surface, as she adopted a serious pose.

Fig. 44: Group activities; *Ajahn* Fuengsin keeps a sober expression.

Yet Fuengsin still saw opportunities to apply her literary background and encourage her students to explore arts and culture, balancing the subject matter of technology and science. She produced traditional Thai drama, including Thai dances normally performed by women, but as there were no women in the college, they were bravely performed by men, much to the amusement of some fellow students.

Fig. 45: College students performing traditional Thai dance.

Fuengsin received copies of some photos with messages. On the back of the above photo was written: 'I give this to my instructor . . . on the anniversary of the college . . . in . . . Thonburi . . . 4 February 2505 [1962]'. She would keep in touch with some staff and students for many years.

In parallel to her professional duties, she also took the opportunity to teach her nephews and nieces, including her sister Wilai's son, Laem, the youngest. He recalled that, when he was about nine years old, in Mor 4, she would tutor him in his homework in the mornings, before she set off for work and he went to school; by his own admission, he was somewhat lazy and unable to understand the materials during the evenings, so he would wait for his aunt to teach and explain things. Suitably edified, he would join Da Hoy, the resident architect/builder, and be escorted to wait for the school bus in front of the soi, whilst Fuengsin would head off to the technical college.

* * *

Fuengsin had maintained her Dhamma practice in her young adult life with Phra Luang Pichit Chalorton, the Abbot at Wat Santidhammaram, until he passed away in 1961. His successor was Ajahn Praderm, who had another centre in Thonburi and became famous in Vipassana practice.[7] However, Fuengsin had already begun the search for another teacher before he arrived and was looking for someone with whom she had rapport. This is very common among Thais as aspirants often seek a person rather than an organisation, someone who will personally inspire practice and whom they feel happy to support. Often potential supporters look also for lineage, some indication that the Buddha's teachings from 2,500 years ago have been transmitted intact right through to the present day. Thus Fuengsin would go from temple to temple and meet various monks, from whom she found inspiration to finding answers to her questions.

Fuengsin thus continued her search in Thonburi, meeting a variety of teachers who taught different methods, some of whom, together with their students, engaged in unusual practices.[8] She later recalled:

> I studied with a good teacher for a while, but he did not have the same influence on me as my last teacher. He is very famous about psychic research as he has a lab at home. And one of his students is a medium. He got in touch with spirits through her. He had special powers. He wrote books about psychic results and he also tried to simplify and adapt Buddhism to every-day life. ... He wrote a book about applied Buddhism.

Fuengsin added that whilst studying with him, she met a monk who was later to become the abbot of Wat Buddhapadipa in England. Yet after Phra Luang Pichit, Fuengsin couldn't settle with any teacher and the methods she was taught didn't click with her and felt unsuitable, so she had to continue her search. It was subsequent to this that Ajahn Prakhong, one of her colleagues at Thonburi Technical College, suggested that she pay a visit to another temple, Wat Paknam.

Wat Paknam (literally 'water gate monastery') was also in Thonburi, not far from the college and home. It had become famous due to the energetic efforts of its formidable abbot, Chao Khun Phramongkolthepmuni. The Chao Khun was more commonly known as Luang Phor Sodh, after his given name of 'Sodh', which means 'fresh'; his ordained name was Candasaro Bhikkhu.[9] Luang Phor was an expert in meditation who taught a method called Dhammakaya, i.e. 'Body of Dhamma', also described as 'Buddha form or essence'.[10] The key aspect was that it taught the Middle Way in a literal sense in that it identified the centre of the human being as the location in which to still the mind. It suited Fuengsin, not least because it was a direct way to become well centred and emotionally balanced.

Fuengsin had just missed seeing the great abbot in person as he had recently passed away, in 1959. So when she arrived at the monastery she was taken to see a nun. Fuengsin subsequently described her:

> The nun that I studied with was a frail looking lady, small. [She] came from a farming community, without much education. 20 years later a lot of people went to study with her and she founded one of the largest centres in Thailand — the most famous centre in Thailand — and her biography was printed. I spent a lot of time with her, meditating, listening to her teacher's tapes.

This was Khun Yay Upasika Chandra, a maechi who went on to found Wat Phra Dhammakaya, the largest temple in Thailand.[11] Through the guidance of this nun, Fuengsin got to know about the founder and his method.

> He was a famous Abbot and founded the method which I am doing. [Practice by this method] means visualisation of the Buddha, visualising a lot of things (the Void in the centre of the body etc.) the whole time you are meditating — Gotama Buddha, all the Buddha forms etc., everything.

The practise of visualisation, which lies at the heart of the method, leads to seeing clearly and brightly, initially taking as the object of meditation something simple like the moon, sun or a crystal ball or — for those who are able — a crystal Buddha, and allowing that object to gently reside at the centre of the body. At first the object is imagined (as recollecting a familiar personal object), and then whatever is in the field of vision is observed, at the centre, *choie choei* (silently, just letting it be, without forcing) as it stabilises, changes and becomes more refined.

The method was elaborated in many of the tapes, which were recordings of public sermons — Luang Phor was an innovator in terms of dissemination and recognised the importance of using technology for communication. One of these sermons that Fuengsin may well have listened to was originally given on the full moon day of 1 January 1955, just a few years prior. It was probably still fresh in the memories of some of her fellow practitioners. In this sermon Luang Phor taught the Dhammacakkapavatana Sutta, the discourse on the setting in motion of the Wheel of Dhamma, the path to the cession of *dukkha* (suffering). The abbot proceeded methodically to explain the Buddha's admonition to avoid the extremes of sensual indulgence and self-mortification by following the Middle Way, a path of purification that always retains this sense of 'middle' as it leads inwards through the centre of the centre.

Fuengsin also learnt how the great Abbot harnessed collective effort by deploying a special team:

And the nun[s] studied with him and he said, "I will use these ladies to study the advanced meditation — very powerful meditation." He started a nunnery. There was a ... workshop and only nuns were allowed there, only the nuns with very advanced meditation. And they take turn[s] to do it all night. They do all sorts of things like curing cancer as well. Meditating, visualising, saving Thailand, to stop the invasion of Mara etc., all sorts of things . . . Some nuns go [on until] about two to three o'clock in the morning and then other nuns take turns. And monks also have their own study and their own teacher. But then the nuns started to teach there in the workshop — they have microphones — to the advanced monks, to their residence, so they can listen.

Fuengsin seemed to have no problem digesting these accounts for she felt the integrity of the practice and she could see how women were empowered to play a very important part in that temple. She was encouraged and studied with Upasika Chandra for a while; and feeling a growing sense of freedom she continued exploring the temple to see who else was teaching. Afterwards she met another nun who appeared young and attractive. This nun gave her a green stone, which was round and very strange looking, but beautiful. She related that the stone belonged to a deity who gave it to her when she was in the forest meditating. Now she wanted Fuengsin to take the stone because she would have to travel — that stone would make her travel.

Fuengsin continued her investigations of the meditators at the temple until she was led to another teacher, a lay man who taught followers at his house, which was very close by. His name was Ajahn Gaew (*gaew* means 'crystal' or 'glass') and he had been one of the disciples of the late Abbot throughout most of the 1950s. When they met for the first time, the Ajahn gazed at her and declared, 'You have a big Buddha within you!' Ajahn Gaew was pleased to accept Fuengsin as a student and Fuengsin knew her search was over.

Ajahn Gaew was of Chinese origin and had the formal Thai name of Nai Gaew Potikanok (the surname is derived from *Bodhi*, which means 'of Buddha nature', plus, *kanaka*, which means 'gold'). Being about 10 years older than Fuengsin, he was similar in age to her siblings. He established a career in the printing trade and then had a chemist shop stocked with Chinese medicines which he bought in bulk; he also taught Chinese language at a Chinese school. He had become active at Wat Paknam towards the latter years of the late Abbot's tenure and had gained a reputation for being a meditation adept, able to attain to penetrative insight with *Vijja Dhammakaya*, the advanced levels of the practice. He had wanted to become a bhikkhu, but when he arrived at the

Fig. 46: Ajahn Gaew Potikanok.

temple he already had a family with children, so he stayed as a lay person, until taking temporary ordination somewhat later, when the children were older. Despite his family commitments, Ajahn Gaew continued to devote a lot of time to the monastery and meditation practice. He had several groups, which included monastics as well as lay people, and committed himself to teaching and practising in evenings and at weekends. The groups would meet in various venues, sometimes in a *kuti* (meditation hut) of an elderly bhikkhu, on the corner, with about 20 students, including monks, nuns and lay people. At other times he would teach at his home.

Soon after meeting Fuengsin, Ajahn Gaew took her to 'meet' the late Abbot, whose coffin was in a special shrine room; his body had been embalmed, not cremated, and remained inside. Ajahn took special interest in her, and her progress in meditation became rapid. He was also convivial, going out with groups at weekends to have something to eat in a restaurant, where he often chatted about China, about politics and about worldly situations. This was somewhat unusual and even questionable for a Dhamma teacher, but he could do so in a way that showed the relevance of the wider context and it fascinated Fuengsin. Fuengsin thus started to consolidate her practice and she drew interest in her family. Although her parents were not inclined to practise, she managed to encourage two of her sisters, Phi Wijit and Phi Wilai, who also came to the temple and started practising, and later some of their children also.

* * *

Ajahn Gaew's international perspective appeared prescient. The college recognised the need for improving the English language skills of its students and Fuengsin attended a British Council Summer School in 1962. However, the major announcement for that year was on 19 December when the college was awarded substantial support from the United Nations Development Programme (Special Funds). Its first project plan, with the unimaginative name of 'Thonburi Technical Institute Project SF Thailand 7', provided for the distribution of educational tools, a number of academic experts (mainly Europeans) and overseas scholarships. It had a total value of over US $1million, with match funding from the Thai government. The scholarships enabled a handful of college lecturers to train abroad and Fuengsin was chosen to be in the first group of five, serving as a UNESCO Fellow specialising in teaching methods.[12]

Fuengsin became eligible having performed sufficiently well in a special examination in which she competed with candidates from other educational establishments in Thailand. They were ranked according to performance. The top candidate had first choice and could select from some of the most prestigious institutions; one of the other candidates, who came just above her, was Supit, a Chula classmate, who went on to study at the Sorbonne, where she obtained a PhD in French and Italian literature. Fuengsin was still left with a number of interesting options and for a while was considering a certain capital city in Eastern Europe.

By now Fuengsin had read quite a lot about world affairs and had been gathering for her scrapbooks many reports about Russia's space exploration that were spearheaded by the cosmonaut Yuri Gagarin, who, in April 1961, had recently been the first human to go into space and orbit the Earth. Being adventurous in spirit, Fuengsin was very curious to learn about life in Moscow. However, her path was intercepted: her brother-in-law was an inspector in the Thai police special intelligence services and one of his colleagues had noticed Fuengsin popping in and out of the Russian Embassy in Bangkok. A short while later Fuengsin was invited to discuss the matter with some advisors, particularly from the United States Embassy. Perhaps she was reminded of certain political aspects — the 'Cold War' and developments along Thailand's eastern borders — and their implications for Thailand's national security. The details remain a mystery, but in any case she was persuaded to think again and the choice was narrowed down to the University of Michigan or the Institute of Education in London. Eventually she opted for the British capital.

Fig. 47: Fuengsin reading photojournals in the Common Room (1962). The article is about President Khrushchev.

Notes

1. At that time, the Faculty of Education at Chulalongkorn University had two pathways to qualification: either a straight four-year degree in Education or a two-year follow-on degree for those who already had graduated from another Faculty.

2. '*choie laek*'. As explained by her friend, Vasana, it means acting or dressing in a style that causes amusement among our friends because it appears old-fashioned and out of date.

3. During the course of his lifetime, His Majesty King Bhumibol Adulyadej has presented approximately 500,000 certificates — according to *60th Anniversary of the First Graduation Ceremony in the Reign of the present King*, Mahidol University, April 2010.

4. The Degree Ceremony photo records 'Royal Graduation Ceremony, Academic Year 2503'. It doesn't indicate which degree and it can't be deduced from the gown because there are only four types of gown, one of which is for a Bachelor's Degree, but the year strongly suggests the BEd. The ceremony would have been very similar for the BA, most likely awarded two years earlier, in 1958.

5. A detailed history of King Mongkut University of Technology, Thonburi (KMUTT), formerly Thonburi Technical College, is available from the KMUTT website produced in 2010 for the fiftieth anniversary.
   http://www2.kmutt.ac.th/thai/abt_history/index.html

   Some information in English at:
   http://global.kmutt.ac.th/about/history

   Videos covering the history are available from Youtube:
   http://www.youtube.com/watch?v=gi8qlGDuPA4
   http://www.youtube.com/watch?v=IYsRgwsdBQ4

   Fuengsin may be seen in a Thonburi Technical College staff photograph, shown about two minutes into a KMUTT 50th anniversary video,
   http://www.youtube.com/watch?v=rmvb97VvcE0

6. The exam day photo was contributed by Mr Phimon Sattabut to the KMUTT archive:
   http://archive.lib.kmutt.ac.th/index.php?option=com_joomgallery&func=detail&id=526&Itemid=55

7. Ajahn Praderm. A description of this monk and his monastery, Wat Pleng, is given in *Bhikkhu: Disciple of the Buddha* by Kristiaan Inwood
   http://d30021575.purehost.com/book_reviews/bhikkhu_phuket_gaz.html

8. On seeking a teacher. According to a friend, when seeking advice on how to go about finding a teacher, one person advised Fuengsin: 'Well, you turn around and around and then go in that direction' and that is how she found her teacher, but the author doesn't recall any such account.

9. For a biography of Chaokhun Phramongkolthepmuni (Luang Phor Sodh), the late Abbot of Wat Paknam, see e.g. *Life and Times of Luang Phaw Wat Paknam*, published by the Dhammakaya Foundation.

10. Luang Phor Sodh gave weekly sermons on Dhamma to the public, many of the more recent ones were recorded on tape. Of the relatively few that have been translated into English, an important collection in two volumes is: *Visuddhivācā, Translation of Morradok Dhamma* [Dhamma Heritage] *of Luang Phaw Wat Pak Nam Phramongkolthepmuni*, 60th Dhammachai Education Foundation, Dhammakaya Foundation: Volumes I and II, published in 2006 and 2008 respectively, which include sermons from 1949 to 1955. In particular, Lesson IX records a sermon in which Luang Phor teaches the Dhammacakkapavatana sutta (the sutta on the setting in motion of the Wheel of Dhamma), where he describes the Middle Way and the Eightfold Noble Path, which lie at the heart of the practice taught by the Buddha.

11. Upasika Chan[dra]. Her full name, which was attributed by practitioners at the Wat, was to be Khun Yay Ajahn Maharattana Upasika Chandra Khonnokyoong. *Chandra* means 'moon'; *maharattana* means 'great jewel'; *khonnokyoong* means 'peacock

feather'. After she passed away hundreds of thousands of people, including the author, attended her cremation ceremony on 3 February 2002.

12. Details about UNESCO funding are taken from the account of the historical development of the university, KMUTT's Archive:
http://archive.lib.kmutt.ac.th/index.php?option=com_content&view=article&id=16 9:2010-01-19-13-10-23

5

First Time Abroad:
Whirlwind Activities

In the 1960s air travel was glamorous; even in Europe and North America it was considered a privilege of the wealthy and influential to take to the skies. Far more so for Orientals, most of whom would not have dreamt of flying to another country, let alone another continent. The images they held about Europe and especially London — Fuengsin's destination — were commonly romantic and idealistic. In reality, transcontinental flights were long and involved several changes and possibly lengthy waits for connections, as illustrated in the film *The V.I.P.s* (1963), which told the story of a group of wealthy people stranded at Heathrow by fog.

So, on her departure in September 1963, a large crowd gathered to say their farewells to Fuengsin. Even though it was a working day there were dozens of

Fig. 48: Fuengsin with monks close to the Sarayutpitag household.

well-wishers from family and extended family together with various friends and acquaintances, colleagues and students, and household staff. Among those who attended there were also many monks from various temples in and around Bangkok, demonstrating that the family was a great supporter of the monastic community; the family's heartfelt respect for the monks, led by Khun Yay Somboon, was well known. So the monastics responded with their presence and gave their blessings to Fuengsin especially as she was travelling to a land where few inhabitants knew about Buddhism. Although most monks committed to staying permanently as a monastic, not all were able to remain in robes. However, whatever their course in life, they often kept connected with the family: one of those who later disrobed went on to work as a clerk for Fuengsin's brother-in-law in Phatthalung and Surat Thani, in the South.

Fig. 49: Fuengsin with her parents,
Capt. Luang Sarayutpitag and Mrs Somboon Sarayutpitag.

Fig. 50: Fuengsin with her mother and cousin, Ven. Chalerm (Suttirak)
and other Sangha members.

Wearing monk's robes at that time was Chalerm Suttirak, who had under-taken the traditional Rains Retreat that summer, which may have been timed to coincide with Fuengsin's departure for England.

Fig. 51: Fuengsin with her sisters, nieces, nephew and other relatives.

There were also friends from university.

Fig. 52: Fuengsin and 'Jao Lek',
a long-time friend from Chulalongkorn University.

And many of her students turned up to add their support in the send-off of their Ajahn. It was also a significant occasion for the college.

Fig. 53: Fuengsin and colleagues from Thonburi Technical College
at Don Muang Airport, 1963.

Fig. 54: Fuengsin and students from Thonburi Technical College
at Don Muang Airport, 1963.

As Fuengsin boarded the plane, Fuengsin's relatives and friends were all very proud of her, and had high expectations of her trip. For many of them believed a shining career in education beckoned.

* * *

After a day-long flight on a De Havilland Comet 4[1] Fuengsin arrived safely in the UK as the plane touched down at London Airport (now Heathrow). One of the first things she noticed was the cool autumnal weather, which felt like the north of Thailand in winter. Entering the airport terminal she navigated through Heathrow's passageways and the crowds, with people of many different nationalities. Very few of them, as far as she could tell, were Oriental, let alone Thai, for this was a land of the fair-skinned Farangs where most non-Europeans were from South Asia or Africa. Don Muang airport had seemed busy, but this airport was a much larger international hub, and the effect was magnified as people were generally a lot bigger. With a stature comparable perhaps to a 12-year-old English girl, it seemed like a land of giants. Many thoughts must have been racing in Fuengsin's mind as she was taking in all the new experiences. Clutching her passport, itself a rare possession, Fuengsin proceeded to pass through immigration, collected her small blue suitcase, and exited via Customs. A visitor from Thailand was still considered quite exotic, and naturally invited curiosity. The UK's border agency and customs officers may well have had mutual feelings of distant worlds, and of cultures so very far apart. Fuengsin then made her way directly from the airport to the Institute of Education in London.

A few days later Fuengsin was a full-time student once more, having enrolled on the Academic Diploma in Teaching English as a Foreign Language at the Institute of Education, founded in 1902 as a teacher training college before it became a college of the University of London.[2] On her record card were typed her family address in Thonburi (177 Soi Taksin 3) and her professional details: 'Teacher, Thonburi Technical Institute, Thonburi, Thailand', and added in pencil was the designation of 'UNESCO Fellow'. Her arrival reflected the expansion of higher education that was being strongly encouraged by the British government at that time, when student numbers mushroomed. The growth of the Institute reflected this drive as it expanded in four disciplines: history, philosophy, psychology, and the sociology of education.[3] Fuengsin was one of several dozen overseas students who had come to study from all over the world — such was Britain's reputation that demand for places was high.

They were housed in hostels for postgraduates with separate accommodation for men and women: the men were lodged at 25 Woburn Square, whilst the women were allocated rooms around the corner at 35–37 Bedford Way. The site was formerly occupied by Meier's Hotel, which the University of London had taken over, repaired and adapted for student accommodation in the late 1950s. In charge of the hostel was the warden, Miss Marian Stephenson, 'a cross between a Russian ballerina and Lady Macbeth'.[4] She was formerly a ballet dancer and in keeping with her imposing character she applied the hostel rules quite strictly: for instance, in accordance with mores of the time, gentlemen were not allowed to stay in rooms after a certain hour in the evening.

Whilst not having streets paved with gold, the central location of Bloomsbury, London WC1, was eminently satisfactory for most students and Fuengsin may well have appreciated its intellectual and literary associations with it being eponymous with the Bloomsbury Group. However, whilst the external facades were grand and fashionable allusions abounded, the hostel's interiors were prosaic rather than impressive. Fuengsin was provided a room on the third floor; it was compact with just enough space for a single bed, a desk, a wardrobe and a sink. For a young wide-eyed student enjoying the adventure of the big city, it probably didn't matter very much and the building could be regarded as a charming terrace. However, for those who envisaged being resident for the longer term, such as some staff, views were different and descriptions were more along the lines of 'dirty and dingy temporary accommodation'.[5]

Some of the rooms were occupied by British students, who were allocated places in Hall on the understanding that they would contribute to the well-being of the foreign students, and help them feel at home. Next door to Fuengsin was one of these students, Judith Powell, who had arrived at the Institute to study for a PGCE (postgraduate certificate in education) after obtaining a degree in Zoology from Birmingham that summer. Judith soon saw the need for the support as she realised that Fuengsin was rather lost in this completely alien environment. Looking at Fuengsin, it seemed to her: 'She had never really had to look after herself physically, or to organise the practical side of her life.' Fuengsin's privileged upbringing was starting to show, but with Judith's help she could regard with amusement her practical shortcomings, the lack of basic services or amenities and the need to do one's own washing.

There were no self-catering facilities, so she was reliant on meals provided by the hostel. However, although the cooks had prepared what they considered an international cuisine, it was institutional and not very flavoursome — Fuengsin found it almost inedible. Whereas she could hide some of her domestic challenges, this was a problem that was almost immediately apparent to those around her because meals were taken communally at set times. To compound the embarrassment, although men and women were segregated regarding accommodation, the men came for all their meals to the hostel canteen in Bedford Way. As recalled by another student, David Bridges, who was studying for a PGCE in History, Fuengsin took drastic action and brought with her fiercely hot red chilli powder, which she kept in a small tin, and proceeded to apply it liberally to almost everything in sight, even to her breakfast. Similarly, for trips out her handbag would include a tube of mustard. Such spices were to prove vitally important because as winter approached Fuengsin struggled with the cold and wearing several layers was not enough for her to keep warm — she needed nourishment and these helped to make bland food palatable.

In addition to far-reaching educational developments, the early 1960s saw immense social changes, with increased mobility and greater openness, particularly with regards other cultures. Dining issues aside, Fuengsin generally managed to settle in well. With a strong curiosity she was eager to explore and quickly overcame any shyness or sense of bewilderment. She made contact and friends with many people, who regarded her as having a natural love of fun and laughter, and she also kept the wicked sense of humour which she had cultivated in earlier student days, though Fuengsin was more restrained as an older student. She took the opportunity to explore the streets of London, taking in famous sites and tourist attractions. Aided by a generous UNESCO grant, which enabled her to zip from place to place in a London cab, Fuengsin was really enjoying her new life in London.

Activities, often undertaken in groups, took in restaurants, the theatre, cinema, concerts, fashionable shopping areas and so on; someone would organise the outing and people would join in. This would have brought back happy memories for Fuengsin of her outings with other students at Chula. Here it was particularly special in that she was mixing with people from around the world who were studying different courses: the young and not-so-young, UK and overseas students together. Among Fuengsin's circle of friends was Goule, an Indian lady who had previously been in East Africa, and then there was Sheila from British Guyana; and Marion from USA and Les, a larger than life character from Jamaica. This no doubt helped foster in Fuengsin a cosmopolitan view of the world.

Fig. 55: Postgraduate Students outside the Women's Hostel:
Terry Walsh (left), Fuengsin (centre), David Bridges (right).
at Bedford Way, the Institute of Education 1963–64.

Yet Fuengsin was also regarded as a private person in many ways; there were some aspects of British social etiquette that Fuengsin found odd and with which she was not so comfortable given her Thai background. Judith, who would see Fuengsin on a daily basis, recalled that a sure way to embarrass her was to give her a hug. Some of the physicality in the gestures may have seemed quite clumsy and perhaps wild. She may even have been a little shocked, but if she was, she wouldn't show it for Fuengsin knew she wasn't the only one experiencing and adjusting to new and unfamiliar situations. Furthermore, Fuengsin anchored herself in regular meditation practise, about which she talked a lot with Judith. One day Judith got to see unexpected evidence of this when she decided to venture into Fuengsin's room without knocking. She saw her Thai neighbour on the bed meditating, turned round and crept out, hoping that she had not been noticed. Judith also became aware of some remarkable mental qualities in Fuengsin: she had trained her memory to be able to retrieve the sort of information that most people would keep in address books. Her mind was highly disciplined and it was obvious she had no problems academically. In fact, Fuengsin was a fast reader of English, though not nearly as fast as for Thai, where she could read each page diagonally in a couple of seconds.

Some of the educational developments that were vigorously pursued after the Second World War related specifically to practical training for teachers of English as a Foreign Language (EFL): to get suitable experience, the Institute of Education sent the overseas students to Wales, and specifically to Caernarvonshire in North Wales. Hence in November 1963 Fuengsin along with about half a dozen other foreign nationals found themselves in Pwllheli.[6] Located in the north-western corner of Wales, on the shores of the Llŷn Peninsula, with cool breezes across the Irish Sea, it may have seemed to Fuengsin a remote outpost, like visiting a hill tribe up-country. It was another mini-adventure, but with further challenges: by now Fuengsin knew how to prepare for autumnal chill and even another refectory, but one aspect that she would not have experienced before was the shortening of the day. Thailand is located within a few degrees of the equator, so the days start and end with only modest deviation in times for sunrise and sunset (around 6 a.m. and 6 p.m. respectively, throughout the year). Here, about 50 degrees further north, as winter approached, days were rapidly becoming short, with sunshine in short supply, and without the city lights of London to compensate.

The group was hosted by the Bangor Normal College, a teacher training college for the region which arranged for teaching practice in local schools.[7] The College was also keen to provide extra-curricular activities and invited the group of students to sample local culture by attending a folk evening. It was organised together with the local community and proved to be a very enjoyable evening of great entertainment and mutual fascination. Although this wasn't the first such group hosted, their presence was still considered unusual and noteworthy; they were photographed and subsequently appeared in the Welsh national press, for *Y Cymro* (The Welshman).

Fig. 56: Visiting students (photo), *Y Cymro*, 21 November 1963.

An approximate translation of the text accompanying the photo reads:

Representing the countries of Cyprus, Ceylon, Greece, Thailand, Uganda and Hong Kong these students are being welcomed at the Folk evening arranged for them on Thursday night by people in Pwllheli and students from The Normal College, Bangor. In the middle is Rev. R. Gwilym Hughes, Penmount Chapel, Pwllheli, and Mr Madoc Ellis, right, the convenor of the meeting.

Whilst not displaying any knowledge of Welsh, Fuengsin remarked that the locals there pronounced her name better than any English people she met (some of her student friends had resorted to the abbreviation 'Fu').

By December, Fuengsin had returned to London, but the term would soon finish. Judith realised that the Christmas holidays were a problem for many of the foreign students and so she decided to invite some of her student friends, including Fuengsin and Les, to go with her and stay at her parents' home. This was at Orchard Cottage in Woodcroft near Chepstow, an English–Welsh border town on the River Wye in Monmouthshire.[8] The house was not very big, but, according to Judith, her parents were used to it being invaded by her friends. News soon got around the local community, with the inhabitants of Woodcroft becoming curious about the foreigners in their midst, the effect magnified by the contrast between a tiny Oriental girl and an enormous chap from Jamaica. Such visitors were unprecedented.

It was a good opportunity to help out, so Fuengsin joined Judith in the kitchen trying to conjure up meals that she found edible, and helping Judith to cook rice for the first time. For Fuengsin this was her first taste of British family life and another reminder of how different was her own upbringing. Having lots of people around was nothing new and Fuengsin would have identified with the close-knit community, but the natural environment was markedly different: Woodcroft was much smaller than Bangor and tiny in comparison with Thonburi; it was more like a village in Angthong, except that here there were no servants to help with household duties.

Judith had a younger sister who was dating a local lad and so they all went to a party one evening in the Beaufort Hotel. It was an opportunity to observe the locals socialising, but also for the locals to observe Fuengsin. Some had come back for the Christmas period from working in other parts of the country. One of them was a tall dark-haired gentleman by the name of Tony Trafford, who had come down from the North West to stay with his family before returning shortly after the New Year.

Fuengsin was introduced to him and they started to learn more about each other. Tony had been brought up in Chepstow and after a brief stint in the Forestry Commission he joined the Civil Service and was now working up in Liverpool as a Customs Officer. His parents were both schoolteachers; his father taught English and Latin at secondary school, having previously served in India in the Royal Army Educational Corps during and after the Second World War, whilst his mother taught at primary school. Some of his father's stories had helped foster Tony's own curiosity about non-European cultures; from his studies in geography, one of his favourite subjects, he knew a little about Southeast Asia, and was interested to know more about life there. Now he had a special opportunity to learn first-hand and they agreed to meet again shortly afterwards in the Three Tuns, a pub in Chepstow. Afterwards Fuengsin gave her address in London so that they could correspond. She subsequently attended other gatherings, including a New Year's Eve Ball in Tintern, but by now her mind was reflecting more on the encounter in Chepstow for when she first looked at Tony, she knew instantly he was the one.

Whilst this was only an initial contact the potential implications were far-reaching and tough questions were soon being asked. It was really unusual for an Oriental to meet someone in the UK, particularly in these circumstances, and was it too soon? At 22 years of age Tony was relatively young, whilst Fuengsin was 27. Tony sought advice from his parents, because chatting with a visitor at a party was not something that could be easily hidden from others.

Being totally out of the blue everyone was surprised. Fuengsin similarly had to inform her parents, but at first they refused to believe that she would even consider marrying a *Farang*.

After the holiday Judith, Fuengsin and the others returned to London. Soon letters started to arrive and Fuengsin received them gladly. She would lean out of the window when waiting for the postman, and say: 'Où est le facteur?!' (Fuengsin had evidently identified French as the European language of romance.) Things escalated very quickly. Tony and Fuengsin visited each other over weekends, travelling by train; Tony would come to London and stay in the men's hostel, and Fuengsin would take the train up to Liverpool, where Tony was staying in digs in 'Cranford', a large rambling building in The Serpentine North, Blundellsands, very close to the Irish Sea.[9]

Fig. 57: Cranford, Tony's digs before the wedding.

It was not long before Tony proposed and with Fuengsin's acceptance they decided they would get married in the summer. Meanwhile, Fuengsin carried on with her studies, with somewhat less focus than before. She managed to complete the course, passing the final examinations. Her record card was amended accordingly, with the status confirmed by the name of the examiner being indicated on the bottom right as Mr Stock. Along the way she was interviewed for a programme for the BBC Overseas Service, as it was known. She was asked about her experiences as a Thai student in the UK, which were relayed positively but discretely as Fuengsin was very much 'on duty'.[10]

The timescales were tight, but for a while there were administrative delays. The legality of the marriage depended on the Thai Embassy issuing a certificate to show that Fuengsin had not been married before. However they were reluctant to cooperate as they did not approve of any of their sponsored students going abroad and marrying locals. For them it was a kind of dereliction of duty to the state, but eventually they relented and the engaged couple could at last turn their attention to the nuptials, which were to present more substantial challenges for Fuengsin.

Preparations for the wedding were a major undertaking, not least because Tony and his father, Alfred, were practising Catholics. Although the early 1960s saw the ground-breaking reforms of the Second Vatican Council, their effects in parishes took a while to trickle down and as Alfred was very active in the local church he was insistent on doing things correctly. It meant that this 'mixed marriage', which the Catholic Church formally terms in Latin, *disparitas cultus*, required special permission from the Apostolic Delegate (the Pope's representative) to Great Britain, who in turn had to obtain permission from Rome.[11] There were major implications for both parties, especially for Fuengsin in terms of the religious practice. Whilst there was no requirement for her to convert, opportunities for sharing the Christian faith would naturally be made available and she was expected to show willing. Although well-intentioned, their knowledge about Buddhism was minimal, so this was not a dialogue of equals and as a result Fuengsin's initiation into the Catholic Church was not particularly comfortable. In following the instructions to the letter, Fuengsin travelled up to Liverpool to receive instruction, which meant being spoon-fed teachings of the Catholic Church in the form of a catechism that included petitionary prayers. She had nothing against the teachings of the Gospels, but she wasn't enamoured by having to recite 'Hail Marys' on a daily basis in front of a nun.

However, a more unsettling implication was the obligation to agree to any children being brought up as Catholic; when it came to religious practice, she couldn't even take them to a Buddhist temple for religious instruction, at least not until they attained legal independence as adults at 18 years of age. This was something that would occupy her thoughts for many years. In fact, in the cold light of day there were many serious implications, including permanently living in a foreign culture, the loss of her Thai nationality, the impact on her career and especially disconnection from her Thai family and friends. In fact Fuengsin was already tasting this as throughout this time Fuengsin heard nothing from Thailand — it was as if no-one wanted to know.

As Fuengsin reflected deeply on this, the extent of this life-changing event became ever greater. In seeking to understand how this had come about she later reflected:

When I was little I used to go with my friends to fish for crabs. This was just a game because the kind of crab we caught wasn't edible. We used a petal of a red flower for bait and a rod made of banana trunk. The petal enticed the crab out of its hole and we grabbed them! Once I caught a whole bucketful of crabs and moved them to another spot and released them which separated them from their families. This was bad karma for me! Because I forced the crabs to live their lives away from their families, I suffer the consequences of living on a small island, thousands of miles from my family!

If there had been serious doubts, Fuengsin managed to overcome them, maintaining her meditation practice and retaining in her mind the love she held for her fiancé, and the certainty that this was destiny. The wedding would go ahead!

The wedding was planned for 4 July and preparations were carried out at a high tempo. Once again Fuengsin relied a great deal on Judith for the logistics. They went together to search for a wedding dress; but whereas Fuengsin's could often fit into children's clothes, wedding dresses were not available for children, at least not in Britain. The streets of London seemed to offer no solution until eventually they found a dress in Dickens and Jones, an upmarket retailer in Regent Street, London.[12] Fuengsin used some of her remaining UNESCO funds to purchase the dress, which was still too big, but Judith was able to alter it to fit. It was perhaps the first indication to Fuengsin that in future she too might find it useful to learn dress-making.

News spread around Chepstow and there were many guests, including quite a number of Fuengsin's fellow students. Orchard Cottage resumed its role as accommodation provider: camping beds appeared and somehow the physical constraints were defied and everyone housed. The much-anticipated day came quickly and the marriage took place in Chepstow's Catholic Church, then in Welsh Street. No members of Fuengsin's family were able to attend as the cost of air travel was prohibitive, so Judith's father offered to stand in *in loco parentis*. In addition, Sean, Tony's younger brother, who had been invited to be best man, was at sea somewhere in the Far East and so couldn't make it; however, Brian Hunt, a friend from Tony's schooldays, agreed to step in. The international flavour was in evidence with the students from the Institute adding colour and variety; Judith and Tony's sister, Elizabeth, were the bridesmaids, once again aided by Judith's handiwork, with their pink satin dresses.

The wedding ceremony proceeded smoothly as planned, but with a unique additional touch. Despite Fuengsin's Catholic instruction before the wedding, she had retained her own beliefs and independence of mind so that when the priest said after the last lesson, 'May God bless you my child', Fuengsin replied, 'And may Buddha bless you!'

Fig. 58: From left to right: Cicely Trafford (Tony's mother),
Tony, Fuengsin, Mr and Mrs Powell.

As was usual in those days, there was a lunch reception after the wedding, which was held in the back garden of the Trafford family home.

Fig. 59: Wedding reception in a family back garden.

The couple finally left for their honeymoon, which they spent in Bristol. Meanwhile, that evening a party was held at Orchard Cottage for all of Fuengsin's friends who had come for the wedding.

After the matrimonial delights of a few leisurely days around the River Avon, the first practical issue was setting up home together and immediately there were adjustments to be made. According to Thai custom, the husband would join the home of his wife's extended family, which is what happened for all three of Fuengsin's sisters; but Fuengsin was obliged to stay with Tony in the UK. At that time Tony did not have a home of his own: he had first gone to work in Liverpool for a few months in 1962, and returned there in 1963 and 1964, each time staying in digs, usually sharing them with colleagues. When he met Fuengsin he was staying in 'Cranford', and he invited his hosts Mr and Mrs Wallace to the wedding. However, the accommodation wasn't suitable for a newly married couple, so they rented a flat.

Tony was very active. He kept fit by training runs on the sand, playing at Waterloo rugby club, and cycling to and from work. Having a dynamic and mobile outlook was useful in those days as staff in HM Customs and Excise were moved about like military personnel: just a week or so into their marriage, Tony received a call informing him that he was to move to Dover. The Traffords duly found some new digs, run by Mrs Slaughter, where Fuengsin was pleased to meet another occupant: the household cat. Fuengsin was very fond of cats!

Fig. 60: Fuengsin with Mrs Slaughter, the landlady, and the household cat.

The rapid relocation meant that Fuengsin lost touch or had greatly reduced contact with most of her student friends, even Judith, who went off to Jamaica before returning to Chepstow the following year. Then after just six weeks of marriage, before they could really settle, Tony and Fuengsin were separated as Fuengsin had to return to Thailand in September to fulfil her contractual obligations with the Thai government.

* * *

Fuengsin's relatives and friends had waited patiently for her return for what seemed a very long time. News of the marriage to a *Farang* had come as a huge surprise and was generally met with disbelief and concern; they didn't know how to respond. Saddest of all was her father. He had hoped that she would continue working in Higher Education so as to develop a successful career in Thailand's public services; he held great ambitions for her, seeing in her the potential to become a professor. Now she was going far away to become a housewife in a foreign land where there were few Thais, no temples, a harsh physical environment, and all he could do was write letters.

Fuengsin also had to deal with the tricky matter of fulfilling her work commitments. When she returned she initially faced the prospect of staying in Thailand for two years as she was expected to work for at least a year on her return and had also drawn a year's salary on top of the UNESCO grant whilst in the UK. It was this money owed to the government that was particularly problematic. Fuengsin managed to arrange for one year's salary to be paid instead to her parents, for which a contract was signed. That left the outstanding work requirement for one year and the impact on Thonburi Technical College, her workplace. Fuengsin encountered difficulties with her boss and colleagues. Fuengsin was not surprised that they were unhappy for her to leave the Tech, especially after the considerable investment in her. Furthermore some other lecturers could have received the grant instead — it wasn't fair on the students or the Tech. Fuengsin was supposed to help the Tech with her knowledge. It left her feeling a deep sense of having failed in her duty.

However, not everyone was disappointed in Fuengsin. Whilst back in Thonburi, worrying how she should handle her work obligations, she carried on visiting her meditation teacher, Ajahn Gaew. Her teacher kindly took a great deal of interest in the situation for he knew that she would come back to very changed circumstances. He took her one day to the coffin of his teacher, Luang Phor Sodh, whose embalmed body remained inside, and gave her encouragement for an unexpected task:

Before I returned to England, Ajahn made a prediction that in future I was to go and spread the Buddha's teachings in England; and Ajahn brought me to prostrate myself in front of Luang Phor [Wat Paknam] in order to ask that he give his blessing to help me succeed in this mission....

He asked me to pay respect and he lit candles and incense and he said he would like the power of communication and teaching be transferred to me....

He said, 'You go ... you are ready to teach now. You will have to teach one day.'

Ajahn Gaew also took interest in Fuengsin's new family. Based on his meditation experiences and particularly insights into karma, he would describe some of their personalities; without ever having met them in person he could sum them up very accurately. It was as though Fuengsin's mission had been planned and as part of the preparation he was introducing Fuengsin to people with whom she would be associating on a day-to-day basis.

Fuengsin was mindful that the usual vehicle for Thais to spread the Buddha's teachings would be a team of specially appointed bhikkhus supported by a Thai lay community. At that time there was no Thai temple in the UK and in fact there were still not that many Thais in the UK. Seeds were just being sown formally through a highly influential organisation called the London Buddhist Temple Foundation.[13] The year Fuengsin got married, an official delegation of monks came from Wat Mahathat in Bangkok led by Phra Rajasiddhimuni (the Most Ven. Phra Dhammadhiraraj Mahamuni). They had a busy programme that included attendance at the opening of the Chiswick Vihara, a Sri Lankan Buddhist vihara, which confirmed to them the considerable potential for a Buddhist mission in the West. So they were greatly inspired to pursue their own goal of establishing the first Thai Wat in England.

Among the delegation was a disciple of Phra Rajasiddhimuni, Phra Maha Vichitr Tissadatto, who returned in 1965 and was later to become abbot of Wat Buddhapadipa, the first Wat in Richmond. He was also assigned the role of Chief of the Buddhist mission in the West, for which he received the honour of the senior title, Chao Khun Sobhana Dhammasudhi. Fuengsin, who also returned to the UK that year, had already come to know Ven. Phra Maha Vichitr in Thailand and would visit him for advice in Richmond. She naturally assumed that it was the role of the Sangha to spread Dhamma, and only the Sangha as they had been formally trained, especially those from Wat Mahathat, which was renowned as a Buddhist education centre.

So when Fuengsin was approached to carry out this mission it seemed a very tall order and she remained deeply sceptical.

> I honestly didn't believe Ajahn at that time, but did not dare tell him. For I thought myself unable to succeed in doing such important work since my knowledge of the Buddha's teachings and my practice were insufficient. And moreover, my English language skills were still too weak to understand any Dhamma books in English. Furthermore, England was also a country with belief in Christianity.

Yet in her response there was already a sense of understanding in what the task would involve and Fuengsin felt duty bound to give it a go. Ajahn Gaew knew well her reservations, so was always happy to support her as best he could, sometimes to the extent of causing embarrassment. On one occasion after a bhikkhu had left the group, he told her in front of those remaining, 'You are stronger than that monk.' Furthermore, Fuengsin had other supporters at Wat Paknam, including some maechis, most of whom had joined the Wat during the tenure of the late Abbot. They knew that Luang Phor had wanted to share his meditation teachings abroad and had responded dynamically to opportunities as they arose. So, from them Fuengsin received various temple materials, including booklets and meditation objects. These were both an encouragement and a reminder of her undertaking.

So whilst Fuengsin continued to belittle her own ability, she was prompted to reflect on what potential she might have.

> I only had faith [in Buddhism] and now and again I talked about it to people who were in distress. I often tried to comfort people. I didn't know why, [but] they always told me their secrets and their misfortunes and I often said to those people, from what I [had learnt by] meditate[ing], "the Dharma will help you — if you practise, come with me and all that" and I persuade[d] them to go to the temple.

Her teacher tried to reassure her: he gave Fuengsin his blessing and said, 'You will be alright' and encouraged her to think of him when living abroad, a long way away. If ever she were in trouble she should think of him and practise, practise what he had taught her.

After further negotiation Fuengsin was bought out of the contract; the stipulation of one year was reduced and Fuengsin was allowed to return to the UK after seven months. However, on this occasion there was no grant or other financial aid. Tony had to use up his life savings just to pay for her air fare.

Notes

1. The de Havilland Comet was the world's first jet-powered passenger plane.

2. For the Institute of Education's early history, refer to their website: http://beginnings.ioe.ac.uk/begsioe.html

3. For a detailed account of historical developments in the programmes of study, see Richard Aldrich. *The Institute of Education 1902-2002: a centenary history: 2002.* http://books.google.com/books?id=GSmFcrdhdb8C

4. *ibid*, page 134

5. *ibid*, page 204. Within a few years the staff got their way and the building was demolished to make way for the Royal National Hotel and the proceeds used for a monolithic 1970s construction designed more in the Brutalist style by the architect, Sir Denys Lasdun.

6. Caernarvonshire subsequently became part of Gwynedd in 1972 (Local Government Act).

7. Goleg y Normal, Bangor (Bangor Normal College) was an independent teacher training college until 1996, when the college became part of the University of Wales Bangor. http://en.wikipedia.org/wiki/Bangor_Normal_College

8. Monmouthshire is a border area that — despite official documents — has retained ambiguity over its identification with England or Wales. Propaganda has flown on both sides: among the English has been the assertion that there are more Chinese speakers in Monmouth than Welsh.

9. Blundellsands was located by the railway station on the shore side, just on the corner where the road forks (the home subsequently knocked down and replaced by a housing development).

10. BBC World Service (Thai) ceased in 2006 after 60 years of operation despite the efforts of Judy Stowe, its former head, to maintain the service. See e.g. http://news.bbc.co.uk/2/hi/asia-pacific/4609860.stm

    If anyone has a copy of the programme recording in which Fuengsin took part please inform the author.

11. For some thoughts on how the official Catholic approach to 'mixed marriage' has evolved, see e.g. the author's *The Catholic Church and Inter-religious Marriages: Reflections on Pastoral Theology and Practice after Vatican II* http://chezpaul.org.uk/chrstian/MSt_essay3.htm

12. Dickens and Jones closed in 2006, with just a House of Fraser label in its name remaining. See the House of Fraser archive at http://www.housefraserarchive.ac.uk/company/?id=c1473 .

13. London Buddhist Temple Foundation. These formal developments appear to have had a quite complex political background. See e.g. the discussions with Sawet Piamphongsant, a meditator, poet and politician, in Chapter 2 of Sandra Cate's *Making Merit, Making Art: A Thai Temple in Wimbledon*, University of Hawaii Press, 2002.

6

Life in the Outer Reaches

Fuengsin returned to the UK to join her husband in spring 1965; Tony had completed his spell at Dover and was now renting a small self-contained flat in Liverpool. She now had to learn the ropes as a housewife without having the help of any maids or servants: cleaning, washing and cooking. Whereas preparing recipes in the kitchen had been a game during childhood, now it became a bread and butter reality. Fuengsin had to learn fast: with very few Eastern ingredients available and an English husband with a healthy appetite, Fuengsin had to prepare basic European dishes about which she initially had no idea. So Tony had to teach her how to cook eggs, boil potatoes and other vegetables, roast a joint, and other staples of the British diet.

The domestic chores were often tedious, but the novelty of life in the UK helped maintain Fuengsin's interest and she gradually received various advice and tips. Some of these came from Tony's relatives; Fuengsin had already got to meet Tony's family on his maternal side, and now as they had settled in the Merseyside area, Fuengsin also got to meet his paternal grandmother who lived in Bootle, along with his aunts and an uncle. Household life generally conformed to the British norm and its usual routine patterns of activity and inactivity, which soon encouraged Fuengsin to join the locals in observing and commenting on the extraordinary variability in the local weather.

However, Fuengsin continued to practise meditation as she had been taught by Ajahn Gaew, so whilst some of her behaviour and conversation was routine, at other times her responses broke the mould. On one occasion the flat had an ant infestation in the kitchen and Tony intended to contact a pest control company with a view to eliminating them. When Fuengsin heard of this intention, she protested: 'You can't do that — that would be killing them!' Tony was somewhat taken aback and pointing out the practicalities of the matter he challenged her, 'So what do you propose we do?' Fuengsin answered simply, 'I'll talk to them.' Somewhat mystified by this response he invited her to give it a go. After all there could be no harm in it and he was curious as to what she would say. Fuengsin duly proceeded to speak to the ants in Thai, uttering words to the effect that they were in the wrong place and that they'd be better off elsewhere. The next morning when Tony and Fuengsin ventured into the kitchen there was no sign of the ants and they didn't return.[1]

They stayed in Liverpool for a few months until the middle of 1965, but it was too cold for Fuengsin, who couldn't stand it. So Tony applied for a transfer to Southampton and was informed that it would likely be in the autumn. To their surprise it came up much sooner and was again at short notice: 'You are to be there next week.' And so they packed their bags and having no car they made the move by train. With so little time to prepare, when they arrived in Southampton with their belongings, they had not arranged anywhere to stay. They left the luggage at the station, and Tony suggested to Fuengsin that she stay at a cinema whilst he went to find some accommodation. Fortunately, he soon found a friendly landlady and they were able to move in straightaway.

Having relocated to the south, Fuengsin started to settle and resumed her hobby of making scrapbooks. As she didn't initially have access to photo journals and as they were relatively expensive, Fuengsin started with newspapers, but she continued with the visual approach, cutting out mainly photographs with brief explanations underneath. Once again the topics were very diverse and ranged from local, though national to international news. The first contribution was an enlarged photograph showing the proposed designs (obverse and reverse) for a commemorative coin, the Churchill Crown; turning the page revealed the first news item, which had been archived a month earlier: the escape from Wandsworth Prison of Ronnie Biggs and three other prisoners. A few months after completing her first volume she penned on the first page: 'No. 1. From August 4, 1965 — Sep. 19, 1965. Fuengsin Trafford April 16, 1966.'

* * *

Just as the Traffords were settling down to married life in the UK, there came an unexpected message. Tony was summoned to London by the Aide-de-Camp to Chalerm Suttirak, Fuengsin's cousin, who had risen through the ranks and was now officially Maj. Gen. Chalerm, a senior figure in Thailand's military communications.[2] Phi Lerm, as he was known by Fuengsin, had come to the UK as member of a SEATO delegation and carried with him a proposition.

Phi Lerm offered both Tony and Fuengsin posts in Thailand at a military camp; there was the prospect of a good career with financial security and no doubt other benefits. However, it was soon surmised that in fact it wasn't his initiative, but rather he had made the offer out of respect and filial duty on behalf of Fuengsin's mother, Somboon Sarayutpitag, who had looked after him for a number of years in Wongwien Yai. Khun Somboon naturally wanted to have her daughter and son-in-law nearby, and the feelings were most likely shared by her husband.

It was a tempting offer, especially given the couple's humble economic circumstances, but, after some consideration, Tony and Fuengsin declined. Whilst acknowledging it could have assured them of a comfortable living, they preferred to stand on their own feet and didn't wish the prospect of a lifelong debt of favour. Mindful of her childhood experiences and the sense of domestic restriction that she had resolved to irrevocably escape, Fuengsin still didn't relish the prospect of her mother keeping a close watchful eye on her.

The decision not to emigrate from the UK to Thailand meant Fuengsin had to continue adjusting to Western life. It was difficult and could be very lonely. Tony was often on detached duty, which meant being away at unsociable hours, sometimes for extended periods. She was unable to readily get in touch with any of her relatives and friends in Thailand, and there was no Thai community in Southampton. As there wasn't anyone immediately available from whom to seek advice, she had to learn by herself, make her way, sometimes by trial and error.

Faced with this situation, Fuengsin was determined to keep persevering and ensure that she wasn't cut off. She sent and received numerous letters, including many from Thailand penned by relatives and friends — for her every week was potentially 'International Letter Writing Week', and so she built up quite a philatelic collection of commemorative stamps, which decorated the envelopes that popped through the letterbox.

At the same time she sought to make friends in the city. However, one of the challenges Fuengsin initially encountered was knowing how to meet people: the weather often sent a hush over the streets and most residents seemed to retreat indoors, so that their homes really did appear to be their castles. Yet although Fuengsin didn't get as many opportunities for socialising as she might have liked, she was already appreciating just how kind British people could be once you got to know them. She found that if she made the right effort with some of the locals, they could become really good friends. Through her naturally gregarious and curious nature, she was able to emerge from her isolation and connect with those around her.

Particularly dear to Fuengsin were the Cooke family. Mr Cooke had served for many years in the army as an NCO; whilst stationed in Burma before the Second World War he met his wife and they subsequently settled in Hampshire. He swapped his army kit for postbags, and military communications for ham radio, regularly keeping in touch with his pals across the Itchen. For both Fuengsin and Mrs Cooke it was a rare opportunity to meet someone from Southeast Asia and the friendship deepened; the Cookes were very welcoming and kind to Fuengsin, helping her to feel more settled and at home. Gradually her connections diversified further. Soon afterwards Fuengsin met an Oriental lady whilst studying shorthand in Basingstoke; her name was Ann Tam and she came from Hong Kong.

Meanwhile, Tony likewise expanded his work connections, where he got to know a mixture of colleagues, some of the older ones having also seen active service during the Second World War. Others were, like himself, still early in their careers and had not even done National Service, but they were still of a generation that knew about rationing. In 1968 Tony worked at Heathrow, where he met Roy Hendy, a colleague in Customs who had a Thai wife, June. Tony and Fuengsin visited them at their home on one occasion by the Thames. Khun June's family owned a teak business in Bangkok and it turned out coincidentally that as a child Fuengsin would play on the logs in their teak yard. Although some of these contacts were some distance from Southampton, it helped to give Fuengsin a reassuring perspective on how immigrants like her could settle in such a foreign land.

Fuengsin also started exploring libraries, which encouraged her to apply her literary skills and read more books in English. The visits to libraries and other civic spaces enabled her to discover what was happening in the area in terms of clubs and societies, but these leads did not enable her to immediately find what she earnestly sought – a Dhamma group. However, by the mid-1960s, Wat Buddhapadipa, a Thai temple, had been established in Richmond on the outskirts of London. Fuengsin got in touch with Phra Maha Vichitr, the abbot of the temple, whom she had met a few years earlier in Bangkok. He gave her the address of a Belgian who was a member of the Hampshire Buddhist Society and a contact address in Paynes Road, on the West side of Southampton, near the docks.

The impetus for the founding of the Society had come during the Second World War. Brian Dyas, a former RAF pilot, had served in North Africa, India and Burma, flying supplies to front-line soldiers. While in India and Burma, he had developed an interest in Buddhism and decided there was a need for a group. After letters of invitation were sent to Hampshire subscribers to the Middle Way, the journal of the Buddhist Society in London, a society was formally founded in February 1965.

Fuengsin subsequently contacted the society and started to enquire about their activities. She was informed that she would be welcome to attend a gathering at the University of Southampton, which was at that time — like the Institute of Education — expanding physically and culturally. The Humanist Society had invited members of the Buddhist society to come and give a presentation. Fuengsin was keen to attend, so she duly made her way to the Highfield campus and managed to find the room where the meeting was taking place. On entering Fuengsin quickly observed that the majority of people were

Europeans, numbering about 40 to 50, nearly half of them university students. What made them interested and what would they be making of the Buddha Dhamma, she wondered? At that time Brian Dyas was the President and the Secretary was Mrs Jane Browne, who had been a Buddhist for more than 10 years and had already been on retreat in Thailand. It was Mrs Browne who was due to be giving a talk and she was watching people entering. When Fuengsin entered she was immediately impressed, feeling that here was someone who would really understand what she was saying. The appreciation was mutual: Fuengsin was inspired by Jane's presentation and soon applied to become a member of the society. She later encouraged some of her friends to join, including Mrs Cooke, who, although originally from Burma, had allowed her Buddhist practice to lapse.

About a couple of months after attending the first talk, Brian Dyas brought Fuengsin to a meeting of regular members at Crabwood Farmhouse, the home of Mrs Browne, to the west of Winchester. The gathering took place in what Fuengsin referred to as the *Buddha vihara*, a converted well-house that was converted into a shrine room. This natural setting served as the main focal point for the Society; it was a Buddhist centre in a single space, including a shrine for the Buddhas, a space to sit in meditation and a library of books. Fuengsin found the space delightful and remarked, 'The first night in this Buddhist centre was the first opportunity I had to join a gathering in which I felt really enthused, where the atmosphere of that place was so peaceful and sacred, just like walking into the chapel of a Buddhist temple in Thailand.' She inspected how the room had been laid out and was very pleased:

> A large white Buddha rupa was placed prominently on a shrine that was beautifully decorated. There were very small Buddha rupas arranged neatly around the side. There were photos of monks, well known in Thailand for their research in Samadhi and Vipassana, including Phra Maha Boowa, Wat Pah Baan Taad, in Udon province, where Mrs Browne had been a disciple of Tan Acharn during a visit to Thailand. I hurried straight over to pay respects to the Buddha with great delight and gladness.

Away from the noises of the city and suburbia, Fuengsin was struck by the silence and stillness.

> The tranquillity in that place is difficult to describe for it is located in the midst of a wood and the farm is far away from traffic and from people travelling back and forth. Sometimes you can hear coming indistinctly from afar the sound of a bird or a forest creature, and then it is quiet until you can just about hear people breathing. So it can really be said to be a Buddhist temple appropriate for the task of sitting and practising true Dhamma.

She was introduced to all the other members and heard about their backgrounds, and where they came from. Some had been to Thailand and so they shared experiences of Buddhism there. Fuengsin's task may have been made easier because meeting a Thai practitioner in those days was very rare, so it was likely the others in the group were curious to know about her background. In any case they appeared very glad to meet her.

Fuengsin scrutinised and noted every aspect of these sessions, using her retentive memory to good effect. The formal proceedings closely echoed the practices she knew from her days in Thailand and their transplantation to Britain must have seemed quite a revelation; they included chanting, the taking of the Five Precepts and sitting meditation practice of about 20 minutes. She observed that most members — apart from the President, Secretary and herself — had to sit on a chair because they were not used to sitting on the floor. Perhaps a little different compared with many Thai gatherings was the reading and discussion on a set Dhamma text at the end, but Fuengsin would have appreciated that too given her literary inclinations. Fuengsin even noted the refreshments at the end.

Fuengsin was mightily impressed and later wrote about their host, 'Mrs Browne, the home owner, is someone whose mind is shining and clear with faith in Buddhism.' She was subsequently invited back to Crabwood Farmhouse and it became a place where she could go and stay, and regularly practise meditation, for which she was really grateful. It helped especially to develop her deep appreciation of the beauty and peacefulness of the English countryside. Fuengsin was happy to stay with the group and started to make some contributions; when the group meditation ended she would spread *metta* (loving kindness) with some words of Pali. As several members were making trips to Thailand, Fuengsin was asked whether she would be prepared to help as a Thai interpreter, to which she agreed wholeheartedly. So she helped those planning on going on retreat in Thailand with the rudiments of the language and customs. She also assisted the Secretary by translating letters to Thai monastics and in administrative duties such as printing.

In subsequent meetings bhikkhus from Thailand and other countries were invited. They would come and give a Dhamma discourse and then lead a meditation practice for about 20 minutes — the society had in fact become a vehicle for a broad range of practices. The group thus provided a vehicle for Fuengsin to hear how these Westerners had turned to Buddhism and what it meant to them. She observed that most had been brought up as Christians, but often an encounter with Buddhism had led to a change in direction: for some it emerged in their travels to the Far East through their contact with monasteries, monastics and lay supporters out of which they developed faith and confidence in their new practice. Others, who had not held a belief in God, even in their early childhood, later converted.

Fuengsin took an active interest in what the practitioners were actually learning, their views and understanding. It was here that she was more critical, especially with regards to the understanding of Samsara, the eternal wheel of death and rebirth according to the Law of Karma. She was alert to the various dangers of syncretism and plain misunderstanding, remarking (to Thai relatives) in very forthright terms about one member:

> In their previous religious teaching, including the philosophy of life, there was no awareness of there being continually imprints that individuals cause by themselves. There were situations that led to Buddhism becoming mixed up with Christianity or attempts to adapt and change Dhamma to suit their own dispositions. Actually, the original meaning of that Dhamma principle was very far from the comprehension of that person.

She must have reflected that it would take a lot of effort for that person to come to a clear understanding, but her sense of duty in helping them was strong as she continued:

> Anyway, when we make the effort to watch deeply, we shall then be able to understand and excuse these eggheads. A person who tends to pursue this Dhamma will read a great deal and have undiminishing perseverance in the task of performing Dhamma.

Fuengsin then established a role as teacher and would meet up with some friends, have discussions and help them. For some it may have been initially uncomfortable to have their discursive reasoning summarily dismissed, but Fuengsin would have been in no doubt about the principles she knew and she would have made a convincing case. There was no messing about on Dhamma matters.

It was also an opportunity for Fuengsin to extend beyond the local scene and gain an impression of the broader landscape in which Buddhist activities were starting to develop. Thus she learnt that prisoners, for example in Winchester and the Isle of Wight, were also interested. They wanted to read and practise Dhamma, for which Jane Browne had already arranged for a teacher to pay a visit and provide assistance. Similarly, she was exposed to other traditions as a few members came from schools of Buddhism distinct from those she knew in Thailand. These schools ranged over so-called Hinayana and Mahayana (Lower and Higher vehicles). There was one such young member who gave up his household wealth to ordain as a novice monk in a Tibetan monastery (Samye Ling) that had been recently established in Scotland. It was thus an early encounter with interfaith and Fuengsin was curious to know more about their spiritual paths.

Fuengsin's own path involved extensive meditation at Crabwood during the course of which she got to learn about other 'guests'. She shared her encounter with Jane, informing her that the farmhouse had two ghosts, who had been previous owner-occupants: a retired sea captain and his sister. They related that they were absolutely delighted that the house had been rescued and restored as a family home because it had been allowed to become run down. Indeed, during the Second World War it had been used to house Italian prisoners of war, but it then became neglected and subsequently abandoned; when Jane and her husband, Ian, had purchased the property it was little more than a shell. The farmer who sold it was quite clever since he cleaned out the whole place and whitewashed all the walls so it looked nice, belying the fact that it was exceedingly primitive. The Brownes did everything to overhaul it, engaging in a full-scale refurbishment that included the externals as well as changing the front windows.

* * *

After a few years in the UK, Fuengsin had started to find her feet as a British wife with various circles of friends and activities. However, just as she might have felt somewhat settled, change was in the air: the year 1968 was to bring radical socio-political ferment on the international scene, but was also to bring personal transition to Fuengsin and Tony. Early in the year, Fuengsin received sudden news from Thailand: her father had passed away.

It transpired that Luang Sarayutpitag (or Khun Da, as he was known within the family) had lost consciousness very suddenly whilst taking his breakfast on 25 February 1968. His wife and children tried to resuscitate him and then called a doctor to come and take a look at his condition, but it was to no avail. The doctor concluded that Khun Da, who was aged 74, had died of cardiac vein thrombosis. It came as a surprise as he had generally looked after his health very well and his medical history had given little suggestion that this might happen and there was no indication of any serious congenital disease.

Family members were devastated; his children felt confounded and later wrote:

> Father departed from us in a sudden manner. We never thought that we would have to face an event like this. We could not prepare ourselves beforehand. Everyone was stunned in amazement. There was no explanation. Anything that we would describe as being afraid of had happened on that day.

Even the grandchildren wore black. It would take a long time for everyone to come to terms with the loss; and to enable people from far away to pay their respects the tradition was observed of embalming Luang Sarayutpitag's body and keeping it in the house over an extended period. In particular, his relatives from his home province, around Angthong, would come and stay, but strangely at this time quite a few of them passed away not long after.

Retaining the body in the home was a custom in keeping with a Civil Servant of high rank, but more pertinently it was a way to express family love as this space became a focal point for offerings and chanting to the Triple Gem on behalf of the deceased. Invitations were extended to members of the Sangha and they responded by coming regularly and frequently so as to receive the offerings and dedicate merit not just to Luang Sarayutpitag, but to everyone in the vicinity — for Thais believe that merit has a wonderful property of being able to propagate and multiply! There were some practicalities in terms of maintenance, but they would be managed and not be an issue: whether regarded as honour or chore, it meant that his teenage grandson, Laem, had the duty of taking care of the body for over a year until the cremation took place in May 1969.

Fig. 61: Khun Yay Somboon (Fuengsin's mother) offering *dana*
to a bhikkhu, probably dedicating merit to her deceased husband.

Also in keeping with tradition, a cremation volume was being prepared, offering a chance to express both sadness and appreciation. Although it may have felt as little consolation at the time, at least the father of the house did not have a prolonged period of pain before his passing, nor did he thereby place a burden on the household, which seemed typical of his thoughtfulness. Such was the care that Luang Sarayutpitag bestowed that his nephew, Maj. Gen. Chalerm Suttirak, was moved to write:

> The benevolence of Uncle Luang Sarayutpitag exceeds any words we may find to describe it. I regard the loss at this time of Uncle Luang as the most momentous occasion of loss in my life, second only to that of my mother who has already passed away not so long ago.

As if to underline his comparatively humble status he referred to himself in his signature as a 'grandson of Uncle', even though he was actually only one generation away.

As to the loss, gradually wise reflection dawned as to the reality of impermanence, as was expressed in the tribute by another nephew, Nikom Suttirak:

> I shall try to restrain all the natural human tendencies that I have by offering a saying that is the foundation to all kinds of Dhamma. It is from the Dhammapada, verses 127-128: 'Regardless of whether the person evades passing away in the middle of the ocean or in a mountain cave or whatever, there isn't any place in the world where he can escape passing away from death.'

Khun Da was a trusted adviser, who kept calm, cool and reasoned. His wife reminded everyone that he was like a source of shade:

> Whilst he was alive, Khun Luang was a person who was fully prepared as well as highly virtuous. He loved tranquillity and was honest. He was a good head of the family, he loved his children and he loved his home. He was like Rom Pho in the sense of constantly providing cool shade and being happy, right up to the last minute of his life. He has departed and there is no way we can ask for him to return and come back again. There remains for us only to keep his goodness, which impresses our hearts as a recollection for all our lives.

His grandchildren likewise described him as a source of shade, but also emphasized how he was close and warm:

> All of us grandchildren still remember the days Grandfather was ever happily engaged in activities with everyone at home. Grandfather offered closeness and warmth, brightness, and good thoughts throughout. We always recall Grandfather's teaching and we shall miss Grandfather as if he were still alive.

The passing came unexpectedly to everyone, particularly to Fuengsin, for whom it was a mighty shock. Ever since she had arrived in the UK, she had carried with her a sense of obligation to somehow fulfil her father's expectations as regards her career potential even if she could not satisfy his specific wishes. She received letters from him which served as reminders of her absence from the Thai household and how her father missed her. Now with his life cut short, she may have felt that time had run out to prove herself to her father. Furthermore, even with the advanced notice, there was little prospect of being able to attend his funeral because the cost of travel was prohibitive. Fuengsin probably felt a debt to her father was unpaid.

Even so, there was still an opportunity to formally say a farewell, show gratitude and observe the Buddhist tradition of offering merit for the deceased. Fuengsin was able to express this succinctly in her own tribute, making clear her father's contribution to her life and career and how she would retain this in perpetuity.

> Father was a strict and complete Buddhist with virtues that are difficult to describe. He was a far-sighted person. He tried to support me in my education as much as he could afford. His manners and dignified personality remained imprinted in the hearts of everyone who got to meet and converse with him. Throughout his life he tried to study intensively and he was always seeking to improve in the areas of his work. His departure has brought great sadness to me. Yet he still lives forever in my memory. He will keep the fruits of his meritorious practice and it is likely that this will inspire his consciousness to go on to a heaven realm.

Furthermore, Fuengsin resolved to make a special effort by contributing to his cremation volume three articles relating to Buddhism in the UK, particularly the activities of the Hampshire Buddhist Society. Two of the contributions were respectively by the President and Secretary, outlining the history of the Society, but the longest and most detailed was her own article sharing her personal experiences. Fuengsin completed this article (in Thai) about a year after her father's passing and gave it the title 'Some Buddhists in England'.

She opened by expressing her commitment to the Buddhist path despite the challenging conditions:

> Ever since I left my homeland to be in England nearly 5 years ago I have not had the opportunity to go to a temple to make merits, to put almsfood in a monk's bowl, or to listen to the Buddha's teachings. Yet I still have faith in the Buddha's teachings. In my free time I am always trying to read books on Dhamma, sit and practise Vipassana meditation, and practise the Dhamma to the best of my

ability. I have been keeping these in mind, thinking that I might yet some day get to meet with other Buddhists.

Fuengsin continued with the theme of merit, which would come to the fore on cremation day. Her article described as far as possible the breadth and depth of her activities so as to be a source of happiness for her father. Some of these she had carried out since her father's passing, no doubt with some extra urgency. Thus she related that in April 1968 she prepared a translation for part of a slim volume of Buddha Desana (collection of teachings) of Phra Maha Boowa, the abbot of Wat Pah Baan Taad, rendered into English for Mrs Browne and other Western disciples.

Fuengsin emphasised how through her membership of the Society she was learning more about Dhamma and the methods to express it in the West. Having now formally discontinued her English language teaching, she might not have intended the report as career-related, but at the back of her mind she may have had the words of her Ajahn. The efforts that she made to demonstrate her Dhamma work in the tributes reflect at least in part her consciousness of the expectations placed upon her. It was thus that she concluded:

> Before I end this article I would like to take this opportunity to invite everyone who has the occasion to go to England to visit the Hampshire Buddhist Society, where you will receive a warm welcome by the President, the Secretary, and all the Buddhists, including myself. I have made firm my constant determination that as long as I remain in England, I shall try to help the Buddhist society and disseminate Buddhist teachings to the best of my intelligence and ability.

These articles, almost like an end of year report, were perhaps the first such contributions to the genre of Thai cremation volumes, but seemed a natural extension, as they fully supported one of the primary goals as conceived by King Rama IV: the preservation and propagation of the Buddha Dhamma.

Eventually the day of Khun Da's cremation came on 6 May 2512 in the crematory of Wat Anongkaram, Thonburi, at the same temple where his wife, now widow, had received her first primary education. To help with arrangements, relatives and close friends congregated from various provinces, including Angthong, Chonburi and Min Buri. Somboon Sarayutpitag coordinated and observed who had come to give their support. Dressed mainly in black, they each paid their final respects, shared their recollections and caught up with other family news. They were joined by other colleagues and associates so that altogether there were hundreds in attendance. Everything was carried out strictly in accordance with received procedure, the ceremony being led by the monastics.

Some of the monastics were relatives, including Ven. Ajahn Yongyuth, to whom Khun Yay had donated land in Bang Phra, near Chon Buri to found a monastery, which he duly did and it was called Wat Khao Mai Daeng, named after its geographical location of a red wood on a hill.[3]

Fig. 62: Ven. Ajahn Yongyuth of Wat Khao Mae Daeng
placing offerings in a cremation fire.
Location unconfirmed, but probably for the late Luang Sarayutpitag.

Those who attended the cremation also received a copy of the cremation volume, a substantial A4-sized book that was printed at the Department of Military Communications, of which Maj. Gen. Suttirak was now Director. Not surprisingly, with privileged access, especially to military records, the details of Luang Sarayutpitag's career were spelt out in meticulous detail across several pages, giving the descriptions of each and every post. Thus a couple of the many entries read as follows (one from the army days and the other whilst in the Ministry of the Interior):

On 1 October B.E. 2458 became acting Second Lieutenant 3rd Class in the same service with salary rates as for Second Lieutenant 3rd Class at 80 baht a month.
. . .

On 28 November B.E. 2477 Section Head, Department of Corrections Department government official 2nd Class, Step 3, with a salary of 220 baht a month. Afterwards he served at step 4 with a salary of 240 baht per month.

Details of awards were also listed, including:

20 September B.E. 2485 Commander (3rd Class) of the Most Exalted Order of the White Elephant

4 December B.E. 2492 Commander (3rd Class) of the Most Noble Order of the Crown of Thailand

These honours were high enough for a representative of the King to officially light the cremation fire, an indication of the standing in which Khun Da was held. It was a fitting farewell from the society he had so faithfully served.

* * *

Whilst the family in Thailand witnessed a cycle of death and passing on, in many ways Fuengsin's life in the UK was still just beginning. At the start of their marriage, she and her husband had enough on their plate just to make ends meet. They rented accommodation, usually just a couple of rooms with a resident landlord or landlady, so there was no immediate prospect of having children. Once they had moved to Southampton, Tony started to earn a little more and the situation became more stable and they started looking for their first home.

At the end of 1966 they found a terraced house in Alpine Close, Bitterne, which seemed reasonably priced and affordable at about £3,300. They subsequently bought the property and Tony took out a mortgage as a first-time buyer. It was quite basic and had relatively few of the modern conveniences; there was no telephone, which was yet to become a universal feature. The family had no motorised vehicle either; Tony used a bicycle to get to and from work and also about the docks, cycling up to 20 miles a day.

The couple maintained contact with Tony's relatives in Chepstow; they would visit his parents fairly regularly at Christmas and Easter, staying at their home in Newport Road. However, there seemed to be something strange going on with inexplicable sounds in the house as though the home had other occupants and it became a topic of local conversation. Not knowing anything about this, Sean, Tony's brother, came back from sea one day and heard the front door open, then close, and then footsteps going up the stairs. Sean thought there was a trespasser, so he enlisted the help of a visiting grocer, who instructed his dog to go up ahead. But they found nothing.

Sean reported this to his mother and she proceeded to relate how Fuengsin had seen a ghost in meditation and described her as an old lady dressed in a long black dress. On hearing this account a neighbour, who had lived in the area for a long time, responded: 'Oh, that's Mrs Lloyd! Mrs Lloyd used to dress like that.' This figure in black had been a previous occupant of the house and had passed away, though not entirely it seemed. These distinctive sounds were often heard. One Christmas there were about 15 people in the room, all of whom heard the front door and the footsteps; the dog was also alerted as though there was a visitor. The mystery persisted until at a later date, when Mrs Lloyd's grandson had passed away, these sounds suddenly stopped.

Restless spirits aside, family life became more feasible now they had a permanent address. In due course Fuengsin became pregnant early in 1968 and the news was shared with excitement, providing a positive counterbalance to the loss of her father. The following months continued generally as normal; gradually the unborn baby grew and became more active, as though 'kicking a football' inside. There were also some slight changes in diet; Fuengsin developed in particular a craving for grapefruit. During the pregnancy Fuengsin went for checks with a consultant at the local clinic, noting in particular his luxurious mode of transport: a Rolls Royce.

Relatives and friends popped by to lend support and in late summer they received a visit from Alan Baker-Jones, who was dating Elizabeth, Tony's sister. Whilst Elizabeth was staying with Tony and Fuengsin, Alan was accommodated at the Cookes' home. He didn't know how to get there, so asked Fuengsin to ride along to give him directions. As she was heavily pregnant by then, she had to be eased carefully into his Triumph Spitfire, a small sports car with low seats, a situation that caused amusement all round.

The baby was expected for early September, but didn't arrive. When Fuengsin finally went into labour with the baby two weeks overdue, the birth process took many hours and eventually required the use of forceps. Finally, late in the evening on 22 September a boy was born at Southampton General Hospital and all was well. Preferring simplicity, Tony and Fuengsin gave him the name of Paul.

Family resources, including no shortage of advice, were mustered from across the generations; Tony's mother purchased a large Silver Cross pram which was often left outside in the garden, with Paul tucked up inside gazing up at the trees and sky. Whilst it was well-made, it was also quite heavy and bulky, and Fuengsin had a struggle pushing it uphill on her way to do her shopping in Bitterne. Fortunately, by the time of the birth, Fuengsin had made more good friends, some experienced in bringing up young children, so skilled help was at hand. Visitors also occasionally came from overseas, including her childhood friend, Tewee Bodhiphala, who visited around June 1969. She was on her way back home after attending her Master's Degree Graduation in Vancouver and was accompanied by a classmate from Chulalongkorn University who had graduated from a university in New York. Fuengsin may have come down to Earth with her life rooted on the South coast, but many of her Thai contacts were flying high.

Fig. 63: Fuengsin, Khun Tewee and a university friend *en route* to Thailand from North America with Paul in the pram.

Paul was also taken to Crabwood Farmhouse to meet Jane Browne's family. Fuengsin was careful not to allow him to cause a nuisance, so she kept him in his high chair rather than letting him roam around. This came as a bit of a surprise to their hosts, especially Jane's mother, but no-one appeared troubled by the end of the day.

* * *

Whilst Tony had married a lady from Thailand, the furthest he had travelled abroad was France. However, his younger brother, Sean, had already navigated the oceans of the world for his training as a marine engineer in the Royal Fleet Auxiliary. In the latter half of 1969, Sean was in Singapore and wondering where to go next as his career was in transition. He decided to return to the UK and then recalled a suggestion from Fuengsin that if he passed through Thailand he could go and visit 'Aunt Ing', the lady of the scrapbooks, as she was able to speak English quite well and had continued corresponding with Fuengsin.

Not having any other commitments, Sean accepted the opportunity and planned a three-day stay in Bangkok. Whilst he had some experience of the Orient, he was not familiar with Thailand's capital and so it was something of an adventure. On arrival he hailed a taxi and managed to give sufficiently clear instructions to the driver to get an affirmative reply and off they went. Although not a huge metropolis at that time, Bangkok and Thonburi were still substantial and the journey from Don Muang was a long one, with each and every turn presenting a new and unknown view. Eventually they came off the main highway and weaved in and out of ever-narrowing lanes until the driver declared 'Here we are!' and pointed to a street sign.

Sean got out and the driver left, only for Sean to realise that he hadn't yet established whether he was in the right place, or that the person Fuengsin had mentioned was at home. For him this was the middle of nowhere! However, after a short while, Aunt Ing duly appeared — contact had been made. She subsequently took him to Fuengsin's family compound and introduced him to Khun Yay Somboon. At first there was a bit of bewilderment, but when they registered his connection he was treated 'like royalty' with her great nephew, Laem, waiting on him hand and foot. When asked why, Laem replied that it was considered a great honour for him to provide this hospitality. Such a visit was an exceptionally rare event, so everyone was naturally curious about the visitor from afar and to learn news from the UK. The honoured guest was then whisked away on various sightseeing trips, taking in a cremation followed by a monastic ordination. It was an immersive experience that he could vividly recall more than 40 years later. The visit was relatively short, but it was highly significant as it re-established at least some contact with Fuengsin and her new British family.

Fuengsin herself had little prospect of such travel, especially with the arrival of Paul. So a few months after he was born Fuengsin decided to keep a personal diary, a private diary that she maintained in Thai, penning the first entry on 6 July 1969.[4]

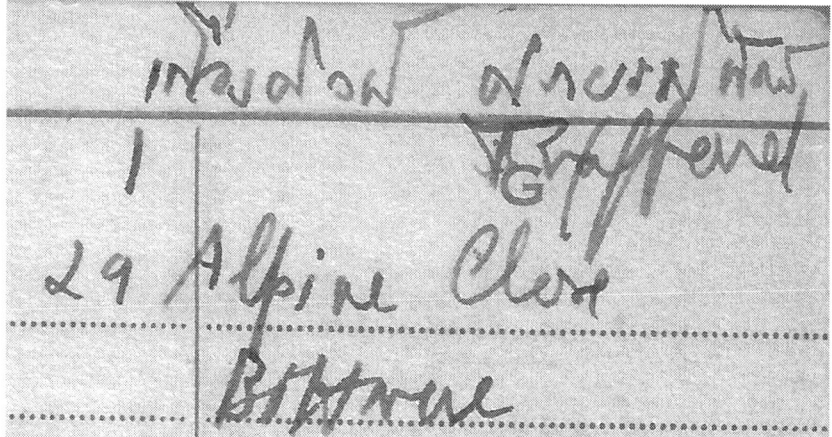

Fig. 64: The inside cover of the first volume of Fuengsin's diary
signed in Thai, เฟื่องศิลป์ ศรายุธพิทักษ์ ('Fuengsilapa Sarayutpitag').

She wrote about matters great and small, — recording events at local, national and international levels — and retained her interest in scrapbooks, so was actively seeking new material. Her first entry included a reference to an article in the colour supplement of The Telegraph newspaper on the ceremonial investiture of Prince Charles, on 1 July 1969. A couple of weeks later, on 20 July 1969, there was a momentous event that Fuengsin recorded with a rare adornment: the first landing on the moon.

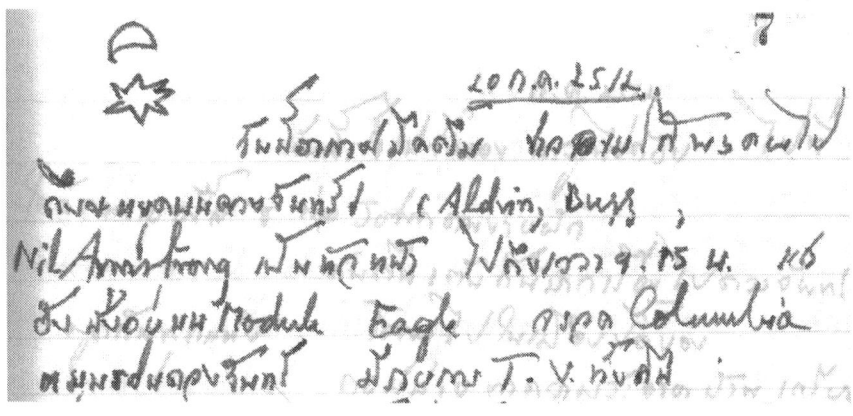

Fig. 65: The start of Fuengsin's diary entry for 20 July 1969.

An approximate translation:

July 20, 1969. It's cloudy today. There is news about three Americans reaching and landing on the moon (Buzz Aldrin and Neil Armstrong, the commander). They landed at 9:15, but are still staying in the Module, Eagle. The Columbia Space Ship circles around the moon. There is an all-night TV broadcast.'

Other events of national significance included UK decimalisation on 15 February 1971, and the General Elections of 18 June 1970 and 28 February 1974. However, most entries were at the other end of the spectrum, typically including her domestic routine of getting up, caring for her son, Tony's work duties and so on — day in, day out. She would describe her meetings with friends in the locality, their situations and activities together, noting their moods and preoccupations. Fuengsin would write largely in a direct and factual manner, describing what she did, and what she observed and experienced, with very little in the way of opinion, sentiment or speculation.

The main themes covered were her domestic chores such as shopping, cooking, and cleaning, and her leisure activities, including reading and writing, meeting friends, listening to music and watching television, all of which she pursued avidly. As in many households in the late 1960s, the television was a recent arrival, rented from a company, and quite a luxury. It was a fairly plain box with a small black and white screen that received three television stations: BBC 1, BBC 2 and ITV. Fuengsin watched TV on a daily basis, sometimes to see important news items, but in her diary as many mentions were given to Crossroads. Fuengsin had discovered soap operas, a new media genre to explore, and which were to become a staple of her household life. The budgets may have been low and some of the plots far-fetched, but for Fuengsin they offered valuable insights into the British way of life and customs, which she could compare with her own experiences in suburban housing estates.

However, Fuengsin still needed intellectual stimulation, so her reading material was generally more demanding. Her list included Dhamma books by Thai Ajahns such as Phra Maha Boowa and Buddhadasa Bhikkhu, but also sophisticated French literature, including a succession of mainly works of fiction, some by Nobel laureates. They often dealt with matters of meaning and human relationships vis-à-vis religion and society, including *Préséances* [Questions of Precedence] by Mauriac, which immerses itself in such themes in the context of the social hierarchies that existed in Bordeaux in the early 20th century. Other works included *La Porte Étroite* [The Narrow Gate] (André Gide), *L'Assommoir* [The Dram] (Zola), *Madame Bovary* (Flaubert) and unspecified works by Balzac. She also read some well-known English classics by authors such as G.K. Chesterton (*The Innocence of Father Brown*), Thomas Hardy's *Far from the*

Madding Crowd and others perhaps less well known, including *The Tenant of Wildfell Hall* by Anne Bronte. Some of her reading came from recommendations, including *Rebecca* by Daphne du Maurier, which introduced Fuengsin to another part of England, Cornwall.

She found some works initially difficult, but she persevered and sustained her commitment until she was able to read several chapters at a time. Apart from the personal, psychological and religious issues, Fuengsin may have been interested in what made European society 'civilised'. This would have echoed an active exploration of Western culture that had preoccupied the Thai aristocracy ever since European powers were actively colonising Southeast Asia. It led in the mid-19th century to the coining of the term *siwilai*, a direct phonetic transcription from English with various localised meanings.

Fuengsin's intentions may have been high-minded, but her budget was limited; she would seek out jumble sales and second-hand shops, sometimes buying items on impulse, which didn't always live up to expectations. Shopping one autumn afternoon she found a row of second-hand French books on sale in an antiques shop. Feeling pleased with the discovery she bought some, including works by Baudelaire, and then carried on with a mini shopping spree that included purchasing an icing set. However, on returning home she discovered that the icing set was rusty and the Baudelaire was not a fairy tale, as she had hoped, but poetry. She was very disappointed; but that feeling soon passed, not least because within a few days Tony had thoughtfully bought a replacement icing set.

Notes

1. Regarding Fuengsin's benevolent communication with small creatures, Tony recalled that this wasn't the only incident that was solved in this way, though not all such cases were dealt with successfully.

2. Subsequently Lt Gen. Chalerm Suttirak, who became Director of Thailand's Department of Signals [Military Communications], 1966-1974.
   http://signal.rta.mi.th/web_signal_new/index3-1-1.html

3. The website for Wat Khao Mai Daeng is on Facebook:
   https://www.facebook.com/วัดเขาไม้แดง-544006572283567/

4. Fuengsin never said much about the diary she kept, so it was a long time before there was any attempt to read it. We hope it has been treated with due care and consideration. One of the French authors she read at the time was André Gide, who himself maintained a journal from the age of 20 and maintained it intermittently throughout the remainder of his life. Fuengsin even translated a portion from Volume 10.

7

Varied Fruitfulness
in the Garden of England

The 1960s drew to a close, a decade that had transplanted Fuengsin from Thailand to the UK, bringing many changes to her life. Yet a further domestic transition was to come as before the decade had drawn to a close, Tony applied successfully to work in Kent. He was initially thinking about Sheerness, but eventually opted for Gravesend, a town situated near the mouth of the river Thames that had for centuries provided a strategic location in protecting against smuggling.

Now the family had the prospect of another move, but on this occasion with the mortgage and baby they couldn't just relocate at the drop of a hat. So Tony transferred there in October and found some digs. A couple of months later Tony and Fuengsin sought the services of Fox & Sons estate agents to put their house on the market and then braved the short days and winter chill of January to explore the Medway area. They employed the services of an estate agent in Gravesend, spending a few days in the generous hospitality of a colleague, Brian Sowerby, and his family. By February, Strood, a town about 7 miles from Gravesend, had been identified as a convenient and affordable location, and eventually a new home was found there. Meanwhile another colleague had offered to buy their house in Alpine Close.

The move was to be effected soon, so Fuengsin quickly informed her friends and on 6 March 1970 she attended for the last time a meeting of the Hampshire Buddhist Society, which took place in Paynes Road. The following week on 12 March belongings were packed and the move was initiated. However, they had not been able to get dates to coincide, so they couldn't proceed straight to Kent. Instead Fuengsin and Paul spent Easter in Chepstow as an interim destination, where they stayed a total of four weeks. It was a good opportunity to mingle with Tony's relatives and friends and to get to know each other better. It was also a chance for Fuengsin to reflect: she had briefly stayed in Kent after their marriage, but this would be the first time that she would really settle there. Would it be as delightful as its coveted title of 'The Garden of England' suggested?

They finally continued their move on 9 April, travelling by train from Newport and wending their way across the South of England via Bristol, Swindon, Didcot and Reading. They reached London Paddington at around noon and after leaving their luggage in a locker did some shopping at a supermarket in Soho. Then in the afternoon they collected their luggage and took a train from Charing Cross to Gravesend, spending the night at the Old Prince of Orange hotel. The following day they continued to Strood and the Blechfords removal van arrived in the early afternoon — details recorded in extensive detail in Fuengsin's diary. At last they could unpack and settle in.

The new home was a standard three-bedroom semi-detached house in Cadnam Close: it was from one suburb to another. The area was within commuting distance of the capital, being situated a little over 30 miles from central London, whilst Tony's work covered various points along rivers and the coast to the East, including Gravesend, Tilbury and the Isle of Grain. The suburb was in Strood and across the Medway were Rochester and Chatham, offering plenty of staple shopping facilities for the suburban family such as Co-op, Tesco, Finefare and Woolworths, though basic shopping needs were satisfied by a supermarket nearer home.

Once again Fuengsin found herself almost back at square one, in a new place where Tony would be away at various hours and where she knew no-one. However, the situation was aided by a few factors: some of Tony's colleagues had been living in the area for a while and Fuengsin kept in touch with friends she had made in Hampshire, receiving cards and letters. There was another fact that helped inadvertently: householders in the close had modest standards of living and were not replete with material possessions, so they would share, including the telephone line, which was jointly rented by the family opposite. One of the few luxuries they had — a television rented from Radio Rentals — broke down within a few weeks.

Fuengsin's gregarious nature enabled her to quickly get to know families in the close. Several of them had young children, including a few around Paul's age, and as the house was located close to a cul de sac, it proved a natural area in which to play. Fuengsin's social life expanded as she introduced herself to her neighbours and then others she met as she wandered around town; most were fascinated by her, keen to learn about her background. Encouraged by the interest, her culinary exploits continued to grow and she even typed up some Thai curry recipes to share: a rare taste of the spicy Orient to excite Kent's taste buds. Soon there were parties to attend, and some to host, as well as domestic duties.

Fig. 66: The Trafford family at 11 Cadnam Close, c.1971.

However, not everyone wished to have much to do with the new arrivals: the lady next door seemed to take a dislike to the family and gave vent to her feelings through midnight sessions of her Hoover, running the vacuum cleaner up against the adjoining walls just to make sure its presence was felt.

Life wasn't plain-sailing, but Fuengsin continued to engage in her spiritual activities including reading Dhamma books and especially practising meditation, which she maintained almost continuously in the midst of these activities both in busy periods and quiet spells. Although she felt bereft on having to leave behind her fellow seekers at the Hampshire Buddhist Society, she still exchanged notes with several members and was generally fastidious in setting aside time for meditation every day, once or sometimes twice. She would meditate typically for between half an hour and an hour, occasionally somewhat longer, usually choosing a time when she was alone, for example when Paul was sleeping and Tony was out of the house, either at work or at church. Not only was there less chance of disturbance, but it meant that when Paul and Tony were around she could make herself available for them.

As there was no Buddhist temple or group, meditation acted like an axis around which everything revolved and she continued jotting her experiences in her diary. Sometimes her practice was very pleasant: 'As afternoon approached I sat in meditation for 50 minutes downstairs. At first I was sleepy, but afterwards the tiredness disappeared and tranquillity arose. I was very hungry.' Furthermore, she would reinforce the practice through her study of Buddhist books. She did not restrict herself to a particular language or tradition, but drew encouragement from a range of teachings, from which she was able to derive much benefit. It was thus that she came to know the work of John Blofeld, her former teacher of English at Chulalongkorn University in the 1950s. She later remarked to a friend, 'It was a long time before I realised that he was a well-known Buddhist!' Blofeld had been living in Thailand, and his practice, which he learnt whilst in China, was very different from Fuengsin's; yet Fuengsin found some resonance in his autobiographical account *The Wheel of Life*, about his experiences there. Later she learnt further from his book *Compassion Yoga: The Mystical Cult of Kuan Yin*, his devout guide to the Bodhisattva who is popular all over Asia. After reading his work, Fuengsin drew inspiration and would note her feelings of gratitude. On one occasion she recorded: 'I immediately practised some Vipassana meditation, and sat for about 50 minutes. It was very peaceful. The book helped a lot.'

With a toddler to care for, Fuengsin had to juggle her time and routines and fit her meditation around other events. Being a housewife and mother obliged her to be more organised and even basic chores sometimes took a lot out of her. When Paul would occasionally hurt himself she'd have to take him to the doctor and the extra travel and worry meant that the relaxation during meditation made her fall asleep afterwards.

There were few holiday breaks and choices were quite limited, but at least there were opportunities to spend time at Crabwood, Hampshire, where she would be reunited with friends in Dhamma and have a chance to take a break and be spiritually reinvigorated. In return, Fuengsin reciprocated with an open invitation to visit her family in Kent. Several took up the offer, which Fuengsin both appreciated and found challenging: a letter would arrive from Hampshire, dates would be finalised and then as the visit approached, it would be all hands on deck to clean and tidy up the house and prepare authentic Thai dishes. The visit itself would involve sightseeing and shopping in the local towns of Strood, Chatham and Rochester. There was usually a lot of catching up to do, with long chats fuelled by coffee and cake.

As global travel continued opening up, Fuengsin started receiving a few more Thai visitors, each with similar Kent itineraries. Among them was Fuengsin's cousin, Lt Gen. Chalerm Suttirak, who a few years earlier had offered Tony and Fuengsin a life and career in Thailand. He visited the family in Strood courtesy of the official Thai Embassy car, which seemed to fill up Cadnam Close all by itself. He came with his wife and an entourage, but this time there was no offer to be made, though the three-bedroom semi in Kent's suburbia must have seemed very humble. They were content enough to see each other, chat and visit some local sights in Rochester and the surrounding area. On such occasions everyone enjoyed themselves in excitement and nostalgia, but Fuengsin usually became very tired from all the activity and lack of meditation (even during preparation, her meditation time would shrink). Once the visit was over, Fuengsin was quite relieved to be able to resume her longer practice. Recharging her spiritual batteries in this manner often yielded results: 'I sat in meditation for 1 hour. It was very peaceful and the mind remained in the sphere of *sīla* and I observed the mind all day long.'

In Thailand there are quite a few occasions for commemoration and cultural festivities, religious and secular, but before the advent of multiculturalism they were not celebrated in the UK. So for Fuengsin, family birthdays became extra special celebrations. Autumn was arriving and now Paul was now two years old, so it occasioned the following entry in her diary:

> Today is our son's birthday. I get up at 8.15am. I hurry to bring the child downstairs to look at the toys piled up in the middle of the living room. He runs to take a look at a bicycle in the middle surrounded by a variety of boxes: a spinning top and books are all around. The youngster runs around to see inside all the boxes, but likes the spinning top the most. He sits playing at leisure for a long time.

Whilst Paul was enjoying the toys, Fuengsin proceeded to read through the morning post. There was a letter from a friend in Thailand who related that her daughter, Kanda (not her real name), was now in the UK to further her studies. The details about precisely why she was in the UK were vague; Kanda didn't know which subjects she would study except that she needed to improve her English language skills. She was staying in Southampton and an address was supplied; it was a house in Highfield, a nice residential area, but it didn't have a phone. Fuengsin received the news with mixed feelings, doubtful about the wisdom of a seemingly indeterminate course of action, but knowing very well that whether she liked it or not there was some responsibility on her shoulders to help the student, if at all possible. She spent some time pondering what best to do.

Later that day Fuengsin became poorly. She recorded succinctly her condition and response.

> I wasn't well. My eye ached and there was a lot of phlegm. It seemed I had a cold and fever. At 8.15pm I quickly got up and went upstairs and meditated for 45 minutes. I perspired a lot. At first it seemed there was no peace, but after 15 minutes things improved and it seemed very good. The mind was cool and calm, one-pointed. The *kilesas* [defilements] tried to enter, but the mind did not stray from the feelings.

Fuengsin's fighting spirit and watchfulness had earned her relief and some ease of mind, but the illness had to run its course. Despite feeling unwell, the next day Fuengsin went looking for a babysitter to free up more of her time. She took Paul with her to visit a kindergarten and found it to her liking with lots of children engaged in drawing and playing; Paul soon joined in. However, the woman running the nursery reported that they were full and in fact Paul was too young — they only accepted toddlers who were at least three years old.

On her return home she was able to meditate for an hour and find some peace. She proceeded to carry out various chores and also typed up a book that she had translated for Jane Browne. But there was another problem: her optic nerves were very tense and she couldn't complete a covering letter. It was to be the beginning of an extended period in which she battled with health issues throughout that autumn and the onset of winter. As the days progressed Fuengsin was increasingly troubled by her nerves to the extent that she had difficulty reading and felt unable to carry on with translation work. She tried to meditate, but the pain was so great that she could only manage half an hour. On a couple of occasions Tony had to break off work to look after Paul and carry out housework, for which Fuengsin was very grateful; some days all she could do was watch TV.

Fuengsin's doctor prescribed some medication, which reduced the pain but left her feeling drowsy. The effects of the prescription often made her sleepy and she felt very lazy, but at least with the respite from the pain Fuengsin could spend more time in meditation and carry on reading Dhamma books. Nevertheless it was hard work and her mind wasn't usually clear, 'I wasn't able to do very much because I couldn't really see the Dhamma body.'

After a while Fuengsin got more used to the medication and experienced some pleasant results in her meditation. However, whenever she found some inner peace, there always seemed to be some kind of disturbance cropping up during the practice or soon afterwards, like an obstacle course. On one occasion she had to get up because there was a loud disturbance from the cot, which Paul was shaking, but it seemed just a bit of boisterousness. On another occasion when coming back home late that afternoon, she got to the junction at the top of Cadnam Close and heard children shouting out and making a racket. Fuengsin went across and found a six-year-old girl who had run away from home. She tried to convince her that this wasn't a good idea, but to no avail. She was unable to do anything and came away frustrated — it wasn't like her childhood experiences in Thailand where she had been taught that respect for adults was paramount. Seeing the anger rise up inside, she sat for 10 minutes in meditation to cool off, but she still went to bed in a bad mood.

Over the next few days Fuengsin read some Dhamma teachings by Ven. Ajahn Paññavaddho and found them helpful in developing *sati* (mindfulness) and *pañña* (wisdom). She also received a letter from an English friend who shared their personal story, an account that Fuengsin found very unfortunate. By now Fuengsin had become a confidante and help to a few friends. Some were in financial difficulties, so that afternoon she went to the market in Gravesend, which was packed that day, and bought clothes to give to several people.

As the pain came under control, Fuengsin was able to receive guests and generally do more. However, in her meditation practice she noted that the eye medication caused her mind to be restricted. Fuengsin was struggling to control the pain, retain alertness, gain space for her practice, and deal with the various personal problems that her friends were sharing with her. One particular issue still hovered in the background: on 6 October, her calm was challenged by a letter from Kanda indicating that she wanted to visit, but hadn't yet got the courage to make the journey. Initially Fuengsin didn't have the space to focus on it as she spent part of the afternoon acting as a marriage counsellor for a friend. However, later on it preyed on her mind and she had difficulty sleeping. Fuengsin was naturally worried for she knew instinctively that Kanda probably needed help, but her health wasn't really improving as the doctor's medication had seemingly done very little to help treat the cause of Fuengsin's eye pain and she had feelings of nausea and giddiness.

Whilst still suffering these symptoms, matters got worse. The toddler, as though picking up the general sense of malaise, was anxious to go outside and once outside he started crying. He then picked up a brick and hurled it at the kitchen window, cracking it. Fuengsin immediately reacted and told him off in no uncertain terms and sent him to bed, but that didn't put an end to the problems. On inspecting the cupboards, racks and fridge, she discovered the house had run short of supplies: 'I can't go anywhere and there are only two eggs remaining for food. There's no bread, potatoes, meat or vegetables.' Tony got back from work and was shocked; a row ensued after which communications broke down. Fuengsin ended up having to go out to find something to eat, barely managing to pick up a few more eggs left outside the old ladies' shop. To cap a bad day, Paul became unwell and Fuengsin was still unwell. On that day the family seemed severely dysfunctional.

The eye pain was still troubling Fuengsin two months after it first being started, so much so that on 23 November she noted:

> My eyes hurt and strain. I have a headache. So I stop and sit in meditation because I'm very much afraid. They have been giving a great deal of pain since last Friday.

When Fuengsin did manage to get out of the house to do some shopping she sometimes had a difficult journey, feeling queasy on the bus and developing a headache. Just as she was improving, there was further trouble around the corner. For a month or so there had been no further word from Highfield until Fuengsin received a letter from Kanda. It was not good news. Kanda was very depressed; she would sit and cry in her lodgings and disliked the landlady; and the monthly rental of £39 pounds was very expensive. She wanted to stay with Fuengsin over Christmas, but was still not brave enough to come. It was probably as Fuengsin feared. She discussed the matter with Tony and he suggested that she collect Kanda from Southampton. Fuengsin immediately penned a reply saying that she would go and collect her on 1 December, but she wasn't sure whether she would come.

Despite prolonged suffering with her optic nerves, Fuengsin remained level-headed through her meditation and was occasionally entertained by TV soap operas. She found some bright aspects — the weather was warm and her child seemed happy, albeit noisy. She even expressed a touch of the poetic:

> At 3.30pm I take the child out for a walk along Crutch Lane. Some of the trees are still red, but the branches are brown. Their outline shapes are very beautiful. The apple orchards have only branches and twigs. They don't have fruit. The grey all around makes it seem melancholy. [Yet] There is fresh green grass coming up. A bush far away is just as in a painting: it's a very dark colour and has a beautiful form.

Fuengsin also received some news from Thailand about marriages and children in her extended family. However, these moments of pleasant distraction didn't last long before issues would assert themselves: soon after receiving the letter a man came along from the TV rental shop to collect some money, the princely sum of £8, without even having sent the usual bill. Such news was not helpful to Fuengsin's problems with nerves, yet despite a lingering headache and painful eyes, she later managed to persevere with her meditation and find peace, whilst Tony dealt with the rental company.

Perseverance and patience seemed to be needed day after day, which (as Fuengsin may have wryly observed) presented opportunities to practice the *paramis*, Buddhist qualities of perfection. On 26 November, another message arrived from Kanda, this time announcing that she would not come because she was scared that she wouldn't be able to return by herself. Who knows what Fuengsin felt at such vacillation, but she simply recorded that she abandoned the idea of going to collect her.

Fuengsin carried on with her daily routines and could see some encouraging aspects: having been very slow to start walking, Paul was now able to walk far and manage inclines. However, her own struggle in meditation practice continued and she tried to refine her practice to cope better with the pain. At one stage she found a technique of drawing her eyes inwards and gazing up, though coming out of meditation the eyes continued hurting. However, the pain increased again until she felt overwhelmed and had to stop reading. Her energy levels continued to be low and she struggled to prepare food and cook, whilst letters remained unfinished and her meditation was suspended: 'I'm still not brave enough to sit and meditate until the eyes get better.'

And then the telephone rang. It transpired that Kanda had changed her mind. Fuengsin quickly made plans to go and pick her up the next day, which meant a return to Southampton, her previous home. Before leaving she arranged for her friend, Christine, to stay at home and baby sit for Paul, whilst Tony rang the railway station to get the train times. All was set, but Kanda remained a mystery: Fuengsin noted that she and Tony were excited at the prospect of meeting her, but they were unable to paint a picture of her. At least she appeared to be polite and very respectful on the telephone.

So the next day Fuengsin left early in the morning and the trip was one of great nostalgia: the train from Strood took her into London and then she caught a bus.

> I spend a long time looking for the place to buy a ticket until I find the bus itself. It's not crowded and I find a comfortable place to sit. The weather is very fine and the view is beautiful. Some trees still have a reddish colour. It becomes beautiful from Woking and from Winchester much more so. I gaze at the verdant scenery which is full of trees. As we reach the vicinity of Southampton I start to feel excited. We arrive at 12.30. I am happy to be back in Southampton again. Everything is still as before.

Fuengsin carried on describing the journey in some detail. The Christmas lights were on display, lining the edge of the road, as she made her way to Highfield. She eventually arrived at her destination, seeing the house on a high mound.

> I had to go up many steps to enter. I caught sight of Kanda standing by the window. She hurried to come up and came to *wai*. She let me in. She was crying and didn't want to be there. The landlady appeared. She seemed to have a bad look about her and wasn't sincere, very dressed up. She made sweet talk. The room decoration appeared luxurious. There was a big black dog. We had a meal — she [the landlady] brought out a packet of noodles for us to eat. I was taken around to see every room. The house was big and looked very cold; there wasn't any central heating, but it was going to be installed soon. Upstairs there was some very old furniture.

Compared with the heat, light and airiness of a house in Thailand, it must have seemed a forbidding environment. Kanda was obviously in the wrong place.

After the initial pleasantries were exchanged, the landlady appeared to be in a chatty mood. However, Kanda related privately how she couldn't sleep until 2 a.m. because she was so nervous. Kanda presented her case to Fuengsin that she should leave the house and soon afterwards sought the landlady's permission for her to accept an invitation to go to Kent. It was granted and very soon they made their exit.

Fuengsin found Kanda polite and kind-hearted. She was easy to get along with and opened up naturally. Her situation was unfortunate and she cried over and over again, but on the way back to Strood Kanda appeared to cheer up a lot and chatted continually. By the time they reached the house in the evening Kanda was happy, and she also got on well with Tony and Paul. Conversations continued until late. At the end of the day Fuengsin had managed the rescue, but was very weary.

The following days featured more chatting and also shopping, especially in preparation for a party that Fuengsin was going to host. Kanda made a generous contribution, which Fuengsin appreciated, noting, 'Kanda enjoys herself very much ... She is a child full of fun, but I am very tired.' At the party there were two tables of food: one outside for adults and the other inside for children, accompanied by Kanda. It was a success, but the youngsters made an awful din, shouting at each other and none of them seemed to know what each other was saying. It became too much for Kanda, so a neighbour came in to help. The party was a success and friends went away contented, but Fuengsin was left with a headache as the price for such a merry gathering.

The week continued in a relaxed manner with Thai-style dining every day. Then on Friday Kanda received a note from the landlady saying that a letter from the Thai Embassy had arrived. The letter was in Thai, so the landlady didn't know what it said. Kanda originally intended to stay beyond Sunday, but on reflection changed her mind fearing that there was something urgent and important. The next two days were packed with further shopping trips; Kanda was initially intimidated by the crowds, but after a while she became absorbed in the shopping and chatting. It didn't seem to bother them that the products weren't cheap, or that they received a rude 'cash and wrap' service in the market, nor that they got drenched more than once on the way home. And so it continued until Kanda returned safely to the south coast and eventually back to Thailand. However, when Fuengsin finally had a chance to sit and reflect she noted: 'This week I didn't sit and meditate and I'm very tired.'

Some while later Tony and Fuengsin tried to help another Thai student in distress. On this occasion it was for a friend, Sukhon (not her real name), who also wanted to improve her English language skills. She found an agency that appeared to offer an au pair opportunity in central London with plenty of time to allow her to study. It was advertised as providing some assistance for an elderly lady, with at least a day off each week. However, in fact the lady was frail and required around-the-clock care, seven days a week, leaving the au pair with very little time of her own. She was being exploited: effectively being used as a servant with very little in return.

In desperation Sukhon got in touch with Fuengsin to seek help. Tony had just bought his first car, a second-hand Wolseley, so with the address in hand they drove off to meet Sukhon in a prosperous part of North London. They took the lift up to the top of the building and were let into a fine penthouse suite by the elderly lady owner. She was not the cause of the problem and seemed somewhat embarrassed; rather, it was the agency at fault and there was some discussion about what to do. Afterwards, Tony and Fuengsin went to pay a visit to the manager of this agency. They found him at his office and Tony started to question him. However, he was an astute character and, eyeing Tony, asked him, 'Are you a policeman?' Tony wouldn't say, to which he followed up with: 'Either you're a policeman or a customs officer!' Despite Tony's years in tackling smugglers and other dodgy characters, the case wasn't properly resolved until a senior connection at the World Bank in New York got lawyers onto the case: they started issuing letters to the agency, a message they seemed to understand as the problem was duly solved with little further delay.

Fuengsin's suburban household life continued with its ups and downs. Just like Charles Dickens, who had a long association with the Rochester area, Fuengsin got to observe many characters, as they emerged through the British mists. Meanwhile Tony had consolidated his position as a customs officer, though in 1972 the Waterguard was abolished and its work was taken over by HM Customs and Excise. When off duty he developed further interests outdoors: the back garden was limited in what it could offer in terms of fruit and vegetables, so he spent quite a lot of time cultivating an allotment. The family now had greater independence and the availability of the car opened up travel options, especially for leisure trips, but there was one other particularly ambitious trip being planned.

8

Thailand and other Family Outings

In 1972, having been married for eight years, Tony and Fuengsin decided that at last a suitable opportunity had arisen for them to visit Fuengsin's family in Thailand. Tony had settled into his job and was able to save sufficient leave, whilst Paul was approaching his fourth birthday, so no longer a toddler, whilst not yet having to attend primary school.

Whereas in the previous decade air travel had been a privilege of the élite, the 1970s saw the emergence of charter flights. Travelling abroad was still quite rare and anywhere beyond Western Europe was considered exotic — that year friends were taking holidays locally in places like Eastbourne and Clacton-on-Sea, with a few days of sunshine and ice-cream. Tickets for long-haul flights, though decreasing in price, weren't cheap, but through scrimping and saving, aided by overtime, Tony had worked out that there were sufficient funds to cover the return trip for the three of them. The next step was to find a travel agency who could arrange flights. Options were limited, but they managed to find one that specialised in the Orient, the Far East Travel Centre (FETC) in Shaftesbury Avenue, central London, possibly the only one in that area at that time.[1] A booking was made for three economy class return tickets at a cost of a little over £250 each, a sum roughly equivalent to three business class tickets today. The outbound flight was scheduled for 20 September and the return was about seven weeks later — it was going to be a trip and a half!

The date duly arrived and in her diary Fuengsin noted rising at 6 a.m. for the journey to Muang Thai. By 8 a.m. the family had left the house to catch the train from Strood to London, on arrival crossing over to Victoria to collect the tickets and then carrying on to Heathrow. There was no time to lose as the departure was at 1 p.m. Eventually the family arrived at Heathrow and having checked in there was a moment to reflect. On this occasion there was no-one for a send-off; for Fuengsin this was a stark contrast with the crowds at Don Muang, whilst for Tony, the furthest trip he had made before was to France. Now he had the prospect of exploring a mystical land that he had only read about in a few items of literature and his geography books.

Whilst jet airplanes had seemingly made the globe smaller, travelling to the other side of the world still required several stops, but in some ways the passage retained a certain freedom and simplicity — and with fewer travellers, airport security was minimal. It was a scheduled flight out of Heathrow with Sabena, the Belgian national airline, though not before Paul had screamed in protest at having a seat belt put on him. Fortunately, once in the air he was quiet and there were no further complaints during the subsequent flights. They landed at Brussels at 2 p.m. and had to wait until the evening for the transfer; baggage checks were made with many of the staff being Chinese and Thai. Thoughts of shopping were soon dispelled on encountering the prices, so the family just had some drinks and idled away the time.

At 6 p.m. the family boarded a Boeing 707 with Sobelair, the charter side of Sabena. It was a much larger plane than the scheduled service and it was packed; Fuengsin estimated that there were about 200 passengers, though in actuality there were probably somewhat fewer.[2] It took off at the appointed time and proceeded on schedule, stopping *en route* to refuel at Tehran, where an armed officer stood at the bottom of the airplane steps whilst an airport officer boarded the plane to inspect it. The crew had tea with sugar ready for him and after a few minutes he disappeared and the plane continued on its way, with one further refuel at Bombay. Fuengsin noted that the service was satisfactory and they arrived at Don Muang Airport at 3 p.m. the following day, half an hour early, but very tired after a journey of 24 hours. They were greeted by a characteristically tropical climate. It was very hot and the sights and smells were vivid — so different from the comparative dullness of Britain.

Waiting in the lobby area to collect the overseas visitors were many relatives and friends: all the close family was there except for Fuengsin's sisters, Phi Umpai and Phi Umpan, who were at work, and also Fuengsin's mother, who stayed at home because she was having problems with her eyesight. It was immediately obvious that Fuengsin was not forgotten; she was still in people's hearts. Initial greetings over, the gathering emerged from the airport and jumped into cars; a couple of them were now fitted with air conditioning, allowing the new arrivals to get some relief and rest.

After a fairly long journey by road, the convoy arrived in Thonburi and made its way to the family residence, which was still located in Soi Taksin 3, not far from Wongwien Yai, the main hub in the district's road network. Winding their way through the narrow streets, just as Sean had done about three years earlier, they eventually arrived at the entrance to the compound. It comprised three homes with the main house at the centre and two further houses for two daughters and their families to the right, surrounded by trees and shrubbery.

Fig. 67: The main family home in Thonburi, 1972.
A little over 30 years after it was originally built. Fuengsin's sister, Umpun,
and her son, Atau, are looking on. On the far right is part of the annexe,
where the builder, Da Hoy, used to reside.

The head of the household, Khun Yay Somboon, was waiting. Fuengsin had wondered what kind of reception they would receive, particularly how her husband would be regarded, given the reservations expressed by family members before the wedding. She needn't have worried; they received a kind welcome with Tony and Paul soon being accepted as family members, aided by token identification with film star namesakes: Tony Curtis and Paul Newman. In particular, it was a relief to Fuengsin that her mother was not fierce or strict as before, but rather was keen to help Fuengsin find and meet up with friends and relatives according to her heart's desire.

Fuengsin sat down and immediately conversations commenced — after a very long absence everyone was immensely curious to hear about her life in the West and the new family. With initial re-introductions over, Fuengsin was shown the room that had been arranged for them at the house of an elder sister, Phi Wilai Posanacharoen, which was opposite the main house. She found it had been very well prepared and had a natural inclination to just stay and rest there, but there were more people to see. Returning, she carried on chatting even though she became so tired that she could hardly speak; for once, a lack of the local lingo had some advantage for Tony and Paul, who were able to just accept the hospitality with some gestures, exchange a few words in English, and then mainly listen to and observe the unfamiliar surroundings.

Fuengsin realised she was truly back in her homeland when it came to the meal, which was taken in the main house; she recorded in her diary that there was a hot curry, fish balls and fried *pakbung* (morning glory). There was still a constant stream of people coming along to give their greetings. Even though her energy was spent, these were happy reunions. Most of the well-wishers were quite animated, but amidst the excitement Fuengsin noted that Shu, her mother's long-time maid, seemed calm and unruffled as usual.

Eventually Fuengsin was allowed to take her leave and a bath, but she had not imagined how disorientated she would be after all the years away: it took her a long time to find things and to get to know her way around and initially she was unable to cope very well with the climate. Meanwhile Paul was very tired and had lost his appetite completely, only taking liquids for what seemed like many days; but gradually he acclimatised like his parents, in his case fuelled by bottles of Pepsi, which Fuengsin protested about, but in vain as she was overruled by her mother.

The next day, Thursday, Fuengsin was taken to a few places by her niece, Jiew. Taking more notice of the environment, she remarked:

> I watch vehicles go back and forth, there are so many of them. The country [*baan meuang*] has changed a lot. It's full of Japanese posters all over the place. Suriwong is still a Westernised area. It has many gift shops.

As a sign of how changes were sweeping the area, only in the previous year Thonburi had formally become subsumed by Bangkok. However, at least there were not yet any town houses in the soi, and the land was still adorned by many coconut palms.

Later that day Fuengsin went to do a bit of shopping and wandered over to the market in Wongwien Yai and was surprised:

> ... It's very expensive. I buy one *paathung* [traditional silk brocade, probably to be made as a skirt or sarong]. The market is very big and crowded. I don't recognize it. The streets are chock-a-block at every turn and it's hot.

Fuengsin was experiencing culture shock in her native land! But despite the rising cost of living, the Thai appetite for trading seemed as great as ever.

There were still other close family members to meet. That afternoon saw a visit to her cousin, Phi Lerm (Lt Gen. Chalerm Suttirak), at his office in the department of Military Communications. She presented him with a gift that she and Tony had bought in the Tower of London: a knight on a horse. They then chatted, catching up on each other's news, which may have included the topic of education as Phi Lerm had developed an interest in children's education. He had become involved with the Mitrapab ['friendship'] Educational Foundation, a joint US–Thai organisation that was founded in the late 1960s with the specific aim of establishing in every province a school with at least four classrooms for deprived children. The organisation provided coordination and some specialist skills, but most of the resources came from the provinces themselves, so projects had local ownership.

When the weekend arrived, the opportunity arose for the first family trip outside Bangkok, to Angthong, with her nephew, Od, the driver. Tony, Fuengsin and Paul were accompanied by Fuengsin's mother. There were many relatives there, including her brother, Phi Lek. After early training in the army he had been unable to develop a career and was generally struggling in life until his mother became exceedingly worried. Ajahn Gaew, who had become teacher and mentor to several members of her family, went to the family home to provide counsel, especially to Fuengsin's mother. He offered to try and help and suggested that Phi Lek ordain as a monk, to which he agreed. He subsequently became an acting abbot of a temple in Angthong that he had helped to establish and practised meditation there.

Fig. 68: Ven. Lek (Surapan) with Paul at a wat in Angthong, 1972.

He stayed for a while at the monastery until he was beset by ill health and had to leave the monkhood.

* * *

Fuengsin was keen to see her teacher again, who was within easy reach as he lived with his family very close to Wat Paknam in Bhasicharoen, Thonburi, which wasn't very far to travel. Fuengsin felt that whilst in Kent her meditation practice had become stale for she lacked fellow practitioners — there was no group and no support. However, her teacher was very happy to see her and gave her considerable encouragement.

Ajahn Gaew was born in Bangkok, but being of Chinese origin his early education was in China, where he studied until he was able to speak and write Chinese; there had long been a sizeable Chinese community in Thailand and this was common practice. On returning to Bangkok he supplemented this by learning English initially at the YMCA. He had a disciplined mind and applied it in his professions, working variously as a teacher, interpreter, and in the printing trade, including work at a newspaper company. He was very fastidious about each character; he would point out that if a character was just a little bit wrong, from a spot of ink, the meaning of that character would be wrong, and would have with extensive ramifications, particularly to important rules and procedures. He would examine carefully his children's notebooks in the same way, and expect them to be in good order.

He got to travel extensively across Thailand until he got married and started having a family at around 28 years old. At the same time he had been searching for spiritual insight and previously had studied Mahayana intensively whilst in China. However he found it didn't suit him and so he carried on searching until he finally met Phramongkolthepmuni (Sodh Candasaro), the Abbot of Wat Paknam, and was able to practise thoroughly with the meditation master in the early 1950s. He arrived in time to meet and get to know a newly ordained monk, Kapilavaddho Bhikkhu, and they spent time together and became good friends. Ajahn Gaew related to Fuengsin about his days with this monk, about their activities together, yet never informed Fuengsin that he was from the UK, only ever referring to his ordained name, so she naturally assumed he was Thai.

Ajahn Gaew's strong faith in Buddhism led him to also observe the tradition of ordaining as a Buddhist monk at Wat Paknam, in a period shortly after the passing of the Luang Phor Sodh. This was somewhat unusual as some bhikkhus decided to move on or returned to lay life. However, his householder's responsibilities were not yet resolved and even though in his heart he wanted to continue in robes, he didn't wish to neglect his family commitments as his children were still only young. So after about a year he left the monk-hood to take care of his family, whilst concurrently continuing his intensive dhamma studies and research in the path of practice. He thus became available for those like Fuengsin who sought a way of peace — lay and ordained alike. It is said that the gift of Dhamma exceeds all other gifts and accordingly he never demanded any payment whatsoever from those who came to study with him.[3] This magnified the respect with which he was held.

Fuengsin duly spent more time with Ajahn Gaew to develop her practice. On one occasion her teacher said, 'I have got something for you.' He then pre-sented her with a small hardback notebook about A5 in size. 'What is that?' Fuengsin was mystified. On the outside it seemed nothing unusual, for it had a fairly plain blue cover with red lettering: 'Leader Standard Book 118/150'. However, opening it revealed about 200 pages of text, all handwritten in ink, together with some additional pieces of paper.[4] Ajahn Gaew explained, 'This is the transmission to you of my knowledge. It's all in the book.' Fuengsin didn't ever see Ajahn Gaew write Thai himself and wondered whether he had the ability as he was Chinese, so she asked him, 'How did you get this book written?' He replied, 'I dictated to one of the nuns and she worked every day to write in long hand.' In fact her teacher could read and write Thai, but he had so much to do that he dictated it over days and weeks to several nuns, which may well have been for their benefit also.

The contents were special. They comprised a collection of advanced teach-ings, like the meditation equivalent of nuclear physics research, and were only to be used by those who know how to practise properly. A few other pages contained astrological charts, including information about auspicious times for giving birth. Fuengsin made sure that she kept the book safely and on her return to the UK she placed it in her shrine.

Ajahn Gaew had often mentioned Fuengsin to his other students. One of the ladies that meditated with him told Fuengsin: 'Ah, now this is the person; I wondered what she looked like because the master always talks about you! He thought a lot of you.' Fuengsin sheepishly replied, 'I don't know why. What does he see in me?' For at that time Fuengsin still felt her meditation wasn't good. On another occasion Fuengsin took Paul with her to see Ajahn Gaew and they met members of his family — his wife, six sons and one daughter. Fueng-sin was concerned about Paul's future as he hadn't shown much ability and wasn't very articulate. Her teacher reassured her saying that his ability would develop by eight years of age. She was further troubled by being unable to bring him up as Buddhist, but Ajahn's response was simply 'It doesn't matter.'

It was also an opportunity for Fuengsin to pay respects to the founder of the Dhammakaya tradition, Luang Phor Sodh, and to catch up on recent developments. It had been over 13 years since the great abbot had passed away, but the Wat had continued to prosper in various ways. In particular, there were still some practitioners who were committed to earnest development of the mind along with devoted students; among them was Ajahn Prakhong, the one who had introduced Fuengsin to the Wat. Fuengsin also received advice and instruction from several others at the Wat, including some senior *maechis*, the white-robed nuns who lived on the premises. She took Paul with her and left him to play with some nuns. Noting that he seemed untroubled and happy in their company, she could relax as she entered inside. The upasikas, like Ajahn Gaew, practised Vijja Dhammakaya, advanced meditation, and they enquired of Fuengsin about her life in the UK. Knowing her potential and having seen that she had been maintaining her practice they were keen to help her further, and furnished her with additional materials. These included the first two volumes of a new magazine called, *Walk Towards Happiness*, which were published by Dhammaprasit House. The magazine promoted a new Buddha Chakra Centre in Pathum Thani Province, which had been founded by Khun Yay Chandra, under whom Fuengsin had first studied Dhammakaya meditation.

It seemed there was significant interest in Fuengsin as the meditation adepts especially wanted her to receive a transmission of the Dhamma lineage to take back to the West. There had been a few Westerners who had returned to the UK and Ajahn Gaew in particular recalled fondly Ven. Kapilavaddho, but Fuengsin knew neither him nor another practitioner, Ven. Ananda Bodhi, who had also explored some of the Dhammakaya practice in the 1960s.[5] Ajahn Gaew may have been mindful that obstacles prevented these two keeping to the tradition, so perhaps he omitted the information so as to avoid discouragement. Perhaps he knew it would not be an easy task.

* * *

As Fuengsin explored the capital, she was gradually reforming her mental map and as she became better orientated her confidence grew. Once more settled, she was able to act as a tour guide for her family. In particular, she brought them to her alma mater, Chulalongkorn University, saying to Paul with great pride: 'This is the university where your Mummy once studied.'

The trips invariably took in other relatives and friends. On one occasion Fuengsin went on a trip with a nurse friend. They visited Dusit Thani hotel, named like many places in Thailand after the Tusita heaven realm, the realm of Bodhisattvas, Buddhas-to-be. They were greeted by a young elephant and its trainer. However, there was a strike by hotel staff and the poor elephant had

Fig. 69: Elephant at Dusit Thani hotel, Bangkok.

Fig. 70: Chomjit (third from left) with her parents at their home,
with Western friends (husband and wife living in Thailand).

no-one to look after it — a situation that later prompted the Thai government to introduce measures to ensure this situation didn't arise again.

The nurse then took her to see a mutual friend, Chomjit, at her family home, and they were also able to meet her parents. Chomjit had Scottish ancestry through her father — his father was a Scottish railway engineer, who married a Thai lady. He had many stories to tell, particularly during the Second World War when the whole family, including himself, were interned during the Japanese occupation.

Chomjit's father looked European, but he was fluent in Thai. Tony was with him one day, which probably gave the impression to most Thais that they were both Farangs. At least that was what a couple of taxi drivers thought as they gossiped in disparaging terms about their potential Western clients. As they were finishing their cheeky conversation, they approached the pale-skinned gentleman, no doubt thinking that here were two potential customers who were looking for less than salubrious entertainment. The opportunists proceeded to offer certain 'extras', touting the sensual delights of the Orient. They appeared confident of the extra trade coming their way.

But it wasn't their lucky day. Suddenly the burly figure of Chomjit's father turned on them and fired a ferocious tirade in the earthiest terms, in fluent and colourful Thai language, which made them run for their lives. Seeing this, he, Tony and all the bystanders burst out laughing. Such situations can be quite common for *look kreung* (those who are half Western/half Thai) and they sometimes play along with people's misconception: one man overheard comments to his wife that he spoke rather good Thai, to which he responded in milder tones, 'Oh, my wife is a very good teacher!'

The family also did the usual sightseeing. Thailand was rapidly developing as a tourist destination, though things were still small-scale, which allowed for leisurely meanderings. There was no need, for example, to beat the crowds first thing to tour the royal temples, not even the Grand Palace. Much to his delight, Tony found he was able to travel by himself up and down the Chao Phraya. He would leave the house and wander down to the pier and catch the ferry boat to the other side. Apparently untroubled by the heat and humidity he wandered on foot for miles, exploring the capital and earning the honorific title of 'the great tourist'. With only a few words of Thai and an imprecise accent, he could still make himself understood with gestures, pre-written addresses, and maps, though sometimes he had to convince would-be helpers of where he was going. Coming back to Thonburi he was met with puzzled and quizzical looks and instructions to turn around: 'You go wrong way! You should go the other way!' It was generally known that Farang tourists didn't go to Thonburi; there was nothing for them there.

Fig. 71: The Grand Palace from Sanam Luang, Bangkok.

The weather was the same, though the rainy season wasn't yet over, so there were frequent deluges.

Fig. 72: Tony at Wat Po.

People were very hospitable, though it sometimes seemed to stretch the notion of work hours. On one occasion Paul was reacting badly to mosquito bites and developed swellings, so he was taken to see a doctor who was known to the family. He inspected the bites, prescribed some treatment, and then promptly closed his surgery to take the family out to lunch — common for visitors from afar, no doubt, but surely not a popular decision with the other patients!

There was even a visit by Ann Tam who came from Hong Kong and stayed with the family for a few days in Wongwien Yai.

Fig. 73: Ann Tam, Fuengsin, Paul and a friend (at Wat Po?).

Travel across the globe was quite rare and so too was touring within Thailand. They stayed at the family house and at first explored only Bangkok, which had many attractions. Various relatives took it in turns to act as guide to some of the most popular tourist destinations, such as the Grand Palace, and less visited surrounds, notably Phra Pathom Chedi, a frequent destination for Fuengsin in her student days.

They then headed further afield on day trips. One such trip was towards Ayutthaya, which lies about 50 miles north of Bangkok and was reached by boat along the Chao Phraya. The group stopped a few miles before reaching the old capital at Bang Pa-In, an exquisite palace complex with gardens, landscaping and water features.

Fig. 74: Aisawan Dhiphya-Asana Pavilion, Bang Pa-in Palace, Ayutthaya.

Fig. 75: Chinese teak house at Bang Pa-in Palace.

On another trip Tony, Fuengsin and Paul accompanied Khun Yay and a relative on a journey west to Kanchanaburi. The destination was an infamous landmark: a railway bridge over the river Kwae that marked the start of the so-called Death Railway, constructed in the Second World War using forced labour involving hundreds of thousands. The majority were Southeast Asian workers, hired or conscripted mainly from Malaysia and Burma, together with substantial numbers of Allied prisoners of war. It was an ambitious project to provide the Japanese military a supply line from Thailand into Burma, much of it carved out through thick jungle. The line was completed in October 1943, ahead of schedule, but at immense cost; of the roughly 300,000 who toiled about a third lost their lives. The bridge then became an Allied target to disrupt the supply line and was eventually put out of action for the remainder of the war in 1945.

Fig. 76: Khun Yay Somboon, a cousin and Tony at the Bridge over the River Kwae, Kanchanaburi, October 1972.

They walked across the bridge, but no further. There was still a great poignancy as it was only a little over 25 years since the Death Railway had been built. They went to a cemetery, where they found a little church, which was well kept. Reminders of the recurrent nature of war were not far away.

Fig. 77: Fuengsin, a cousin and Paul, Kanchanaburi
(Paul is more interested in the steam locomotive).

On another occasion Tony and Fuengsin joined a Thai coach trip going east to the town of Aranyaprathet, just five kilometres from the Cambodia border.

Fig. 78: Fuengsin stands by a sign to Cambodia, with Aranyaprathet
railway station in the distance. October 1972.

There was no plan to cross the border — this required visas and they didn't have their passports. However, when the tour guide got everyone back on board he said they would go a bit closer. Next thing they knew, they had crossed the border and entered Paoypet — the driver had already obtained clearance.

By 1972 the country was already in the throes of civil war and the Thais or, at least, government forces were fighting the Communists. This meant that Tony and Fuengsin had landed themselves in what was effectively an armed camp. Even so, there were still places to eat, though the behaviour of some clientele was not quite what they expected. As they sat in a restaurant ready to dine, a jeep pulled up, a man got out, and brandished a gun. However, this wasn't a threat to the newcomers, but a signal to insiders; seconds later the rest of his family emerged and joined him for lunch at the restaurant. Tony and Fuengsin looked on bemused, and probably didn't have the same appetite as usual; they felt a bit stuck and wondered how they would return. However, somehow they got back over the border safely without being questioned: fortunately it was a government-controlled area of the Khmer Republic and the border guards were happy to wave them on, probably thinking Tony was an American.

Some of the outings took in the tropical forests with their lush vegetation and waterfalls. One trip was with Khun Vasana and her husband, Capt. Jamras,

Fig. 79: Khun Jamras, Khun Vasana, Khun Songsee and Fuengsin, Chantaburi.

who worked for Thai International Airways as a pilot, later going on to train pilots. On this occasion they were joined by Khun Songsee, a childhood friend of Vasana. It was a nostalgic trip to Chantaburi, southeast of Bangkok, an area that the three of them had explored, roaming free during student days at Chulalongkorn. One of the first stopping points was Wat Khao Mai Daeng in Chonburi, a little bit inland, where they paid respects to the abbot, Ajahn Yongyuth, the cousin who had established the monastery through a donation from Khun Yay Somboon.

Fig. 80: The residence (top floor) of the Abbot, Ajahn Yongyuth, at Wat Khao Mai Daeng, Bang Phra.

Thailand's rich landscape also allowed trips to the coast, sandy beaches and islands. Chantaburi was still a delightful haunt as it had been more than 10 years ago. Wherever they went they took with them copious food supplies for unhurried picnics, and there was hardly another soul in sight.

On this occasion, the sea wasn't the only attraction: this was a good place to buy gemstones from Cambodia, and Khun Vasana had an eye for potentially excellent purchases. She spent several hours in the jewellers, exercising her bargaining skills to great effect. Considering an item she would ask the price and on being given a figure would express surprise at its cost. Some haggling might ensue and then, as though she had completely lost interest, she would start the process again on another item . . . until the salesperson, unaware of Khun Vasana's stamina, might get quite worn out or impatient, and significantly drop the price, at which point a deal was struck. Fuengsin had other friends with similar abilities — *caveat vendor*!

Fig. 81: Khun Songsee, Khun Vasana and Fuengsin by the coast, possibly Rayong.

The Traffords' stay in Thailand overlapped with a visit by Jane Browne, who invited Fuengsin to go with her to Udon Thani in the North-East to spend some time at the monastery of Wat Pah Baan Taad. Fuengsin accepted and they were driven up to the Wat by a friend, whose sister owned a large restaurant in central Bangkok, which meant they were in a good position to offer *sangha-dana* (donations, especially meals, for the monastics). Although Fuengsin had got to know quite a lot about the Wat and its incumbents, especially through chats with Jane and her readings and translations, she had not visited the monastery before and didn't personally know any of the monks. Furthermore the meditation method taught there was quite different from her own. Nevertheless she recognised the opportunity to cultivate various aspects of her practice in an environment dedicated to release from suffering.

Fig. 82: Fuengsin at the entrance to Wat Pah Baan Taad, 1972.
Ven. Paññavaddho Bhikkhu is approaching in the distance.

On the back of this picture, Fuengsin noted:

An opportunity to go back and visit all the family in Thailand and to go and cultivate sīla [moral virtue] in Udon Province, Thailand (1972).

Phra Maha Boowa was the Abbot of this forest monastery, a disciple of the late Luang Pu Mun, who was highly revered, especially in that region. Although Fuengsin practised in another tradition, she was very respectful of monastics that put their heart into their Dhamma practice and was happy to support them and encourage their followers. Furthermore, she was familiar with the ascetic practices and peripatetic lifestyle of dhutanga monks since many had camped in the garden of her family home in Thonburi. So she gladly joined Khun Jane in her various activities to cultivate virtue and to spread the teachings and practices. They were a minority for at that time the monastery received little attention beyond its devoted disciples, who recognised the value in leaving the household life in order to work on eradicating defilements in the mind. Hence there were only a few tables for offering food, whereas in the decades to come the numbers increased more and more until there was a huge covered area for this purpose.

Fig. 83: Alms offering in the morning at Wat Pah Baan Taad.
Udon Province, Thailand (Fuengsin's description).

Fig. 84: Khun Jane is offering alms to Tan Ajahn Maha Boowa
at the front of Wat Pah Baan Taad, Udon Province, Thailand, 1972.

Fig. 85: Ven. Paññavaddho Bhikkhu, near the entrance to Wat Pah Baan Taad, 1972.

Also resident at the monastery was Ven. Paññavaddho Bhikkhu, an Englishman, who was originally ordained with Ven. Kapilavaddho as Preceptor at Wat Paknam — but again Fuengsin may not have been informed about that as he had changed his tradition. Fuengsin knew primarily that he was English and trained under his present Abbot, Phra Maha Boowa, to whom he remained loyal for the rest of his life. Fuengsin got to speak with the Abbot and Jane noted in her diary that they chatted like old friends. A connection was maintained so that when two years later in June 1974 Phra Maha Boowa made a visit to London Fuengsin recorded developments in her diary and already knew quite a few of those who would go and pay respects.

Fuengsin spent only a short while at the monastery before returning to Bangkok to continue reconnecting with friends and to carry on her own training with Ajahn Gaew at Wat Paknam.

* * *

As autumn advanced, it was time to pack their bags and face the prospect of returning to the UK and cooler climes. The colour of the tropics was left behind and after another long flight the family was back in Kent, with a return to grey skies and cool breezes. The experience had been wonderful, intense, and thoroughly absorbing, but in the end too much for the body to take and on returning to Cadnam Close the whole family came down with a fever.

It took a while for Fuengsin to write diary entries again. She had stopped on 24 September 1972 and her next entry was on 13 January 1973. She explained:

> Today is Saturday. I've just started making notes again having stopped for several months because I was too busy. I went home and saw Mother and all my siblings, nephews and nieces, and many friends. It meant I didn't have enough time to return to the diary plus I was continually ill for about a month. Also the child often had a fever or a cold. On top of that I was really lazy. So I didn't write. Today I have gathered my wits to write again.

Life back in the UK was comparatively dull and relatively inactive, yet Fuengsin didn't express any desire to remain in Thailand; her visit only seemed to confirm that her destiny lay in Britain. Fuengsin reconnected with her milieu in the close and continued receiving occasional visits from friends in Thailand, particularly Khun Jamras; in between flights he would stay a few days in London, allowing some time for a visit. His wife, Khun Vasana, would ensure that he would not come empty-handed.

Family life became more oriented around their growing child. When Fuengsin resumed her diary she noted that Paul was now four years and three months old, had grown taller and could speak two languages, but would not speak English with his mother. Her hopes might have been raised, but Paul's conversation did not progress: whilst other children at that age were expressing themselves volubly, Paul hardly spoke at all. The situation seemed serious enough to require medical advice, so Tony and Fuengsin consulted a doctor. He concluded that their son had become confused and thus advised speaking only English in the family, a response that was typical at that time. However, it was particularly tough on Fuengsin because she had already conceded religious responsibility to her husband and now it seemed that the chances of cultural exchange were further diminished. Fuengsin reluctantly followed the advice by and large in general conversation, but still kept repeating a few rhymes and choice phrases in Thai in the hope that the sound would not be completely lost.

However, whilst Paul's speech development was slow there were some encouraging signs: one teacher at the nursery school remarked that he was adept at jigsaws and doing sums. Tony and Fuengsin ensured that he led a balanced life, encouraging him to spend a lot of time outdoors; and he could sometimes be seen perched on his father's shoulders, which seemed miles up in the air. Outings included visits to a local wood, where Paul would collect bark and bring it back home. He also played with other children in the close: there were two boys the same age, Geoffrey and Stephen, with whom he would race around the close on bikes, and across the road were Michelle and her younger sister, Nicola, who would gather at children's parties.

The following autumn Paul duly took his first steps in the mainstream UK education system and attended Bligh Way School; his form teacher was Miss Woodruff and the headteacher was Mrs Smith. Fuengsin would go with him, catching a bus part of the way and walking the rest. On some other days he would receive a lift in the car from Mr Butler, whose daughter, Lucy, a few years older, was also a pupil. The family were kind, but they usually would leave just a few minutes before the school was due to start.

Paul generally enjoyed his first school; whilst there he started to read more, but it was noticed that he held the book up close to his face. An eye test established that he had astigmatism and required glasses, which came as a surprise as neither of his parents needed them. However, once he had glasses he was able to progress more and at the age of five he was assessed as having a reading age of seven — he was starting to show some signs of promise. And so suburban life continued with little incident apart from a bomb scare which led to bomb disposal experts coming in.

A few weeks after Paul had started at Bligh Way news erupted from Thailand. In October 1973 thousands of students had poured onto the streets to protest at the country's political restrictions. Some of the protest movement had origins among students of political science, contemporaries of Fuengsin in the 1950s, who were pressing their socialist ideologies. Fuengsin readily admitted in later conversations that if she had been there she would have joined them. This would have been seen as quite rebellious as her family was in many ways part of the establishment. Indeed, her cousin, Phi Lerm, was in the unenviable official position of directing the army's communications at that time.

Whilst there were explosive events in the background, life was generally more settled in the UK. The holiday of a lifetime meant that it would be many years before the family could even contemplate another expedition abroad. So they contented themselves with a series of local trips: a day's outing in February took in Tunbridge Wells, the Sussex border, Maidstone, West Malling, Aylesford, and Wrentham; a few days later the family wandered through Upnor and Allhallows; whilst another trip took in Southend Pier and Leigh on Sea, on the other side of the Thames Estuary. Perhaps it was to get a break from the impending General Election, in which Labour narrowly beat the Conservatives (Fuengsin duly exercised her democratic right, but never divulged her voting intentions; it seems she liked to keep people guessing).

In 1974 one large family saloon was replaced by another: out went the Ford and in came another second-hand model: the British-made Wolseley 16/60, a well-fitted vehicle with a fair amount of luxury, though already looking a bit dated. Leisurely day trips included an outing with friends to St Margaret's Bay near Dover. As the car cruised along, it came up behind a vehicle that was progressing slowly, veering from one side of the road to the other, back and forth. Each car that came in the opposite direction had to take evasive action to avoid collision. The driver eventually pulled into an empty forecourt (it might have been a disused fire station). Tony followed. The driver opened the car door and struggled to his feet and could hardly stand as he was heavily inebriated. He left the car keys in the car and Tony lost no time in taking them, as was his professional training. Shortly afterwards, a police car arrived on the scene, and the policeman seemed to know the driver. The family left at that point and heard no more afterwards, preferring to continue with meanderings of the more sober variety.

Easter often meant visiting relatives in Chepstow and taking in the sights in that area or *en route*: hence visits to Abergavenny, Sugar Loaf, Raglan Castle, and Sudeley Castle in the Cotswolds. Tony and Fuengsin both had a deep appreciation of the beauty of the British countryside and a fascination with the nobility that historically owned it. This fuelled Fuengsin's imagination, encouraging her to read works by Anthony Trollope, particularly the Palliser Novels.

Fuengsin continued to keep in touch with her Buddhist circles. There was no temple in Strood, so she occasionally made her way into London and frequented both the Hampstead Buddhist Vihara and the Chiswick Vihara, usually on special occasions such as Vesak (the birth, Enlightenment and final passing into Nibbāna of the Buddha), where they could make offerings for the special occasion and listen to Dhamma talks. It was here that she could meet and catch up with members of the Hampshire Buddhist Society, usually Jane, Brian and Sue, plus Freda Wint and Irene Quitner. These centres, which hosted many visitors from around the world, had strong Oriental connections, sometimes mysterious and unknown to Fuengsin. It was on one such occasion that she noticed a picture of Chao Khun Phra Monkgol Thepmuni and wondered how it had got there.

Then at a later date came a re-connection with her visit to Wat Pah Baan Taad. Between 14 and 16 June 1974 Fuengsin noted in her diary a 'long weekend' in Hampstead involving quite a number of Hampshire supporters, including Jane Browne, Irene Quitner, Rob, Freda Wint and Dorothy Wilkinson. They had gone to pay respects to Phra Maha Boowa who had come on a visit to the UK, one that proved a significant step in the founding of the Thai Forest Tradition in Europe.[6]

Notes

1. The Far East Travel Centre (FETC) in Shaftesbury Avenue was acquired by the Omega Travel Group in 2007 and is still going strong today at the same location.

2. Sobelair Sabena Boeing 707. According to the official specification, the capacity would range between 141 and 189 passengers depending upon how many were flying First Class.
   http://www.boeing.com/history/products/707.page

3. The quote 'Dhamma exceeds all other gifts' comes from the Dhammapada verse 354, Sakkapanha Vatthu. See e.g.
   http://www.tipitaka.net/tipitaka/dhp/verseload.php?verse=354

4. Blue book (meditation manual). It was surmised initially that most of these teachings had been copied from another handwritten source because they are so close to teachings that were subsequently published as *Vijja Mokpon* [*Maggaphala*] *Pitsadaan*, which translates approximately as: *The Special Path and Fruits of Vijja*. Only in May 2014 did it come to light that Ajahn Gaew had dictated these teachings, which makes Ajahn Gaew's knowledge all the more remarkable. We don't know when these teachings were recorded, but it may be that they were initially recorded for Ajahn Gaew's own use several years earlier. It is not known over what period the book was compiled; the astrological details could have been added much later.

5. Ven. Ananda Bodhi later practised in the Tibetan tradition and was recognised as an incarnate lama by the Karmapa and given the name Namgyal Rinpoche.

6. Some of the talks and Q&A for Phra Maha Boowa's visit to the UK in 1974 are recorded at: http://www.accesstoinsight.org/lib/thai/boowa/london.html

9

New Prospects in the Midlands

Tony had been a Customs Officer for almost 15 years, over the course of which he had seen a lot of activity and gained considerable experience, so it was a good time to look for further progression. However the Waterguard offered few opportunities for promotion. Meanwhile VAT had replaced purchase tax from April 1973, and this created a need for more staff, so Tony prepared himself for a change in the nature of his work. There were some vacancies in the London area which Tony could have undertaken, enabling the family to remain in Strood, but he did not fancy the prospect of working in and travelling to locations in and around the capital. So he explored further afield and found the Midlands region more appealing; they offered less of a commute, with reasonably priced housing and good areas within easy access. It wasn't long before Tony had received news from HM Customs and Excise that his application for promotion to Senior Officer had been approved: from being based by the coast, he was now going to be located about as far away as you could get from the sea, at a VAT office in Dudley, in the West Midlands. As he was still relatively early in his career, such an opportunity conveyed quite an incentive, so after some deliberation Tony and Fuengsin decided to commit to the move.

Once again the family needed to find a new home. So in February 1975 Tony went up to Dudley by train and hired a car to look at some houses. Meanwhile Fuengsin stayed at home to look after Paul, who became infected with a virus that Fuengsin herself caught soon after. They were both unwell for a week or so and Fuengsin's diary entries reduced to a trickle, describing her struggles with illness and eventually her signs of recovery. On 10 February, having kept her diary on an almost daily basis for more than five and a half years, Fuengsin penned her last entry. During that time she had produced 10 volumes amounting to about 2,000 pages, but no-one else seemed to know their contents even less why she decided to stop. It might have had something to do with the coming transition, sorting through belongings and routines being affected. Or perhaps she had an inkling that new vistas lay ahead.

Tony and Fuengsin were not familiar with this central region, though they knew that the county of the West Midlands was an industrial area and that Dudley was in the heart of the Black Country, which was historically an engine of heavy industry. Tony did most of the scouting and suggested that rather than live in another suburb they could look further afield for somewhere more rural, beyond the natural break of the Wychbury and Clent Hills. The village of Hagley was identified as a potential location: it was served by good road and rail links, a row of shops provided essential groceries, and there were highly regarded schools for pupils of all ages. Situated on the edge of the Worcestershire countryside the area seemed pleasant and it even boasted local gentry, the Cobhams at Hagley Hall, a Palladian mansion sitting in extensive grounds. Generally impressed, they explored the market and found a three-bedroom detached house with additional features including a sun lounge and a well-maintained garden at the back. It had the name of Darnley, which was coincidently the same as that of a road near their home in Strood. The only significant detraction was that it looked onto the A456, a heavily used artery between Kidderminster and Birmingham.

The purchase was duly made and the family moved in at the end of May. Being situated further north and more inland it was going to be somewhat colder than Strood, but they were still surprised when it snowed on 1 June! This didn't matter. They were charmed by the house and its garden, which was broad as well as long. It contained well-maintained borders and several mature fruit trees, including the sweet Worcester Pearmain and a cooking apple tree. Towards the rear there were a large pear tree and three further apple trees with a crisp taste that surrounded an open-air swimming pool and an adjacent chalet. The pool was above ground, open air and unheated, which severely limited its use, but within a couple of months it had warmed up sufficiently for people to take a dip; and the following year saw a heat wave, so the pool entered was regularly used and became popular with neighbours. There was also a double greenhouse to encourage them to be self-sufficient, and it was used especially for tomatoes, cucumbers and peppers.

Inside, the house was reasonably spacious, though the kitchen was a bit cramped. Worries about noise disturbance from the road in front were eased as the family got used to its monotony and the rooms at the back were well insulated, so visitors could rest in comfort. The home was equipped with a few conveniences, but in some respects it was basic: bedroom windows were yet to be double-glazed and the central heating was used sparingly so during winter the windows regularly iced up. Downstairs, there were gas fires, but they were kept on a low setting, whilst a padded snake draft excluder kept out unwelcome breezes. Initially, Fuengsin did a lot of washing by hand in the kitchen, with only a spinner rinse to assist — until Tony's mother showed her the benefits of an automatic washing machine, which then became a priority on their household shopping list.

The house may have been cold at times, but the family received a warm welcome from locals. The previous owner was Mr Cyril Goode, who gave kind assistance to the new arrivals. He was well known in the local community as he had been treasurer of Hagley Village News, a monthly publication distributed to all the village households.[1] Next door was Mr Hadley, a widower, who had the distinction of being an occupant since the 1920s: he and his wife had moved into their home as soon as it had been built. He recalled that originally each house had a front gate to prevent cattle straying when farmers drove them along the road. The other neighbours were similarly welcoming. In fact, around the village the pace of life seemed gentler and people generally seemed more approachable and had time for each other.

Hagley was quite large as villages go, with a population of between 2,000 and 3,000. It was also stretched out, causing some confusion about names: 'Hagley' was primarily the area near Hagley Hall, together with a swathe of land that stretched south through 'top Hagley' and down to what was originally called 'lower Hagley', but now called West Hagley. When locals referred to the 'village' they usually meant the shops along Worcester Lane, which was in West Hagley. As a result of its expansion, Hagley was covered by two parishes, the Hagley parish and also the Clent parish to the east, part of whose boundary was Worcester Road itself.

There were also linguistic changes with a new local dialect and accent to tune into: instead of Cockney and Medway derivatives, along came the Hagley accent — which was not Brummie (unless someone from Birmingham had moved into the area), nor Black Country (which might have applied to the nearest town of Stourbridge), but had its own distinctive intonation. Fuengsin also drew on regional TV soap operas, particularly Crossroads, to gain further familiarisation. She greatly enjoyed the way these fictional characters were depicted, the emotions they expressed, and how they related to each other, particularly 'Benny' and 'Miss Diane'. If Fuengsin felt somewhat disoriented by strange conventions and accents, then Tony was on hand to provide illuminating explanations based on a lifelong interest in history and human geography. However, at first both Tony and Fuengsin were perplexed at the ITV schedules as they seemed to vary from what was listed . . . until they discovered that the channel was actually ATV (the Associated Television company), whose daily listings were squeezed into one of the inch-wide boxes reserved for 'regional variations'.

Gradually Fuengsin got to know who was who, their daily routines and rhythms of life, their backgrounds and aspirations. People in the village got to know about Fuengsin, whose diminutive Oriental figure could often be seen striding back and forth on trips to the shops, with bags balanced in both hands. Fuengsin remarked that because of her family's military connections she didn't walk — she marched, a trait that had long been recognised, earning her the nickname back in Thailand of *Taksin's Warrior*, after the former King of Thonburi. Among the villagers who had spotted her distinctive frame was Mrs Brenda Harding, who like Mr Hadley, was a long-time resident. She noticed the figure of Fuengsin passing by whilst tending her front garden and that, in keeping with the military tag, she seemed to bear a serious or perhaps inscrutable expression on her face, absorbed in concentration as she maintained a brisk pace. Mrs Harding felt a strong desire to catch this stranger's attention and was determined to make her smile. And when it duly happened it came very naturally. She and her husband, Tom, subsequently became Fuengsin's good friends and further demonstrated the kindness of the villagers.

There were some very distinctive personalities and Fuengsin usually kept an eye out for an opportunity to meet and speak with them. She found one such character down Summervale Drive: turning left brought her into a rambling nursery and following the track round to the right she'd find Mr Vaughan among greenhouses in his garden gear; from his humble nursery, which was free of any the fancy services offered by modern garden centres, he simply supplied fruit and vegetables, wrapped in brown paper bags. In the village there was Mrs Barns, an elderly lady who lived alone in a terraced cottage between Church Street and Chapel Street. She had collected a large assortment of items for her home, an eclectic selection that could easily have been turned into a bric-a-brac shop. Mrs Barns would give some of these as presents to Fuengsin, included clothing and a large print entitled 'Midst Pine and Bracken', which was gratefully received and hung up on display in the dining room.

The family soon heard about the doorstep milk deliveries: early each morning there would be the sound of an electric motor whirring on and off, followed by the clink of bottles and footsteps. This was Tony the milkman and his milk float; Fuengsin soon introduced herself and received a friendly response, for he was all too pleased to have another customer. Tony was well known as a cheerful chap with a loud and clear voice, earning him the nickname of 'The Microphone'. It wouldn't matter where you were in the house when he called, you could always hear him. 'Good Morning, Mrs Trafford! How are you today?!' he would boom in his natural voice. As an accompaniment to his voice was the tinkling of coins in his satchel, as he searched for change. Tony was particularly friendly because, in contrast to a few others, Fuengsin would invariably settle the bill every week; Tony would mutter about them, especially if they lived in big houses. His travels around Hagley and interactions on the doorstep made him a good source of informal news which Fuengsin readily digested. Another useful source was Lawrence the hairdresser, with a salon above an optician, from whom Fuengsin could form a general picture of the kinds of psychological profiles among some locals.

As part of the settling in process, Paul was swiftly registered at Hagley First School, which was about half a mile away — a good walking distance — and he joined before the end of the summer term. Fuengsin accompanied Paul for a while, taking the opportunity to get to know one of the lollipop ladies, Mrs Dyas, who helped children cross the road at the junction of Worcester Lane and Park Road. When Paul had become familiar with the route he was allowed to make his own way, but his mother urged him to take care when crossing the road, warning him, 'I have my spies in the village!' It was unwise for Paul to doubt this for wherever his mother came into regular contact — be it with the butcher, the pharmacist, post office counter staff, or various tradespeople — she got to know people on some level. Fuengsin was always open to expanding her circles, so she gradually managed to get to know a long line of people along the Worcester Road, and their interests such as classic S-Type Jaguars and Volvos. Fuengsin had little interest in cars herself but she was interested in the fact that people had these various activities as hobbies; it was a distinct facet of local life.

Similarly, villagers became increasingly curious about Fuengsin and once they had met her she came across as informed, stimulating and articulate so they were happy to chat and get to know her. One was Harry, the window cleaner, who very much appreciated that she always had a cup of tea ready and he never heard a bad word about anybody. Harry was an ardent fan of country music. Most years he would put aside his cleaning cloth, buckets and ladder, and make his way to Nashville, Tennessee. Since her days in Kent, Fuengsin had been listening to a few albums from the likes of Jim Reeves, and was open to expanding her selection. So Harry would come back enthused with those country sounds and bestow upon Fuengsin a cassette tape so that she'd hear the latest from stars such as George Jones, Tammy Wynette, Boxcar Willie and Ricky Skaggs. Fuengsin accepted these tapes with excitement and tuned into country music programmes on local radio stations such as BRMB, Beacon Radio and Radio Wyvern, and also on national radio, particularly Country Club hosted by Wally Whyton, who was one of Harry's mates. She was particularly engaged by the lyrics, which covered so many of the ups and downs of life.

The 1970s saw the rise of home hi-fi systems, with a flood of silver models from Japan, but the family could not afford brand new equipment. Initially, they made do with a turntable for records. However, one of Tony's colleagues was an electronics and music enthusiast and sourced some good quality second-hand items, including a Sansui stereo receiver and some sizeable loudspeakers. Fuengsin would usually take her seat on the settee next to the stereo and near the fire, and gaze through the French windows, through the sun lounge into the garden. From this comfortable position she would then put the stereo through its paces, cranking up the volume, especially when she was by herself, though occasionally forgetting to turn the volume knob back down when powering off. When listening to music on the radio she would also switch very rapidly between channels; her mind could access different music almost instantly, but the channel hopping was a bit disconcerting for anyone else who happened to be in the room. Fuengsin really enjoyed Country: the tip of one slipper would go up and down in time with the lively rhythms. In her younger days she might have joined in, but by this time her guitar was stowed away in a cupboard and her mouth organ was in a drawer. It was fun, though she readily conceded that the melodies interfered with her meditation practice — the tunes would play over and over again in her head.

Meanwhile in the classroom, Paul started his learning tentatively. He didn't find it so easy to make friends and seemed a bit confused about some of the activities when he tried to fit in. It was a period in which he was being made more aware of his mixed background, which was unusual at that time. It was highlighted when Christopher Thomas, one of Tony's first cousins on his mother's side, came to visit whilst passing by on the motorway. He enjoyed discussions with Fuengsin because he had an interest in the Orient, particularly in martial arts. They chatted in the kitchen whilst Fuengsin was preparing some food. Paul entered and Fuengsin spoke to him in Thai, but to her surprise he flatly rejected the invitation to show his bilingual aptitude saying, 'Mummy, please don't talk to me in that scribble — I'm an English boy now!' Indeed, over a period of several years Paul was not amenable to much Oriental culture: a hat he had been given in the style of Thai hill tribes was eagerly passed on to a classmate and when Fuengsin playfully suggested a traditional Thai hairstyle of *hua jook* (gathered up in a topknot) he was against that too. In his early schooling he was the only non-Caucasian in his class and he was evidently self-conscious of this and wanted to conform.

Yet overall Paul was not unhappy; he enjoyed being outside during breaks and seemed to have generally more energy. The following year he made much greater advances in his studies under Miss Jones, who allowed him to work through a series of mathematics textbooks at his own, now rapid, pace. Tony and Fuengsin received encouraging news on their son's academic progress at a summer parents evening. He was showing an aptitude for mathematics, and there was an astute observation: 'Paul doesn't have many friends, but he has good friends.'

Fuengsin was further encouraged when he put his mathematical ability to practical use. Chinese supermarkets were starting to open more widely, with some large stores in Birmingham providing essential and more exotic Oriental ingredients. On one occasion the family did some shopping and then paid the bill. For some reason Paul asked to see the bill and having inspected it queried an item of £2 at the bottom. Tony and Fuengsin took a closer look, but weren't sure what it meant, so they asked about it at the till. The cashier conceded it was a surcharge that should not have been applied, and so issued a refund — Paul had duly earned his pocket money (which was considerably less than £2).

It was necessary to stock up from such shopping trips to cater for the increasing number of Fuengsin's friends who came to visit the family singly, in families or small groups. One of the individual visitors was a lady with a powerful mind and a strong and forceful character, which was fairly standard among Fuengsin's friends. On such occasions Paul was minded to be on his best behaviour. The traditional phrase, 'children should be seen and not heard', had been repeated by Tony until it lurked somewhere in Paul's consciousness. However, after the visitor departed Paul volunteered to sum up her particular traits in a few words. Tony and Fuengsin were surprised by his powers of observation — he had her down to a tee — though this shouldn't have surprised them greatly because they were both very observant themselves, able to discern people's characters.

Fuengsin could then recall Ajahn Gaew's prediction that her son would show promise from the age of eight. As though on cue, Paul then took up chess and displayed some initial aptitude; it was Tony's second attempt to get him interested as he had already tried to teach him when he was five without success. It was around this time Fuengsin stopped playing any indoor games with him as they were both competitive and in these recreational jousts she always lost. Tony's tactics were shrewder, so games were more evenly matched, but he recognised that Paul needed to face more experienced opposition. So he took Paul up to the road to join Hagley Chess Club, which held weekly sessions on Friday evenings in an upstairs room of the Hagley Free Church. At first Tony reluctantly accompanied him for evening games across the chequered board, but he was soon spared the extended periods of concentration and would just come later in the evening to collect his son. Fuengsin didn't ever go herself, but was interested to hear about the characters at the club, many of whom had long-time associations with the club and the church. One such guiding light was C. Leslie Heathcock, a former Worcestershire champion, who was generous in sharing his time and experience both across the board and in the pews, giving much encouragement to everyone.

Paul continued to prosper in Hagley Middle School, particularly under a form teacher, Miss Sharman, who was strict but supportive and tried to stretch all her pupils. Fuengsin generally observed from a distance and just ensured that he did his homework on time. Whilst she was delighted to see him thrive academically, she also wanted him to mix more. She encouraged him to play outdoors, and he enjoyed riding his bikes with friends, sometimes in the housing estates at the back, including Sweetpool Lane and the adjoining nature reserve, but he was generally self-contained, more often absorbed playing by himself with Lego. Tony also had a bike, so as Paul grew older they explored the country lanes, occasionally going on picnics. However, Fuengsin never had a bicycle, so she couldn't join.

Whilst Paul seemed to favour mixing with only a few, Fuengsin already had many friends. As she did not initially undertake any paid work she often frequented village spaces and got to know individuals, personally, one by one. She would receive an invitation to have morning coffee or afternoon tea and then reciprocate, cherishing their company. This process was not new to her, but the village seemed to make it easier to get to know more people than she had experienced previously. Thus Fuengsin got to know some neighbours on the other side of the road, especially a spinster, Janet Eadie, another of the long-time residents and a former teacher with an 'old school' outlook that Fuengsin greatly respected. She often went round for tea and learnt about how life in Hagley had evolved over generations. It was still the case that there were quite a few residents whose ancestors had been in the area for many decades and this gave many of them a stable and sagacious view; being well-settled they were very accommodating to visitors.

As in Strood, Fuengsin developed a reputation for being a good listener and being sound in her advice. When she listened, her body was still and she gave her undivided attention, maintaining steady eye contact. Her friends knew that she properly understood what they were saying, so they began to place a great deal of trust in her and share their problems. She would often act as counsellor and confidante regarding relationships; one lady was moved to ask: 'Fuengsin, do you think will I ever find someone?' And Fuengsin replied, 'Well, you might do, but you might not, because not everybody finds that right person. [For] Some people . . . the destiny is just to go through life alone.' She would frequently encourage independence of mind, encouraging her listeners to be 'an island unto yourself', to keep expectations realistic and not depend on others for happiness. When Fuengsin expressed her views on very serious matters such as drug addictions in families, depression, neuroses and many other kinds of problems, the words had an impact because they were spoken directly with conviction and she invariably hit the mark.

Fuengsin appreciated the general kindness and hospitality, but was sur-prised at how some affluent westerners, despite their many material comforts, could be emotionally insecure and in such a psychological mess. She was also not afraid to point out what she regarded as inappropriate behaviour, particu-larly rash activities that harmed existing human relationships. Her audience knew something was seriously wrong when in emphatic voice she expressed her disapproval, 'Oooh that is bad, very bad!' It was not a knee-jerk reaction to scandal, but the understanding of the negative karmic consequences that would ensue. Yet she didn't merely dismiss these people, but tried to be constructive, in a way that echoed the example of her father. Her approach had a lasting impact as long afterwards when deliberating solutions to problems some would wonder what Fuengsin would have said to them or would have done.

The Community Centre was an important focal point — as well as being a place for obtaining delicious items from the Women's Institute. Here, Fuengsin acquired practical skills such as dress-making and knitting clothes for family members, which were much needed in a household on a very limited budget. Fuengsin would be very careful with her shopping, avoiding most luxury items and brands. She assiduously collected Green Shield stamps, filling the books after doing her shopping at International, the supermarket on a prime location in the centre of the village.[2] For a greater range of products and more competitive prices she also wandered into Stourbridge market and would buy fresh fish such as a whole mackerel, which would cost about 40p. On her return, she would fry the mackerel and prepare home-made chips from potatoes grown in the back garden.

Fuengsin continually expanded her culinary repertoire so meal times included pasta dishes, such as spaghetti Bolognese, traditional roasts, and casseroles. She would still try to treat the family with some sweets and put a lot of effort into various creations, including pies, steamed puddings and an array of cakes, including requests for school favourites. She'd announce their appearance cheerily with, "Here you are!", and then see them disappear almost as fast as food coveted by Tom and Jerry in their cartoon duels. All along Fuengsin also refined her knowledge of Thai cookery with various recipes, especially curries. In true Thai fashion, she retained her fondness of dry salted fish, something that Westerners find very smelly. In order to prevent its premature disposal, Fuengsin stored items she received — especially from Vasana — out of sight, saying: 'When my friends bring it to me from Thailand, I keep it in the shed until my husband is out at work and then it reappears.' The same treatment was reserved for some spices and durian, a quintessential delicacy that is sometimes banned from aeroplanes because of its intense smell.

Meanwhile there was a growing interest in Thailand as a holiday destination and when prospective visitors from Hagley heard about Fuengsin they sought her help in learning elements of the language, usually just spoken Thai. Fuengsin willingly taught them and once she had got to know them she also allowed extensive contact with her family in Thailand. One of her first pupils was Mr Jack Moulder, who used to run the Forge and then Cross Keys garages in Hagley in the 1950s and 1960s. Whilst in Thailand in March 1979 Mr Moulder met Fuengsin's family and sent a postcard reporting that he had dined with her mother and was taken to Ayutthaya and then to the sea at Bang Po.

Long before helping to create demand for visa applications for the Thai consulate and even before she had really consolidated domestic matters, Fuengsin had started to investigate whether there were any Buddhist centres in the area. The West Midlands conurbation had a population of over two million, with many immigrant communities from South and Southeast Asia, so she was optimistic about finding practitioners somewhere. Her enquiries did not take long to bear fruit. Her initial lead was a Chinese Mahayana Buddhist tradition and from there she was directed to Bearwood in Sandwell, to the home of Mrs Dorothy Bailey, who was a professional acupuncturist. Mrs Bailey was better known as Vajira, an ordained name she had received a few years earlier from Ven. Maha Sthavira Sangharakshita, whilst she had been a member of the Western Buddhist Order (and thence of the Friends of the Western Buddhist Order). Vajira was now a Soto Zen lay minister, who trained under Roshi Jiyu-Kennett, the first female to be sanctioned by the Soto School of Japan to teach in the West, and had subsequently become a member of the Order of the Buddhist Contemplatives. She acknowledged all her teachers for their contributions to her religious development and continued to welcome teachers from many different schools.

One of these teachers was Ven. Dr Rewata Dhamma, a Burmese bhikkhu who had come from India at the suggestion of Sister Palmo, a Tibetan Buddhist, and in response to an invitation of the Birmingham Buddhist community. Fuengsin's timing was uncanny because the venerable monk had arrived for the first time in the UK just the day before she turned up. Bhante Rewata Dhamma's circumstances were unusual. Being Burmese he had practised in the Theravada tradition, as is the norm in most of Southeast Asia, and being a particularly bright student he had advanced rapidly in Abhidhamma, higher Buddhist learning, leading on to his studies at Varanasi University. However, whilst in India he had associated with many Tibetan lamas and came to appreciate deeply their traditions.[3] It was in that light that when a request was received from supporters to establish a centre in the Birmingham area, the Karmapa, spiritual head of the Karma Kagyu order of Tibetan Buddhism, backed Bhante in a petition.

Vajira also had a background distinguished by the confluence of traditions. In her professional life she had been a laboratory scientist at the Atomic Energy Authority, where career advancement for women was at that time severely restricted. The work brought her to Birmingham and in her free time she attended lectures by Ninian Smart, a great pioneer in the study of world religions. She went on to explore Buddhism and trained in the Theravada school, subsequently becoming Chairman of the Birmingham Buddhist Society in 1967. Two years later she was ordained as a member of the Western Buddhist Order and given the name Vajira by Ven. Sangharakshita, the Honorary President of the Society. It was also during her tenure that she invited Rev. Master Jiyu Kennett to lead a weekend retreat in the Birmingham area, from which Vajira obtained incisive help.

Fuengsin's spirits and sense of purpose were given a real boost on meeting such people and she would subsequently make many trips into the Birmingham area. Not being able to drive, she would sometimes be given a lift by Tony, but more often she would catch the 192, 292 or X92 bus service that ran up the A456 through Hagley and into the city centre. By the end of 1977 the West Midlands Buddhist Centre was established at 41 Carlyle Road. It was largely a Burmese vihara, but Bhante was keen to welcome other traditions too, so it became a hub for Theravada, Tibetan and Zen. The Tibetan presence was particularly significant with the subsequent arrival of Lama Thubten and Lama Lodro in Karma Ling, the seat of Tai Situpa Rinpoche in England.

The practicalities were not so straightforward. Initially, there was a single communal space, whose usage alternated mainly between Theravada and Tibetan groups (the Zen group met at Vajira's home). It was cumbersome, so a Theravada shrine was arranged upstairs and a Tibetan one downstairs. Some resources were shared, but there were still difficulties: arriving for a regular meditation session sometimes revealed a shortage of cushions as the majority would have gravitated either upstairs or downstairs, depending on which was the last group to gather. Bhante, the main instigator, may have observed everything with mild amusement, seeing it as part of everyone's training. Fuengsin, who was there all along to give support, certainly saw plenty of humour in these situations. Many of these observations were freely expressed in the kitchen, as were shared joys for the unveiling of luxuries — such as the first electric rice cooker, which was worthy of a great celebration and also a few jokes.

Thus, an unusually 'ecumenical' Vihara was established in the mid-1970s, finding a home in Carlyle Road. Meanwhile Fuengsin explored further afield and visits followed to the Thai consulate and Thai temples; certain bus routes soon became as familiar as her skin. Yet Buddhism remained quite a novelty for several years and Fuengsin's experiences led her to write:

> If one looks back, even as far as the Sixties, one can see a large number of people of different nationalities and religions in London and other big cities. However, the sight of a monk in [a] saffron-colour robe was rare enough for a Buddhist to be surprised and excited. On the other hand most people here would be wondering who the shaven man in the robe was. There were some stories of curiosity, resentment, ignorance and rudeness when the encounters between

the monks and some local people took place. A monk on his alms round about 12 years ago [in the late 70s] in Birmingham was stared at while some people thought that his begging bowl was a drum — they didn't realise that he was walking around in silence according to the Vinaya or monks' rules.

At that time the majority of the British had not been to the East before. There were only two temples, the main Buddhist Society in London and a dozen smaller groups all over the country. As a result there were not enough communities for a lot of overseas students and the ones who could not speak good English would not be able to understand lectures or take part in various discussions on the profound philosophy. Moreover, in the beginning, most English Buddhists were from the middle class and intellectual, though some were hippies.

Since many of these early initiatives were on behalf of immigrant communities, there was a natural inclination to charitable purposes. Karma Ling was active in contributing to Rokpa, a charity founded in 1980 by Dr Akong Tulku Rinpoche, Lea Wyler and Dr V. Wyler to provide humanitarian help, especially for the poor, and supporting disaster relief, education and training.

As Fuengsin's exploits became more widely known, early in 1981 Jill Skelding, a journalist, visited her at home to conduct an interview. A photo was taken in the dining room and Fuengsin was invited to include in the shot some sacred objects. So Fuengsin went upstairs to her shrine, which was in the visitors' bedroom, carefully located in a cupboard above a wardrobe. It was deliberately placed high up out of respect, but so high she could only reach it by standing on a chair and she often needed Tony's assistance to retrieve items. On this occasion she brought down three Buddha rupas, varying in shape and material, including a large crystal Buddha from Wat Paknam.

The outcome was a 'Woman to Woman' feature for The County Express, a regional paper that was based in Stourbridge, whose circulation included Kidderminster. It was entitled, 'Buddhism as a Way of Life', and was published on 13 March 1981.[4] The article conveyed both her distinguished family background and earthiness, celebrating spotted dick steamed pudding. Fuengsin's reflections on Thailand were nostalgic, commenting on its different pace of life and lack of traffic. However, the heart of the article was about her Buddhist practice, and a statement in characteristically no-nonsense fashion was recorded thus:

It isn't a Sundays-only type of religion, and I know it's hard for people who know nothing of Buddhism to even to begin to understand what it's all about, but basically, no one can tell you how to practise Buddhism, it's something the individual must learn for him or herself.

It has to come from inside a person, and it is a very personal thing — no one can help you with it, and you can only practise Buddhism though life itself.

Fig. 86: Fuengsin at home. Photograph by Phil Loach
for the County Express, March 1981.

Fuengsin wanted to share about her meditation, and tried to keep it simple for her interviewer and readership. She was very much aware of the challenge in trying to communicate a lifelong tradition in a few words to someone from a completely different background. It was even more of a challenge to expect this person to pass this on to a general audience. Some of the phrases that made it to print were a little mixed up, yet Fuengsin was happy as the overall message was consistent and showed how meaningful it was in her daily life:

It is closely linked with meditation and when you meditate you look at a figure of a Buddha and bow — that way you are aiming to suppress your ego, and get rid of any pride. Once you are rid of that you are at one with the universe.

. . . Buddha taught us to do things in moderation, and there is a strong accent put on family life — I feel it is important for me to do what is best for my family, whether it be cooking, cleaning or whatever. All the time I have to think of others and try to get rid of any selfishness.

. . . Your behaviour is only a reflection of your mind. When you meditate you become single-minded — that doesn't mean narrow-minded, merely that your mind is opening up and you are more capable of appreciating and understanding things.

The article also related that at that time Fuengsin was teaching English to Asian immigrants. These were elderly Pakistani ladies living in Lye who started with no knowledge of the language at all, but there was nobody available in the community to teach them. So a volunteer scheme was introduced, which Fuengsin joined as she was already qualified to teach English as a foreign language. When she went along to the preparatory meeting, she was surprised to see that out of perhaps 30 instructors she was the only non-white person in attendance. There was no pay involved, not even travel expenses, but Fuengsin signed up and proceeded to teach on a weekly basis for several years. She even went to visit one of her students in hospital in Bromsgrove. Apart from such necessary journeys, her students didn't travel much as a rule, but an exception was made for Fuengsin when a car pulled up at the house and one of her students got out and delivered some sweets as a present.

Fuengsin had plenty of opportunity to put her Buddhist principles into practice with situations in and around the house. Paul was seldom really idle, but still had unspent restless energy and acquired a bad habit of throwing tiny apples that had just emerged from bud: he would hurl them high into the air, trying to clear the pear tree. One morning the doorbell sounded and Fuengsin went to answer. Standing at the door was a policeman, who asked, 'Is your mother in?' Fuengsin, who was around 40 years old, answered, 'I *am* the mother.' Undaunted, the constable then asked whether he could come in and have a word. On entering he explained the reason for his visit: at the estate at the back a lady had been hit by small apples fired by a young boy and this house had been identified as the source of the offending missiles. Paul was the suspect and was unable to deny the accusation, so the constable advised, with Fuengsin firmly agreeing, that he go and apologise to the lady in question.

So Paul joined the officer in his car and was taken round the back. He was brought to the lady who had been subject to the bombardment and instructed to apologise, which he duly did. However, the lady in question looked a bit puzzled and expressed surprise: 'He's a bit smaller than I imagined.' Even so, she accepted the apology and Paul was returned home by the policeman. The PC then returned to the house, the scene of the apple crime, and on wandering into the garden his helmet was promptly knocked off by an apple projectile. But this projectile had not been thrown — it had been fired by a catapult. Looking over the fence, it was obvious he had grabbed the wrong suspect and actually there were two miscreants. In fact, it turned out that the house on the other side was nowhere near the Traffords; it was more than 200m further along the Worcester Road. A somewhat sheepish PC returned the next day to give an apology to Fuengsin, which was later relayed to Paul as he had been at school. It was a relief, but the case was enough to persuade Paul to abandon his apple throwing. For the police officer it was just one of those days; at least it showed that there was still time for community policing in Hagley, to deal with these disturbances of the peace.

Fortunately there were alternative options to relieve childhood boredom during long summer holidays. Paul was enrolled in the Hagley Holiday club, run out of the Community Centre, which offered a wide range of activities, including trips out and about, with parents volunteering time (and forbearance) to look after the young charges. Hence Paul went to the theatre in Birmingham and met the Swain family, who were also Catholic: Alan and Wendy, their son Christopher and daughter Helen. Alan Swain was a highly skilled engineer, with the kind of expertise that was sadly vanishing. Fuengsin enjoyed Wendy's pragmatism and cheerfulness, which she seemed to have inherited from her mother, who was 90 years old and still very alert.

Summer offered opportunities to roam at leisure. Tony and Fuengsin had chosen Hagley for its rural location and good transport network, which enabled them to explore the natural environment and visit many fine sights. Stepping out of the house it would take only a few minutes to reach some fields. The tiny village of Broome was a little over a mile away and very sheltered, where most activity seemed to be coming from ducks in and around a pond. The undulating landscape offered excellent views: Walton and Clent Hills could be reached in little more than half an hour on foot, and from the top could be seen their neighbours, including Abberley and Clee.

The River Severn, with which Tony was familiar from his childhood, is prominent in Worcestershire, snaking its way through several towns such as Stourport and Upton on Severn as well as sweeping through the county town of Worcester, with its impressive cathedral. The city was also home to Royal Worcester porcelain, which Fuengsin greatly admired, so she would frequent an outlet where high quality 'seconds', which had slight irregularities or blemishes, were sold at knock-down prices. The eponymous Severn Valley Railway provided a very scenic route from Hampton Loade (and later Kidderminster) to Bridgnorth, and friends and family would usually join at Bewdley. Further away were Evesham, and Broadway, the Western edge of the Cotswolds in Worcestershire, all of which were explored.

The countryside, with its fresh air, varied scenery, stately homes, formal gardens, shops and tea rooms, was the focus for many day trips where Tony and Fuengsin could show friends the beautiful environment. Tony took up rambling and through the Birmingham Catholic Ramblers he was introduced to many routes, some of which he extended during his own explorations from Worcestershire into Herefordshire, on or around the Malvern Hills, and beyond to Ludlow and The Welsh Marches. He became familiar with the whole stretch of land down through the Wye Valley to Monmouthshire, the county of his childhood. Fuengsin did not generally join these rambles, but on day trips in the car Tony would take her to many points along the route — to garden centres, nurseries, and to hedgerows to gather fruit for making jam (raspberry and damson were the staple favourites) and filling pies.

However, Fuengsin's enjoyment was hampered by car sickness in twisty lanes and by serious bouts of hay fever, for Hagley is in a valley and the pollen accumulates in high density. She tried many kinds of treatments including antihistamine tablets, which helped to clear her runny nose, but she still used up boxes of tissues at night and later old bed sheets were repurposed, cut up into makeshift handkerchiefs. Tony was unaffected, whilst Paul had some occasional trouble, but for Fuengsin it lasted several months at a time and impacted on all her activities; at night she would end up sleeping by herself in the back bedroom in order not to cause disturbance.

Holidays offered an escape, particularly to the South West via the M5 and M50. The Wolseley provided a smooth and comfortable ride, but it wasn't particularly nimble and was expensive to maintain. Within a year of arriving in Hagley, Tony traded it in for a Volkswagen Beetle, which was smaller, more economical to run, and easier to service. It was not long before the popular 'people's car' had its first major outing. In summer of 1976 Fuengsin received a visit from Khun Vasana and her daughter, Dongjit. Arrangements were made to stay with the Brownes, who had moved a few years earlier from their home near Winchester to a farmhouse in the tiny village of St Erme in Cornwall.

Unable to afford a holiday abroad, the invitation to spend summer in Cornwall was readily accepted. So five holiday-makers and luggage were packed into the little car, which made its way down the M5, stopping at Chepstow *en route*. It became a ritual to tease Tony on the associations of Chepstow with Wales: less than a mile from his parents' home, drivers who came off the M4 and headed towards the town passed by an official road sign of welcome. Its appearance was greeted with the chorus '1-2-3 Welcome to Wales!' Even so the detour meant very welcome refreshment, especially for Tony, who had to continue his solo driving as no-one else had a license. The car then proceeded along the dual carriageway as far as Exeter. Weighed down by its heavy load, with the engine underpowered it struggled up the hills, crawling up the inclines hardly faster than fully-laden lorries. Yet the German engineering was solid and the car was equal to the challenge: the Beetle duly progressed through the Devon and Cornish moors, following a procession of caravans. It eventually reached the outskirts of Truro and finally arrived safely at Resugga.

Resugga was to provide a wonderful holiday base for the years ahead, offering everything a family could want: a farmhouse building with centuries of history located away from urban developments, remote enough so that at night the Milky Way could be seen vividly, with satellites clearly discernible making their measured way across the starry sky. The nearest neighbours were

Cornish locals; there were two sons, Brian and Simon, with whom Paul could play and ride his bicycle along the lanes. Yet the county town of Truro was just a few miles away from this rural idyll, and both the north and south coast within easy reach by car.

These holidays were delightful — a peaceful and beautiful location away from the hustle and bustle of urban and suburban living. The environment was fresh and the county's tourist traps were largely confined to particular areas. The Brownes quickly identified quieter spots, such as Porth Joke, a small beach on the other side of a peninsular from the expanse of Newquay. The sea may not have been particularly warm, at least not compared with the coast of Thailand, but this was still carefree leisure in which the usual sense of time was lost, affording reminiscences of days of youth. Eventually it was time to get changed and for children to pack up shovels and spades. As the sun started to fade, the family would trudge back up the cliff to the car park and head back, but not before fish and chips had been collected for evening supper. There were also more sophisticated outings to stately homes and gardens and to the Minack Theatre, with the sea an impressive and fitting backdrop for the staging of plays such as *The Admirable Crichton* and *Twelfth Night*.

In addition, the home had a large shrine room that Fuengsin could use at any time for meditation. On one occasion their stay coincided with that of Freda Wint and her grandson, Shiva, who was a similar age to Paul. Shiva was extrovert and enjoyed performance; he persuaded Paul to join him in putting on a puppet play, but Paul was not a performer so, inspired by the undulating Cornish landscape, he designed scenic stage backdrops whilst Shiva worked the puppets. Freda, Jane and Fuengsin were all practitioners of Thai traditions, but Shiva was later to abandon the theatre and become ordained as Gelong Thubten, a monk in a Tibetan tradition.

Whilst Hagley was a semi-rural community, it was large and urban in comparison, and that meant people had more varied backgrounds. One of the ladies whom Fuengsin got to know was called Rosemary and she in turn introduced Fuengsin to Francesca, who was originally from a tiny village in the Basque Country, a very rural and mountainous environment, more remote than Resugga. She had first come to the UK in the early 60s, a similar time to Fuengsin, so they compared notes on adapting to the British way of life and on adopting Britain as their home — they didn't want to remain forever as just foreigners. Fuengsin was also very interested to know about her farming background, about the village and the mountains, and the general environment. She was pragmatic and took into consideration many qualities in the people she met. Her experience of being in the UK for more than 10 years made her realise that it wasn't status that was important in a person; indeed, she herself was in some ways living far humbler than when in Thailand, prompting her to quip that she was 'downwardly mobile!'

Francesca and her daughter, Yolanda, often hosted Fuengsin at their home; hearing a distinctive single firm knock on the front door, they knew immediately who had arrived. Conversations were wide-ranging. If there were problems Fuengsin would listen very carefully before giving advice. If they seemed weighty, she would point out: 'Paquita, remember that in this life all is transient, everything will pass, and better things will come.' It would have been a lot to ask if it were just words, so Fuengsin taught them meditation in the comfort of their lounge. She instructed them in basic posture, sitting upright, and then would lead them in their practice, keeping it simple. She might start by asking them to take a couple of deep breaths and then guide them to focus on a single object so as to become one-pointed, allowing the mind to empty and just be aware. When struggling to concentrate, she would point out: 'Look Paquita, your mind is like a monkey jumping from branch to branch!' Paquita would laugh because her friends would tell her it was just so and that she couldn't concentrate on one thing for more than two seconds. Fuengsin assured her that meditation would help her to concentrate on one thing at a time.

The topics weren't always serious for much of the chat was light-hearted. Grateful for Fuengsin's company and advice, Paquita gave her a specially made Harris Tweed jacket, of herringbone design. Its slim fit was ideal for Fuengsin and she made good use of it for trips in the cool British weather. She acquired quite a few donations this way. Fuengsin also got to know Sancho and Chico, Yolanda's cats, who would purr contentedly on Fuengsin's lap and claw at her trousers, but Fuengsin would come prepared with thick jeans.

* * *

Hagley is a little over 10 miles away from Birmingham and was to feature increasingly in family life, not just the temple activities. Tony and Fuengsin had both given a great deal of consideration to Paul's education. With Tony's father being a deputy head and Fuengsin's own family being highly educated, it was natural for them to give priority to this matter; they were ambitious for their son.

Paul enjoyed his studies at Hagley Middle School and Fuengsin was pleased that they operated a system of streaming because she believed that all pupils should strive to achieve according to their capabilities. Paul's performances appeared to bear this out as he continued to do well and he seemed content with the prospect of continuing to Haybridge, another school with a fine reputation. However, Fuengsin and Tony had other ideas. Tapping into Paul's interest in puzzles they gave him a book of aptitude tests and encouraged him to tackle them and see how he fared. This was followed early in 1980 by a trip into Birmingham, where he sat an examination at a school in Edgbaston. He performed sufficiently well to be offered an assisted place, where fees were reduced through means testing so Tony and Fuengsin could just about afford them. They were delighted because this was an independent school that had an excellent reputation; they were very willing to undergo material sacrifice and a tight financial discipline. Thus the remainder of Paul's secondary education was now to be at King Edward's School, Birmingham.

Paul was somewhat ambivalent and became a little nervous once the penny dropped. Nevertheless a few weeks later he said farewell to friends at Hagley Middle School, realising that he would not be returning in autumn. Over summer Fuengsin was, like most other mothers, keen to get her son ready for a new school — for one thing it meant a new smarter uniform, complete with blazer. When September came, Fuengsin proudly accompanied Paul on his first afternoon in Birmingham, but his subsequent journeys by train and bus were with other newcomers from Hagley and other stops *en route*. He was duly stretched as he found some of his classmates far better equipped than himself both in the subject matter and in life in general. Fuengsin remained very pleased and attentive as the school's broad curriculum emphasised a balance between cerebral study, sport and other extra-curricular activities.

Thus, Friday afternoons were spent out of the classroom and one of the first choices Paul had to make was which activity to join. He showed no military inclinations so the Combined Cadet Force was not an option; he soon settled on the Boy Scouts as the school had a Group comprising a troop for 11 to 15-year-olds and a Venture crew (16+) run by several of the science masters. Fuengsin had plenty of fun talking about *look seua*, the Thai phrase for scouts, and even learnt a few practical aspects. Every year the Group had a summer camp, Paul's first being in the Brecon Beacons. Furnished with a detailed list of what to prepare and take, the family went shopping for a rucksack, waterproofs and other clothing, first aid, plastic plates, cheap cutlery, a torch and so on. It was Paul's first experience of camping and the organisers had devised a programme packed with exercises, which he generally enjoyed. He came back with new knowledge to share, some of it very simple: having learnt from his mother to tie socks together like pieces of string he showed her how to fold pairs neatly inside each other. Fuengsin laughed at her own clumsy method and dropped it immediately to gain a bit more space in cupboards. A couple of years later Paul set up his own patrol and called it Tigers, without realising that *look seua* literally means 'tiger cubs'.[5]

Paul managed to settle in, though he still could only count on his fingers those he regarded as close friends. However, his academic results improved and he was soon playing chess for the school; in his second year he was also representing his school in rugby and athletics. Fuengsin learnt of his progress at parents' evenings, an occasion she looked forward to as it offered a chance to meet some of the personalities that Paul variously depicted as intelligent, strict and occasionally eccentric. The gathering took place in the main hall, Big School, where parents would identify a number of teachers to meet and then select a queue to join. In waiting her turn, Fuengsin had the chance to look around and observe other parents, the way they dressed and their behaviour. She found the teachers generally friendly and courteous, conversations were relaxed and interesting, and evidently they enjoyed meeting her as it was still relatively rare to meet an Oriental parent.

Paul also reported on other aspects that the teachers wouldn't know about: on one occasion he related that he had been given the nickname of 'Gandhi', to which Fuengsin replied that in her younger days in Thailand she had been called 'the female Gandhi.' She probably didn't realise it at the time, but just a mile down the road was a centre that had played an important historical role in connection with Gandhi's work and Fuengsin would be working there.

Notes

1. For Cyril Goode's role in the Hagley Community Association, see e.g. Hagley Village News, June 1969:
    http://hhfs.org.uk/hhfs/documents/Societies/Linked_Docs_2_HCA/69_6_donations _community_centre.pdf

    Mr Jack Moulder was another well-known figure. See e.g. *Stourbridge Old Edwardian's Club: Golf Society History*, http://www.oldedclub.org.uk/history.html and *Hagley in the 1950s: Down Memory Lane*, Hagley Historical and Field Society, http://hhfs.org.uk/hhfs/documents/Hagley1/down_memory_lane_20110419.pdf

2. The International supermarket chain was sold in the mid-1980s to the Dee Corporation, and the plot subsequently taken over by Lo-Cost.

3. In conversation Bhante Rewata Dhamma would emphasize the commonality of Tibetans and Burmese by stating that ethnically they were related, with the mountains of Burma being the foothills of the Himalayas.

4. A copy of Fuengsin's interview, 'Buddhism as a Way of Life', is available online: an introduction and the transcript plus photograph are available from Paul's blog and personal website:
    http://paultrafford.blogspot.com/2011/06/county-express-interview-with-fuengsin.html
    http://fuengsin.org/articles/buddhism-as-a-way-of-life/

5. *look seua* was established as a junior division of the paramilitary Wild Tiger Corps by King Rama VI, based on Baden Powell's boy scout movement.

10

Emergence

Fuengsin engrossed herself in the activities of the Birmingham Buddhist Vihara in Carlyle Road, assisting Bhante Rewata Dhamma in various ways. It was a wonderful opportunity to practise generosity and be of service; having been in the UK for more than a decade, she really appreciated the chance to see a Buddha rupa as a focal point to pay respects to the Buddha, just as she had done at Jane's home. She could also listen to sermons, all of which helped her to find Dhamma within; and she could make offerings of food and other requisites to the Sangha to sustain the holy life. If there were visiting monks, she would go especially to listen to their teachings, keen to see and hear not only what they taught but also how they taught. This brought Fuengsin much joy, so she readily extended this appreciation whenever setting foot in other places of worship and meeting with holy people.

Frequenting the vihara on a regular basis encouraged Fuengsin to maintain *sila*, a Buddhist term for virtuous conduct, particularly observance of the Five Precepts. Her ongoing attendance enabled Fuengsin to get to know very well the supporters closely associated with the vihara, including a Burmese medical doctor, Dr Mar Mar Lwin, who managed to combine her professional work with providing daily household assistance. Historically, there has been chronic rivalry between the Thais and Burmese, so here was a good opportunity for Fuengsin to test her personal commitment to dialogue and it proved to be no problem. She travelled extensively among different groups so she had to take care about her speech. Fuengsin, an avid viewer of soaps, had seen many examples of how not to conduct social affairs. Somehow she managed always to maintain her integrity.

After a while the nature of her involvement at the vihara changed. In the late 1970s she became a teacher at a Buddhist Sunday School and suddenly found that she was able to apply her teacher training in a new field. Soon after she became co-editor of the magazine, Children's Dhamma, an occasional publication that was launched around 1980. Among its varied contributions, Fuengsin provided a tale to encourage a virtuous life. It was about Kruba

Srivichai, a well-known monastic who lived in Northern Thailand and who had already displayed many virtuous qualities in his childhood, a fine example for younger members of the vihara:

> At the age of seven Faa Hong was very good and quiet and did not enjoy playing with children of his own age. He was very kind, never harmed animals and looked after the family's buffaloes very well. Once he freed the fish which his father had caught and kept in a jar of water. He showed deep compassion for every creature. He refused to eat meat and was content to have rice and a variety of chilli sauces for his meals.

She went on to narrate his exemplary life and concern for the welfare of everyone. He became famous for his dedication to the local community, able to rally thousands of people together not only to restore temples and pagodas but to make them more accessible; it was thus that he directed the construction of the first road that wound its way up the hill to Wat Phra Dhatu Doi Suthep. The life had much to commend it for the young centre operating in the urban jungle.[1]

There were even a couple of contributions from Paul. One was a poem about autumn, which he had written at school, describing the leaves in a multitude of colours falling on the ground; but for publication it received a Buddhist rebranding so that its subject became 'change'. The other was a maze, a variety of which he had been designing for some while, challenging his schoolteachers to try and solve them. Here it may have been chosen to symbolise the labyrinth of life, but Paul saw no more in it than a puzzle with an ultramodern design. Afterwards Ven. Dr Rewata Dhamma invited Fuengsin to come and help teach beginner's Vipassana meditation to newcomers. So every Monday she gave a class to locals, who were usually Westerners. The introductory technique was based on mindfulness of breathing, paying attention particularly to the rise and fall of the abdomen.

Fuengsin recognised this was an important development, but it was not like the Dhammakaya method in which she had been trained. She admitted as much to a Tibetan Buddhist friend, saying, 'That's not my practice. My practice is [like] Vajrayana!' Teaching a method from another tradition is generally problematic and it was to become an ongoing concern for Fuengsin. Perhaps it inadvertently affected her own practice, for after a while she realised that something was not quite right with her meditation. It then dawned on her that, beyond sending a few New Year cards, it had been about 10 years since she had communicated with Ajahn Gaew, her meditation teacher. She had been assured that he would willingly give assistance, but they hadn't been in communication at all.

So one day Fuengsin wrote to him to suggest if he wasn't too busy then his daughter or someone else might write to her, because she would like to hear from him. Ajahn Gaew responded through Darunee, his daughter, with the message that something was wrong in the way she was practising her meditation. Her teacher reassured her: 'Now don't worry — I am going to lend you tapes to correct you.' Four tapes subsequently arrived through the post, including an audio recording of a guided practice by the great meditation master, Luang Phor Sodh. Fuengsin found they contained instructions that dealt exactly with the problem so that Fuengsin knew where she was going wrong and how to correct it, which she duly did. The tapes also featured Luang Phor Sodh leading some chanting with further tapes of other monks chanting, especially from the Khuddakapātha, one of the books of the Khuddaka Nikāya in the Pali canon. The timely help prompted Fuengsin to reflect that it was her teacher that had got her to write, so that he could draw attention to the issue. Furthermore, by instructing his daughter to write Ajahn Gaew also looked beyond Fuengsin as an individual and was helping to maintain family connections through the generations.

Fuengsin also heard about another temple, the Wolverhampton Buddha Vihara. It had been established in 1976 by followers of Dr Ambedkar, the Indian Buddhist convert who is beloved by the Dalits and by others who reject the caste system. However, there was no permanent resident monk as Indian bhikkhus could only come for a few months at a time. So in 1982 the Dr Ambedkar Memorial Buddhist Committee approached Wat Buddhapadipa, the Thai temple in London, seeking help. In response they sent Phramaha Somboon, who had been in the UK since 1968, and he arrived in Wolverhampton the following year. He was a Dhammaduta monk, that is to say a Dhamma Ambassador, one trained in being a messenger wherever there is a need. On hearing of his move Fuengsin went to pay respects, adding a train journey to her bus journey. She knew it was not easy for a Thai monk to serve an Indian community for although Thai culture has many Indian roots, the Thais have evolved their own customs, tastes and, of course, language. Yet Phramaha Somboon's kept his base in Wolverhampton and so Fuengsin went to give him support and became greatly impressed at his calmness and patience; he gained the deep respect of the community he served in the UK and in the Punjab. She also had a connection with him as he knew well Ven. Ajahn Praderm, one of Fuengsin's former teachers.[2]

Fuengsin also made connections with monastics who were born and brought up in the UK. During the late 1970s, Fuengsin met a young English bhikkhu by the name of Ven. Khemadhammo, who was staying in the Birmingham area. He visited her at home in Hagley, met the family and afterwards they all went for a walk together in the Clent Hills. The monk subsequently established a small monastery on the Isle of Wight, which Fuengsin visited in 1983, sending a postcard to Paul, commenting, 'We are having a peaceful time though the weather is dull. There are 2 goats who became good lawn mowers for this big garden. Our cottage is behind an old mill.' Fauna and flora were always to feature in Ven. Ajahn's monastic residences.

About a year later Ven. Khemadhammo moved to Warwickshire at the invitation of a group of Buddhists and within a couple of years he initiated many developments. One of the most important of these was Angulimala, a Buddhist prison chaplaincy service named after a serial murderer who completely reformed on meeting the Buddha. At a preparatory meeting Fuengsin strode into the room and the monk, a little surprised, questioned her presence. She responded directly, 'Why shouldn't I be? My father was a prison governor!'

Fuengsin was subsequently one of the first to join and in the mid-1980s accepted appointments by the Home Office as Buddhist Chaplain to a couple of establishments, including HMP Long Lartin. There was now a substantive connection with the initiatives about which she had heard more than a decade earlier in Hampshire. Initially it was conceived that support would be needed mainly for immigrants from traditionally Buddhist countries, but soon there was wider interest. The fact that these were criminals didn't deter Fuengsin from teaching and she would have been proud to offer her services in memory of her father. She delivered Dhamma teachings in her usual inimitable style, which was punchy and dynamic. It certainly had an impact as the prisoners enjoyed her presentations and, according to some reports, they would be in hysterics before she left.[3] Then, when Ven. Ajahn Khemadhammo became abbot of The Forest Hermitage, a new monastery in the Warwickshire countryside, it was Fuengsin who came up with the Thai name of Wat Pah Santidhamma and she continued to offer support, bringing along friends as well as food and other requisites.

In supporting the various Sangha members and circulating at gatherings where Orientals gathered, Fuengsin naturally extended her network of Thai residents. Some were students and staff, particularly at Birmingham University; one friend was a tutor in Mathematics and married a lecturer in Economics; others worked in the service sector, particularly in restaurants and the NHS. Fuengsin had been in the UK longer than almost all of them and they looked up to her for advice. Among them was Pranee Sunasavenonta, who came originally from the South of Thailand, with whom there was an immediate rapport. She had a bold spirit and was used to riding a motorbike until she had an accident that seriously shook her and she stopped immediately. Her situation became difficult so Fuengsin arranged for her and her sister, Preeya, to go and see Ajahn Gaew, who taught them meditation according to their aptitudes. They were impressed for it transformed their outlook and they developed their practice, later going on retreats. Once they had established roots in Birmingham, they set up a popular Thai restaurant in Selly Oak called Pranee's and became more involved in supporting the Buddhist centres. They hosted relatives and friends, including Darunee, Ajahn Gaew's daughter, who studied and gained work experience.

Whilst the Southeast Asian communities continued to strongly back the Birmingham vihara, its reputation spread and it generated wider involvement beyond the specific communities it had originally been set up to serve. Fuengsin's own activities in Birmingham also grew; initially she had got to know other Orientals who were from traditionally Buddhist lands including some Thais, mainly through the Thai consulate, together with some western practitioners, but after a few years she started to receive invitations to share her practice and culture with people of other faiths.

Around the time Fuengsin was adjusting to life in a Christian country, a certain Catholic nun had been welcoming the momentous changes that emerged following the Second Vatican Council, dubbed 'Vatican II' for short. Her name was Sister Mary Hall, a member of the Congregation of Jesus and Mary. She sought wholeheartedly and with great determination to embrace people of faiths from all round the world, leading her to teach in Europe, South Asia, North and South America. It also led her to declining to wear the nun's habit so as to reduce barriers to engagement — she really was intent on removing barriers. After heading a school in Pakistan, she returned to the UK and responded to a request from the Catholic Bishops' Conference of England and Wales in 1978 to initiate a research project into dialogue between people of different religions in Birmingham.

Sister Mary arrived in Britain's industrial heartland with a vision of people of faith coming together to learn from each other, to work together and to develop programmes of benefit to the community as a whole. She saw this as absolutely necessary, especially for communities which are new to cultural and religious pluralism. Sister Mary then immersed herself in a three-year intensive research project involving people from many walks of life, including the registered unemployed. Fourteen communities participated, with representation from Anglican, Baptist, Buddhist, German Evangelical Lutheran, Hindu, Jewish, Methodist, Muslim, Pentecostal, Quaker, Roman Catholic, Sikh and United Reformed traditions. The project, under Sister Mary's direction, developed an educational methodology for interfaith and intercultural dialogue that encouraged participants to first become aware of variations in their own cultural and religious heritage. This helped them to recognise that differences of the 'other' already existed closer to home than they may have realised and that such differences were not as hindering as they may have imagined.

A tangible fruit of the project was the Multi Faith Resource Unit (MUFRU), which was started in January 1981; its initial home was in Selly Oak, in rooms rented from a student hostel, together with a converted garage and air-raid shelter. Sister Mary presented a powerful case for her work and the financial timing was good. Grants were obtained from many sources such as governing bodies, religious charities in the UK and overseas, with additional donations from generous individuals and groups. The aim of the unit was to provide 'education by encounter' (often written in capitals in introductory leaflets), through a team of trained multifaith, multicultural educators and resource personnel working from their own communities to address first hand some of the most painful problems in society.

Sister Mary possessed a doctorate, but knew from experience that conceptual discussions — especially when they became comparison of doctrines — were problematic. She went further in believing that scholarship alone was ineffective, which she expressed very firmly in an article she later wrote:

> The staff believes that an honest sharing by practising members of living religious and cultural traditions does more to combat racism and prejudices than any amount of dry, academic explanations given by well-meaning, but uncommitted, neutral experts.

It was difficult to argue with this pioneer, especially in person, as she had an imposing physical presence as well as a forceful conviction. There was no room in this organisation for dusty cobwebs or shrinking violets.

The administrative structure was made simple and oriented around six world traditions: Hinduism, Islam, Sikhism, Buddhism, Judaism and Christianity, each of which had a designated faith representative who formed a team that designed and implemented a variety of programmes. These included special study days, workshops, seminars and lectures to introduce its methodology to people from many walks of life — social workers, doctors, nurses, prison officers, chaplains, teachers, university lecturers and other professionals. Sister Mary deliberately chose representatives who had been born into a tradition and lived it; in her mind converts may have been problematic because they often still carried unhelpful mental baggage.

During this period Fuengsin was being invited to go and give talks on Buddhism by various associations, schools, religious youth groups and colleges. Sister Mary heard favourable reports about her and in 1983 invited her to come and teach, leading to further invitations to hold classes. The approach of direct engagement appealed very much to Fuengsin, who saw that she could learn a great deal from this forthright nun; likewise, Sister Mary was impressed as here was someone who fulfilled all the criteria and knew quickly what the organisation was about. However, Fuengsin was initially daunted at the prospect of giving classes because some of the students who came already held degrees in theology or religious studies whereas Fuengsin's specialist qualifications were not in these fields.

By now she was in the habit of writing more frequently to Ajahn Gaew, who always replied through Darunee, his daughter. She told him that she wasn't up to it, feeling that it was a very advanced course for her to teach, especially the theory, and that in particular she feared the highly educated attendees. He replied, 'You will be alright — you can carry on. It doesn't matter, even though someone is very intellectual — knowing the language and all that — if he is not a born Buddhist then he won't know everything.' Indeed Fuengsin needn't have worried because she already possessed considerable knowledge from her Thai upbringing together with studies at school and university, and she had extended this knowledge in the UK, reaching out to other traditions in the process. More importantly her authority was based on practice and Ajahn Gaew offered some specific advice to improve her efficacy and ease her worries:

> Before you teach, give compassion to the whole class and think of them as your own body, as if they are one with you. Visualise them in you and fix here and try to visualise their five aggregates at one spot. The visualisation that we do — each of the aggregates condensed like a crystal — tiny spot like a crystal — and it gets so everybody's aggregates condensed to one point, here at the centre of the body. Each person has one — has five aggregates and the five aggregates condense into one — it is like a ball — and it's over the four elements — floating in the middle of four elements. Yours is theirs. So imagine the 5 aggregates of your students as one spot and at the same spot as yours. So they will understand more.

Fuengsin was in fact already an experienced teacher able to work with different groups according to their background and temperament; and reassured, she developed further her unique combination of skills and experience. Speaking about a group from the Swedish Theological Institute, whom she found reserved, she remarked, 'You have to break the ice!' having probably chosen some everyday situation to apply her characteristic humour. The Institute later proved to be very loyal in sending its students every year, so they must have felt the teaching was appropriate.

The Unit also extended its work beyond the usual spaces. Over a period of several years it organised an annual multifaith concert at Birmingham Cathedral, under the banner, 'Festival of Faiths for Peace', with many local performers from different religious communities. They were in touch with local media and one year there was an introduction by Tom Coyne who worked for the BBC and ITV.

However, much of the Unit's expertise was consolidated in a new one-year course, the Certificate Course in World Religions, advertised as a way to help 'understand the ethos, customs and practices in our multi-cultural society'. The course was designed so that each of the six traditions was studied in a series of six-week modules and the lectures in each module would 'speak from within the experience of their tradition'. Classes were given once a week in the evening and lasted two hours. As the course rolled on from one year to the next, the course could be joined at the start of any module, so it was relatively easy to fit into someone's schedule. However, to try to convey the essence of so many religions in such evening classes was ambitious and for students there was a lot of study at home, as Fuengsin had discovered when she went on to undertake the course herself.

Friederike Rice was the Coordinator. She took care of many of the operational aspects and ensured that everything ran as smoothly as possible, from setting up the lecture space to managing the course assignments. Modules were designed to allow a range of views to be expressed; each session involved one or more resource people, who were comfortable with providing supplementary information or even presenting part of the session, explaining their most treasured practices. Friederike was there in attendance, observing what was going on and making notes.

Fuengsin became responsible for the Buddhism module from 1985, giving her first session on 9 December, with Ven. Chander Bodhi, an Indian Bhikkhu, as the resource person. As with all the modules, Fuengsin's syllabus comprised six sessions, which covered both the doctrinal foundations and the way Buddhism is practised in its cultural context. Initially she didn't know whether or not she would be up to it; she could see that it was a very advanced course to teach, especially the theory of Buddhism. However, reassured by the supportive words already offered by Ajahn Gaew, she carried on. In fact she had a great opportunity to apply her professional training in the various tasks: in this case she had to prepare a syllabus that was suitable for the contemporary scene, which in Birmingham meant many different traditions. As well as covering the basic tenets of Buddhism to be found common to most schools, she read extensively from traditions other than her own — covering Northern Schools, including Tibetan and Zen traditions — so that she could communicate some of their distinct flavours. She would then try to make the lectures stimulating and assign the students thought-provoking essays, whose scripts she marked as well.

Whereas most academic courses might set out with a philosophical overview about what is Buddhism, Fuengsin immediately grounded her course with an introduction 'as seen through its art and architecture by slides of temples with background music'. She had brought from Thailand 35mm slides that depicted important sites dating back to the sixth century CE, and also had audio recordings. Fuengsin substantiated her accounts through a variety of sources, including lecture notes she had received whilst at Chulalongkorn University, which included detailed diagrams explaining the significance of each aspect in pagoda design. She proceeded to cover the Buddha's life story, the formation of the Sangha community, and an outline of the Buddha's administration and day-to-day running of his ministry. Only then did she tackle the fundamental teachings: the Four Noble Truths and its connection with Dependent Origination, Karma and The Eightfold Noble Path. Then Fuengsin went on to discuss scripture and schools, including a brief account of the Buddhist Councils. Finally she concluded her discussion by showing the impact of Buddhism in present-day society through ceremonies, rituals and festivals, ensuring that it would remain vivid in people's minds.

One of the topics that Fuengsin dealt from the outset was the role of women. In her teachings she related that in Indian society in the Vedic period they were honoured first and foremost as someone's mother, but in Buddhism women could be single and lead their own lives, not having to be someone's wife. Furthermore, followers were accepted from every class of society. Fuengsin gave a quote from a text in which the Buddha gave a reassurance to King Pasenadi of Kosala who had been disappointed at the birth of a daughter:

> A Woman child, O Lord of Men,
> may prove even a better offspring than a man.
>
> Verse 16: The Daughter, Saṃyutta-nikāya 1.3

She emphasised that women have the same potential to become Enlightened. There was added poignancy because Thailand had been getting a bad name from sex tourism. This had become a vicious circle, drawing on impoverished Thai people looking mainly for a means to support themselves and their families in rural provinces. This put into the spotlight the status of women in Thai society, and Fuengsin was conscious of highly critical views with accusations about women's mistreatment. It had a contagious effect among some, which led to implicating the whole country.

Fuengsin saw how damaging was this selective and often poorly informed critique — often conveying the impression of Thai women as subservient stereotypes who were helpless victims. Whilst Fuengsin accepted that there was shameful exploitation, this was certainly not the experience of herself or anyone else in her family, so she felt a responsibility to show in person that the Buddhist heart of Thai society was ennobling. She gave witness to the close support of the monastic community, showing aspirations to the highest ideals; the provision of meditation was a key to success and fulfilment, which was freely available to anyone in Thailand, and now increasingly so in the West too.

Thus her students were benefiting from a classical Thai education rooted in long-standing traditions, with a fresh interpretation. Fuengsin used two kinds of libraries for her research: the physical one and her mind, especially through meditation practice. Occasionally she sought advice internally when coming across a passage in Buddhist canonical texts whose meaning was unclear to her. One such passage was the following teaching of the Buddha, originally recorded in Pali, a language of which Fuengsin had some knowledge, but is here translated into English:

> I tell you, friend, that it is not possible by travelling to know or see or reach a far end of the cosmos where one does not take birth, age, die, pass away, or reappear. But at the same time, I tell you that there is no making an end of suffering & stress without reaching the end of the cosmos. Yet it is just within this fathom-long body, endowed with its perceptions and thoughts, that I declare that there is the world, the origination of the world, the cessation of the world, and the path of practice leading to the cessation of the world.[4]
>
> Rohitassa Sutta, Anguttara Nikaya 4.45

Fuengsin asked Luang Phor Sodh for help in explanation. In response, Luang Phor appeared, stood and stretched out his arms either side, forming a cross. In this way he indicated the extent (from hand to hand) but also that the body could trace a disk, rather like Leonardo da Vinci's 'Vitruvian man' inscribed in a square and circle.

As well as the language issue, Fuengsin had some other challenges. The physical problems that she had with her nerves, which had given her eye problems in Kent, now affected her body in other ways, resulting in shaky hands. The use of PowerPoint was still rare, so flip boards were provided for teaching and Fuengsin prepared sheets in advance. Sometimes she also asked for assistance; the photograph above shows the elegant writing of Friedericke with three essay titles:

1. A Bodhisattva and His Ideals
2. The Six Directions and their application to modern life
3. In Buddhism there is a saying: 'You are the architect of your own destiny.' Please explain.

Fuengsin considered it important to do her best and to look the part, often wearing traditional Thai costume. In her mind she was not only representing the Centre, but Thailand, so she would try to convey in words, pictures and actions her Thai Buddhist heritage. To her it was evident that Buddhism could not be practised shorn of culture, for culture was necessary to the Centre, but Thailand, so she would try to convey in words, support the practice; and students could see this in actuality as during the course a visit was arranged to a local Buddhist centre. There was much to prepare beyond the texts and Fuengsin was not without worry, but once she had started, she was generally in her element, relaxed and dynamic in delivery, drawing on her considerable knowledge and cracking jokes on the vagaries of life and the merry-go-round of sense-based experience. She also received considerable help from Ramona Kauth, who had emigrated to the UK from Iowa. Ramona assisted her in developing the syllabus and provided some materials, particularly from the Tibetan tradition, and also came to many of Fuengsin's sessions to boost her morale.

Fuengsin didn't use books as furniture but read them avidly — as evidenced by the many pieces of paper and bookmarks that were sandwiched between pages, usually deep into the heart of the work. She found reading the Dhamma an energising activity and her reading spanned traditions across the world. These works typically originated in countries that were predominantly Buddhist (such as Sri Lanka, Burma, Tibet, Japan, China, Vietnam and Thailand), had orientations to the West, and were particularly notable for their recent adaptation and enculturation. For the foundations she drew on explanations of early canonical texts expounded by Sri Lankan bhikkhus, Ven. Walpola Rahula's *What the Buddha Taught*, and Ven. Narada's *The Teachings of the Buddha*. Reading these texts reinforced her sense of common heritage and values in Southeast Asia and helped her to feel more at home in the various viharas.

Among her many books on meditation traditions, she read about SN Goenka, who was Burmese, but is perhaps best known for popularising what he termed 'Insight Meditation' in India. From Thailand, in addition to her volumes from the Dhammakaya tradition there were guides and reflections from the Thai Forest Tradition, such as Ajahn Sumedho, *The Way It Is*, and surveys of well-known Southeast Asian masters such as Jack Kornfield's *Living Buddhist Masters*. Fuengsin could compare these meditation masters with the famed monks and nuns which her teachers had spoken about. There were also other, more philosophical and specialist works such as *Abhidhamma Papers* from the Samatha Association. From the Tibet traditions she delved into works such as *Crystal Mirror* from Dharma Press, *The Myth of Freedom* by Chogyam Trungpa and Sogyal Rinpoche's *The Tibetan Book of Living and Dying*.

She came to appreciate that Britain was one of the few places where so many traditions were being practised, a curious legacy of what she teasingly

Fig. 87: Fuengsin lecturing at the Multi-Faith Centre.
Topics include the Brahmaviharas (Sublime States), the Eight Worldly
Conditions, and the Six Directions of the Sigalovada Sutta.

referred to as the 'British Raj.' Yet some traditions seemed to have prospered more readily in other Western countries and Fuengsin also wanted to learn about these. To extend her introduction to Mahayana in the Far East, to which she had been introduced through John Blofeld and works such as *Compassion Yoga*, she added *Zen Mind, Beginner's Mind* by Shunryu Suzuki, who trained in Japan and settled in the US, where he became very influential, and *The Miracle of Being Awake*, which expounded the teachings of the Vietnamese Zen master, Thich Nhat Hanh, who left Vietnam and established a tradition that gained a following in France and Plum Village. Fuengsin was intrigued as to why this was the case and was motivated to observe more closely the different groups she taught, particularly the temperament of her students. She was thus able to gain a first-hand perspective, as well as a general knowledge of what affected the transfer of Buddhism in different countries.

At the end of the module Friederike would gather her notes and carry out an assessment before reporting back to Sister Mary. Fuengsin was somewhat hesitant in her first attempt, but the content was good and she got the nod for delivering the course the following year, where she improved markedly. In her second end-of-year assessment (early 1987), Friederike wrote:

> I am very pleased with the way the course went. Fuengsin was good, much better than last year when she was under the vigilance and probably some stress when the Venerable Chandrabodhi sat in on her presentation. This time she was much more relaxed and the whole atmosphere was transformed.

Fuengsin would have been in some difficulty in having a Theravadin bhikkhu serving as a resource and not the other way around since she would ordinarily have deferred to monastics on any matters relating to Buddhist teachings. However, by the second series Fuengsin had become more familiar with her new role and was able to bring in a wider selection of resource people from different traditions, whose contributions were also well received by the students. She was also pleased when on several evenings some participants requested a short meditation to end the session. Fuengsin's initial discomfort eased and as her confidence grew so did her network. A later assessment declared that Fuengsin was the only one of the course leaders to arrange for all the resource people by herself.

Friederike made sure that all faith representatives took the course to help them, and especially to fulfil Sister Mary's expectation that they work as a team. So Fuengsin too was required to sign up. Once again Fuengsin became a student and started gathering references and visiting libraries, writing notes, making photocopies, and filling up folders with primary and secondary sources. At home assorted papers and books appeared on the dining room table, arranged neatly in piles, and it was time to buy another ream of A4, dust off the typewriter and insert a new ribbon.

The course presented a creative opportunity and Fuengsin generally embraced it with enthusiasm. She had developed an ability to read and absorb a wide range of Eastern and Western views, covering historical–objective and personal–subjective. This was evident in her extended essay on Hinduism, which concerned the Epic of Ramayana. In just a few pages Fuengsin summarised the original Indian context, its authorship in the fourth century BC by a saint called Valmiki, and its subsequent ever-expanding circles of influence. As Fuengsin approached the conclusion of her essay she indicated that it featured in Mahayana Buddhism (in the Lankavatara Sutta) and in Thai culture through its adoption by the Royal Courts:

> The Epic's influence on Thai culture was and still is profound. People of all classes and education levels know the story from their childhood. King Rama 2nd translated the Indian version into Thai and it is included in school and university curricula. It has become part of Thai literature and has been adapted to suit Thai culture.

Like many Thais of her generation, Fuengsin became familiar with it as a child, but unlike her contemporaries, she had the opportunity to study in depth during her Liberal Arts degree at Chulalongkorn. This trained her to be systematic and to respect the subject specialists, putting first the works by specialists in the field, Vedic scholars, and then gradually drawing on her own background through Buddhist and then specifically Thai reflections.

Finally, having summarised the historical perspective, she'd bring it up to date by indicating the contemporary response:

> The story of Ramayana is currently being shown on television in India and is watched by virtually the entire country's viewing population. When it is shown, life in the cities, towns and villages comes to a standstill. Conches are blown in celebration and incense sticks burnt on top of T.V. sets. Until an episode is over, milk goes undelivered, telephone calls remain unanswered and political rallies have had to be postponed in order to avoid clashing with the series. . . . People are always spiritually uplifted when they hear the story as it was blessed by God Brahma saying, "As long as the mountain peaks stand and the rivers flow, so long will people find solace by listening to the Ramayana."[5]

This and her other essays — on Christianity, Sikhism, Judaism and Islam — were all well received and prompted further respect from colleagues. It helped her to become more fully a member of a close team.

That Sister Mary's venture took root was due in no small part to a long history of benevolent education. Swathes of Birmingham had been touched by the hand of philanthropy, especially educational colleges. Members of the Society of Friends, more popularly known as the Quakers, were prominent benefactors, among them the Cadbury family who had set up Bournville, a village for staff at their chocolate factory, providing a holistic environment in which to live and work. Members also looked to the future and saw a need to educate future leaders. Thus, at the turn of the twentieth century, George Cadbury and other local members of the Society of Friends founded Woodbrooke College in Cadbury's former home. Westhill College was also begun by Quakers, founded in 1907 as a Froebel Training College to train Sunday school teachers, and its remit soon expanded to train youth and community workers; it became a pioneering teachers training college. Other religious organisations such as the Methodists followed in setting up other centres, many involving missionary work.[6]

From these beginnings the Selly Oak Colleges emerged as a federation of nine colleges, covering many dimensions of Christian mission and promoting open exchange. Since their early days the colleges had students and academic staff from many parts of the world and inter-cultural influences permeated right across the college. Indeed, in October 1931 Woodbrooke College had hosted Mahatma Gandhi. He had been brought to Woodbrooke for a weekend by Horace Alexander, tutor in international relations, whom Gandhi had described as a 'Friend of India', after some sessions of the second 'round table' conference on Indian independence, which was taking place in London.

Fuengsin probably didn't know the history of the colleges, but her interest was naturally sparked when another door opened as she was invited to teach weekly at Westhill College. Here she got to meet pilgrims of Abrahamic faiths, people who were committed to seeking deeper meaning through belief in God. Fuengsin was not troubled by the fact that these were Christian institutions engaged in mission with different world views as she could sense their collegiality and openness. She especially appreciated the opportunity to share the principles of Dhamma, to give another perspective on perennial topics such as the nature of suffering and non-violent action.

So Fuengsin contributed as fully as she could and after a while became familiar with Westhill, the USPG College of the Ascension and Woodbrooke. Fuengsin's willingness to respond to expressions of interest and exchange led her to receiving valuable support and to developing close friendships. One of her supporters was the Reverend Andrew Wingate, the Director of Ascension College, who had spent many years in South India and was warmly accepting of cultural diversity. He appreciated Fuengsin's natural abilities:

Fuengsin was a born teacher, and could make Buddhism understood at whatever level was required. She would always defer to those she saw as more learned, but it was Fuengsin whom people remembered. This was partly because she evidently lived what she preached; it was partly because she was a very good listener, who wished to learn from others, without feeling in any way threatened; it was perhaps above all because of her joy and sense of humour. Her use of everyday illustrations reminded me of Jesus' way of teaching. If people could not accept Buddhism from Fuengsin, they could not accept it from anyone.

Fuengsin was certainly down to earth, and she had an instinctive sense of humour that could pick up very quickly on topical currents, making her a memorable speaker. It was reported that one missionary student, on returning from a period away, came back and asked immediately, 'Where's Fuengsin?'

However, she was also stimulating company for the more intellectually inclined and those who had more professional experience. At Selly Oak Colleges, Fuengsin got to know and respect Prof. Aasulv Lande, a Norwegian priest who had spent many years in Japan before being based later on at Lund University in Sweden. She also met other teachers of Buddhism, including Dr Elizabeth Harris, who was a Methodist and a recognised authority on Buddhism, having spent many years in Sri Lanka. They taught side by side and Fuengsin regarded their teaching as complementary — Dr Harris was the educated academic authority and she was more concerned with the everyday practical application. Another connection with Sri Lanka was through Prof. Antony Fernando, who was a champion of interfaith dialogue in Sri Lanka. He was Christian, but his wife, Sumana, was Buddhist, which had naturally encouraged him to explore the inter-religious encounter, leading to several books, such as *Christianity and Buddhism, Their Inner Affinity*, a copy of which he inscribed with a dedication and gave to Fuengsin.[7] For centuries the people of Sri Lanka and Thailand have fostered cultural ties and Fuengsin was continuing this process, developing a rapport through professional collaboration and family visits.

Within this environment Fuengsin was constantly reflecting on her encounters with differing world views, particularly Christian ones. She also tried to validate her approach by observing how other experienced Buddhists viewed those who crossed boundaries between religions. When reflecting one day on the question of dual belonging, Fuengsin was prompted to recall the response from Bhante Rewata Dhamma:

One of the Dutch asked Bhante: "Can a Christian become a Buddhist at the same time?" And he said, "Yes, a good Christian can become a good Buddhist, but a good Buddhist can't become a good Christian because when you have the morality, you have the eightfold path, you meditate and all that; a good Christian is the same as a Buddhist, but a Buddhist does not have the belief[s], so he can't be a Christian at the same time."

She was impressed by his handling of such questions and took the opportunity to probe further, remarking, 'We learned a lot that day, and I asked him to explain about craving and attachment and karma.' Fuengsin found these visitors from overseas well-travelled in that they had learnt to be receptive, which made fertile ground for mutual enrichment. They contributed significantly to an open ethos and environment in which Fuengsin had the freedom to work with many different colleagues and where this openness within the colleges poured out naturally to the surrounds. It made a positive impact on the local communities; the area had a quiet and positive buzz.

However, not all outings went quite as expected. As part of their Buddhist encounter, Fuengsin brought her students to some of the local centres, including the Birmingham Buddhist Vihara. One of these groups came from Woodbrooke College and in this group there was an Egyptian nun who had some difficulty understanding English culture, particularly when it came to making arrangements for hospitality. She expressed her problem at the vihara and a locally-born bhikkhu tried to help, explaining that the English like to fix a day and time, otherwise a seemingly open invitation of 'any time' might sound insincere.

The nun was pleased with the answer and wanted to give something to the monk as a token of gratitude. As the group were making their way through the hallway, the nun came towards the bhikkhu, putting out her hand to shake his. As she made the gesture Fuengsin thrust out her arm, which went crack! The poor nun was in a state of shock, but the young monk tried to explain that he was not to come in contact with women otherwise a great demerit would be caused. Fuengsin had seen the risk and acted swiftly and directly to ensure he kept this rule. It was to become an abiding memory for the young monk, Ven. Bodhidhamma, who was a practitioner at the vihara from the late 1970s. He was originally a student of Vajira and then went on to explore Theravada Buddhism, leading to bhikkhu ordination in 1986. Thus he was given the same name as that of the bhikkhu accredited with bringing the Buddhist tradition of Ch'an (or Zen) to China.

Fuengsin was very protective of the monks she served and was watchful about the restrictions on their physical contact, especially with Western bhikkhus, whom she saw as particularly vulnerable. On another occasion Fuengsin was watching people emerge after some function and saw from a distance a lady handing out presents to everyone who came, including another English monk. Fuengsin put him on the spot, enquiring how he had dealt with the situation. He responded that he managed to have some cloth ready, as appropriate; with some relief, his answer was accepted.

In February 1987 the Multi Faith Resources Unit changed its name to The Multi-Faith Centre to reflect the growing importance of its outreach programme. It became a registered charity and an affiliated Centre of the Selly Oak Colleges, Birmingham. The Centre began to draw increasing numbers of students from other countries, especially where new waves of immigration, combined with economic problems, had heightened tensions caused by racial and religious prejudice. This led to major cities adopting similar methods and programmes to those in Birmingham. The Centre had helped place Birmingham on the world map.[8]

With the Centre formally established at Selly Oak, plans were laid for a permanent home. The Trustees of Selly Oak Colleges agreed to make available at a peppercorn rate considerable land for the construction of a new, purpose-built Centre. An architect drafted plans for a building based on an Alpha/Omega concept, with a geodesic dome in the centre and two 'A' frames at the extremities. A brochure for these plans referred to a prayer/meditation room as the centrepiece located in the upper half of the dome, and talked of five full-time and five part-time staff to run the centre.

Such a project was very ambitious and even if everything could come together it would take years to come to fruition. Sister Mary did not rely on this option and continued to explore other possibilities through her extensive network. Her powers of persuasion did not take long to bear fruit. Nearby was Harborne Hall, a large residence owned by the Sisters of La Retraite of the Sacred Heart, a movement that originated in France whose aim was personal sanctification of others in a life of action and prayer. The Sisters had bought the Hall in 1925 for use as a convent, but were finding it difficult to maintain its estate.[9] Seeing the merit in Sister Mary's organisation they allowed the Multi-Faith Centre to take over the premises and so the Centre moved there in 1988. There commenced an ongoing programme of upgrading, refurbishment and decoration of the Hall and its buildings. The grounds were overgrown, but the emphasis was on tidying up rather than landscaping. It was a remarkable outcome for the Centre to be based at and associated with such a historic site, and an ideal setting for its work.

* * *

Fuengsin kept in touch with Ajahn Gaew, who continued staying in Thailand near Wat Paknam. He never visited the UK in person, but apparently often visited in his mind. Whilst Fuengsin had originally got to know Ajahn Gaew as a spiritual guide closely associated with a temple, he also had a volunteer background that was very relevant to her work in the UK and was someone who was able to promote good community relations. He had encouraged members of the Chinese community, for centuries a significant presence in Thailand, to give valuable support to the monastery at Wat Paknam, especially through the Thai–Chinese Pracha Association, which organised gatherings and published Dhamma teachings. This enabled exchanges among monastics of the respective Thai Theravada and Chinese Mahayana schools.

The Association also hosted guest lectures, one of which, in October 1954, was on the topic of 'The Essence of Dhamma' by a certain English bhikkhu with the lay name of William August Purfurst, who on Vesak, May 1954, was the first Westerner to take full bhikkhu ordination in Thailand, receiving the formal name Kapilavaddho. Among those in attendance on this momentous occasion was a highly regarded specialist in Chinese Buddhism — John Blofeld, who sat in close proximity, meditating, whilst the new monk was receiving gifts after his ordination.[10]

In fact the mid-1950s was an exciting time for international relations at Wat Paknam. In 1954, the wat's annual magazine of the junior bhikkhus was published for the first time in both Thai and English; with more than 350 pages, it included many articles, annotated photos and other materials. Ven. Kapilavaddho was exceedingly active, being central to this publication and giving lectures in many parts of the country. Ajahn Gaew spoke a lot about 'Tan Kapilavaddho', about their travels together, but never mentioned his origins to Fuengsin even though there was similarity in their approach to outreach. However, he did hint at how he was challenged in his mission.

As for Fuengsin, he had predicted she would succeed and she reflected on her teacher's prophecy about spreading Dhamma in the West especially in the context of her work in and around Birmingham:

> From encountering these situations, I was able to see that Ajahn had a very powerful mind and was really able to predict things that will occur in the future. Whenever I went to give a talk, when it came to giving instruction, I tried to spread the honour of Ajahn on a regular basis by making the British and people from other countries understand.

In some of his letters Ajahn Gaew would talk about healing, how he would heal himself. He had some problems with his stomach and through meditation he could treat the situation at the molecular level; he gave descriptions as though passing on instructions. He had twice been successful in using this to treat serious conditions, but he eventually lost this battle and passed away in 1986.

His passing was a major blow for Fuengsin, who related deep sadness at her teacher's departure as she contributed the following reflections in his memorial book:

> The departure of Ajahn has brought such sadness and grief to me that I am unable to find the words to express it. The loving-kindness, compassion and interest he showed in every one of his pupils, his mental attainment in the knowledge of Vijja Dhammakaya and also his methods of instruction will impress me forever. He was an exemplary lay person who, even though they may have very many responsibilities, yet still they devote time to performing Dhamma and can perform it well and are able to instruct their disciples. It gives me moral support to follow his observance of Dhamma. I think that I myself will have the opportunity to return Ajahn's kindness by maintaining moral virtue, developing concentration and mental cultivation as he kindly taught me. I will also try to disseminate Buddhism in Britain and then the continent of Europe in accordance with his intentions.

Just as with her contribution to her father's cremation volume, Fuengsin signalled her resolution to propagate Dhamma, but this time aspired to share this still further afield.[11]

Notes

1. Fuengsin's article (first instalment) on Kruba Srivichai is available on the Web at: http://paultrafford.blogspot.com/2011/07/childrens-dhamma-kruba-srivichai.html

2. A synopsis of Phra Maha Somboon's life and a collection of his teachings is given in *Odds and Ends*, available online at: http://www.scribd.com/doc/37070834/Odds-and-Ends

3. Fuengsin's bold entrance into Angulimala was recalled by Yann Lovelock, the secretary for the organisation, and her ability to humour the prisoners in her Dhamma teaching is according to Khun Vasana's account in *Chulalongkorn Faculty of Arts 2497-2501 50 Years Anniversary*.

4. With reference to the origins and cessation of 'this world', 'world' is a translation of the Pali word *loka*, which means 'a space', here a created space, or perhaps sphere of extent, more than just a planet.

5. *The Ramayan* was an Indian TV series that originally ran in Hindi between January 1987 and July 1988. *The Mahabharat* was an Indian TV series that originally ran in Hindi between October 1988 and June 1990. It was broadcast on BBC2 between April 1990 and April 1992: https://en.wikipedia.org/wiki/Mahabharat_(1988_TV_series) http://ftvdb.bfi.org.uk/sift/series/18561

Fuengsin's essay, *The Epic of Ramayana*, is reproduced at:
http://fuengsin.org/articles/ramayana/

6. A detailed history of Westhill College is set out in *The Lumber Merchant and the Chocolate King* by Dr Jack Priestley, a past Principal of Westhill College. It is available for download from the Westhill Endowment website's *History* page:
http://www.westhillendowment.org/about-us

7. Prof. Antony Fernando founded the Intercultural Research Centre in 1961, an English language school for low-income students, as featured in the Initiatives of Change:
http://www.forachange.co.uk/profile/2049.html

   Buddhism and Christianity, Their Inner Affinity was first published in 1981 by the Ecumenical Institute for Study and Dialogue 490/5, Havelock Road, Colombo 6, Sri Lanka. The full text of a revised addition co-authored with Leonard Swidler, entitled *Buddhism Made Plain: An Introduction for Christians and Jews*, is available from Temple University at:
http://astro.temple.edu/~swidler/swidlerbooks/BUDDHISM-X.htm

8. The origins of the Multi Faith Resource Unit (and hence Multi-Faith Centre) in Birmingham are described by Sister Mary Hall in an article in *The Harborne Society NEWS*, Number Twenty-One, Summer 1991, Pages 6-7:
http://www.theharbornesociety.org.uk/uploads/3/9/5/2/39529175/1991.pdf

   The far-sightedness of her work is described in a tribute in the Birmingham Council of Faiths newsletter of October 2008:
http://www.bhamfaiths.org.uk/docs/newsletters/5.20Oct.202008.pdf
   (However, it contains a typo regarding Paul: for 'six' read 'sixteen'.)

9. A history of Harborne Hall since its foundation is given by William Dargue in *A History of Birmingham Places & Placenames*:
http://billdargue.jimdo.com/placenames-gazetteer-a-to-y/places-h/harborne/

   Details about the period when it was a convent are given by Sr. Elizabeth Ann in *Harborne Hall: 60 years of retreat*, The Catholic Herald, 24 January 1986.

10. Photograph from Richard Randall, *Life as a Siamese Monk*, Aukana, page 100.

11. A complete translation of Fuengsin's tribute to Ajahn Gaew is available from:
http://fuengsin.org/articles/ajahngaew/

11

Further Visits to Thailand

ony and Fuengsin had sacrificed a great deal to support their son's education, just as their parents had done. Given such an investment, Fuengsin followed closely Paul's progress in his studies, making sure that he continued to complete his homework consistently and participate in the life of the school — Fuengsin didn't want him to be a crammer as she had once been. He generally performed quite well across a wide range of subjects, though seldom came top in any. When it was time to choose 'A' levels for the Sixth Form Paul initially opted for a mixture of humanities subjects, showing similar leanings to his mother and his paternal grandfather. However, time-table restrictions combined with his mathematical leanings eventually led him to undertake a double dose of Mathematics together with Latin and the compulsory General Studies, a combination that was somewhat unusual, but not unknown at that school.

Fuengsin chatted with Pranee about Paul's future, with full expectation of him going onto Higher Education; they wondered whether Paul would choose Oxford or Cambridge, but they didn't inform him of their ambitious wishes. Paul initially explored the possibility of mathematics at Oxford, but abandoned the idea on the advice of the school's head of mathematics. He looked at other universities and eventually decided that he would apply for courses in mathematics and actuarial studies. On filling in his UCCA application form he put Southampton as his first choice — it was his birthplace and he had already sampled a little bit of study there through a Sixth Form taster course, which he quite enjoyed. Paul duly sat the exams and achieved the grades he needed. At the end of September 1987, Tony took Paul down to Southampton and his undergraduate life began at Glen Eyre Hall of residence, just a couple of miles from where he was born.

Even though most meals were provided, Fuengsin was concerned that Paul might not have sufficient to eat, so she jotted down some essential items of Chinese steamed food such as *sa see pow* (dumpling) and *sue mai* (prawns stuffed in a pastry case). It was the first time that Paul would be away from home and she wasn't sure he could take good care of himself, so she added the address of Mrs Cooke, who was still living in the same house in Bitterne. But Paul had little trouble. Once registered for his degree course, Paul's life away from home was underway. His first term as a fresher began well; like most students he found an assortment of societies to join: in his case the university chess club, the film society and the Catholic society. Fuengsin was pleased to learn that he had settled in and noted that he tended to mix more with overseas students. Within a few months Paul obtained a scholarship from Bacon & Woodrow consulting actuaries, with the prospect of a grant, book token and work experience. Everything seemed to go smoothly and he had plenty of leisure time.

He also kept in touch with a few of his school friends, particularly David Yau, whose family ran a Chinese takeaway in Acock's Green. Paul had met David at King Edward's School, but in the Sixth Form he had left to go to Matthew Boulton College, because he had been uncomfortable with the formality and felt out of place, even though he was liked by classmates. David came to visit Paul a few months before they were due to sit their 'A' levels and as he got on with just about anybody, in line with Birmingham's multicultural scene, it was easy for Fuengsin to chat with him; she was happy that Paul had some friends with other backgrounds to expand his horizons.

* * *

As Paul was supported by a local authority maintenance grant, Tony and Fuengsin were freed of much of the financial burden of his education and the family had more disposable income. Thus, at the end of summer 1988, it seemed a good opportunity to take another family trip to Thailand. This time Tony could not take more than four weeks of leave in one block, so Fuengsin and Paul went in advance in mid-July.

A booking was made with Gulf Air and the flight was scheduled to depart from Heathrow airport shortly after midday. There was a coach to Heathrow from Birmingham International Airport and Tony agreed to come along. The service was not frequent, so it meant having to catch one at 3 a.m. But being so early traffic was minimal along the whole route; the coach reached its destination well before 6 a.m., allowing a very leisurely breakfast in a very quiet concourse. As crowds started to gather at check-in, Tony planned to hop back on for the return bus as soon as they had confirmation of the flight. However, a couple of hours before departure it was announced that the plane had apparently 'gone tech' and they wouldn't fly until the next day. It was inconvenient, but only a minor dent for an extended holiday and Gulf Air arranged for affected passengers to be whisked away to the Excelsior Hotel with a departure at the same time the next day.

Fuengsin and Paul were duly in the air after a comfortable night's rest and the first leg of the flight to the Middle East was pleasant. There was a short stop at Doha to take on more passengers before going on to Muscat, where the Oman terminal's distinctive Arab décor was basking in floodlights and simmering in summer heat. On arrival, everyone had to disembark and take their hand luggage with them into the terminal. Inside it was less appealing: after a slightly anxious wait there was a rush to board the plane as there was no seat allocation. Fuengsin and Paul were left bringing up the rear and ended up in the smoking section. The onward journey was bumpier and less agreeable, but after several further hours in the air Thai rice fields could be seen through the windows and at 10.30 a.m. the plane touched down at Don Muang Airport.

Anticipation was growing, but became muted as there was another delay at the immigration desk: staff took exception to Fuengsin filling in her landing card in Thai because she carried a British passport. The fact that she was born and bred in Thailand and spoke fluently was deemed irrelevant; rules were rules and so she had to step aside and fill in another card — in English. At least the delay meant a shorter wait for baggage and they exited through Customs without a further hitch. Having battled through the taxi touts (to which the answer was always, 'Someone is coming to collect us' [in Thai]), Fuengsin could not find a familiar face. However, after a phone call a white Volvo pulled up and Fuengsin could breathe a sigh of relief as its two occupants were immediately recognised — Vasana and her younger son, Tor, at the steering wheel.

Vasana had visited the UK only a few months earlier and so she and Fuengsin simply picked up the conversation from where they had left off whilst Paul was left to gaze at the fleeting landscape. The airport was some way from the centre of Bangkok, so the expressway leading into the capital was initially just flanked by palm trees and large bill-boards. Within 10 minutes they had arrived at Vasana's home, not far from Chatuchak market, and were greeted by their maid, Daeng, and two friendly dogs, Pepsi and Yew. The home was spacious, had a modern design with a stone exterior, and various trees and flowering plants around the edges. Inside it was a mixture of East and West: the room was quite airy, as is typical for Thai homes, but among the furniture were a piano and display cases full of fine bone china, including Crown Derby porcelain and numerous other European articles. It was about as much as Fuengsin and Paul could take in before they retired for some rest.

They stayed overnight and spent the following day taking it easy before departing in the evening to the family home, where Khun Yay Somboon, Fuengsin's mother, was waiting. They found her quite well, though substantially deaf. Despite being over 90 years of age, she had made a great effort to make the house comfortable for her Western guests, going so far as to refurbish the bathroom and install a new ceramic toilet, though it was still in a traditional Thai design. The soi had changed enormously since the family's last visit, for suddenly looming over the compound were eight-storey town houses, which might have been even higher if regulations had not prevented them. The streets felt even narrower. Yet as evening descended, the humdrum urban noises eased somewhat and familiar sounds of birds, insects and other creatures became more distinct.

Fuengsin and Paul initially stayed in the main house, but as they had found on the previous stay some 16 years earlier, it was disorientating. After a couple of days Fuengsin reported that she was unable to find her glasses anywhere; neither could anyone else, until about a week later they suddenly reappeared. Meanwhile Paul had mosquitoes to welcome him back, leaving him with swellings. He also quickly encountered problems with the diet, having to rush to the toilet with a loose stomach, not just during the day, but also in the middle of the night. As well as having to navigate in limited light, Paul had to be mindful of another resident in the house: Dic, a stray dog which Khun Yay had felt sorry for and rescued. It could see only in one eye and tended to be fierce if it couldn't see someone clearly, so approaching on its blind side was not a good idea.

Paul struggled to cope and was feeling ill — he ate nothing on the trip out, nothing on the restaurant menu sparked his interest. So after making her first visit to Wat Paknam, Fuengsin took him to see a doctor, Mor Dee (literally Dr Good), who prescribed some medicine. This was the same routine as on Paul's previous visit to Thailand as a toddler. In view of the situation, he was moved to the house of Fuengsin's niece, Ead, who was familiar with the comforts of the West as she worked at the American Embassy. English-style breakfasts were served, complete with scrambled egg, tomato ketchup and sweetened white bread, and Paul's appetite and health improved. Paul was able to feel more at ease in a relatively modern home where he could keep company with some young cousins, learning Magruk Thai (Thai chess) from Ead's son, Gate, who was the school's teenage champion. Gate was also talented at art, like his father, Khun Dum, and showed photographs of a large mural he had produced at his school.

Yet that house was already crowded: a nephew, Ad, and some of his family lived in just the one room, with a fair number of their eight children staying with them, from 12 years old through to adult. Then there was Ead's elder sister, Yui, with her husband, Khun Chaiwat, and their two children, Ad and Ink; there was also one other cousin, Od, and furthermore a couple of servants. As the house was not particularly extensive it made for complicated family dynamics, but in typically Thai fashion a way of living together was somehow worked out. One reason so many were gathered together was the recent loss of Wijit, their mother and Fuengsin's eldest sister. During her stay, Fuengsin attended her cremation, a reminder that time had advanced considerably since her last visit.

Next door, directly opposite the main house, was another of Fuengsin's sisters, Wilai, and her son, Laem, and daughter, Jiew. Neither Laem nor Jiew had families, so this was a quieter household and had a different pace of life. Jiew was a schoolteacher and had a very modest income; her health was poor, but she was kind and appeared with a ready smile for visitors, just like her late father. Jiew took Fuengsin and Paul to visit Ajahn Gaew's widow and her daughter Darunee, who still lived in the same house, a former pharmacy, next to Wat Paknam. Some family members still had an association with Wat Paknam that Fuengsin had initiated long ago. Fuengsin would have liked to have spent longer in and around the temple, but she had various family obligations, which invariably meant many outings in and around the city.

In the neighbourhood there was a lot of change for Fuengsin to update herself with. The effects of urban modernisation were pervasive, though still in transition: the odd global branded Western-style fast-food outlet was in evidence and Paul got 'treated' to McDonalds, an experience he found very disappointing; there were far tastier options in the markets, and street stalls offered very affordable menus. However, apart from foreign brands there was a more significant development in the shape of shopping malls, including Central. These competitors sold all kinds of products in air-conditioned spaces, conveniently located under one roof, but they were relatively expensive compared with street prices. On the other hand, traders generally seemed to be thriving; apart from the usual food and domestic items, fake goods were everywhere — a couple of T-shirts in the most desirable labels were on sale for 100 baht, and automatic Rolex watches. Fuengsin would buy a few items, but didn't dwell long.

Life here was generally more hectic. Outside the malls the roads were packed with motorbikes, tuk-tuks, buses, taxis and personal vehicles, weaving in and out, many of which had discovered marketing — various stickers on the back of cars sported trade names and slogans, some composed of English words randomly stuck together to comical effect. When signals turned red at large road intersections, motorbikes would amass and young boys would stroll along and peer through the windows of vehicles that had come to a standstill, trying to sell garlands. Despite the smog, these were regarded as signs of the city's 'progress', and the population had exploded in large part due to economic migrants. Some dwellers complained about excess immigration, claiming that only the pre-1761 generation were true Thais, when they had fought for the land against the Burmese, until Ayutthaya was ransacked by their foes. There were also accusations that immigrants put family business before the country; the first and second generation worked hard, but by the third generation their offspring had become far less energetic, enjoying easy and luxurious lifestyles. Once comfortable they were often lazy, driving everywhere, walking little, and complaining about the heat. The striving for material prosperity had taken hold, but although many had become well off, most were not: in slums the accommodation was makeshift, only rented, and sanitation was poor, and gambling and drugs were prevalent.

Even in Thonburi, which was still largely residential, as Fuengsin absorbed the surroundings she realised the extent of the change, especially in the vegetation. She later remarked:

> In the past, there were vegetables growing free in the hedgerows all over Thailand for anyone to pick. A green vegetable called 'kathin' was a big favourite. It was eaten with a sambal of chillies and prawn paste or with other sauces and served with rice and plathoo fish.
>
> Nowadays many of the hedgerows have been cut down to make room for more and more houses. The orchards have disappeared and pollution has made it hard for things to grow in the cities.

This last sentence is particularly poignant for families who grew up in the soi. Younger generations have often wanted to move out, but everyone is mindful of the more senior members, who know nowhere else and for whom the upheaval would be too great.

Fuengsin continued:

> There also used to be lots of wet areas where Chinese watercress used to grow. Also there were plenty of fresh water ponds where fish and fresh water prawn were abundant, but there aren't quite so many these days.

However, Fuengsin remained upbeat despite all the modern developments:

> In spite of all these things, Thailand is still a land of food, not famine. Because of the climate and soil, things grow easily. If a bird eats a bit of aubergine and swallows a seed, it's not unusual that an aubergine plant should grow from the bird's droppings.

Whilst much of the soi was giving way to concrete, Fuengsin's relatives still cultivated their land. Her eldest nephew, Od, had a small business cultivating plants in the compound, which he delivered to offices. However, whilst Thailand was still very fertile, the diet was not so healthy. Few vegetables were eaten in the family outings; they were often just served as decoration in restaurants and left untouched because of fears that they were unclean or contained too many chemical fertilisers. And whilst fruit was eaten a great deal, the Thai sweet tooth was now pandered to with new selections of cakes, beautifully decorated, and the emergence of commercial brands such as Dunkin Donuts, all of which could be washed down with fizzy drinks. Thai people, fuelled by consumerism, were getting fatter, and cholesterol levels were rising.

Nevertheless, Fuengsin had reasons to be optimistic. Beneath all the external transformation, upheaval and the bewildering array of distractions, personal cleanliness was excellent, even in slums, and the streets were not as smothered in litter as in the UK; people still took off shoes before entering the house and personal spaces; and the 'Wai' greeting was observed by juniors to seniors and then returned, though perhaps more grudgingly than in the past. Almost everywhere His Majesty King Bhumibol Adulyadej was still highly respected, with photographs of the Royal Family placed in prominent positions in homes and in businesses. There were still familiar activities, like boys kicking Tak-roh bare-footed with much dexterity, and houses still overrun with cats and fed the staple diet of rice. Furthermore when Fuengsin re-established contact with many of her friends she found them hospitable and ready to take on the burden of looking after others. Even their distinctive personalities and problems seemed very familiar.

Likewise, the family compound, though developed, still retained the same topography. The more noticeable changes were inside, where there were burgeoning electrical goods complementing the traditional items. 'Home entertainment' systems were also beginning to encroach: as well as powerful stereo music receivers, there were now colour televisions with five TV channels (3, 5, 7, 9 and 11), given odd numbers for the sake of auspiciousness. The TV companies were mainly state-controlled and the schedules were oriented to the latter part of the day. There were a few early morning university programmes, then closedown until 4 p.m., and between 4 and 7 p.m. there were many Thai and Chinese dramas (poorly dubbed) plus a few cartoons from the US. Later programmes included news and sports coverage, such as badminton and boxing. There were also a few imported dramas (usually dubbed) and quiz shows. At 8 a.m. and 6 p.m. the Thai national anthem was broadcast, the only times when you could be sure that there wouldn't be interruptions from comical advertising. Demand for electricity was mushrooming but Bangkok's urban planning, or at least the domestic electrical plans, were inadequate: it was not uncommon to have prolonged power cuts, some lasting half a day.

Despite the extra efforts of his relatives, Paul's health was generally weak during the first couple of weeks, which culminated in a day in hospital on a salt water drip and *cow dom* (rice porridge) as the only food. The following day he was diagnosed with a fever and was consigned to bed. Looking pallid and out of sorts, his young cousins got worried; it was time for another consultation, to seek another opinion. That afternoon, whilst Paul lay in bed, one male family member, who was a medium, entered a trance and channelled a local spirit, who was called 'Grandfather'.[1] Grandfather was familiar with the area and the domestic situations, so they asked him various questions. He reassured them that Paul would recover within three days, and indeed he did. By Sunday he was back to normal.

Fuengsin's presence was generally a catalyst for heightened activity among her relatives, friends and former students. She had many hosts in Bangkok, each determined to offer something special and for Fuengsin the experiences brought back all kinds of memories, some quite nostalgic. One distinguished friend was now a senator. He collected Fuengsin and Paul from Wongwien Yai and drove his vintage Mercedes at the sedate pace of a bygone era. They dined at Methavalai Sorndaeng, a well-known restaurant on the Rajdamnoen Klang roundabout, a familiar landmark for Fuengsin's family and a setting as good as any for reminiscences of times past. Whilst Fuengsin was progressive in outlook she steadfastly maintained traditional roots and she made sure she did not neglect a visit to her alma mater, Chulalongkorn University.

Many of her outings had academic connections. Among her students from Thonburi Technical College was Khun Narong, who collected Fuengsin and Paul from the soi in his car and took them to a restaurant. He apologised that the car wasn't new and wasn't air-conditioned, as Paul discovered instantly with mosquitoes milling about. Narong's high regard for education was evidently passed on through the family: on the back seat there was his 15-year-old son's mathematics textbook, which Paul browsed through. Paul announced that it seemed densely packed and looked more substantial than the 'O' levels he had sat. At the restaurant Narong listened attentively to Fuengsin's news and updates, as though back in the classroom.

Fuengsin was more at ease with individuals and small groups. Many of her friends now had families and were living a modern lifestyle. One of them introduced Paul to his son who was in his mid-teens, a similar age to Narong's son. Paul became intrigued when it appeared he was trying to reprogram the operating system of his IBM computer. Paul considered that on the face of it the task seemed far from feasible, but he didn't dismiss the idea — indeed, the lad subsequently gained early entry to study engineering at university. Fuengsin had already made it clear to Paul that many Thai families were ambitious about pursuing education and where parents could afford it children often received additional private tuition. Paul had a chance to do a little bit of teaching himself and gave some English language instruction to a couple of youngsters in the soi.

A succession of sightseeing outings were arranged, some of which were planned in haste or met with unexpected obstacles: there was one abortive trip to a temple in which the car broke down and half the group had to return. There were also some trips to the provinces, including to Rayong, the area Fuengsin frequented as a student and on her previous visit. On this occasion a visit was made to a Memorial park to Sunthorn Phu, perhaps Thailand's most famous poet from the Rattanakosin era, in the first half of the nineteenth century CE. Further whistle-stop tours included Sukhothai Open University and various temples, often with interesting tales about their monastic residents.

One major excursion was towards the South, which began at around 6 a.m. on a Saturday, with two Nissan Carryboy 4x4s packed with family members. The convoy made its way through Hua Hin, an area where His Majesty the King liked to stay for extended periods. However, any thoughts that the overseas visitors might have had about palace grounds were dissipated when they continued south to Pranburi, an area reserved for the Thai military; Ead's husband was in the army and this was where the largest Thai regiment was stationed. Finally at noon they reached their destination, Ao Manao (Lemon Bay), which was again an area for military families.

The accommodation was quite basic, but was fine for a beach holiday and came with some distinctive features and more spirits to acknowledge. One of the houses had a pair of big wooden pillars, both of which were thought to have been possessed by the spirit of a fierce old lady who acted as guardian. Garlands would be hung around the pillars as offerings and it was said that sometimes oil leaked from them. In Thai society ghosts or spirits are usually believed to be female because women are landowners and family leaders — their residential associations are thus stronger.

The beach itself was welcoming, with fine sand, a lot of space and few people. The urban crowd took in the sea air, which was pure and refreshing, and everyone could relax. Some, including Khun Chaiwat and Paul, were even inspired to go jogging at dawn. Out at sea, offerings were made to other spirits: during a boat trip, family members burnt and threw incense, garlands and money into the sea.

However, all too soon the group had to set out on the return journey, which started in the morning and went via Nakorn Pathom, another familiar haunt of Fuengsin, especially when she had been an undergraduate. As with many other sites, Fuengsin was the principal guide; this time she was leading Paul, another undergraduate, into Thailand's most famous temple, Phra Pathom Chedi, a highly revered Buddhist site of more than 2,000 years. Moving towards the central chedi they peered inside the colonnade that went right round the circumference and found a class in progress, in which an Ajahn was instructing novices. Fuengsin introduced her group and asked whether Paul could take a photo to which the Ajahn smiled in assent, so Paul took a couple of snaps — one of the Ajahn and one of the students. Having paid their respects, they made their way east towards central Bangkok and, a little reluctantly, returned late on Sunday evening. After the open spaces of the sea, the soi felt claustrophobic in comparison.

A couple of days later, Fuengsin went with Paul to visit another friend, who stayed in a lodge on palace grounds. Fuengsin's visit was not just a social call — there was food in mind for the friend was one of Queen Sirikit's cooks. The menu for the overseas delegation from the village of Hagley was *khao mun gai* (chicken steamed with garlic and rice) and it was served straight out of a rice cooker. It was delicious. Fortified, Fuengsin made a trip to a naval hospital and then to Tewee, her childhood friend, and some of her family who also had naval connections. She also went to visit Kruanoi Suttirak, the wife of the late Lt Gen. Chalerm Suttirak, whose home was also in a family compound, but it was a far more open layout than that of Fuengsin's family. A pair of elephants greeted visitors at the entrance to their home and inside was a serene orderliness. As with many of Fuengsin's older relatives and friends, Khun Kruanoi was dignified and spoke in measured tones, taking care to observe proper conduct.

* * *

After a few weeks Tony arrived, somehow emerging through Customs only half an hour after touchdown and reaching Wongwien Yai after just a further half an hour. On arrival he greeted Khun Yay and all the other relatives, who remarked how fit and strong he still looked. Their perception was strengthened as he tucked into whatever dishes they put his way and demonstrated his continued appetite for fresh fruit. Tony quickly settled in and started exploring the local area, shopping in the nearby markets and then wandering across to central Bangkok, including Lumbini park. Paul accompanied him and they nipped back and forth on ferry boats along the Chao Phraya; the charge for crossing the river was 50 satangs (about 1p).

Soon after the family took a trip to Nakhon Pathom, to see Phra Pathom Chedi and the Rose Garden, but just as the family schedule was picking up, Fuengsin was stopped in her tracks. One day, as she was making her way to the bathroom, treading softly, Dic was surprised and attacked her and bit her leg, leaving a deep cut. Fearing infection, she was rushed to hospital and given a large dose of injections, but after treatment and tests she was cleared. To compound the family angst that day, a young cousin's school friend was shot following an argument in the playground. Plans to visit Ayutthaya were put on hold and for the moment everyone had to make do with local travel.

With Fuengsin needing to rest and recuperate, Tony and Paul decided that they could wander off by themselves and so they caught a train from Wongwien Yai to Mahachai, a town that was about 25 miles to the south-west. They enjoyed a pleasant journey, seeing a lot of life with homes, schools and traders right next to the line. However, when they reached their destination they opted for a paltry lunch, much to Fuengsin's dismay, prompting her to write later:

> My husband and son . . . decided to take that train — except now it's an electric one — the Mahachai to eat some seafood at one of the many fish restaurants there. I think I should have gone with them because they, being Westerners, couldn't tell the good restaurants from the bad and ended up at one of the very few bad ones in the district.

Outside most Thai buildings is a spirit house, a miniature home in the form of a traditional Thai house, complete with characteristic gables and small statue figures inside. It was just so with Fuengsin's relatives and (again as is usual) they had shrine rooms inside the homes, full of rupas and amulets, some Buddhist and some non-Buddhist, but mixed up in a way that Fuengsin wasn't keen on. Both the spirit houses and shrine rooms were regularly supplied with flowers and burning incense. Spirits appeared to be very active in the soi and some seemed unsettled: there were numerous local disturbances, including frightful sounds coming from a neighbour's house. A day or so later monks could be heard chanting, to dedicate merit to the spirits. It was believed there were many spirits such as hungry ghosts (*petas*), in that area, particularly of deceased soldiers who use to live in the army camps when the capital was being established in Thonburi in the late eighteenth century. Fuengsin's relatives were anxious enough to plan their own response to placate the spirits. It involved an elaborate ceremony that took place under the guidance of two monks in which a feast was laid out on a long table and offered to the spirits. Fuengsin was uncomfortable and quietly remarked to Paul that monks shouldn't be involved in a ceremony of spirit worship, and pointing out that the complexion of the monk leading the ceremony had darkened by unskilful deeds. He might have been well-meaning, but the animistic practice was not in accordance with the Vinaya, the rules of training for monastics.

In later years, although the spirit houses remained, there was no repeat of the grand ceremony and the area became more peaceful; the cousin who had acted earlier as medium stopped his practice. Instead, he used his psychic abilities to teach the spirits who visited him in his daily meditation session, which he started at 4 a.m.

With domestic duties completed, Tony, Fuengsin and Paul could concentrate more on exploration. After a few days wandering around Bangkok, Khun Jamras and Vasana came to collect them and they set off for the floating market in Damnoen Saduak, Ratchaburi, to the south-west of Bangkok. Although the market was starting to attract tourists it was still busy as a local trading point, with many tradesfolk selling fresh produce early in the morning. Whilst there, they hired a boat and were paddled slowly and silently through the market areas, along the main canal and then down a narrow side canal until they stopped by a house. Khun Jamras explained that this was where he had been brought up as a child. His relatives still lived in the same house, which provided further glimpses of an older style of life; the distance seemed reinforced when some of the more elderly relations were very shy and avoided group photographs.

Tony's reputation as an intrepid explorer went before him and travel plans became more ambitious. After Fuengsin's bite was properly bandaged and medication applied she was fit enough to travel, so a 'long weekend' was arranged in Chiang Mai in the North, involving a road trip of over 400 miles each way. It was organised by a lady whose nickname was Moo, another friend of Fuengsin who had spent time in the UK. She had a clever business brain and worked for Japanese organisations, making sure she practised her golf in the increasing number of driving ranges and 18-hole courses.

Due to work commitments the journey started in the early evening. Inevitably it was not long before there was a food-related stop, as Fuengsin recounted:

> I went to the north of Thailand with my husband, son and a group of friends. On the way we stopped at a village where every stall was laden with bananas. They were hanging everywhere and were sold in gigantic hands, made up of many bunches. They were extremely cheap and very fresh.

The van was making steady progress until it suddenly broke down along the single carriageway. It was 9.15 p.m., dark, and with little traffic; to the passengers it seemed like the middle of nowhere. The driver got out and went off to search for help, leaving a strangely quiet vehicle by the roadside. After a while he returned in a truck and they were towed to a service station. With the sun having set several hours ago, there was the expectation that it was already closed for the night. However, some garage staff emerged who were persuaded to start work on the van — perhaps because they were drunk. Their inebriation was a cause for concern and the travellers were sceptical that the problem would be fixed before daylight, so they prepared to settle down for the night, Fuengsin finding a bench to lie down on.

But some time after midnight the group was woken up from its slumber by the sound of the van's engine starting up; the problem was fixed and the group were off again. At 8 a.m. they reached their destination of the Phucome hotel in Doi Suthep, the site of the famous monastery perched on top of a hill, the one whose road had been built under the direction of Khruba Srivichai, about whom Fuengsin had written for the Birmingham Buddhist Vihara's children's magazine.

Time was limited, so rather than sleep, Fuengsin and Paul took breakfast, had a little rest, and then later that morning commenced their whistle-stop tour. They met up with another of Fuengsin's former students, Khun Jornsuk, a lecturer in electronics at Chiang Mai University, and in the afternoon the group toured an orchid garden; and in the evening there was an excursion into the hills. The next morning the group visited Wat Phrathat Doi Suthep, climbing the stairs decorated with nagas, pausing along the way to take photos of Lahu hill-tribe children who were posing for a few bahts. At the top, Fuengsin entered the temple compound, paid respects and made some offerings. Later in the afternoon, the group explored a silk factory that made umbrellas, and they rounded off their excursion with a visit to some hot springs. The next morning Paul and Tony went off to Mass, and by late morning they departed for the return, waved off by Khun Jornsuk and his wife.

The return was uneventful — there was no repeat of the vehicle breakdown. Back in Bangkok, Fuengsin and Paul crossed the Taksin Road to watch Niu Chinese drama in an open-air theatre. It was free, fun and noisy: the outsized characters boldly delivered their lines in sharp and distinctive tones, the musicians clashing cymbals and banging drums in time to deft movements on the stage. Thais enjoy a good show.

However, not all trips were filled with merriment. One of the saddest encounters was when Fuengsin and Paul went with the family's long-serving maid, Shu, to see a mother and son who were originally from an aristocratic family in Cambodia. They had been running a successful business and owned factories, but they lost everything in the Communist revolution and had to flee to Thailand. They subsequently came into contact with Fuengsin's parents, who allowed them to stay a short while at their home in Wongwien Yai, and the families remained in contact afterwards. Their prosperity never returned: mother and son stayed in a small house next to a yard that made Buddha statues, which was noisy and pumping out unhealthy fumes. For a while they chatted as a group, Fuengsin hearing further accounts of life's wide-ranging experiences and the workings of karma. Despite having little time to digest the stories, she could usually come up with some practical advice; but here the circumstances seemed intractable. The mother was elderly and weak, and her middle-aged son, although highly educated and fluent in French, was only able to secure a modest position as a hotel butler. Nevertheless, the family retained a grace and dignity, and the son had enjoyed perfecting his work as a butler; he had sufficient savings to pursue a few hobbies, particularly assembling hi-fi systems from locally sourced components.

The next day saw a return to jollity as Fuengsin joined a Chulalongkorn Alumni reunion for lunch at the Imperial Hotel, a gathering of intelligentsia that engaged in animated conversation fuelled by an extravagant selection of food. Fuengsin shared her stories from the UK, much to the delight of those around, quite a few of whom had studied or worked in Europe. However, Fuengsin couldn't linger as she had to get ready for the next excursion.

Early that evening Fuengsin, Tony and Paul, departed for Hua Lamphong railway station, where they met up with Khun Vasana. With tickets in hand, they were heading south on the overnight service. They chose second-class compartments with seats that converted into bunk-beds; there was no air conditioning, but the fans lining the ceiling kept the air circulating so that it felt quite comfortable. It was another view on local life without the gloss — and of course with plenty of food options available. At 6 a.m. they arrived at Surat Thani and disembarked. With luggage in tow, they found a restaurant and had breakfast, but not before complaining about hygiene. The tablecloth was dirty and so a replacement was requested, which duly arrived, but it was just the same. The cloth came with matching glasses of water featuring tiny ants. Paul felt very weak, but Surat Thani was not the final destination. Lingering no more, they made their way to the ferry for Ko Samui, an island that was just starting to become popular. After a bit of sun and sand, most enjoyed by Tony, it was back to Bangkok.

Fuengsin's itinerary continued to flow like this right through until it was time to return to the UK. By the end of it she had strengthened again long-standing ties and witnessed much of Thailand's transformation, with varying qualitative results. However, she was quite looking forward to the relative tranquillity of the Worcestershire countryside and very soon she was back in Hagley.

* * *

However, only a few months after the family returned the spectre of life's uncertainty manifested again when Fuengsin received news that her mother had passed away. It was not unexpected as she was 94 years old, but it marked the end of an era. For the family in Wongwien Yai it was like a candle going out and there was a great emptiness. Yet, her departure came with a surprising consolation: she appeared in dreams to some neighbours and conveyed numbers to them. They needed no encouragement to remember the numbers and use them in the lottery. They won.

Fuengsin decided that this time she ought to go back to Thailand to attend the funeral, so in July 1989 she flew once more to Bangkok. The funeral was attended by about 400 people, with many distant relatives. Afterwards Fuengsin received a celestial vision of her mother who appeared happy, asking only for a glass of water, which Fuengsin duly offered.

Fuengsin now had a couple of weeks of free time. It had been three years since Ajahn Gaew had passed away, so she went to Wat Paknam to find another meditation teacher. She met up with her long-time friend, Assistant Professor Prakhong, who accompanied her, just as she had done almost 30 years ago. Fuengsin arrived at the temple on Friday 14 July and carried out some practice with Phra Bhavanakosol (Veera Kanuttamo), who was Director of Meditation Affairs. It didn't go smoothly as Fuengsin experienced severe pain in her stomach, but she persevered. Following a recommendation, she then visited Luang Na San Tippasanto, who was a friend of Ajahn Gaew, and was also a senior meditation teacher (Luang Na is a term of respect for a revered uncle). He resided in the Vised Dhammakaya building, which housed the temple's museum, named 'Mor-Sor-Jor', an abbreviation in honour of the temple's founder, Luang Phor Sodh.

Fuengsin arrived there the next day, again accompanied by Ajahn Prakhong. On display in the museum were many Buddha rupas as well as objects relating to the history of the temple and especially the life and work of Luang Phor. She greeted Luang Na San, paid respects, and introduced herself and her background, particularly her connection to Ajahn Gaew, through Ajahn Prakhong. She mentioned what had happened concerning her meditation the day before and asked whether Luang Na would consider taking her on as a student. Luang Na San was only interested in people committed to meditation, especially advanced meditation, so he got Fuengsin to sit and meditate to gauge her experience and to see whether she was suitable.

Satisfied, Luang Na San agreed to teach intensive meditation over several days, along with some supporting Dhamma talks, which included a concise history of Vijja Dhammakāya. He had with him a tape recorder and started recording the guided sessions. Knowing that Fuengsin would not be able to stay very long in Thailand, saving these sessions would be useful for her to play back in the UK, something Ajahn Gaew had already done previously. As if to emphasise the historical importance of the event, Luang Na started Sunday's session with the following introduction:

So far today up 'til now we have been listening, we weren't sitting. We have already heard that today is Sunday 16 July B.E. 2532 [1989]; yesterday was Saturday 15 July, which we note was the first day when Khun Fuengsin came to meet Luang Na San Tippasanto at Wat Paknam, Bhasicharoen, where Luang Na usually resides in the 'Mor-Sor-Jor' museum of the Vised Dhammakaya building — 'Mor-Sor-Jor' being an abbreviation, where 'Mor' is short for Phra Mongkol Thepmuni; 'Sor-Seua' here is short for Luang Phor's name of Sodh [= 'fresh']; 'Jor' is short for Luang Phor's ordained name of Candasaro. Hence Phra Mongkol Thepmuni Sodh Candasaro is abbreviated as 'Mor-Sor-Jor.'

Luang Na San then went straight into summarising the practice of Vijja Dhammakaya, starting with recollection of the various kinds of *kayas*, a succession of increasingly refined bodily forms from the human to the 'clear crystal Buddha with the crown topped by a Lotus bud'. It was a short prelude to the kind of approach they would be taking, as though surveying salient features of a route up a mountain.

He then started the sitting practice with some orientation:

Since we already have a fairly good understanding, Assistant Professor Prakhong along with Khun Fuengsin, who has been able to make the journey from England, we can come to practise vijja together so as to scrutinize and compute[2] our body and the special Dhamma dhatu [elements] in utmost detail, a task which we have already been able to carry out previously and, also, further practice [also] thoroughly.

He then addressed posture and indicated that this practice could be done anywhere with eyes closed or open:

So that we don't regress, we can sit in a posture that we find comfortable for sitting; it is okay to sit with the eyes open and it is okay to sit with the eyes closed because in Vijja Dhammakaya we can keep our eyes open, we can practise with our eyes open, until it is time for us to close our eyes and practise with our eyes closed. This is because we are in control when practising with our eyes open. We are capable of doing this everywhere — it doesn't matter whether we close our eyes when sitting — whether we sit in a car, we sit in a boat, in a great variety of places. We can do so whatever our deportment.

Preparations over, he then launched into the practice, in which Fuengsin applied sustained *satipañña* (mindfulness with wisdom) successively to whatever arose in her mental purview. Fuengsin followed Luang Na's guidance closely and was able to carry out whatever was instructed, entering successively more refined states, removing blemishes in her mind. The pace and work rate was exceedingly fast, but Fuengsin was able to keep up; so quick was her mind that on occasions it was as though the meditation teacher was giving his student instructions to go ahead — like a scout on reconnaissance — and to report back what she had seen. The practice deployed special techniques, at one stage including the use of a musical sound from a family of percussion instruments called *ranard*, which could help overcome certain obstacles.

Afterwards Luang Na San checked her progress and asked how Fuengsin felt about her practice. She was very pleased, expressing how good and thorough it was. A more general conversation followed in which Luang Na enquired about the situation in England. Fuengsin answered by relating the spiritual landscape, describing the activities in Birmingham, mentioning that the Burmese vihara taught the method of Mahasi Sayadaw. They pondered how long it might take to spread Vijja Dhammakaya teachings; it wasn't easy as even experienced practitioners might not be supportive because they could be fixed in their views. Even so, Luang Na told her that she had sufficient skill in the practice to be able to communicate Vijja Dhammakaya in English.

Fuengsin expressed doubts, feeling that it was because of Luang Na's guidance that she could undertake such advanced practice, and saying that there was no such expertise in the UK. She also felt that the English language was still inadequate, its vocabulary insufficient to express this meditation. It seemed that she lacked some confidence in her abilities. Luang Na conceded that England was a long way away, but they could use the telephone and he could gain special permission to obtain copies of audio recordings of Luang Phor Sodh leading meditation. Fuengsin was also concerned about authority, conscious that she was a housewife and not someone with any formal teaching title, so she felt she wasn't the right person to teach. In response, Luang Na pointed out that it was not like a royal or noble title that was passed down from one generation to the next. There was no conferral as such, only the duty for an individual to do the practice and conduct to the utmost of their ability, and Luang Na was trying to reassure Fuengsin that she was very capable in this regard.

After the session of intense concentration, Fuengsin and Ajahn Prakhong were left to reflect by themselves in a more relaxed manner with Fuengsin joking in her characteristic fashion. They recalled some features of the meditation and then discussed a few practicalities — including photographs, as Fuengsin sought some souvenirs. There was a selection available which Fuengsin was able to take, particularly photographs of Luang Phor Sodh and Luang Na San, but she was concerned that they might get damaged. The temple offices had a facility to laminate cards, but they were cautious about treading on people's toes or drawing attention to themselves as they knew the procedures could be strict and required observing the proper etiquette. They carefully planned how they would approach the office, indicating clearly that they were disciples of Luang Na, and making sure that they put Luang Phor's photo on top, with Luang Na underneath. Ajahn Prakhong provided further guidance, knowing about Luang Na's schedule and what he would and wouldn't do to help. The preparations bore fruit and Fuengsin was able to take back home laminated photographs of these cherished teachers of Vijja Dhamma-kaya.

Luang Na San also taught Fuengsin the following Saturday. On this occasion there was quite a lot of general discussion after the conclusion of the sitting practice. Fuengsin came with a request. Sister Mary had a wish to install a Buddha rupa at the entrance to Harborne Hall and Fuengsin indicated that she could arrange it. The import and export of Buddha images to and from Thailand, even small ones, is subject to strict controls. Accordingly, a formal letter was drafted to indicate the intended purpose of this image, which Fuengsin sent to a number of temples in Thailand. Whilst at Wat Paknam Fuengsin was given the name of a contact, Khun Treetar, and she asked Luang Na whether she could meet her.[3] He assured Fuengsin that she would come and arrangements were made accordingly.

Fuengsin received further support from nuns, and two volumes of an advanced meditation manual that was published in 1974. It was remarkably similar to the contents of the Blue Book that Ajahn Gaew had dictated for her a few years before the publication, which in turn had been prepared from a manuscript of Phra Bhavana Kosolthera (Ajahn Veera Ganuttamo, later to receive the title of Chao Khun). She brought these and other items back to the UK and kept them in her shrine, helping her to maintain the link with the temple and most of all with the meditation practice itself. Fuengsin returned renewed, and everything seemed to be well set, but before she left the temple she was given a warning: 'Watch your stomach!'

Notes

1. Thai mediumship. The fact that the family medium was male is unusual. Generally, women have key roles in ceremonies and rituals with respect to taking care of spirits of ancestors.

2. Fuengsin's meditation with Luang Na San. The phrase 'compute' (the body) comes from the Thai word *kamnuan*, which usually means 'calculate', 'measure' or 'compute'. Luang Na actually goes on to use the English term 'super computer'.

3. The contact provided was probably Ajahn Treetar Niemkham (Thai: อาจารย์ตรีธา เนียม ขำ), the Chairperson of Wat Paknam Alumni Association.

12

Flourishing

Fuengsin's recent trips to Thailand had offered plenty of evidence that the country's tourism was booming and becoming increasingly popular with holidaymakers from Britain. There was certainly interest in Hagley, where Fuengsin was invited to give a talk about Thailand at the Hagley Free Church, which was a nonconformist church that had opened its doors at the beginning of the century, welcoming a diverse group of believers in Christian unity.

Fuengsin had routinely passed by its front gate every time she went shopping in the village, but had not ventured inside. However, she had already formed a good impression about the church, partly because it was well known for its shared facilities, as with the chess club that Paul had been attending. So she was happy to speak and accepted the invitation.

Equipped with 35mm slides, and now up to date with some of the latest developments, she was in a good position to reflect on the country's traditions and modernity. She depicted a colourful land with a long and proud history, where spiritual and temporal were closely linked, the King being defender of all faiths. The audience enjoyed her talk and afterwards she had an opportunity to chat with some more villagers. It was there that she met Alfred and Elsie Crabtree, who invited Fuengsin to their home, just a couple of hundred yards up Newfield Road. The Crabtrees hailed from Lancashire, but had spent most of their working lives down south. Alfred had initially trained as an engineer and became a specialist in chain-making. Then in later years he developed his career in management consultancy for which Elsie provided her organisational skills to do most of the administration. They had two grown-up children and now, with a wide range of personal interests, they devoted a lot of their time to voluntary work to support the church and the life of the village.

Alfred and Elsie were keen to learn more about Fuengsin's background and how she had adapted to life in the West. Alfred was particularly interested in her Buddhist practice as since before he started his first job he had been nurturing a deep interest in psychology and 'what makes people tick'. He had not had the chance to study formally, yet he had amassed a large collection of books in the field and more pertinently — at least to Fuengsin — he had developed many observational skills from his vast experiences, working his way up from the shop floor to senior management. Fuengsin enjoyed very much the company and kindness of Alfred and Elsie and her hosts in turn were very pleased to spend time with Fuengsin. For several years she was invited to spend an hour or two together each week. They talked about spirituality and how it contrasted with dusty religiosity. Alfred was very interested to see how Buddhists believed and practised, recalling especially Britain's encounter with Asia and the Far East in the 1960s, the period when Fuengsin was encountering the West. In their dialogues they explored what it meant to be human, the consciousness of all kinds of life forms, the relationship between body and mind, the capabilities of mind, the soul and so forth, and then what all this meant with regards to communication. There was discussion about the use of language, the meanings behind words and phrases, and the interpretation of scriptures (hermeneutics). Permeating all the serious talk they had a lot of fun and laughter, shared many stories and anecdotes, and life's coincidences. Alfred and Elsie were delighted by her sense of humour, and how she could crack jokes in English.

As in Strood, Fuengsin took a keen interest in the welfare of village residents and quickly knew their circumstances. Most people in Hagley were generally prosperous, but there were some who fell on hard times and she did not shy away from asking friends for help on other people's behalf. Alfred recalled:

> She put us to shame because on one occasion she came in and she was talking about somebody ... between here and Hagley Free Church, where I go, of course . . . who had virtually no money. So we gave her some money to take to that person. But what struck us: here are we, Christians, supposed to be helping other people, but your mother knew what was going on and she *did* know what was going on in the village.

Fuengsin had to be careful because her earnings were little more than pocket money and so the family was dependent on Tony's income. His salary was modest and there was little scope for overtime. Furthermore, Tony was always someone who enjoyed getting out and about and would often encourage others to get fresh air and exercise, prompting Fuengsin to remark that he was 'very vigorous'. It was not surprising then that he found life in a VAT Office, even with his visits to companies, quite confining. Looking around for alternatives, he saw that Birmingham Airport was developing as a regional hub and some opportunities were arising there in Customs, which was similar work to his earlier career in the Waterguard.

Tony applied for a transfer and was successful. It meant a longer commute, initially via central Birmingham and then along a newly opened extension of the M42, which he travelled on the day after it was opened. At night there was so little traffic that he could switch on the headlamp and use main beam most of the way, confident that there was no traffic coming in the opposite direction. The airport was located next to the National Exhibition Centre (NEC), which boasted far more exhibition space than Earl's Court and drew the national motor show, which Tony and Paul attended one year. It was a hub of innovation and even boasted the world's first magnetic levitation rail system to run as a public service: the Maglev shuttle service between the airport and the NEC. Tony soon established himself with a team of about 15 staff.

Paul was still yet to start his career; his experience of 'team-building' was — like most Southampton undergraduates — formed mainly by sharing a house, as he spent his second year with four other students in one of the many properties owned by a Mr Singh. The end-of-terrace property along Woodside Road in Portswood was quite international. Enock, the eldest, was from Zambia, one of a group on a healthy sponsorship from Zambia Consolidated Copper Mines. The rest were making do on a mixture of grants and parental support: Geoff, of Welsh origin, was born in Rhodesia and then moved with his family to South Africa; Gary hailed from Wales; and Andy was from Birmingham. Paul enjoyed their company and Fuengsin was happy with this arrangement, though it was to last only a year and then everyone went their separate ways. Meanwhile Fuengsin's street cred was spotted by one of Paul's other university friends, Carl, who told him one day, 'Your Mum was on the radio. She has a nice singing voice!' He had heard her on Radio 1, when a DJ was asking listeners to recommend restaurants, after which he would phone the restaurant, inviting the staff to sing on air for charity. Pranee's restaurant was tipped in this way and received a call, but only Fuengsin had the nerve to respond, singing the rhyme 'Daisy, Daisy' in Thai.

Paul returned to Glen Eyre for his final year, but could not settle and this time found it difficult to get on with some neighbours. He became fatigued, his health deteriorated and his mid-term exams were a small disaster. Yet he remained determined, as though the importance of education had been encoded in his genes. That summer he sat his final maths papers and waited, unsure whether he had performed sufficiently well. Fuengsin was also anxious, but assured Paul that in her meditation she had seen a quite bright light; and so it was, as before he had packed his bags for the return home he had received unofficial news that he was to be awarded First Class Honours. A few days later, towards the end of June, Paul and Tony went off on a week's holiday in the Isle of Skye, during which he received confirmation that he had been accepted for a place at Glasgow University, to start a research degree in Pure Mathematics. On their return at the beginning of July, Tony and Fuengsin travelled to Southampton to attend Paul's graduation. Fuengsin was very proud.

During a leisurely summer the family spent some time in Chepstow with Tony's parents. Fuengsin took the opportunity of phoning Judith Powell's mother and was delighted to know that Judith was there at the time with her family, so she made a quick visit to Orchard Cottage on the afternoon of 12 August 1990. They reminisced — this was the house from where she had got married — and then shared more recent developments. Fuengsin talked about her family and mentioned Paul's studies ahead of his continuation at Glasgow University.

Paul duly arrived in Glasgow and met his supervisor, Professor Robert Odoni, who would guide him in his studies of Number Theory. However, there seemed to be some confusion as Paul had originally intended to spend only a year pursuing a Master's, but he was greeted with the words, 'For your PhD . . .' Somewhat taken aback he then changed his mind and prepared for the long haul. He was initially fascinated by the city's landscapes and architecture, and was somewhat in awe of the tenement blocks. Glasgow was undergoing rejuvenation spurred on by being the designated 'European Capital of Culture'. The locals seemed friendly and he found that getting around was quite straightforward on the underground; understanding the local accent was more challenging, but he persevered, partly by watching Rab C. Nesbitt, Govan's antihero.

As this was by the far the furthest Paul had lived away from home, Fuengsin was keen that he remain in touch, so he usually phoned home once a week and letters would be sent back and forth every few weeks. Fuengsin would encourage him and regularly informed him of life at home and work activities, which continued to keep her busy. The Multi-Faith Centre in Birmingham was proving to be a delightful home for interfaith work. It was now consolidating its brand with the strapline, 'A Partnership for Education and Training', accompanied by a logo of intersecting circles of six faiths. However, it was still operating on a limited budget and could not afford to produce glossy brochures so the advertising materials still had a home-made quality about them.

Despite these budgetary constraints, the 12-page A5 programme for 1989/90 was advertising its Certificate in Religion with an added air of confidence, starting its pitch with: 'Would you like to know more about other Cultures and Religions? The Multi-Faith Centre's Certificate in Religion is a long and well-established one-year course that will help you understand the ethos, customs and practices in our multi-cultural society . . .' The cost per module remained modest: it was £22, or half price for the unwaged.

The Multi-Faith Centre
— A Partnership for Education and Training —

Harborne Hall
Old Church Road
Birmingham
B17 0BD England

Tel: 021-427 1044

Harborne Hall

Would you like to know more about other Cultures & Religions?

Fig. 88: Header for the front cover of a Multi-Faith Centre programme.

The sequence of religions began in October with Hinduism, and proceeded to cover Judaism, Buddhism, Christianity, Islam and finally Sikhism in July. Fuengsin's teaching was scheduled for January and February, which were the coldest months of the year, where central areas of the UK always saw sharp frosts, which left Fuengsin's hands icy cold as she had poor circulation. Her schedule was similar the following year, which saw a particularly severe winter; she succumbed to a virus, requiring her to cancel lectures and other work.

Fuengsin generally maintained the syllabus she had devised, but with gradual refinements. Thus she continued introducing students to the fundamentals of Buddhism such as the Five Precepts, the Ten Perfections, the Four Noble Truths and the Eightfold Noble Path. However, as she accumulated more materials, she was able to go into greater depth: in her treatment of Karma she discussed the Five Niyamas, the many factors that make up phenomena such as the weather and biological processes as well as our intentional actions. At the same time, Fuengsin also indicated the importance of intention by focusing on the karma that operates at moment of death: the weighty karma, the habitual karma and the death-proximate karma.

Fuengsin also described in greater detail the life of the Buddha: his ancestry and family as a prince, then his renunciation, his search for Enlightenment with different yogis in Bihar, his practice alone in Uruvela, and under the Bodhi tree until his Enlightenment. She continued with his life of teachings, starting with the First Sermon, the 'Turning of the Wheel' given to the five companion ascetics. She made more use of visuals, creating a map of the Buddha's life on an A1 sheet, showing his wanderings across India, the Southern continent (or as it was termed in Buddhist circles, Jambudipa).

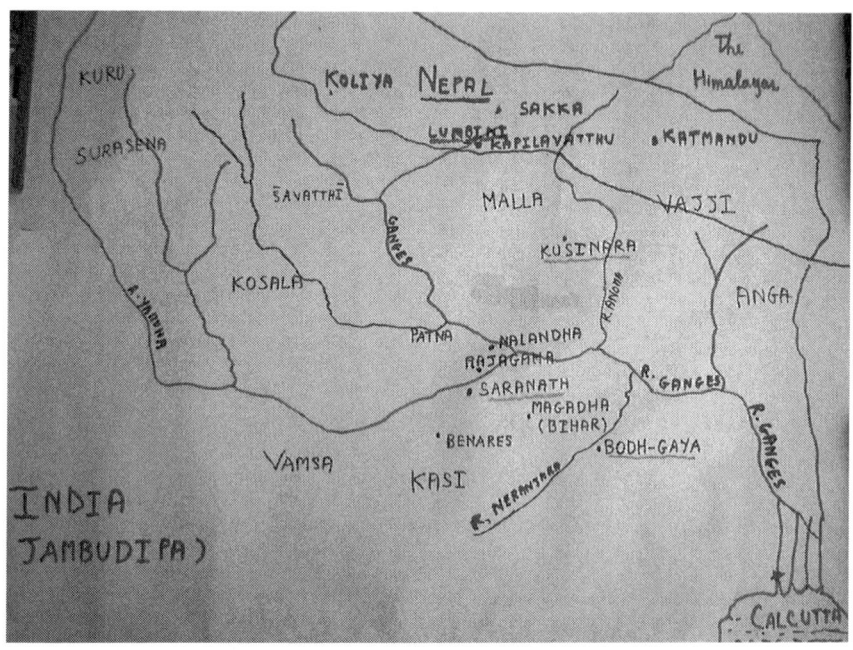

Fig. 89: Fuengsin's map with the locations where Buddha Gotama taught.

She also charted historical developments as Buddhism spread in the early centuries CE beyond India and the Pali texts. Hence she explored the Prajnaparamita or Perfection of Wisdom sutras, which are core to Mahayana Buddhism. They were rendered in English by Edward Conze, whom she referred to as 'the great translator'. She also studied some texts of Pure Land Schools to be found in Northern and Eastern Asia, including the Amitayurdhyana Sutra (Meditation on the Buddha of Infinite Light), the Sukhavati-viyhu Sutra (Array of the Happy Land).

She continued with the subjects of tantra, mantra, mudra, puja and mandala, which were most popularly associated with Tibetan traditions, many of which developed in the eighth century CE when they were transmitted by luminary figures such as Padmasambhava. Fuengsin admired the way Tibetan practices transformed physical and emotional energies in the body, as she often had to deal with negativity herself. She was particularly fascinated by the account of yogis in caves keeping themselves warm by practising *caṇḍālī* (*Tummo* in Tibetan), that focused energies to generate heat. In this case it was a practical application to keep the body warm, but beyond that there were deeper states of mind and the neutralisation of defilements. In all this research she drew on personal contact with practitioners in the respective traditions and would seek clarification.

Fuengsin ventured still further in her reading material. Not content with books from different branches of Buddhism and primers on the world religions; she also enjoyed spiritual works from outside the established institutionalised religions: the *Teachings of Don Juan* and related works authored by Carlos Castaneda were a big hit with her, especially the stark training exercises in mental clarity. Whether they were fact or fiction (or a mixture), something resonated with her and she would share her fascination with Paul, joking that a native South American in an immaculate suit could be just around the corner ready to introduce himself. Similarly, she was enthusiastic about adepts in Tibetan tantra and read works by Chogyam Trungpa such as *Cutting Through Spiritual Materialism* together with articles in the *Crystal Mirror* journal of the Tibetan Nyingma Meditation Center, Berkeley. Fuengsin's interest in knowing the mind's extent led to her to search far and wide.

In addition she received various magazines and newsletters, many delivered by friends from Thailand. The fusion of religion into Thai culture runs very deep and has a number of interesting manifestations such as the many magazines that have sections devoted to Buddhist practice and interesting tales told by monks. One theme that drew a lot of interest concerned Nareepol trees, where the fruits were in the form of young women. Several pages were devoted to descriptions of meditating yogis who were able to enter into Himavanta, a heavenly forest high up in the mountains beyond the Himalayas where these maidens could be found and picked off trees. Some made love to them and then fell unconscious and lost their powers, their craving having got the better of them. It was just as related in the Thai version of the popular Vessantara Jataka, one of the many accounts of the Buddha's previous lives in which the trees were planted by the god Indra as a distraction for men so that Princess Maddi, the wife of Prince Vessantara, the Bodhisattva (Buddha-to-be), would be safe in the forest while gathering food and water for her family. Fuengsin had a stock of such narratives to spice up her presentations.

Fuengsin would not, of course, settle just for reading. The Buddha's teachings were an oral tradition communicated through chanting by members of the monastic community. The chants were the primary vehicle to preserve the teachings to the letter and so were chanted in monotone, in one voice; they are not melodies or harmonies, but to help memorisation their intonation has rhythmic qualities. For a long time Fuengsin had been listening to recordings of chants from Wat Paknam. She also had recordings of Dhamma talks by famous Thai monks, including one or two Westerners such as Phra George Anavilo Bhikkhu at Wat Mahathat in Bangkok, as well as Thai practitioners at Wat Paknam.

She was always looking at ways to enhance her communications and since her arrival had been giving specific attention to Westerners in their homeland. She had for a long time been fine-tuning her instruction, trying to find the right kind of language and means of expression. It was in this context that Fuengsin became very interested in the work of Sangharakshita, who had established the Friends of the Western Buddhist Order — this was perhaps the most popular Buddhist organisation in the UK, with centres in most cities. She knew that the FWBO's exposition of Buddhism had taken on a form that had radical differences from those with which she was brought up in the Far East. Fuengsin's background was reflected in her staunch support of the monastic heirs in their saffron robes, particularly to those who were fulfilling the vision of the English Sangha Trust, keeping the Patimokkha (the 227 rules of training instituted by the Buddha, as recorded in the Vinaya section of the early Pali texts). On the other hand, Sangharakshita had instituted an order in which ordained members didn't have robes and observed 10 rules of training, the dasa-kusala-kamma (ten wholesome actions) rather than the Patimokkha.

Some of Fuengsin's Dhamma associates expressed strong reservations about this organisation and its founder, but Fuengsin recognised that Sangharakshita had a special ability to communicate and stimulate interest in Buddhism and make it appealing, so she wanted to investigate. It was thus that she approached the FWBO and visited their centre in Moseley, which had been founded in 1987. She was encouraged by the orderliness of the shrine room and was initially struck by the Western face of the Buddha rupa, but realised that throughout the world Buddha images have often been made as a reflection of their creators. She then observed what it was that members sought from religion and how they applied it in their daily lives. However, perhaps the most significant step was when she started borrowing cassette tapes containing audio recordings of Sangharakshita's many lectures. It was then that she appreciated just how effective he was in engaging the listener. It was not surprising that his exposition appealed to Fuengsin, for both had literary minds, but Fuengsin was still striving for further ideas on how to approach the subject, and how to select the right topics for the audience that would appeal to Westerners and be relevant for their everyday lives. Furthermore, she was interested in how he delivered his material, how it could be unfolded. So Fuengsin started borrowing tapes on a regular basis and proceeded to work her way through dozens of them, on topics such as 'Buddhism and Psychoanalysis' and 'Breaking Through Into Buddhahood', in which Fuengsin heard how a few choice words and combinations — such as 'clock time' and 'organic time' — could make distinctions easy to understand. Very soon she added them to her teaching repertoire.

Conscious of being a consumer with a big appetite for knowledge, she would 'dangle carrots' by taking doughnuts and other cakes for the order members, a strategy that she knew worked very well for she herself was partial to chocolate cake. Fuengsin had of course a lot more to offer than sweet treats, for in the exchanges order members could learn from Fuengsin by example that Thai people were practitioners worthy of respect. Fuengsin learnt about the wider activities outside of the Centre and particularly how it was supported, so as to compare with the *dana* activities associated with Thai Buddhism. She was informed about Windhorse Publications, the FWBO's publishing house and the right livelihood businesses that promoted ethically sound practices. This led naturally to her becoming a regular customer at the Evolution shop in Birmingham, one of the flagship initiatives that the FWBO was running in the area, which sourced products with careful attention to the processes by which they were made. Having got to know several of the dharmacharis, the ordained members, Fuengsin enlisted their support in her teaching over several years: Dh. Satyapala and Dh. Vimalvajra were her resource persons in 1987 and 1991 respectively, joining others from Zen, Theravada and Tibetan traditions.

Fuengsin also wanted to meet people from non-Buddhist backgrounds who embodied a bold spiritual outlook and her resolution yielded many interesting seekers. Among her colleagues at Harborne Hall was Ada Margaret Pask, who was Birmingham born and bred, had made her career in the print industry, and now lived semi-retired in a flat in Erdington. Fuengsin referred to her as 'Senior Ada' because she knew another Ada, of Irish origin and younger in years who also worked at the centre. Senior Ada was a member of the National Federation of Spiritual Healers and had psychic abilities; she had visions both of the past and of the future, and she perceived different realms of beings living in parallel, sharing space, but unseen to the physical eye. Meditation was part of her daily routine and she recollected a time long ago that she had spent in deeper practice in solitary meditation in a hut. She and Fuengsin got on very well, talking not just about the sublime and ethereal, but also about struggles in daily life in which they would deal with troublesome mundane matters and difficult personalities. Fuengsin never found it easy to make her way despite her qualifications and apparent confidence in her professional teaching. She knew Senior Ada had special attributes and was trustworthy, so allowed her to become a confidante.

There were also other kinds of works, which were less magical, yet still attracted Fuengsin's curiosity. In 1988 Fuengsin made a trip to Hudson's book shop in Birmingham and made her way to the information desk. She asked where she might find a copy of a certain novel by Salman Rushdie. The counter assistant stared at her, perhaps wondering whether she should get ready to set off the fire alarm, but said nothing. She merely pointed her finger downstairs. Fuengsin eventually found a copy, but was underwhelmed and left it on the shelf.

Staff at the Multi-Faith Centre sought to discover new ways to cooperate, especially in situations where interfaith relations were either non-existent or actively hostile, always insisting on *education by encounter*. This led to courses on topical issues such as 'How Green is My Dragon?' which ran for 10 weeks. It raised awareness of environmental concerns. Fuengsin was sympathetic to the eco-activists and joined Friends of the Earth in Stourbridge. A few days after Paul had moved to Glasgow, Fuengsin wrote about a meeting she attended which featured the rainforests of Southeast Asia. Fuengsin was interested to hear how they interpreted the situation and was ready to give her own views.

Last Tuesday evening I went to the Rain forest talk by a Friends of the Earth member. He was very good + the slides were impressive. I gave my view + put a man's opinion right as he said that the people who cut the trees down were poor + wanted only to survive. I said that it was not always economic[s] since the ethnic minorities in Burma, e.g. the Karens, Mons wanted to fight their government. So they gave concession to the Thais to cut their trees in order to get some money to buy weapons. It is politic[s]. The man agreed . . .

She was well engaged that evening as she conversed with both the speaker and the man who had made the comments, establishing further connections and interest in meditation.

Later I talked privately to the speaker about the Japanese who were Buddhists who would not even cut flowers because a lot of them were Zen. I really could not understand why they destroyed the world's environment like that. Later that man whom I contradicted earlier came to introduce himself to me saying that he was a Buddhist and meditates every day. He also went to Vajira's for a few years. He was delighted to meet me + wanted me to start a meditation group here. A lady who went with him that evening was also a meditator. They belonged to Stourbridge Friends of the Earth. The man talked a long time to me. I am trying to find a venue.

Fuengsin was probably referring here to Edward Davies, who lived in Stour-bridge and was also a member of Friends of the Earth. He joined the ranks of resource people at the Multi-Faith Centre, and contributed the following year to the Buddhism module.

The Centre also hosted gatherings at the weekend, including workshops on popular religious figures from various continents, such as Antony de Mello, an Indian Jesuit priest and psychotherapist. Among the participants was Bishop Patrick Kalilombe, a popular character who eagerly promoted his goal of 'Black and White together', becoming Director of the Ecumenical Centre for Black and White Christian Partnership at Selly Oak. Occasionally Fuengsin used her language skills: among some French speaking delegates she found herself having a conversation with the Archbishop of Monaco (she wasn't afraid to name-drop afterwards). Fuengsin readily accepted everybody of faith as she firmly believed that every religion had something good to offer. However, diverse gatherings like these didn't always achieve a degree of harmony: on one occasion the assembled group found little in common and couldn't seem to get beyond this sticking point. Fuengsin then intervened and suggested that everyone bring their holy books and find the teaching on not taking life — every religion had such a teaching. From this point of commonality, dialogue could begin and easily extend to other teachings.

The services of the Centre were now increasingly in demand from public sector organisations, notably in multi-ethnic urban areas. This was often where differences came to the fore and the sense of the shared was diminished or even lacking through the lack of communication. In summer Fuengsin contributed to a Race and Culture Awareness course run by the South Birmingham Health Authority at the Nursing Staff Development Unit, Selly Oak Hospital. She had an opportunity to present considerations for treating Buddhists, including aspects such as diet, which was not generally an issue for Fuengsin as she would eat most things, but she knew that many Buddhists are vegetarians; culturally, Fuengsin's Thai background meant she was not comfortable in mixed wards, but by and large the requirements for lay people were not burdensome; there were more constraints when treating monastics, who had to maintain a strong discipline. Afterwards she received a letter from Alison Coates the Staff Development Officer on behalf of the Unit in which she wrote that Fuengsin's talk had been 'well received and evaluated well'.

Similarly, international connections were being established with associated groups in municipal centres abroad, including Washington DC and Melbourne, Australia, all of whom faced similar issues in the public sector. The Centre also sent representatives to participate in high-profile conferences such as the 27th Congress of the International Association for Religious Freedom (IARF) in Hamburg, 1990, in which Elnora Ferguson, the Chairman of the Centre at the time, and Sister Mary, Executive Director, gave a paper in response to an exposition on dialogue by Eshin Nishimura, a Japanese Rinzai Zen priest and Professor of Buddhist Studies at Hanazono University in Kyoto. The message of the congress, which received strong support from the Centre, was that a strong conviction for one's faith does not preclude an outlook that is oriented to dialogue.

The Centre also actively promoted research, organising and hosting an annual international conference workshop. It ran for 10 days that summer and the theme for 1990 was 'What happens to Dialogue in Dialogue?' One of the presenters was Dr Alan Keightley, who was a philosopher of religion who had gravitated towards the East for quite some while. He had authored a few books, proceeding from 'Wittgenstein, Grammar and God' that developed out of doctoral research in 1970s at Birmingham University. His later work aspired to an Oriental outlook and resulted in a book with the flowing title, '*Into Every Life a Little Zen Must Fall*'.

Dr Keightley became increasingly interested in the Buddhist non-conceptual view and practice, so that when he was appointed as head of religious studies at King Edward VI College in Stourbridge, he sought to share this radical approach with his Sixth Form students. He even published on this theme in academic journals, offering his colleagues ways of introducing 'non-ideas' into teaching.[1] It seemed he was really trying to break free of the conditioning and clinging he perceived in contemporary Christian belief. It was no surprise then that when he met Fuengsin there was a spark; learning that she lived in Hagley and could teach meditation, he attended some of her sessions and kept in touch. On 9 February, Fuengsin wrote to Paul about Dr Keightley's proposal to teach religious studies classes at King Edward's in Stourbridge.

> Dr A. Kiethley [Keightley] at King Edwards, Stourbridge wanted me to teach meditation there next [academic] year. He is very pleased with my performance. Next month there will be 17 students to attend the class. There are at least 40 students who are waiting to learn to meditate. As they are not free at the same time, they have to take turn. Most are girls, though.

Fuengsin agreed and started her preparations for the autumn term. She decided to teach them the Dhammakaya method, encouraged by Luang Na San's endorsement. She wondered how best to guide them and decided that she needed a visual aid for the meditation object; but where apart from a temple might she find something? One day whilst shopping along the High Street in Stourbridge, she popped into Mark and Moody, a well-known general purpose store with a long history in publishing. Among the various knick-knacks she found a small transparent crystal ball about an inch in diameter, roughly the size of an eyeball. It was just what she was looking for and she returned home very pleased and showed off the acquisition to Paul.

As Stourbridge is only three miles from Hagley, almost on the doorstep, Fuengsin was glad to have the prospect of daytime work so close by. She proceeded to teach meditation and Buddhism to dozens of students, with about two dozen in a class one term and a similar number the following term. To illustrate impermanence, she bought from Evolution another prop: a paper skeleton, several feet long, made up of multiple cards, which could be suspended like a Christmas decoration.

In contrast it was bitterly cold outside and caused severe problems in her body. In the same letter she wrote:

> It is warmer today and a lot of people are about. I have not been to work since last Monday night when I had temperature and the pain was intense. I cancelled a lot of lectures + other work. Today I felt better though the pain is still there. Today also we are supposed to visit the temple but a lot of students will be missing. So it is also cancelled. Dad swept the drive for us + for Miss Edi [Eadie] as well. I am lazy and do not do very much. Judith's father, Steve, has just come back from Italy + the snow there was heavy too. There is nowhere we can escape to except the East.

Despite the early freeze, 1991 was especially busy for Fuengsin and the Centre as it brought the 10th anniversary. Sister Mary reflected on achievements in an article for The Harborne Society News entitled 'The Multi-Faith Centre at Harborne Hall', complete with a photograph of the entrance by John Pratt.[2] Never one to waste an opportunity, she ended by saying: 'The Multi-Faith Centre hopes that its friends, old and new, will help it continue its work to change attitudes and build a cohesive multicultural society where people live in peace.' To demonstrate the Centre's commitment to the local community, the Centre joined in the centenary celebrations of Harborne village, with a Victorian Garden Party for the public and an exhibition of the Centre's history and the Hall's history. It received formal recognition in December, when it was visited by the Lord Mayor of Birmingham (William Henry Turner). Fuengsin also met and chatted with him beforehand at the New Clergy Reception at The Council House.

Other special events included an art exhibition by local artists and students at Birmingham Polytechnic's Institute of Art and Design. It was during this heightened period of activity that Fuengsin's project of arranging for a life-size Buddha image to be commissioned and brought over from Thailand to the Centre bore fruit. Arrangements were eventually made with Wat Sanghathan, and the new Buddha rupa was eventually installed at the entrance to the

Multi-Faith Centre in 1991, bestowing a serene and benevolent presence for all who wandered through.

Fuengsin also wanted to keep in touch with people who had moved on. In a letter of 10 March 1991 she wrote:

> I hope to visit S. Ireland after Easter. Dad will find out about the fare for me. Ada may visit us again soon + I will write to her. She sent me a card on St. Patrick day. I miss her very much + the office is not the same since she left

> Other activities that had grown out of the Centre continued to progress . . .

> I am relief that the Certificate course is finished. It is much better not to teach at night. The class at King Edward Stourbridge is going well as there are 17 students meditating. Many more want to do it but they are not free at that time. Dr Kiethley invited [me] to teach there again next year. He also wrote a book about Witkensteine (wrong spelling). It is translated into Japanese + Dutch. He will give me a talk about the philosopher.

Fuengsin's workload continued to grow, so much so that on one occasion she wrote:

> I have been so busy that I lost my "awareness". This morning, I went to King Edwards [Stourbridge] + was an hour late. I got mixed up + thought that it was the first lesson. I felt awful about it. Dr Kiethley was very kind and patient with me — This week I will have 3 more sessions there, Wednesday + Thursday for Buddhism + Taoism, a special week. I will also get pay as well.

In general, though, it was a happy burden and her teaching never becoming too intense or serious. She would humour her audiences with reference to contemporary characters: for example, she would advise them to practise mindfulness or else they would be stumbling along like Mr Blobby![3]

Fuengsin's involvement at the Selly Oak Colleges was also burgeoning and over time connections continued to be established between her home and workplace. Among the participants was Alfred Crabtree, who studied at the College of Ascension, and remarked:

> She put across a message and she had this sort of joyous, bubbly attitude. At the same time people recognised her for the depth of her spirituality. . . .

He also had a chance to meet some of Fuengsin's regular colleagues who also worked at the Centre including Ramona and Sharada Sugirtharajah, who was a lecturer in Hinduism. Among her missiology colleagues at Selly Oak was

Werner Ustorf, a scholar who carried out research into European missiology to distant lands. He was particularly interested to observe Fuengsin's response to certain animistic beliefs. Fresh from her experiences in Thailand, she did not hesitate to qualify the certain popular customs and traditions as 'superstition'.[4]

Meanwhile Alan Keightley was encouraging her to publish in academic journals, to help Fuengsin overcome her hesitancy as she thought she was not sufficiently qualified as a scholar. She had a book review published in *Journal of Beliefs & Values: Studies in Religion & Education*[5]. Fuengsin wrote to Paul saying she felt 'very flattered + embarrassed as some of them teach at Oxford, Bristol + other distinguished Institutions'.

The Unit's reputation as an authority on interfaith education continued to grow and demand for its programmes spread. The Centre began to draw increasing numbers of students from other countries, spanning America, Europe and Oceania, and developed formal contacts with a number of organisations around the world. The programmes succeeded in meeting the specific needs of particular groups that came to the Centre. It was a close-knit community and the staff became genuine partners and friends. However, whilst there was balance in the way teaching was distributed, Sister Mary took on too much of the day-to-day organisation by herself, including the finances. She did not avail herself of some offers of assistance from people, especially those experienced in financial planning and management. Many efforts were made to bring in extra revenue, some exploring the hiring out of Harborne Hall's premises for business courses. The need was becoming urgent as competition was increasing and demand for the Centre's expertise was falling — other organisations were adopting the methodologies, customising them to their own needs. However, Sister Mary was not persuaded of the appropriateness; sometimes she simply wouldn't turn up at meetings and nothing further could be done. Ironically, in some practical matters the executive in her title of Executive Director diminished her power to direct what she was most skilled at — the programmes. The organisation sometimes had a chaotic feel as a result.

Indeed, even during the anniversary year, not all had been sweetness and light. The underlying tensions continued to be fuelled by ongoing financial difficulties; against the generally depressed economic backdrop the organisation was not being run on sustainable lines. This was despite the considerable efforts of some very experienced and long-time supporters such as Tom McCready, a civil engineer by profession, who Fuengsin often praised for his excellent organisational support. Challenging the harmony were clashes of principles and personalities, including complaints about poor treatment. A few staff resigned, whilst some others continued reluctantly. On returning home, Fuengsin often reported the internal ups and downs alongside the formal dialogues; it was in itself a bit of a multicultural multifaith soap opera, but the Centre's value in many spheres of society was real and substantial and Fuengsin remained committed. She carried on with the work and studiously avoided the politics.

Among the students of the Certificate in World Religions were members of the Society of Jesus who were resident at Manresa House in Harborne. Several Jesuit novices came to undertake the Certificate in World Religions at Selly Oak Colleges, including Peter Tyler, Ian Coleman, Chris Bowles, Slavic from Poland and Colm. The Jesuit novices were all impressed by Fuengsin and invited her for lunch at the novitiate, to which she agreed. Fuengsin wanted to know more about Western thought and the novices were keen to learn more about Eastern views of mind. So they came to an agreement whereby Peter would teach Fuengsin Western Philosophy and Fuengsin would teach several of them Buddhist 'Philosophy'.

In the subsequent meetings Fuengsin was taught about Descartes, Locke, Berkeley, and Hulme. She was also introduced by Peter to the ideas of Wittgenstein, with which she found some particular resonance. Coincidentally, he had been educated at King Edward VI College, which brought up a connection with Dr Keightley, who had published on Wittgenstein — 'trendy views' according to Peter. In return she would explore Buddhist concepts such as the three marks of existence: *anicca* (impermanence), *dukkha* (unsatisfactoriness), and *anatta* (not-self). She knew her audience was highly educated, so she would indicate that it was easy to gain intellectual understanding, but realisation was a different matter. She drew on imagery, particularly the lotus, which is replete with meaning of practice in the Buddhist context.

> As the flower of a lotus,
> Arisen in water, blossoms,
> Pure-scented and pleasing the mind,
> Yet is not drenched by the water,
> In the same way, born in the world,
> The Buddha abides in the world;
> And like the lotus by water,
> He does not get drenched by the world.[6]

Fuengsin followed a traditional interpretation that contrasted the unopened lotus bud of one stuck in the mud of ignorance and defilements with the fully opened bud above the water, like the fully Enlightened, unblemished in conduct, with various stages in between. The image was appreciated and led to jokes and some mischievous speculation about states of attainment among members of various religious orders.

Fuengsin also taught meditation at Manresa House. She would arrive about an hour early and make her way to the chapel upstairs, which had a beautiful view, the effect magnified by the emptiness of the room. She would then meditate for an hour before meeting the novices, who would sometimes join her to meditate together in the chapel. Fuengsin led the meditation, starting with relaxation of the body, focusing on the breath.

To this standard practice Fuengsin added a few choice words: 'Dispel all bad thoughts from mind — like British Rail or Bull Ring shopping centre!' Fuengsin regarded these as quintessential English examples for she had already re-marked in a Dhamma talk: 'It's very easy for English people to understand the truth of *dukkha* because you have British Rail!' As with her talks, she used humour to relax people for meditation and loved to crack jokes that were to the point. She hit the nail on the head about the unsatisfactoriness of these two fixtures in many a Brummie life: British Rail gradually became privatised in the mid-1990s, whilst the Bull Ring was redeveloped a few years later.

Fuengsin also met others at Manresa House. Greeting her at the entrance was Brother Bill Jordan and she would chat with him about practical aspects. She also had conversations with Father Gerard W. Hughes, who was impressed by her spirituality. He had been interested in the work of Fr Aloysius Pieris and his dialogue with Buddhism in Sri Lanka. Now was a chance for him to engage first hand with a Buddhist from a country that had close links with Sri Lanka. Fuengsin often enjoyed her lunches at Manresa House, meeting a variety of interesting characters, with varying degrees of openness. They were all polite and they never seemed to lack good catering.

She was later to latch on to the reputation for fine dining by arranging a meet-up with Peter for afternoon tea at Fortnum and Mason in Piccadilly. In the course of her teachings, Fuengsin gave Peter an inscribed copy of the Dhammapada, succinct verses encapsulating fundamental insights expressed by the Buddha, adding further Dhamma foundations. Afterwards, he left the Jesuits, but continued his explorations with Fuengsin and they became good friends. He stayed for a while in Liverpool with the L'Arche Community, an international federation that supports people with learning difficulties, where he started running the House of Prayer, in autumn 1991. Peter was reviewing his life at the time, so Fuengsin went to visit him one weekend in November, travelling there and back by train. Fuengsin knew that he was finding the transitional period tough and noticed that he had lost a lot of weight. As though to symbolise his fading away, Peter reported having seen a ghost at the end of his bed, peering at him. Fuengsin affirmed his vision and wrote about this to Paul, indicating that if she were to return and stay there she would practise *metta bhavana* (the cultivation of loving kindness) for that being.

Fuengsin had a very long conversation with Peter, in which he expressed serious interest in becoming a Buddhist. However, Fuengsin advised him: 'Best way for you to be Buddhist is to be a good Roman Catholic!' Peter was stunned because he expected her to have encouraged him to be a Buddhist, especially as he recognised there was a kind of missionary aspect to what she was doing. But it wasn't the kind of missionary activity with which most people are familiar; she wasn't going to force him to become 'a Buddhist'. After recovering his wits, he reflected that Fuengsin was right because everything he was looking for in Buddhism he began to find in the Christian mystical tradition, especially in the life and works of Teresa of Avila and John of the Cross, which led him to author and publish several books.

Fuengsin wrote to Paul about her visit, saying that she had a really good time and it ended all too soon. She enjoyed the varied dynamics of the environments in which she was circulating. In particular it suited her that there was no clinical separation between different Buddhist groups; practitioners in the Birmingham area had a comparatively broad exposure to different views. Hence the Multi-Faith Centre also ran weekly meditation sessions under the direction of Ven. Dr Rewata Dhamma at the Birmingham Buddhist Vihara, the practice being Shinay, traditionally a Tibetan practice, organised by Karma Ling. It was often in the context of meditation that Fuengsin continued meeting people, among her students and in the Birmingham multi-religious milieu. These included quite a few Catholic Sisters, of whom several were from St Paul's convent in nearby Selly Park; she noted their address and phone number on her copy of the timetable for the 45 and 47 buses, which ran along the Pershore Road.

Among other groups was the Buddha Light International Association, affiliated to Fo Kuang Shan temple in Taiwan. It was established in 1992 and Fuengsin was one of the first to be put on their mailing lists. Shortly afterwards the Buddhist Fat Yue Temple, a temple in the Chinese Ch'an tradition, was established in Amblecote, Stourbridge. The opening ceremony, which was televised, took place in 1994 and was attended by Vajira, who had a natural association as a practitioner in the Soto Zen tradition and as a professional acupuncturist.[7]

* * *

In the midst of this plurality Fuengsin kept sight of being a representative of the Theravada tradition. In 1988, the year that her family was in Thailand, two Thai monks arrived in the UK and founded a Thai temple initially in Perry Barr, a suburb of Birmingham. They named it Wat Sanghathan after their main temple in Thailand. It was set up in response to requests from the Thai community, which by this time had grown enough to be able to provide the necessary support to maintain the property and look after the monastics, who in accordance with their training could not earn a wage. Fuengsin herself had a few Thai friends such as Khun Kai, Khun Preecha and Khun Supawan, all of whom married Englishmen and maintained a wish to contribute to the maintenance of the Thai Buddhist tradition. It was through this organisation that Fuengsin was finally able to realize the objective of sourcing a Buddha rūpa for the Multi-Faith Centre.

The abbot of the main temple was Ven. Ajahn Sanong Katapunyo, who came from Suphanburi Province. Before he had reached adulthood his father had been ordained and his mother urged him to follow his example, to which he willingly agreed. Under the instruction of the Most Ven. Sangwahn Khemmako Mahathera, Luang Phor Sanong trained hard in his *kuti* for a period of three years at Wat Nong Pai in Suphanburi. During this time he remained silent and stayed put; only his teacher came occasionally to check progress every few months. His practice was earnest, being of the Thai Forest Tradition characterised by ascetic discipline — he intensified his meditation practice for 18 years by not lying down to sleep, but maintaining a sitting posture instead.

In the 1970s, on the advice of Luang Phoo Song Brahmassaro at Wat Arevut in Bangkok, he took up residence in an old, abandoned temple which had a large sacred Buddha image in the Bang Pai Sub-District of Nonthaburi Province. It was chosen for its suitability for meditation. Coincidentally, it was only about two miles away from Wat Bot Bon Bangkuwien, where several decades earlier Luang Phor Sodh had made a breakthrough in his meditation, leading to the (re-)discovery of the Dhammakaya tradition. Luang Phor Sanong settled and his temple, Wat Sanghathan, became well established and active in fostering the Dhamma all over Thailand, with teachings broadcast on their own radio station.[8]

The arrival of the two monks in the UK was thus a natural extension of this mission and they soon realised that many British people were interested as well. However, their materials were almost all in Thai, they had very little they could share. Into the scene arrived Fuengsin who offered to assist with some translations. It was decided to make available a translation of a booklet of basic teachings of Luang Phor Sanong, suitable for the general public. As with all such publications, these would be prepared entirely through voluntary effort and distributed free of charge, one of the many expressions of *dana* that is promoted by the Thai Buddhist community. As a devout Thai practitioner Fuengsin was well aware that it is said in the Dhammapada, a famous treasury of sayings, that the gift of Dhamma exceeds all other gifts.

Whilst Fuengsin could understand the teachings well, she wasn't confident about producing polished English, so she sought editorial assistance. Fortunately, she did not have to look far as Alfred and Elsie had a son, Andrew, who was staying with them at that time. Later on she received assistance from Simon Romer at Karma Ling. The booklet was given the English title of *The Taste of Dhamma* and it comprised about 30 short chapters, often only a few short paragraphs long, more like a book of verse. The content was devoted to meditation and mind training, starting with a brief overview of *anapanasati* (mindfulness of breathing). The book was published by the temple in May 1991 and printed using its own facilities. Whilst not as sophisticated as Windhorse, they could easily run off 1,000–2,000 copies and distribute them through the temples and supporters.[9]

Fuengsin also introduced some residents in Hagley to meditation, but always on request; whereas talking about Thailand was readily accepted, introducing this kind of inner practice was for many something too strange. Alfred had tried to persuade members of the Hagley Free Church to explore meditation and contemplation, and to enter deeper into God, but he met with resistance. He expressed some discontent to Fuengsin: 'And that comment in the Bible where it says a peace beyond all understanding and you feel it and yet the Church doesn't teach it.'

So Fuengsin had a strong impetus to show the way and started a meditation group in Hagley in autumn 1990. She wrote to Paul about the first meeting, on 29 October in Ferndale Close, which was to be one of several venues as members took it in turns to be host. She remarked that five women attended and they found it extremely difficult to sit still. Within a few months the group expanded and on 9 February 1991 she wrote:

> The group in the village is stable — at least 9 people. More people want to come — even from Pedmore. We have to hire a hall soon. Also the midday group at Harborne Hall is doing well as students from Woodbrooke came to join us. An Australian girl with a Yorkshire man came + enjoyed it.

Later, Paul joined in on one occasion. He didn't often meditate with his mother because of his Catholic upbringing, but once he went to university he started to become more interested. By then the group had dwindled in size to about four or five, but one person who tried hard to maintain a regular practice was Mrs Mollie Pauli, a lady who had special sensitivity to the natural environment, perceiving that different buildings radiate energies on different wavelengths; she remarked that some older buildings, such as those in Oxford colleges, radiate a tranquillity that is lacking in many new buildings.

Everybody knew how to meditate, so Fuengsin didn't spend much time with the introduction; she merely indicated the clock on the mantelpiece and suggested that the group should sit for about half an hour. Then the practice began, but after five minutes Fuengsin said, 'Now it is time to finish.' She was greeted with perplexed expressions, so she glanced again at the clock and was surprised to find that the minute hand had hardly advanced; she was convinced they had used the allotted time as she had such a deep experience, being 'soaked with bliss'. Her access was so quick that she had, as it were, greatly extended organic time in very little clock time.

Whatever time Fuengsin had, she used purposefully, in matters spiritual and mundane. A few hundred yards along the Bristol Road, just over the brow of a hill, heading into Birmingham's city centre, was Pranee's Thai restaurant, a new business which was doing well in catering for the growing appetite of British households for Far Eastern dishes. Being from Krabi, Pranee and Preeya specialised in Thai cuisine from the south, which had a reputation for being especially spicy. Like Fuengsin they had excellent cooks in the family; Preeya's matron at school was Khunyai Jieb, a famous chef who used to cook for royalty.

With fresh ingredients from Wing Yip, now well-established as a reliable supplier from the Orient, they could get all their supplies first thing in the morning. They generally served only in the evenings and then it was action stations: onto the large stoves in the kitchen were placed huge woks and within a few minutes the irresistible flavours of Thai cuisine were sparkling and sizzling in chilli, garlic and fish sauce, and then whisked straight onto plates and the tables of guests. Using everyday vegetables such as carrots Preeya was able to carve vegetables in the shape of butterflies, flowers and leaves, sculpting intricate decorations to adorn the plates, so that meals were visual as well as gustatory treats. Preeya made it look simple, but few were able to emulate her as it required special skill: the consistent application of the right amount of pressure in the right place.

Oriental restaurants are family businesses. Among those who helped out over the years at Pranee's were their sister, Khun Eig, and a niece and nephew, who came to the UK to receive the benefits of a British education, whilst still maintaining their Thai culture. However, whilst the restaurant delighted most of their clientele, it was hard work and difficult to find good Thai staff because of the difficulty of obtaining visas. After a while, Pranee consulted with Fuengsin about the possibility of producing a cookery book — they both had the necessary knowledge and Fuengsin was gifted at writing. By the mid-1980s a demand for Thai food prepared in people's homes was clearly emerging. Yet it was still regarded as unusual and exotic, so there were few books available. Here then was a great opportunity to share authentic recipes and perhaps create a business from it. Furthermore, Fuengsin would make it a unique offering by peppering the prose with stories from her childhood (many of which have been included in this biography).

The idea seemed a winner, but neither Pranee nor Fuengsin were familiar with the publication process. Fortunately, Fuengsin found among her many connections in Selly Oak a colleague who was willing to offer editorial assistance. Margaret Breiner, who was originally from Canada, worked at Westhill College's RE Centre and had acquired a taste of the Orient after living in Malaysia for a while. In her professional work she had edited a number of publications, including Hinduism resources such as the *Hindus Photopack* prepared with Sharada Sugirtharajah (Westhill Project RE 5–16). Equipped with a desktop computer with word processor software on which to prepare and edit documents, she kindly agreed to offer her services.

And so they proceeded to prepare dozens of recipes and Fuengsin started jotting down stories. The layout was generally conventional and followed the sequence of preparation; it was fairly comprehensive and left little to chance. After an introductory section just on rice, the next section was devoted to curry pastes. Recipes were grouped under about 10 categories, ranging from starters and soups through to noodles and desserts. These were followed by the stories, arranged under topic headings such as 'Food for free' and 'Hot, hot!' Margaret worked her way through the text, applying her editorial eye, making sure that it all made sense. Occasionally it didn't and she'd point this out by inserting comments such as 'Fuengsin — this story doesn't fit under the topic.'

It took years to compile; only in summer of 1992 did Fuengsin declare that the final draft of the book had been completed, much to her relief. At last they had reached the point of approaching potential publishers, but Fuengsin was doubtful that it could make it to print: 'I think it may be difficult to get it published because of the present economic climate.' Margaret was more optimistic and used her connections and knowledge of the industry to draw up a list of about 30 suitable candidates. Among them was the BBC, who had already scored a big hit with Ken Hom's Chinese cookery. Discussions were held, even going as far as considering the format for television presentation in the nearby Pebble Mill studios. However, after getting tantalisingly close the talks foundered and the project went on the back burner; the book never made it to print. Fortunately, the recipes were at least kept on disk and permission was later given to a few people to distribute them.

Inadvertently, the restaurant was a very useful source of recruitment, as quite a few of the clientele asked about Thai language studies. Having taught the Buddhism module for several years, Fuengsin could devote more time to her other activities outside her scheduled teaching, so in autumn she responded to the growing demand by offering evening classes in Thai language. This was billed as a course of 10 lessons in conversational Thai for beginners, providing a basic introduction to the language and culture. Fuengsin soon had quite a number of students as news about the course spread through various connections and there were very few opportunities elsewhere. The Brasshouse

Language Centre, part of an Adult Education Centre run by Birmingham City Council, did not offer Thai so Fuengsin had a captive market. Noting that the students were invariably male, she remarked, 'I think, in a previous life I was an army officer in charge of a regiment of soldiers!'

Fuengsin was in her element teaching Thai and soon had her students acquainted with the basic structure, phonetics and the five tone groups. She gave them some drill practice in which they had to repeat the alphabet and practise the intonation; and through repetition they soon became familiar with simple phrases. She chose examples from typical daily life, covering the basics such as checking into hotels, navigating around streets and shopping, through to travelling up country and seeking out hill tribes. Example after example would flow forth as she drew on her own varied background with observations about the different ethnicities, including memories of her childhood spent playing with Chinese neighbours. Whilst this wasn't a formal course, Fuengsin inserted linguistic references, understanding especially the origins of assorted dishes such as the Cantonese *chow mein* and Hokkien *gwytieow* (stir-fried and watery noodles respectively). She also contrasted the way the Thais adopted foreign terms and how they sounded compared with neighbouring countries in the region. In this way the teaching was immersive and provided a vivid picture of what the prospective visitors could expect.

Fig. 90: *Krob Krua* — the immediate family.
Illustrated in English and romanised Thai
(from Fuengsin's papers — unknown artist, probably a student).

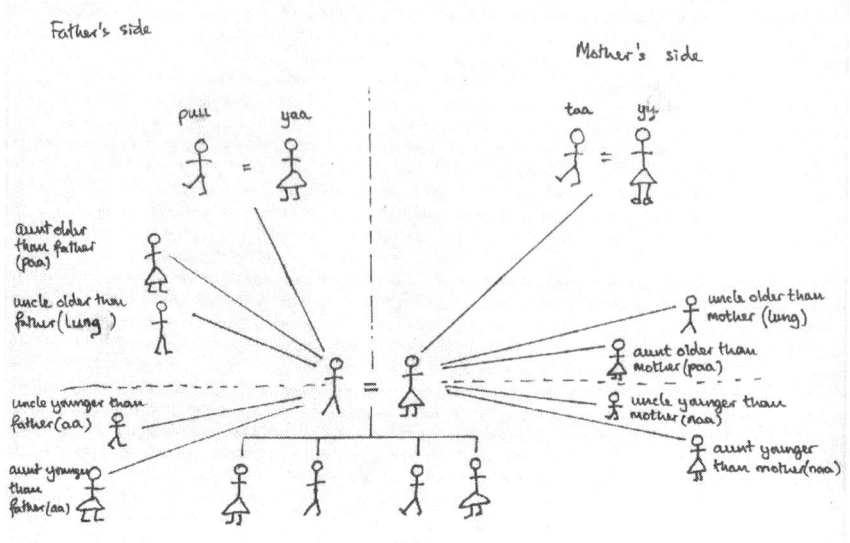

Fig. 91: *Krob Krua* — the extended family.
Illustrated with English and romanised Thai (from Fuengsin's papers —
unknown artist, probably a student).

Fuengsin made sure they also learnt some Thai etiquette — for personal conduct was an important aspect, it wasn't just about the words. She was keen that students were engaged and was very attentive to their responses, whether to affirm or correct; she was delighted whenever they showed initiative and was often prone to laughter. Fuengsin generally enjoyed getting to know her students and could remember them all, identifying them in a simple way either by numbers as in 'Martin' and 'Martin (2)' or by their profession, hence 'Malcolm the Scientist' and 'Malcolm the Photographer'. There was no selection process as she accepted anyone who turned up, but she found some of the less able students hard work and required 1-to-1 instruction.

> My new Thai language student is certainly not intellectual. He came without a
> pen or paper + expect to learn by parrot-fashion only. Anyway, he begins to
> improve + works hard. I teach him once a week on Wednesday.

Fuengsin was interested in their varied trades and backgrounds and what had prompted their interest in Thailand; some were highly qualified and keen to explore the traditional cultures in remote areas. However, after a while Fuengsin saw a depressing pattern to what some other students shared. In one of her first letters to Paul in Glasgow, on 6 October 1990, she wrote:

Last Wednesday, an English man (about 50 years old) met me at Pui's [Pranee's] and asked me to translate his love letter to a young Thai woman whom he met in Pataya. She was a prostitute there, he told me. He wanted to marry her + adopt her 2 sons. I translated his letter + gave it to him next day + I charged him £15 as it took me 2 hours altogether. He is going to Thailand in a few days.

About a month later she wrote on the same theme:

I finished translation of a love letter last night. I met the man . . . where he was working . . . I gave him a lecture about Thai women because he had a very naïve view about us. He seemed to pay attention to me.

And again on 9 February, 1991, by which time Fuengsin was despairing, seeing some men succumbing to what she regarded as honey traps, in almost identical circumstances:

I also translated more love letters. An English man is going to Bankok on 17th March to meet his Thai girl-friend. She was a prostitute in Pataya + had 2 children. I think he wants to marry her + bring her here. They only knew each other for two weeks. He is besotted by her. . . . Just hope that this woman does not spread Aids here.

In the same letter, from her experience as an interpreter, she gave evidence of the sad outcome that could happen to such couples later on:

I worked for the Probation Office last Monday + it was the same couple again. They still live in the same house but put it up for sale. They want either a joint custody of the little girl or just sole custody.

There was worse to come. A year later one of her students reported that his wife had committed suicide thinking that she could not join him here; he was crying on the phone when he told Fuengsin. The media got wind of the story and caused him further disturbance. Fuengsin felt really sorry for this poor man.

In the course of her teaching she got to know many Western men who had visited Thailand to seek Thai brides. Some had been heartbroken as their relationships broke up; quite a few had naively assumed that they had discovered 'true love' when in reality they were being manipulated. Fuengsin got to know the familiar patterns: initially the bride couldn't come because the visa would need to be arranged, so the husband would return to the UK, whilst the wife would stay behind. Then he would be asked for funds to support the family, more and more; and then the marriage would be broken off. Older men were especially vulnerable for in many cases when their new wives did come across they would pursue someone younger. With reluctance Fuengsin ended up translating quite a few letters from these hapless Englishmen to their wives, but was ashamed of their behaviour. So when Paul discovered a newspaper advertisement for a scheme promising Thai brides, Fuengsin expressed strong condemnation and urged Paul to report this to the local MP and Thai Embassy in London.

Nevertheless, these tragic cycles did not discourage Fuengsin from teaching, though she gradually devoted more attention to business people and others who had a serious intention to learn the language in greater depth. She had many teaching resources available, including some authoritative tomes such as *Fundamentals of the Thai Language* by Kumchai Thonglaw. However, she could see that a systematic course with a simpler hands-on approach was needed. With the encouragement of several of her friends, she started to plan a book, *Talk Thai!* It had two stated aims: to produce a sound but basic introduction to the Thai language which would be functional to the traveller, and to provide a basis for the learner wishing to gain a thorough knowledge of the Thai language. It consisted of written materials, with an accompanying cassette tape featuring a cast of four people: enter Mr and Mrs Smith and their two children, who were depicted finding their way around, ordering meals, shopping, exchanging money, having conversations with relatives, sending letters and having medical appointments.

Fuengsin produced all the written and audio content, recording the conversations with a simple microphone and the home stereo. As with the cookery book, it was close to completion, but the project stalled when one of her supporters pulled out because he became too busy. Another project was put to one side.

Notes

1. Dr Alan Keightley's radical Zen-inspired paper on teaching was *Teaching Buddhism in the Upper Secondary School Part I: Ideas for Introducing Non-Ideas.* In: *British Journal of Religious Education*, Volume 9, Issue 1, September 1986, pages 4-16.

2. Sister Mary's tenth anniversary article for The Harborne Society News was *The Multi Faith Centre at Harborne Hall*, Harborne Society News. Number Twenty-One, Summer 1991, pages 6-7:
   http://www.theharbornesociety.org.uk/uploads/3/9/5/2/39529175/1991.pdf

3. Mr. Blobby was a large clumsy pantomime-style character who first appeared alongside Noel Edmonds in one of his BBC TV shows around 1992.

4. Thai superstitions. Werner Ustorf mentions Fuengsin in his book *Robinson Crusoe Tries Again: Missiology and European Constructions of 'Self' and 'Other' in a Global World 1789-2010*, page 226 footnote 26.

5. Volume 12, Issue 2, 1991.

6. From a poem by the Elder Udayin and recorded in Thag 15.2: *Udayin Thera — The Blooming Lotus* (excerpt), translated by Olendzki, from the *Groups of Sixteen Verses*, Theragathas 673-704. Translation available from Access to Insight: http://www.accesstoinsight.org/tipitaka/kn/thag/thag.15.02.olen.html

7. Buddhist Fat Yue Temple was subsequently renamed the Fa Yue Buddhist Monastery in 1999 and moved to Cottage Street in Brierley Hill.

8. Luang Phor Sanong Katapunyo's biographical details were sourced from: https://sites.google.com/site/dhammawavenet3/71

9. *The Taste of Dhamma* by Ven. Ajahn Sanong Katapunyo may be accessed online at: http://fuengsin.org/translate/sanong/taste/

13

Transition to New Projects

Whilst Fuengsin was fully occupied with her literary and pedagogical pursuits, some concerns and questions were starting to surface relating to careers — her own and Paul's. It was to be a transitional period, a somewhat bumpy road, but with important indicators for the future. She was certainly keeping an eye on Paul's progress. The first few months in Glasgow had been quite comfortable, but afterwards as the days shortened and clouds gathered life became less smooth. In his studies he was finding the subject matter abstract and intangible; it wasn't quite what he had expected. Outside his studies he was struggling to make friends; as before he looked to international students, the first being Alireza, a pharmacology researcher from Iran whom he had met on his first visit to the city when looking for accommodation. However, whilst he found Glaswegians friendly for general chitchat, as a 'Sassenach' it seemed hard to get to know them.

Then in late January Paul received a letter from Susan Yau with the shocking news that her brother, David, had been knocked over by a bus and lost his life. Paul went back down to the West Midlands to attend the funeral a few days later in the Chinese section of Quinton cemetery. He did not dwell with David's family, but met up with other former classmates, Andy Killeen and Karl Pillage. After the service had finished, they reminisced over a drink, reflecting that David never had an ill word for anyone. Paul had wanted to continue the conversation, but couldn't stay long as he had to return to Glasgow.

He then fell ill as the weather deteriorated around the British Isles. Meanwhile his landlady, who had been widowed more than 10 years, had decided to get married again — at the age of 71. Paul needed to find somewhere else to stay, but not much was available because it was midterm. Fuengsin sent a letter on 9 February, asking him how he was and trying to encouraging him to persevere: 'Enjoy your youth + make the most of it. Try hard — get a qualification behind you.' However, his health continued to be poor, so Fuengsin tried again to reassure him in her next letter in March: 'Hope you will be stronger soon. The sun will shine + it will make all the difference in a few weeks.' After a while Paul found another place to live, in Church Street opposite the Western Infirmary, within easy walking distance of the University. It was a small flat comprising two bedsit rooms, a small shower room and kitchenette. His flatmate, a mature student who was attempting to complete a Law degree in 18 months, described it as a 'hovel' and spent as little time there as he could. Initially Paul wasn't concerned, but it didn't help his limited social life as he became ashamed to invite anyone there.

News from Hagley sometimes didn't sound any more salubrious. In May Fuengsin wrote:

> Hagley is becoming a seedy or rundown place. The other day, 3 glass windows at the railway station were smashed to pieces by drunken youths. These youngsters have too much money + drive good cars to school here.

Fortunately Fuengsin kept Paul informed about other more encouraging developments concerning work and family. She wrote about weddings (with a commentary on the guests, the food, and attentiveness of staff) and various journeys. If anyone had a connection with Southampton, she would briefly be lost in nostalgia. Paul's activities also provided some cheer as he enjoyed occasional mealtime gatherings with Alireza and his friends who shared a post-graduate self-catering apartment. They included a Burns Night supper and an outing in April to Ben Lomond with stunning views over the loch set against a clear blue sky and snow-topped mountains. He also found some encouragement at the Mathematics Department. He successfully gave his first seminar and was further motivated when he was joined by another research student, Etuka Onono, the two of them later dubbed the 'Number Theory twins'. His finances also received a boost as he earned some extra money tutoring first- and second-year engineering students in algebra and calculus, which he enjoyed doing — a little bit of self-sufficiency that Fuengsin approved of.

Perhaps of greater interest to Fuengsin was when Paul managed to complete a course of six weekly classes in Buddhism and meditation. It was held at the University and run by the FWBO. He subsequently visited their centre in Sauchiehall Street, where, in evening sessions, he continued with the regular practice of mindfulness of breathing and *metta bhavana* (the cultivation of loving kindness). As Windhorse Publications was based in Glasgow it served as the venue for some book launches, including *Facing Mount Kanchenjunga*, the second volume of the memoirs of Sangharakshita. Paul went along and bought a copy, and asked the author to dedicate it to Fuengsin. He also fostered a bit of dialogic reflection at the centre: one of the Order members made a habit of contrasting the meditation with Christian prayer, giving the impression that there was only petitionary prayer. Paul informed Fuengsin of this, saying that he showed him a newsletter from his parish quoting St John Chrysostom (Homily 6 on Prayer):

> As our bodily eyes are illuminated by seeing the light, so in contemplating God our soul is illuminated by him. Of course the prayer I have in mind is no matter of routine, it is deliberate and earnest. It is not tied down to a fixed timetable; rather it is a state which endures by night and day.

The point was taken, at least for a few weeks, as the Dharmachari chose his words more carefully in his introductions. Fuengsin would have known this quality of contemplative practice well through her various dialogues with the members of Christian orders she met in her work; when discussing with the nuns at St Paul's convent in Birmingham she had discovered many similarities.

Paul found the atmosphere at the Centre agreeable and enjoyed the meditation practice. There was also pleasant conversation, but there seemed to be only one person who offered more than token friendship outside of its communal spaces. This was a local middle-aged man who gladly shared insights into Glasgow life, but he proved to be problematic. He was a chatterbox who had difficulty dealing with changes in his family circumstances and seemed unable to get out of a rut. Paul ended up giving him extensive counselling, which involved listening to many hours of philosophical reflection and procrastination going into the wee small hours of the night. Effective action was much less forthcoming. Paul lacked his mother's experience in handling the situation in a canny way and it was draining him of energy and nullifying the benefit of his meditation practice. Eventually progress was made, but when Fuengsin spoke to him on the phone she often heard reports of his being ill and generally unsettled.

Feeling concerned, Fuengsin went to see Alfred Crabtree, seeking advice. Alfred was a member of the International Order of St Luke the Physician, whose members practise the laying on of hands for healing. On that occasion she was somewhat disturbed and not her normal self, so she asked him to lay hands on her, to which he agreed. He had laid hands on dozens of people, yet felt such serenity in Fuengsin that he had never felt in anybody else, prompting him to remark, 'She meditated peace in person'. It made him ponder how, with her meditation, she would not normally let things upset her, but here things were certainly getting her down and she couldn't put them to one side. How come then that he felt such peace? It was, he surmised, simply that Fuengsin was a mother reacting like all other mothers worrying about her son. Yet he remained puzzled at how Fuengsin showed no bitterness or anger when life was not going well in Scotland; she was just anxious.

They continued to exchange on these matters at different levels — physical and the more significant non-physical healings. Healing was closely related to the different ways of expressing love and compassion; 'gifts of the spirit' as Alfred would term them. Alfred would lay on hands on people, sometimes with only a mild response, at other times with remarkable results, especially in improved mobility. He took a down-to-earth view, where healing was not restricted to religious halls, but was practised in the street. He declared, 'People will lay hands on people and they will get well' and maintained, 'It isn't me who is the healer, it's God working through me who is the healer.' In this way Alfred described to Fuengsin how he would place his hands and then just leave them 'until the hands come away automatically'. He also applied his management consultancy shrewdness by scheduling healing sessions in such a way that he wouldn't be delayed so much that he'd miss the following appointment; he would, for example, plan sessions shortly before people were due to have meals. 'Really Christian attitude!' he joked. Such joviality would be accompanied by tea and cake, which Elsie usually arranged and Fuengsin found a particular treat. They would likely break off to chat about family matters and life in the village. Fuengsin felt very much at home and came to regard Alfred and Elsie like parents.

These sentiments about spiritual healing in everyday situations echoed what she had shared in the interview with Jill Skelling. She indicated that there were Buddhist parallels, though the practice and explanation would be different. For instance, monks might chant and the listener would share in the merits and thereby would make a faster recovery, but much more revolved around meditation and developing a healthy state of mind. Fuengsin described some of her own experiences and they both knew other people who had special gifts so they were brought into the discussions, which could be extended still further to include other cultures. Thus when Alfred mentioned the First Nations people of North American (so-called 'Red Indians') who revered nature and were sensitive to harming plants, Fuengsin could cite Mahayana practitioners, especially in Japan, and recounted experiments by one of her former meditation teachers, a Thai scientist who showed how plants are sensitive to the way they are treated. Alfred himself held a scientific outlook on the world and demonstrated a systematic approach in his spiritual investigations. He probed a great deal with questions as to why, but was open to mystery and incomplete explanations, leading him to explore many kinds of phenomena and practises (such as laying on of hands, dowsing and *feng shui*). Much of the conversation was concerned with wholeness and interrelatedness, a holistic spirituality. Alfred cited a range of studies, quite a number drawing on advances in psychiatry, including research by Stanislav Grof, particularly his work on consciousness, *The Holotropic Mind*.

Fuengsin greatly appreciated the support she received and in turn she carried on trying to encourage Paul in her letters. In August, she wrote: 'I hope you are feeling better and settle down. It is very difficult for you not to feel homesick as you had a very good time here.' Whilst Fuengsin tried to remain upbeat she didn't refrain from sharing unfortunate events. That same month, she informed him by letter:

Dear Paul . . . I must tell you this extremely sad news. Last Thursday at 11.00 pm, I was getting ready to bed when I heard a car break [brake] and crash. It was quite loud. I rushed to the front bedroom + looked through the window. Your father was at work. I saw 4 cars stopped — opposite us + there was glass everywhere, though none of the car hit any others. A young man got out of his Morris with both hands covering his face + was really shaking. A lot of people got out of their cars + rushed to the last car.

A man from the second house on the left came out + rushed back home to phone the police. So I went across to have a look + saw a body which was covered except the one arm, looked like a female. It was very still + I knew that the person was dead instantly because the car went over the body. Nobody knew who he or she was. The police + ambulance came + they took photograph + put it in a plastic container + left just before 1.00am. I offered the young man a cup of tea but he declined.

Today, Brenda rang me up + told me that the deceased was Miss Eadie!!! I could not believe it + was deeply shocked this morning. She was crossing the road — after visiting Ruth, the old lady near us. The young man was from Malvern + was driving back when it happened. This evening, I went to see her cousin + we talked for 1 hour. She is still very shocked.

So I just let you know + hope you will not be too sad.

Fuengsin ended by reflecting on the reality of the situation, and what could still be done to help:

It was her karma with the young man to meet him at a certain place + time. As she was a very good + kind lady, she will take rebirth in a better realm. So please meditate and pray for her.

Paul moved again in autumn and the subsequent accommodation in Hillhead Street was better, far more spacious and even closer to the office. This time the landlady was Miss Macaulay, who had retired from running a nursing home. Its décor was distinctive, in fact rather eccentric: it was full of brass acquired over many years from the Barras, a very popular market in Glasgow's East End; it had wall-to-wall tartan carpets accompanied by matching curtains and even a teddy bear sported a tartan tie. In addition there were chandeliers, stags' heads and a Latin motto to crown the effect: *dulce periculum est* ('danger is sweet'). Yet, the landlady was not fearsome and compared with his previous residence, Paul found this relatively luxurious. With the extra space he invested in some second-hand computer equipment, including a printer, which was good enough for writing up his research. It also enabled him to start writing a few programs to support his research — an activity in which his supervisor was curious only about the results, as he generally left his office computer unplugged and contented himself with pen and paper. Miss Macaulay later let another room, which was taken by a medical student, Martin. It turned out that he knew Peter Tyler from volunteer work at L'Arche.

Paul returned to Hagley for the Christmas break and whilst there Fuengsin received a New Year card from a friend and put it on the mantelpiece. It depicted a monk, seated cross-legged, and gazing afar. Paul did not recognise the monk, but the figure appeared to him in three dimensions and he felt some connection. So he enquired, 'Who is this monk?' Fuengsin replied, 'Luang Phor Wat Paknam' and proceeded to explain that he was the one who discovered dhammakaya meditation in Thailand and that her teacher, Ajahn Gaew, was one of his disciples. He then told her that he connected this with a question he had recently been earnestly pondering, 'Why am I here?' Soon he made up his mind to finish his studies, much to his mother's relief. Although his supervisor was satisfied with his progress towards a doctorate, he would write up what he had and submit it for a Master's. It would not be the pinnacle of achievement, but all being well with just a *viva* to come there would be at least something to show for his efforts.

Meanwhile Fuengsin was engaging in much writing of her own. *The Taste of Dhamma* was well received so in January 1992 Luang Phor Sanong asked Fuengsin to help out with a further translation of a more in-depth meditation guide with lengthier explanations and a glossary of Thai and Pali terms. Fuengsin was prompted to search for more Thai–English dictionaries until she found some huge volumes in Foyles bookshop in Charing Cross Road, London. She also had delivered a complete set of the Thai version of the Tipiṭaka, whose bulk weighed down a couple of large shelves. Just to make sure she didn't get the wrong end of the stick she consulted further with others, especially with Simon Romer.

She commented in a letter to Paul:

> It is very difficult work but really worthwhile. The rest of the time I read Thai scriptures and become more learned and meditation helps me to understand them much better. I now know a lot about the Buddha's environment, teaching + climate of India + the way of life in the 6C B.C. It was very interesting period. The vast knowledge of the Buddha + his disciples astonished me.

Fuengsin faced obstacles, many of them health-related, though within these constraints she was anxious to apply herself effectively. In April she started to suffer from hay fever and it continued for three months, hampering her efforts. Her other work for the police, Immigration and various colleges consumed most of her energy, yet by her own admission she sometimes used the hay fever as an excuse to get up late. As a result, the translation was neglected and she developed feelings of guilt especially when she considered that Tony worked many kinds of shifts, often getting up at dawn, and he was sometimes on call during the whole night. He occasionally admitted to tiredness, but he didn't complain. So she increased her resolve and got up earlier to spend at least 2 hours every morning on the translation and continued with further sessions during the day and evening.

However, more intractable were organisational health issues, with longer-term implications that would prove insoluble. By the early '90s the Multi-Faith Centre had established many international links, but it still had not addressed serious financial problems at home. In a letter to Paul dated 13 March 1992 Fuengsin wrote of an irrevocable consequence:

> Yesterday I heard a very bad news that Harborne Hall is to be closed down. The Conference Centre will be closed within a fortnight but the Multi Faith Centre can remain there till September. We cannot make ends meet there as recession hits us hard. Sister Mary is broken hearted. The nuns will take over the place soon. Last week, a computer was stolen from the reception room when somebody broke in. Unfortunately there was no copy at all + we lost all the records.[1]

The period saw quite a lot of unsettling news, but the clouds had some silver linings. Paul submitted his thesis in May 1992 and promptly returned to Hagley. Whilst it meant he now had no source of income, Fuengsin was glad to see him safe and sound. He brought with him his computer and printer and helped her with typing and also taught her the basics in how to use the equipment, which she very much appreciated. She was soon generating articles and letters.

Fuengsin also gained impetus from seeing Simon Romer at Karma Ling, who would spend one or two hours with her going through what she had written for Luang Phor Sanong and correcting her English. It was just as well as Fuengsin accumulated other tasks — she knew they could be viewed as ways of meritorious action, but she didn't always relish the prospect. Given her knowledge of life in Britain the monks at Wat Sanghathan expressed their gratitude by conferring further opportunities to help, which Thais feel obliged to accept. In June the monastics needed to deal with the Home Office immigration department to invite another monk, Phra Pibul Kantasilo, to come across to the UK. So Fuengsin assisted by answering a raft of questions from the Home Office, one by one. Aware of the different mindsets and not wanting to leave the situation to chance, she went out of her way to make it as clear as possible: on her copy of the letter Fuengsin pencilled responses in English to each question, and highlighted in blue ink three of them, with some explanations in Thai. She then typed up a letter for the monks to send before resuming the translation work.

By the end of July she had completed almost all the chapters and could see: 'The end is in sight. I still have to soldier on to complete the whole book.' The process was also extended when Luang Phor Sanong occasionally visited Birmingham; whilst there he sometimes would make changes to the texts, trying to improve them. For Fuengsin this added further to the translation work, but she dutifully persevered and eventually the final version was settled and *Oneness* was published, with the front cover adorned by a close-up photograph of a lotus bud.[2] The effort was worthwhile as readers really appreciated the insights and, being compact, copies would end up in people's bedside drawers. Fuengsin was delighted to hear one reader admitting that they even hugged the book because it was so helpful.

Despite the uncertainties at the Multi-Faith Centre, Fuengsin continued to make connections. The monks were very grateful for her help and were happy to receive visits from Fuengsin's regular interfaith contingent. In addition, the colleges arranged for visits by students from places other than Birmingham, including religious studies students from Bath College, secondary schoolteachers from Rotherham LEA, and teachers from Sweden. On one occasion they had the opportunity to ask questions directly of Luang Phor. He received queries about the practice and development of Buddhism in Thailand and answered in simple terms, maintaining a calm expression, until he suddenly smiled and seemed somewhat surprised when one person asked whether he was Enlightened. To this enquirer, he returned a question: 'How can you verify the answer?' Fuengsin acted as interpreter, but was not shy about chipping in when it came to reflections on modern society. She opportunistically and enthusiastically added that the Dhammakaya tradition was flourishing in recent times.

For a few moments it was like a rare portal connecting different worlds. The satisfaction rate was high and the temple received several letters of appreciation. Fuengsin was welcome at almost any time and took other visitors. On one occasion she was accompanied by Edward Davies, who had been deepening his interest in Buddhism and felt the time was right for some formal commitment. He consulted with Fuengsin on how this might be done and she suggested a visit to Wat Sanghathan. He was fortunate in having available Luang Phor to preside. A simple ceremony took place in the shrine room, the Abbot seated before it, with Edward in front of him and Paul to one side, ready to assist. The proceedings were simple in structure, but not trivial in practice. Kneeling in a respectful posture, Edward took refuge in the Triple Gem and recited the Five Precepts. Then he was given the age-old instruction for ordinands on non-attachment through reflection on the constituents of the body, reciting *kesa* (hair on head), *loma* (hair on body), *nakha* (nails), *danta* (teeth), *taco* (skin), and then in reverse. He had to recite it several times until Luang Phor was satisfied. However rather than continue to the internal organs, this was followed immediately by a short meditation and blessing.

Throughout these events Paul was himself searching spiritually and had been composing a work of spiritual philosophy reflecting his experience and perceptions of Christianity and Buddhism. He shared extracts with Fuengsin, who was naturally interested in its treatment of meditative aspects. She proudly told her friends about the project; in a letter to Jane she summarised:

> It is his biography about being brought up by both Buddhist and Christian parents without conflict. He has written about two third of the book. If it gets published, he will send you a copy.

It wasn't a biography in the conventional sense, but rather a very personal work on what he called 'spiritual philosophy'. Whatever its description, it seemed that Buddhist readers and those from traditionally Buddhist countries could follow easily what was expressed. Among those who gave encouraging responses was Prof. Antony Fernando, who urged him to publish his spiritual work. However, it wasn't that straightforward for some Western-educated Christians. He had shown some chapters to one clergyman, who after expressing initial excitement later declared reservations about it sounding dangerously close to 'dualism'. Perhaps troubled by Paul's enthusiasm for the gnostic Gospel of Thomas (from which Paul had picked out some Zen-like quotes), he subsequently directed him to some methods of prayer and a standard textbook on the principles of Christian theology. However, Paul couldn't identify with these perspectives, and as they failed to answer his questions about the nature of mind he was frustrated by them; he only came to a more satisfactory position by also embracing other views that struck a chord with him.

Fuengsin continued introducing Paul to her various religious circles, notwithstanding his different qualifications, for she saw his potential for contribution. Yet, whilst supportive of Paul's spiritual explorations, through her natural pragmatism, Fuengsin continued to worry that Paul had come back exhausted and couldn't raise much energy beyond writing. However, slowly there was some resolution. Over the summer he also had to prepare for his

Master's oral examination, which required concentration because although the thesis was only 50 pages long the subject matter was abstract. Paul made a final return trip to Glasgow in September and survived the *viva*; his supervisor, Prof. Robert Odoni, was in a relaxed mood and in a statement of curious symmetry with his first greeting, he bid him farewell at Hillhead underground station with the words, 'It was not far short of a PhD.' It was a pleasant trip for Paul as he caught up with a few friends and colleagues; Etuka had now moved to Falkland Mansions, one of the largest tenement blocks Paul had ever seen, so he was able to stay there in a spare room.

With another qualification bagged, Tony and Fuengsin urged Paul to start seeking work in earnest, but he found it difficult to even get job interviews and the possibilities of the actuarial profession had by now disappeared. As locally advertised positions seemed to elude him, Paul registered for unemployment benefit so that he could at least make some meagre contribution to the household budget, and Fuengsin tried to lift his spirits by blessing him when he handed over the small sums, 'May you be Enlightened in the next life!'

His failure to get a foot on the career ladder at least brought more family time, time that was to prove more precious than they may have realised. There were in particular opportunities for Fuengsin to provide local illustrations of Buddhist themes. Sometimes Fuengsin and Paul would go for walks along the country lanes. On one occasion they were making their way along Thicknall Lane and then turned onto a narrow lane to head towards Broome. Over on the right was a large field where horses were roaming and one made its way over to the fence to greet the walkers. This horse appeared approachable so Fuengsin started speaking to it. As she spoke, it would repeatedly cock its head to one side and then the other. Fuengsin noticed that it was particularly attentive so she came to the point and asked, 'Why have you been born a horse so that you are not your own master? What karma did you do?' The horse seemed to register the question and suddenly a troubled expression crossed its face. It took fright and bolted, galloping hundreds of yards to the other end of field. Fuengsin's directness had hit a sore point and she had lost her equine listener.

At home, Fuengsin and Paul would often chat about karma and related Dhamma topics in the lounge, sometimes to help make sense of life's everyday struggles, whilst at other times to probe more deeply into one's spiritual purpose. When Paul was preoccupied and lost sleep at night, Fuengsin merely advised him: 'Just observe.' He should know that the situation would change through the impermanence of conditioning, and that it was dependent on causes: this being ... that becomes; this ceasing ... that ceases. These are widely known Buddhist observations, but Fuengsin added lesser-known facets:

she described the Buddhas as 'innumerable' and related that Buddha Gautama had reached Buddhahood relatively quickly and was especially analytical. Even so, all Buddhas had been accumulating *paramis* (perfections) over many aeons and — bringing things down to earth — the *paramis* were acquired through developing qualities such as generosity, patience and loving kindness.

Fuengsin continued to develop such qualities herself when she undertook a third translation project for Wat Sanghathan, which was somewhat different from the others. It was a calendar for the Thai year 2536 BE (1993 CE) to explain the 12 links of Dependent Origination, which is a teaching that comes from the earliest Buddhist texts. In a quite daring move, the Abbot borrowed a visual representation from Tibetan Buddhism: the calendar depicted concentric circles starting with the three fires of greed, hatred and delusion that power the cycles of existence; and this was surrounded by segments with depictions of different mental states, realms and stages in the process of becoming and re-becoming. The calendar carried with it a blessing:

> May all who are virtuous and possess good qualities remain virtuous and of good qualities. May they have good thoughts, good actions, mindfulness and wisdom. May all of our goodness remain and increase throughout the New Year.
>
> Everyone should strive to do good for oneself, one's society, one's relatives and should be prepared to be self-sacrificing. Such behaviour is considered to bring good fortune throughout the year.[3]

Fuengsin again asked Simon Romer for assistance on the translation, which he readily provided, intrigued by the transplantation. However, he expressed a touch of unease, remarking that in some aspects the interpretation he had learnt was different!

* * *

Fuengsin also had to juggle her work with further responsibilities at home. Vasana had an elder brother, Khun Chalitapakorn Virabalin, who lived next door in Chatuchak. He was married and had a daughter, Rajanipa (nickname 'Ann'), who had recently graduated from Chulalongkorn University. Ann wanted to undertake postgraduate studies in the UK, which required her to pass IELTS with a certain mark, so she needed first to gain greater in proficiency in English. Tony and Fuengsin were approached and asked if they could host her, to which they agreed. Arrangements were made for her stay in Hagley and in January 1993 she duly arrived to start her English language studies at Linguarama, in Birmingham. The house became fuller than normal and Fuengsin was somewhat ambivalent about the extra chores, anxious that it took time away from her Dhamma activities, though she was pleased that Ann kept her room neat and tidy, especially since that was the room where the shrine was kept.

Ann also tried to encourage Paul in his job search. He started to think more laterally, seeking to combine his formal background in numerical disciplines with a growing interest in the field of religious studies. It led to his writing occasional letters in response to articles on related themes, including the Computers in Religious Education project at University College of Wales, Lampeter. He wanted to know more about their software to teach about the life of the Buddha and was hoping some opportunities might arise, but nothing materialised in response to his speculative enquiry.

The global recession of the early 1990s was hampering Paul's job prospects and it was continuing to cause difficulties for the Multi-Faith Centre. Having lost the prime location of Harborne Hall, the Centre relocated to more modest premises along the Hagley Road. Yet Sister Mary was determined to keep going as she had felt for a while that the methodology she and her multifaith team had developed would be usefully applied elsewhere around the world, particularly in urban areas with multiple ethnicities. Having already established international links, it was now time to take the project abroad, complete with her faith representatives. Thus in spring 1993 (20–26 March) she took her team to a snowy New York state where they ran a week-long programme, entitled 'Multifaith Dialogue in a Multicultural Society'. The event was hosted by the Stony Point Center, a gesture that befitted their strapline, 'where the world becomes an open house'. It was co-organised by Auburn Theological Seminary and comprised a series of workshops designed to give participants grounding in the Centre's approach and methodology, promoting common citizenship in the wider community.[4]

There was also a session at the United Nations headquarters, which was only about an hour's drive away. Whilst the UN had been established with no explicit reference to religion, the role of religion had long been recognised for its importance in society with close cooperation at many levels, involving international faith-based and interfaith organisations. Yet Sister Mary still felt that the Birmingham team had something especially well-grounded and integrative that could offer something fresh and new. Her team represented the grassroots — they were not high-ranking leaders of religious communities. They did not need a red carpet or operate according to refined protocol, but were practitioners who were active in settings in which the majority of people lived their everyday lives, and they were available to share insights based on their experiences of working together for the common good.

Fig. 92: The New York team (from top left): Bahadur Singh (Sikh); Mary Hall (Christian); Khalid Alawi (Muslim); Fuengsin Trafford (Buddhist); Ronald Levi (Jew) and Madhuri Lahiri (Hindu).

Fig. 93: Fuengsin standing outside the main entrance to the United Nations building, New York state.

However, the team were made to work hard: participants had paid a $265 programme fee and certainly sought value for money. Fuengsin remarked how on that programme and at the UN the Americans asked many questions and expected well-informed and engaging responses. There was also the occasional linguistic issue: Fuengsin learnt that whereas in England 'homely' meant somewhere cosy and comfortable, it was a derogatory term in the US, and 'homey' should be used instead. One member of the team experienced problems with his sense of humour, which apparently didn't travel well across the Atlantic.

Sightseeing provided some light relief and although it was limited by wintry weather, a bonus trip was arranged to the military academy at West Point, and on a postcard Fuengsin reported with delight the chance to see soldiers in uniform. Sent from Bethany Retreat House on 21/3/93, she wrote to her family in Hagley in typically earthy fashion:

> The snow is still very high. We visited Sister Mary's Order & found the place very spiritual + the nuns delightful. On the same day, we visited WestPoint + my dream had become true. I cannot express it esp. when I talked to a very smart & polite cadet. Everyone was impressed with him <see photo>.

> Love, Dang

Fig. 94: Fuengsin and Madhuri Lahiri flanking an officer at
West Point Academy, United States.

Team members were given various souvenirs, including a 20-page booklet published by the Center that provided a complete programme for that year. Fuengsin also brought home some sweets and doughnuts, which tasted refreshingly different, and gave Paul a T-shirt for the New York Mets Baseball Team, helping to keep fresh his student memories.

Fuengsin performed well, but overall the success of the trip was mixed and it did not provide much extra impetus to operations in the UK. The Multi-Faith Centre was still not being used optimally so did not grow to fulfil its potential and there were continual doubts about its economic viability, prompting a review for 1993/94. If it were not for the generosity of Sister Mary's order, it might not have survived even this far. Against such a backdrop there was unease among Centre members, some of whom wanted major change. Fuengsin herself was not an agitator, but there were increasing demands on her time from other activities, especially translation work.

The situation caused Fuengsin to take stock and question the relative merits and eventually she reached the uncomfortable conclusion that it was time to leave. It was thus with sadness that she penned her resignation letter to Sister Mary and informed her of her decision, saying that after 10 years of service, for which she was deeply grateful for all that Sister Mary had done, she felt it was time she moved on. Sister Mary was moved to tears, but respectfully accepted the decision.

Fuengsin had sensed that the Multi-Faith Centre was in decline and within a few months it formally closed. Yet there continued to be many positive legacies pervading her life. One of her students there had been Tony Blundell, who was formally Roman Catholic, but enjoyed learning from many traditions — one of his favourite works was *Journey to Joy* by Robert Shiarella, who presented on nuclear physics and siddha yoga as taught by Swami Muktananda. Tony built a lovely cottage at a tranquil spot by the river in Welford-on-Avon and made it available for people to pursue spiritual activities; Ven. Dr Rewata Dhamma led meditation there, joined by Fuengsin, Ramona and other friends. Paul also benefited from the location as he went there on a writer's solitary retreat for 11 days, to continue with his spiritual philosophy.

* * *

Whilst the move away from Harborne Hall had a detrimental effect on the Multi-Faith Centre, contributing to its rapid demise, interfaith was still actively being researched at Selly Oak and Fuengsin was increasing her participation. Having been established for many decades with contacts in many parts of the world, it responded to its social imperative to promote faith cohesively. Towards the end of 1992, the colleges organised an interfaith prayer and candle-lit vigil for communal harmony in the Indian subcontinent following the razing of the Babri Mosque in Ayodhya. The organisers knew that international events had regional and local repercussions, so they advertised the vigil as also being one for the West Midlands. They gave it a high priority and senior figures, including the President, Dr Martin Conway, made sure they were present. There were contributions from many faith and interfaith representatives, including Fuengsin, who offered a Buddhist reflection. The gathering prefigured in many ways the pattern of communal events in years to come.

Fuengsin participated in another vigil in May, which concerned refugees and took place in Birmingham Cathedral. She had been invited by Elnora Ferguson, who granted Fuengsin a slot of 15 minutes, 'for you as a woman, from Southeast Asia, a Buddhist to reflect as you wish, inside the Cathedral'. She was well-qualified to give a response as she was well-informed about ethnic minorities and other marginalised groups in Thailand. Having lived more than 25 years far away from home, she could also relate naturally, with her early years in England being deprived of relatives, friends, and the material and spiritual culture in which she had been brought up. Such experiences led her to developing a response rooted in compassion.

The following month she gave a two-hour lecture at Westhill College on 'Religion and the Environment — a Buddhist Perspective' to around 40 second-year trainee primary teachers of varying religious backgrounds; it was a good occasion to emphasise our interrelatedness. For the students this was part of a five-week series of lectures on 'Religion and the Environment'. Fuengsin was advised that it might be difficult to maintain student attention and was encouraged to make use of visuals and student participation. She was given plenty of preparatory materials and suggestions of what to do, and the staff gave their guest lecturers a great deal of support.

After a decade lecturing at centres and colleges in and around Birmingham, Fuengsin was in a position to write papers and invitations started to arrive. One of her contributions was 'Buddhist students in the United Kingdom', which was published in The Journal of International Education, Vol. 4, No. 1, March 1993.[5] It was an opportunity to reflect on how far the acceptance and development of Buddhism had progressed in the UK, based in large measure on her own experiences since she had arrived as a student 30 years earlier. Overall, there was far greater awareness — nowadays a monk in saffron robes was more familiar and the bowl he used on alms rounds would no longer be mistaken for a drum. There were more facilities to support born Buddhists, and the people who had come to the path later on had become more diverse, and were no longer just the preserve of the middle-class intellectual or hippie. Dharma discussions and meditation were widely available from many different traditions, particularly at universities and colleges. Fuengsin went on to briefly summarise the historical development and salient qualities of three main Schools of Buddhism — Theravada, Mahayana and Vajrayana — indicating a few significant differences. She also highlighted the varied functions of the temple:

> The temple is a very important place for Buddhists because it is a social, cultural and spiritual centre. Some lonely students go there to meet others, or to volunteer to do various jobs for the monks. They may attended chanting sessions, meditation classes, discourses, stay for a weekend retreat and perhaps be ordained as monks, novices and nuns for a fixed period, such as during summer holidays. Students can take some food to offer to monks and share with others as part of the practice of supporting the spiritual communities. The monks and nuns are spiritual teachers who can also fill the roles of psychotherapists or even the Samaritans.

Fuengsin saw the need more for a generally amenable location rather than any special treatment.

> Students also have need of "quiet zones" or "rooms" in which to meditate but they should not be offended by religious symbols of other faiths being present in such rooms. After all Buddhism is a very tolerant religion. Not all Buddhists meditate but a lot do regular chanting and venerate the Buddha with Puja regularly. There is no hard and fast rules about what foods should be eaten or avoided. What is important is that spiritual guidance should be available to students, and this becomes very important when a person is very ill or dying. A monk or spiritual friend should be there to guide or support him or her. This is why the appointment of Buddhist monks or lay ministers to the Chaplaincies would be appreciated.

More support could be provided, but overall Fuengsin thought that Buddhist students were fortunate to be in such a tolerant society. She had certainly seen a transformation since she had arrived.

Evidence of this transformation was to be found throughout the country and occasionally there were connections with Fuengsin's own background. One day Paul and Ann went on a day trip by train to Bath, a city made famous for its spa by the Romans. They explored as tourists, taking in the views and admiring its fine classical architecture, followed by a spell of shopping. This included a wander into Waterstones bookstore, where they made a quick visit to the section on religion. On arriving, Paul stopped and asked rhetorically in his mind whether there was any book that was really worth reading. Immediately his eyes were drawn to a particular shelf and alighted on a volume with the title 'Life as a Siamese Monk' along its binding. He pulled it out and read on the back cover:

In May, 1954, 10,000 people gathered at the outlying temple of Wat Paknam in Bangkok to witness the ordination of 47-year-old journalist-photographer Richard Randall. Known henceforth as Kapilavaddho Bhikkhu, he is the first Englishman to enter the monkhood in Thailand.

Paul was surprised and intrigued. He had never heard about this man, let alone his biography, so he made the purchase and stowed it in his rucksack. When he got back home he showed his mother. Fuengsin looked at it and remarked, 'Ah. That explains why I saw a picture of Luang Phor Wat Paknam hanging on the wall at the Hampstead Buddhist Vihara!'[6] She then recalled that Ajahn Gaew had often spoken of his friendship with Kapilavaddho Bhikkhu and their travels together, but she had assumed he was Thai. Now she had a clearer picture and the significance of Ajahn's recollections were slotting into place, almost 30 years after she had first arrived in Britain.

The manuscript for this work had apparently languished for a long time in a waste paper basket, only to be salvaged posthumously and kept for years until an opportunity arose for publication. The account described his ordination at Wat Paknam in 1954 with the Abbot, Chao Khun Phramongkolthepmuni, presiding over the ceremony as Upajjhaaya (Preceptor). The new bhikkhu then practised assiduously for several months until he had explored his mind to considerable depth. He also showed great vigour in his teaching activities, and so impressed the Abbot that within a year he was granted special dispensation to go and teach the Dhamma in the UK, as he had been taught at the temple. He was such a talented student that he became much appreciated by the Abbot and others at Wat Paknam; they really had high hopes that he would be able sow Dhamma seeds.

When Ven. Kapilavaddho returned from Bangkok he continued his extraordinary efforts by laying the foundations for a bhikkhu Sangha in the UK; those who studied under him were greatly impressed by the careful attention he gave to their particular circumstances, and how he was able to use his vast knowledge to good effect. However, he faced battles, manifest in illnesses which were so severe that after a couple of years he was forced to disrobe and he disappeared from the Buddhist scene for more than 10 years. He eventually made a comeback and the Hampstead Buddhist Vihara was reinvigorated with industrious practice. However, whereas he had previously taught as standard the Dhammakaya method (referred to as the 'Wat Paknam' method), he then dropped it and taught other methods. With no-one available from the temple to provide guidance it meant a fundamental break with the training that Ven. Kapilavaddho had received and the path of the Middle Way became lost.[7,8]

Back in Thailand Ajahn Gaew had followed the Englishman's progress with interest and knew about the obstacles. Recalling that period, he commented to Fuengsin, 'Mara had a go at him.' Fuengsin may have wondered how she might fare, especially as she faced illness, but she always retained the method and kept in touch with a teacher at Wat Paknam. She also continued to teach the Middle Way to her students, including those at King Edwards in Stourbridge. Fuengsin was liberal in her acceptance of others, but very strict about her own practice, following instructions to the letter and — as young Western bhikkhus had discovered — trying to protect the Vinaya, the monastic code. Her up-bringing undoubtedly contributed to valuing tradition and preserving it, which was manifest in small things such as protecting books with temporary covers as well as in the most significant matters of guarding religious ortho-doxy.

A few months later another connection was established. Fuengsin and Paul accompanied another group of students to Wat Sanghathan. Among them was John Randall, the son of Richard Randall, the lay name that Ven. Kapilavaddho adopted on disrobing.

Paul was finding spirituality and the history of his mother's meditation tradition fascinating, but there was a pressing need to earn a living. He contin-ued to focus on Information Technology (IT) as a career path, albeit he could sense it wasn't conducive to the best of health. However, he was unable to find a suitable opening: if he applied to a company he lacked relevant experience of particular programming languages and the more academic posts required specialist knowledge (but not in algebraic number theory). He wasn't getting much response from his applications. After a while of signing on the dole, Paul was obliged to join Stourbridge Job Club, which meant a daily commute to Stourbridge to spend half a day with a contractor looking for jobs. The idea was that it at least got claimants into a regular Monday to Friday rhythm and the time could be spent preparing CVs and applying for jobs. It led to a three-month employment training course in Computing Applications run out of MOST (Midlands Oak Skills and Technology services), which was set up after the sale of the Roundoak Steelworks. Paul got to meet local people from various backgrounds, ranging from teenagers through to highly-qualified technical staff, some close to retirement age. It was a friendly environment, and at least gave some work discipline, and Paul seemed reasonably content.

Fuengsin was pleased that he didn't get stuck at home, but continued to worry, wondering how a highly qualified graduate could struggle to find employment. For a while it seemed little more than filling in time, but in March Paul spotted an advertisement in The Guardian, in which Kingston

University was advertising an MSc conversion course in IT (software engineering). It looked up-to-date and would provide the bridge with industry, so he applied. However, with funding not forthcoming, discussions at his interview gravitated to research. The department needed mathematicians and Paul's background appeared a good fit; he was subsequently offered a PhD studentship in Computer Science. After some further soul-searching he decided to have a second attempt at a PhD. Once again everyone in the family could breathe a sigh of relief as Paul had another chance to engage in something purposeful.

It allowed a spell of relaxation and before he started his research he went youth hostelling in Cornwall with Paul Godfrey and Greg Howard, friends from Southampton University Catholic Chaplaincy. Paul took with him his UB40 to claim a discount off the already modest YHA rates, so Fuengsin dubbed it the 'pauper's holiday' on account of its very limited budget. Yet despite occasional downpours and long walks to get to a few of the hostels, the weather was generally fine and Paul enjoyed it. Suitably refreshed, he moved to Kingston upon Thames to start life again as a full-time student. However, as with Glasgow, Paul had difficulty finding a suitable place to stay. After just seven months he was obliged to find his third accommodation, but at least life and the weather in general were more clement. The PhD also provided an opportunity for Paul to attend a couple of specialist courses, including one held in June 1994 at the University of Twente in the Netherlands. On his return Fuengsin seemed distinctly pleased, remarking, 'Now you know how to travel abroad by yourself.'

Fuengsin was particularly encouraged when Paul informed her that he had become involved in setting up a meditation group affiliated with the university's Guild of Students. It was run by members belonging to an association whose founder, Nai Boonman, had originally come to the UK from Thailand about a year before Fuengsin. After his arrival Nai Boonman had been invited to teach meditation in London and Cambridge, leading to the establishment of the Samatha Trust, an organisation that had meditation groups around the British Isles. Paul subsequently became President of the KUGOS Meditation Society and Fuengsin was very pleased; even though he didn't provide the instruction, Fuengsin apparently regarded it as his group.

At the same time, Paul was continuing his spiritual investigations more broadly, many of which had some cross-currents that Fuengsin followed with interest. He was still attending Mass on a regular basis and came to learn of a pilgrimage to Walsingham, arranged by a lady called Georgina. Paul found Georgina a very sincere and devout Christian. She and her husband had a large family of eight children, but many who met her for the first time thought she was a nun because of her refined demeanour. Meanwhile, Paul was exploring around the edges of contemporary Catholic practice, which led him in 1994 to attend an introductory talk about meditation for Christians, held at a church hall. It used a mantra, but the speaker seemed oblivious to the significance of the way he was incorrectly pronouncing it. Paul followed it up by attending a session where parishioners gathered to practise the same technique by listening to a tape, but when the tape came to an end the lights were flicked back on instantly and the 'practice' was stopped abruptly. There was no-one to offer any guidance. Fuengsin received a report from her son and she shared his concern — it was dangerous that they didn't know what they were doing. In parallel to that Paul shared his experiences with Georgina and she too had reservations, saying it was 'bad news' having seen some ill-effects in hospital (she was a nurse).

Fuengsin had meanwhile received an invitation to give a talk in Birmingham to the Interfaith Society at King Edward's School, Paul's alma mater, a society established by the Reverend Weaver in September 1992 after the Birmingham Interfaith Council's Youth Day. As several of Fuengsin's friends and associates were members of the Council, it was a natural connection. In the 1994 Chronicle, Matthew Price recorded: 'The most recent guest speaker was Fuengsin Trafford, a Buddhist lady who fascinated all who were present with her talk.' She also received a letter of thanks, which she very much appreciated.

Among the plethora of Fuengsin's activities, it was important to have a new sense of direction following the loss of the Multi-Faith Centre, and for this to bear suitable fruit. There were new developments in her work at Selly Oak Colleges that were to provide much promise of this. At Selly Oak, she liaised closely with Aasulv Lande, who had by now been Lutheran lecturer for four years.[9] During this period he was much involved in cooperation and co-teaching with Fuengsin, and it was mooted that it would be interesting to develop further Christian-Buddhist dialogue, particularly with Southeast Asia. So, along with other colleagues they started to explore possibilities and Fuengsin began making enquiries. This led to ground-breaking cooperation with Mahidol University, who were partners with Selly Oak's Department of Mission and Islam Centre. Together they organised an international two-day workshop on 'Death and Dying: Cross-Cultural Perspectives', held in Birmingham on the 26 and 27 October. Fuengsin was instrumental in communications with Thailand, liaising with academics at Mahidol, particularly with Dr Pinit Ratanakul and Dr Araya Phonghanyudh. Quite a large group came from Thailand, including a monk who said little, but took many photographs. However, when he saw Fuengsin he gazed intently and then pointed at her, declaring: 'She is no ordinary woman!'

The workshop was a success and shortly afterwards a meeting took place at Selly Oak Colleges to discuss the future of Christian–Buddhist studies. It included an item on how to continue the dialogue with Mahidol, for which Dr Phonghanyudh was present. The discussions reached an advanced stage as Fuengsin drafted a two-month residency programme. This was to help develop relations between Sweden and Mahidol University in Thailand, culminating in visits by Dr Gerhard Köberlin.

Fuengsin continued participating in a wide range of events, particularly dialogues with other religions. Programmes at the College of the Ascension were flourishing and becoming very creative. On 21–23 June 1994 she was a speaker at an innovative conference on the comparative study of the Bhagavadgita, selected Buddhist Texts and St John's Gospel. The conference started in the afternoon, after a preparatory meeting in the morning that all the speakers attended. Fuengsin participated in several sessions. Alongside two representatives of other faiths, she offered a brief reflection on the place of scriptures; at the end of the day she was involved in the Buddhist chanting and meditation.

The following morning Fuengsin introduced and chaired a session on the theme of 'suffering'. Before lunch, she contributed to the issue of how people in various religions have been influenced by the scriptures of other religions. One of the speakers at the conferences was Dr Alan Keightley, who spoke on Zen Buddhism and Christianity. Fuengsin also had to consider other themes of 'Paths of social action' and 'Liberation/Salvation', which were chaired by her co-lecturer, Elizabeth Harris. Sacred Texts — Hindu, Christian and Buddhist — were discussed by three colleagues Fuengsin knew well: Alan Keighley, Elizabeth Harris and Sharada Sugirtharajah.

She enjoyed the seminar greatly, remarking:

> Heaven is like now, on a sunny morning, being with people like you of various faiths, on an exciting course like this!

These nascent developments had celestial visions, but an accumulation of earthly troubles were about to take their toll.

Notes

1. Harborne Hall was subsequently used as the VSO headquarters and then was put on the market by the Sisters of La Retraite (on 13 May 2010): http://www.theharbornesociety.org.uk/uploads/3/9/5/2/39529175/summer_news-letter_2010.pdf

It continued as a training centre for VSO and then was variously used as a conference and wedding venue.

2. *Oneness* by Ven. Ajahn Sanong Katapunyo may be accessed online at:
    http://fuengsin.org/translate/sanong/oneness/

3. Ven. Ajahn Sanong's teachings on Dependent Origination are available online at:
    http://fuengsin.org/translate/sanong/wheel/

4. The Stony Point Center, http://stonypointcenter.org/

    Auburn Theological Seminary, http://www.auburnseminary.org/

5. The *Journal of International Education* was produced by the UK Council for International Education (originally UKCOSA, then UKCISA) with support from the British Council from 1996 to 1999, having previously been published by PEPAR publications. See *The Experiences of International Students in UK Higher Education: a review of unpublished research* by Caroline Pelletier, who notes it did not have a high circulation and is no longer published, but nevertheless contains many articles that are likely to be of interest to researchers.

6. The Hampstead Buddhist Vihara was formally established in 1962 by the English Sangha Trust. Its founding owed much to work carried out in the mid-1950s by William Purfurst (later Ven. Kapilavaddho). The Vihara later came under the direction of Ven. Ananda Bodhi, who, like Ven. Kapilavaddho, had received training, though separately, at Wat Paknam. In the early 1960s Ven. Ananda Bodhi helped to establish a Thai Theravadin temple, whereby arrangements were made for the abbot of Wat Mahathat, Phra Rajasiddhimuni, to come and spread Dhamma to the locals under official Thai patronage. The method of that temple was actually derived from Burmese practices, particularly those of Mahasi Sayadaw. Similarly, Ven. Ananda Bodhi's first meditation practice had been with a Burmese monk, U Thila Wunta Sayadaw, also in the tradition of Mahasi Sayadaw.

7. An in-depth autobiographical account of Ven. Kapilavaddho's experiences at Wat Paknam were published posthumously as *Life as a Siamese Monk*, written under his second lay name of Richard Randall and published by Aukana:
    http://www.aukana.org.uk/book/browser/booklsm.htm

8. An appreciation of Ven. Kapilavaddho's life and work is given in *Honour Thy Fathers,* compiled by Terry Shine, available at:
    http://www.buddhanet.net/pdf_file/honourfathers.pdf.

    For the Wat Paknam perspective, please see *The Life and Times of Luang Phaw Wat Paknam*, published by the Dhammakaya Foundation, available at:
    http://en.dhammakayapost.org/book/?p=25

9. Fuengsin's cooperation and co-teaching is described by Prof. Lande in *Swedish Missiological Themes*, Svensk Missionstidskrift Vol. 90, No. 1, 2002.

14

Faltering Health and Grand Finale

Teach us to care and not to care
Teach us to sit still.

Ash Wednesday, T.S. Eliot

Fuengsin battled with a number of health issues; as well as the seasonal hay fever, she had chronic problems with her circulation so that her hands often felt icy. She tried various treatments, including acupuncture, which she received from Vajira on a weekly basis during spring 1992. Fuengsin found her a very good practitioner and her rates were affordable, but more than that they could always view these conditions from a dharma perspective.

Fuengsin also had trouble with her eyes; as well as the problems with the optic nerve, which had manifested within a few years of arriving in the UK, she developed glaucoma, which required an operation to reduce the pressure. Afterwards she had further unrelated problems, resulting in her left eye becoming so painful that she could not move it, severely restricting her reading and writing. The doctor gave her some drops to put in for 10 days and the pain stopped; it turned out that the cause was dry skin on the eyelid and it was nothing to do with the pressure or the operation. Fuengsin was relieved, but these were warning signs of the fragility of her health.

She was also conscious of ageing, especially as she entered her fifties, when she admitted to pulling out grey hairs. And then she remarked casually, 'I don't want to live to old age.' Very occasionally when she was in a bad mood she asserted strangely to Tony, 'Well, you will outlive me!' She even went on to recommend that he remarry after she had passed away, but nobody around her took much notice of what seemed a statement in jest. For several years she experienced sustained heat in her body, often whilst just sitting at leisure; it may have been hot flushes related to the menopause, but Fuengsin didn't refer to the heat in this way and these were prolonged states. She also started having problems with excessive rumblings of her stomach and she became very conscious of the noise being made in meditation practice, but all of this was put down to entirely normal and natural biological processes.

Fuengsin simply carried on, continuing with her usual activities, domestic and work-related. At home she hosted more visitors, especially from Thailand, including Ajahn Chusak and his wife — Ajahn Chusak had originally been one of Fuengsin's students and then became a lecturer at King Mongkut Institute of Technology. As with most visitors, it meant shopping for fresh ingredients, bringing out the large saucepans, cooking various dishes and serving them on hot plates. There were also day trips to the countryside, usually with Tony acting as chauffeur. In addition she and Tony were making more frequent visits to Chepstow as Tony's mother was not in good health.

When not playing the host and undertaking household duties, Fuengsin continued with her teaching and literary work. Following the publication of the calendar, there was a fourth project lined up at Wat Sanghathan. Luang Phor Sanong asked Fuengsin to translate another set of teachings, which focused this time on the theme of attachment and contained many reflections on how to face the transience of life and the cycles of birth and decay. Fuengsin applied herself conscientiously as before to the translation and was now more fluent, this time aided by Andrew Campbell, another friend from Karma Ling.

However, having been deeply involved in the temple's activities Fuengsin had noticed that the monks in residence still had difficulty interacting with locals. She reflected that even though the temple was regarded as friendly and welcoming, it was only slowly integrating in the local community. There were ongoing problems in communication that seemed to limit the beneficiaries mainly to Thais and their British spouses. When other residents in the area expressed an interest in meditation the Sangha members struggled to explain concepts in a way that they could easily understand; no matter how insightful they were, their Dhamma teachings and meditation instruction were not reaching the local population.

Fuengsin felt that the Thai monks needed especially to be more open to the host culture and to learn how to communicate effectively in the Western context. She herself had been listening to Western teachers for decades as well as working alongside people from all walks of life. From observing the responses of practitioners she had a keen sense of how to engage people. It was thus that she came up with the idea of a publication in Thai aimed at monastics illustrating how to be effective communicators. At around the same time she learnt about a forthcoming biography, *Sangharakshita: A New Voice in the Buddhist Tradition*, being prepared by Dharmachari Subhuti (Alex Kennedy), who was a senior disciple. Having seen and heard how Sangharakshita was able to stimulate interest among his listeners, Fuengsin identified this book as one that would be useful and decided to discuss the possibility of a translation with senior FWBO members.

In September 1993 Fuengsin travelled into Birmingham and took Paul with her. It was a typical journey that included a stop for refreshments in Druckers overlooking some outdoor market stalls in the Bull Ring shopping centre. The café was one of a chain that had been serving Vienna Patisserie to Brummies since its founding by Andre Drucker in 1964; it was one of Fuengsin's favourite spots for satisfying sweet cravings and watching the world go by. Here she chatted at leisure with Paul, reflecting on urban life, feeling very much at home; in many ways it felt similar to Wongwien Yai in Thonburi. Then they carried on to Moseley where there was a celebration at the FWBO Centre, with their founder in attendance. They met up with Vajira, who took them to meet Sangharakshita, who was sitting at a table greeting guests and well-wishers. Vajira, having been ordained in the FWBO more than 20 years earlier, facilitated the introductions and then Fuengsin took the opportunity to express her appreciation of his teachings. She then delivered her project proposal to translate Subhuti's biographical account into Thai. Sangharakshita's eyes lit up: he was pleased and gave the project his blessing.

Having been given the green light, Fuengsin later wrote to Subhuti, but for some reason she did not find it easy to draft even a short letter: in a rough manuscript, she wrote two lines of the first paragraph and then crossed it out. She tried again underneath, this time managing three lines before abandoning it. Only at the third attempt did she complete the paragraph and the following draft before the final version was sent.

> Dear Dharmachari Subhuti,
>
> I am a Thai Buddhist who has lived here for a long time. Since I was very young, I have been very interested in meditation and study. So I have the opportunity to propagate the Dharma in the West by working at the Multi Faith Centre in Birmingham. I also visit the F.W.B.O. Centre at Moseley.
>
> I am very impressed with Ven. S. and his work. Last September, I was very lucky to meet him for the first time. So I expressed my gratitude for his tapes & books which help me to put B. across to Westerners effectively. I then told him that I would like to translate his biography into Thai as very few of my fellow countrymen hear about him. He was delighted and said that I could translate the book which you are writing & it will be finished in February.
>
> So I would like to ask you permission to translate it.

Subhuti replied and readily agreed to the project. Fuengsin subsequently met up with him at the Sangharakshita Festival held in the Bishopsgate Institute, London, on 7 July 1994, where he launched the book. Fuengsin had already received an advance copy and had started the translation. Paul went along also, coming across from Kingston, and whilst Fuengsin was discussing the book with Subhuti, Paul took a seat in the main hall. The programme included various talks, with many speakers expressing their devotion to Sangharakshita and his work. However, Paul found some speeches straying into condescension about other traditions, which he found distasteful. Feeling unsettled he left the building and went for a walk. On his return he met up with Fuengsin, who asked, 'Where have you been? You have missed a puja with good energy!' There was not much Paul could say to that. Fuengsin knew there were issues, but didn't let them prevent her from drawing the positives and working towards her far-sighted objectives. Soon after returning home, Fuengsin wrote back to Subhuti saying how she found the book 'Both interesting and rewarding . . . It will be a real challenge for me.'

* * *

Fuengsin's outlook stretched beyond Buddhist denominations. In the early 1990s she had more opportunity to travel abroad and visited Italy three times with Tony, attracted by the vitality of the people and finding that among all the Europeans, the Italians were the closest to the Thais. She was fascinated by the country's various cultural and artistic expressions relating to Christianity. Fuengsin was encouraged to learn more and was grateful to Peter Tyler and other friends who could explain the works of Renaissance masters such as Fra Angelico, allowing her better access to discerning the meaning in iconography and other forms of religious art.

None of the stays were very long, but they made a lasting impression and this part of southern Europe became her favourite holiday destination. Fuengsin admired some of Italy's saints, especially St Francis of Assisi. On her final trip in September 1994 she had the opportunity of visiting the great basilica where his tomb lies. At the time she was severely constipated, which was perhaps an indication that her health was already failing, so she 'prayed' to St Francis for help. Immediately after making the request, she had a sudden urge to rush to the toilet — indeed her prayer had been answered! Perhaps Fuengsin knew that St Francis himself had suffered severe stomach trouble in his later years. This prompted her to look for a little statue of St Francis, but for some reason she was unable to obtain anything suitable before boarding the return flight.

However, her intention was yet to be realised. On her return to England, she went to visit Brother Bill Jordan, S.J., at Manresa House, who had a gift for her, which he presented on her arrival. It was a small wooden statue of St Francis holding two doves, yet he had not known that she had been looking for such an object. The dear memento was then placed affectionately on the mantelpiece at home.

Fuengsin was fond of gazing at this statue, especially for the compassionate expression on the saint's face, as she had been suffering since June from stomach problems causing chronic pain. She knew something was not right, so she saw several doctors and an X-ray was carried out, but it did not reveal anything. Based on the symptoms and lack of other visible evidence, the only diagnosis they could reach was 'irritable bowel syndrome', which was notoriously vague and lacked definitive treatments. She knew that this diagnosis was inadequate and was hinting to them about this, but she couldn't pinpoint exactly what it was or at least not communicate it in a way that convinced them to explore further.

Fuengsin didn't make a fuss and hid much of the pain she was experiencing, but she started getting in touch with friends as the problem increased. She called Paquita, who noticed that Fuengsin's voice sounded extremely weak on the telephone. Paquita went to visit her straightaway and Fuengsin described some symptoms, particularly problems with her bowels. Her Basque friend looked at her and saw that her face was very drawn and her skin had become yellowish from jaundice. She told Yolanda, 'No, I don't like the look of Fuengsin, she does no look well at all, she has got something else.' The illness got worse and her suffering, particularly the diarrhoea, was making it very difficult to carry on with her usual activities. There were perhaps other indications of Fuengsin's struggles: in her shrine she placed no fewer than three statues of Kuanyin — echoes of Blofeld's *Compassion Yoga* — spreading compassion in people's suffering.

Fuengsin tried to continue with her work schedule at Selly Oak, teaching and attending meetings, but the problems intensified so that sometimes she had to return home early and unless Tony was available, it meant a couple of bus rides, with waits in between. Meanwhile Tony's mother was becoming frail, and on a visit to Hagley an ambulance had to be called as she struggled to breathe.

One of Fuengsin's last formal gatherings in which she participated was in late October and took place at Woodbrooke College. It was on the theme of silence in the world religions. Fuengsin was able to make a contribution that was well received and Chris Lawson, who was Director, wrote a letter of thanks on 28 October. After the typed letter he added a handwritten note:

Thank you so much for sharing so easily with us — I was aware that you weren't feeling as fit as you'd like to be and do hope you will find the right help soon. Hope your mother-in-law is getting on alright after her accident too.

Yet, Fuengsin continued to largely play down her illness and the pain she was experiencing. Even in November when Paul wrote a letter to a former school friend, Robert, he did not mention anything about his mother at all. However, when he returned to Hagley for the Christmas holiday he got a shock on arriving home: Fuengsin greeted him at the door and was distressed in a way he had never seen before. She was struggling to hold off tears, in a terrible physical state, very thin and weak. Yet even in this condition she insisted on preparing a meal of prawns and rice. It was to be the last one she cooked for him.

On Boxing Day Fuengsin became so ill that Tony called out the doctor, who on seeing the seriousness of her condition rang Kidderminster General Hospital. A couple of days later she was seen by a consultant who promptly ordered an ultrasound scan. Early in January Tony took Fuengsin to the hospital, where she was admitted for a few days during which the scan and further tests were carried out; a correct diagnosis was needed urgently as her condition continued to deteriorate.

Whilst waiting for the results to come through, which would take a few days, she received further nursing from hospital staff and from Tony, who would try to spoon-feed her broth to give her strength; sometimes she accepted, but at other times refused — her body couldn't take it. Meanwhile she had beside her a few items to help her continue practising, including a statue of Maitreya Buddha, the Buddha-to-be (currently, as she explained to Paul one day, a Bodhisattva in Tusita heaven waiting for the right time to take rebirth in human form many years hence). It had been lent to her by Sister Mary, who had received it as a gift on her travels to the Far East.

At last on the morning of 18 January the results were made available. Fuengsin was diagnosed as having cancer of the pancreas and it was at an advanced stage. It was inoperable and chemotherapy was not likely to help because the cancer was very 'aggressive', partly because of her relative youth. The doctor's prognosis was grim: going by statistics of similar cases, it was only a matter of months, but it seemed even this was couched in cautious terms.

Now there was an urgent need to inform people, so Tony and Paul (who was by now back in Surrey) began contacting relatives, close friends and a few of her colleagues. As neither of them really knew the extent of Fuengsin's network, they were dependent upon news spreading across the grapevine and the message duly propagated. Among the first to know were Alfred and Elsie, who went to the hospital that same morning. Alfred later reflected on the work of Elisabeth Kubler-Ross, a Swiss American psychiatrist who was a pioneer in near-death studies and the process of death and dying. He found that Fuengsin didn't seem to require any stages to work through the grief and when recalling the bedside encounter later on he noted: 'She immediately accepted that that was the case ... and she was very clear about it ... she wasn't crying or anything like that. She just gently said I've got 3 to 9 months and that's it.' Alfred found Fuengsin's continuation very striking: ' ... She went on to say that she would put her faith in the Buddha ... she felt that she wished that she would suffer [pay for her unskilful karma] so that she may come back in a higher state or form. We thought that was quite some feeling, the experience to find a person who was thinking like that and able to express it like that.' Alfred and Elsie were soon joined by Prof. Aasulv Lande and other colleagues from Selly Oak, people who had known for some while that something was wrong. They came very quickly to visit Fuengsin, exemplary in their practice of pastoral care. They were reciprocating the way she had travelled so often to the college, for now it was as though the college travelled to her.

Among the other visitors from Hagley were Joyce Slusarczuk, Paquita and Yolanda. When they arrived they found Fuengsin sitting cross-legged on the bed. Yolanda ventured to help her by trying to give her some home-made chicken soup, but Fuengsin didn't want it. She was looking surprisingly well and they were both amazed how serene and beautiful she appeared with her hair still shining and cut in the same bob. She actually looked young — there was some form of acceptance there as to the illness and her face appeared flawless. Paquita drew on her experience working with older people and found it contrasted with the contorted faces of those who are terrified of death. Fuengsin also benefited from accepting people of other faiths very happily, able to recognise good in everything and this was especially so in these times of trial. It wasn't a sad occasion even though some felt deep down that it might be the last time they saw her.

Reverend Andrew Wingate came with Sharada Sugirtharajah and they presented her with a Thai orchid and a book of interfaith readings. Fuengsin shared with them serious reflections on her situation; she emphasised that having talked so much about suffering in her lectures, now she must show the way. She expressed a wish to revisit Thailand, but remarked enigmatically, 'It may be that I will go there only in the spirit.' Fuengsin had been practising assiduously: each morning at around 6 a.m. she would pay respects to the Triple Gem and meditate. At other times she was cultivating *satipañña* (mindful wisdom) and whilst her physical frame continued to wither, her mind was becoming more aware. Reverend Andrew noticed that she was able to follow the condition of patients nearby despite being confined to her bed; knowing that a patient was struggling, she would ask a few of her many visitors to go over and give them support. Fuengsin was still being instructive too, as Reverend Andrew observed:

> There was never any self-pity. She told another friend, in a puzzled way, who asked if she was not angry that she had not been diagnosed earlier, "What is the point in being angry?"

And on leaving there was purpose: Sharada suggested: 'You and Tony will pray, and Fuengsin and I will meditate.' They continued in hope, even though a cure was not feasible, but rather healing.

Meanwhile down in Surrey, Paul was combining Buddhist and Christian practices; he continued his practice of *samatha* meditation at Kingston University, whilst still practising devotions as a Catholic. Georgina, who had continued to offer support, suggested attending a healing service. Paul was amenable to the idea and accompanied her to a special Mass of healing led by Monsignor Michael Buckley of the 'El Shaddai' community with assistance by other priests. The church was already quite full, so they sat on a long bench towards the back; Paul was content to just observe, but then it came to the point where priests started going up the aisles inviting people to come forward for healing. At the end of their row was a man in a wheel chair and it was expected that he would be approached first, but as the priest came up to the row he gazed straight at Paul and enquired of him of any healing requests. On being informed about Fuengsin, the priest anointed him and gave him instructions to pass on the blessing to his mother. He also invited him to join a group at the front, which Paul accepted. There he was received by Father Michael, who got Paul to put his palms together and pray for healing. The service went on for four hours, yet the church remained full throughout.

Paul then hastened back to Hagley and went with his father to see Fuengsin. When they arrived they found already present at her bedside Reverend Andrew and Reverend George, a West Indian Methodist minister; there was thus already a small interfaith gathering. Paul recounted briefly his attendance at the healing Mass and went over to his mother, but paused as he didn't know how to transfer the anointing — it seemed a rather strange thing to do. Fuengsin readily accepted the offer of help and simply guided his hands over the stomach and expressed appreciation. He was supported in prayers by Reverend Andrew and Reverend George, who proceeded to read from 1 Corinthians 13, the quality of love, which Fuengsin greatly appreciated, bringing to her mind the *Brahmaviharas*.

Having conveyed the spiritual healing which he had been granted, it was not clear what Paul should do next, so after consultation he returned once again to Surrey. At the end of January he wrote a letter from his address at Acre Road in Kingston upon Thames to FWBO members Dharmapani, Sunanda and Viracitta at the Birmingham Buddhist Centre in Moseley. After reporting the situation, he tried to look on the bright side:

Yet there is a lot of positivity to report as well. First and foremost, my mother has throughout been compassionate and calm — she has not protested. Also, she has demonstrated considerable will power and intends to make the most of the time ahead. Her mind remains as clear and alert as ever and those who have visited her have been inspired by her fine spiritual example.

The range of support she has had is remarkable — friends and colleagues from such a wide range of backgrounds have been wishing her well. There is certainly a lot of optimism and light.

I think she will be coming out of Kidderminster General today and will spend a few days at home in Hagley, before proceeding to stay with Thai friends at Pranee's Thai Restaurant in Selly Oak. I'm sure that she would like to hear from you once she gets there.

However, it also meant cancelled projects:

> One important consequence of all this is that my mother cannot perform the translation from English into Thai of Subhuti's book about Sangharakshita. She has requested that I write to Subhuti to notify him. I would be grateful if you could let me know of his current address (Norwich?).

As there was nothing further the hospital could do for her, a few days later Fuengsin was discharged and then went to stay with Pranee in Selly Oak as she was a trained nurse with the right skills to look after her and she also had hospice experience. Further assistance was provided by other family members; a young relative by the name of Thip patiently attended to her everyday needs. It was still hoped that even with the terminal diagnosis there would be some remedy found through Thai herbal medicine, meditation or miraculous intervention, but the disease was very advanced. Another Thai friend, Kai, offered to take care of Fuengsin, but she lived in Rugby, which was too far away. Attempts were still being made across many fronts — modern and ancient — to restore Fuengsin to full health.

It was not an ideal rest home as there was a recording studio next door, just the other side of the wall of the small bedroom where Fuengsin was sleeping. When the sessions were being recorded the room was overwhelmed with sound. Yet Fuengsin became calm and seemed strangely detached. On one occasion, when seated downstairs by the dining room table, she gently re-marked to Paul: 'At least I'm going up there' (her finger pointing upwards). Paul said nothing, still hoping for some miracle cure or at least prolongation, and clinging to the prospect that she would be like her mother, Khun Yay Somboon, who lived until she was in her mid-90s. However, he already had a sense of the inevitable also and asked her in the context of Dhamma: 'Is there anything else I should know?' She shook her head.

Any solution was more in hope than anything; Pranee's herbal medicine was not really having the desired effect. Everything was done to find a cure, but it seemed that Fuengsin fully knew and accepted her destiny. She continued cultivating merits by clutching coins in her hand and making resolutions, but the emphasis seemed to be on receiving as many visitors as possible. Now those apparently throwaway remarks about not wanting to get old became prominent and could not be brushed aside. Among her regular reading was Sogyal Rinpoche's *The Tibetan Book of Living and Dying*. In case Paul was in any doubt about the coming transition, Fuengsin continued, 'Look at all the people I have gathered for you', referring to her contacts in interfaith and beyond. She also remarked about Tony, 'How is it that he has been so devoted?' She was amazed at and really appreciated her husband's support.

News continued to spread further afield and reached Peter Tyler, who was now earnestly seeking meditation in the Christian tradition, partly prompted by Fuengsin's advice. He had just joined the Benedictine monastery of Christ the King in Cockfosters when he received a phone message of Fuengsin's illness and her stay in hospital. It was very unusual to let somebody out so soon after their arrival, but the abbot was very understanding. When Peter told him the news and her significance in Peter's life he said, 'You must go and see her at once because of the nature of the cancer . . . she won't have long.' He knew because he had done a lot of hospital visiting.

Just a few weeks after the diagnosis, on 15 February, Fuengsin was admitted to St Mary's Hospice in Selly Park. The hospice movement in the UK is a wonderful enterprise and this hospice is one of its fruits. It was a pleasant and caring environment, not as clinical as a hospital, and with attentive staff highly trained in palliative care. Fuengsin was initially placed in a ward with several others and settled in quite easily as the staff enabled everyone to feel a sense of calm and dignity.

The move signalled the last days and the last chance for people to see Fuengsin, which presented personal and logistical challenges, and left many of the visitors not sure how long they should stay. Yet it unfolded naturally enough so that everyone could have some access — just as for public treasure. Fuengsin remained calm and composed, so much so that several nursing staff thought Fuengsin was in her late twenties or early thirties, as all the scales of age seemed to have slipped away. Her practice was being noticed in other ways too: one of her visiting friends with an inner eye perceived Fuengsin's body swathed in green crystals. As Fuengsin's physical health waned, she remained alert, her awareness becoming very pronounced. Tony and Paul spent as much time with her as they could. The interactions were generally limited, with the odd exception. At one point Fuengsin asked Paul, 'How old am I?' Paul proceeded to compute: 58 years, 1 month, and the exact number of days. On hearing this she nodded acknowledgement and said nothing further.

Well-wishers still offered advice to Tony and Paul, some very practical — Pranee was particularly concerned that they ate enough to maintain their energy levels. More of the advice was at a spiritual level: one of Fuengsin's Thai friends suggested that Paul encourage her with the mantra 'Buddho...' However, Paul knew that this was not used in Fuengsin's practice. Even so he went over and half-heartedly recited this. Fuengsin immediately shook her head and responded, 'Samma Araham' and Paul readily accepted. He was in fact already repeating the mantra himself. Fuengsin also received monastic visitors, including Ven. Ajahn Khemadhammo, who came with Ven. Suthep, a monastic in the Forest Tradition of North-East Thailand. He went across to Fuengsin's bedside and gazed at her face, and remarked, 'She is practising padhāna', that is to say, meditating in earnest and striving for liberation.

Among the regular visitors was Ramona, who lived close by. On one occasion Fuengsin gripped Ramona's hand extremely tightly, drawing blood, showing her how strongly she was fighting. However, gradually Fuengsin's gestures became more subtle and reduced to slight movements of hands, mouth and eyes. Gradually she receded, as though moving into a back room; and her physical engagement diminished, but she retained awareness. Peter arrived, having taken the train from London, and dearly wanted to speak with her, but at first it seemed he couldn't hold any conversation with her for although she was conscious, she couldn't talk. However, when he saw her and actually spoke to her, her eyes were very attentive and she knew; she was well aware of his presence. Peter felt sure she heard what he had to say.

Meanwhile there were many activities taking place focused on helping Fuengsin. Reverend Andrew visited the Burmese Vihara with some of his students, where they were invited to join in a practice of metta bhavana, the meditation on 'loving-kindness', specifically for Fuengsin. The whole group did this together for about ten minutes, Buddhists and Christians doing this each in their own way, to powerful effect.

Within a few days Fuengsin indicated that she wanted the monks to be called for the remaining moments of transition. The hospice had a chapel, traditionally used for administering the last rites in the Christian tradition. Staff had no problem with the chapel being used by practitioners in other traditions and so arrangements were made for 22 February. On the day there was some strange weather: there had been signs of spring, but snow came and lay all round and about, covering the flowers that had been emerging. By this time Peter had arrived in the area. He had spent the night in Edgbaston, next to Selly Oak College, and then the snow had fallen heavily during the night. The next day he made his way to Manresa House and walked through the snow. When he arrived he went upstairs and sat in the chapel and just meditated and remembered Fuengsin.

At 2 p.m., Fuengsin was moved on a stretcher to the chapel and placed along the length of the room with a large crucifix behind her, above the altar. This was to be a ceremony of ceremonies for not only were there Buddhist chants in Pali, but many other kinds of chants and prayers — Vajira was there together with Anita, reading passages of Zen; there was also Tibetan Buddhist chanting in progress. It was like a symphony with many players of different instruments working diligently and in harmony under the direction of the conductor, the frail figure of Fuengsin at the centre. Tony and Paul entered, Paul joining at the head of the bed, opposite Senior Ada, who was trembling as she channelled healing energy. Many people continued to come for the ceremony; Reverend Andrew came with Sharada and gave Tony the twenty-third Psalm, suggesting that he whisper it to Fuengsin. This was the grand finale.

Several monks arrived, including Ven. Dr Rewata Dhamma, and Ven. Khemadhammo. They brought a statue of the Buddha, some incense sticks, and a bowl of water containing two carnations. They asked where they should put them, and Reverend Andrew indicated they could put them on the altar. They then created a *sima*, a ceremonial boundary, and indicated how they would proceed. They proceeded to chant in Pali and further well-wishers arrived, including Alfred and Elsie. The dramatic nature was heightened as a freak storm struck in the course of the proceedings; the sky went dark and hail-stones clattered on the ground, adding to the strong sense of crescendo.[1] There was speculation that she would pass away imminently, perhaps even during the ceremony.

However, Fuengsin made it through. The monks led everyone to practise metta bhavana and then took the flowers, full of water, and dashed some of the water onto every part of Fuengsin's body. She registered the water hitting her brow. Next, Paul held her hand, and repeated quietly, '*Samma Araham . . .* ', while Pranee spoke quietly into her other ear. The three monks each spoke to Fuengsin, reminding her of her meritorious deeds, especially what she had done to spread 'dharma'. She should have nothing to fear. Now was the time to be courageous and let go. As the chanting continued, each one went up to Fuengsin, said farewell in their own way and left the chapel.

The experience had a profound effect on many who attended. Reverend Andrew was moved to reflect:

> The experience almost made me repeat the words of Mother Julian of Norwich, 'All shall be well, and all shall be well, and all manner of things shall be well.'

After the ceremony, Fuengsin was moved to her own room and joined by a smaller group of friends and relatives. Ramona, Colm, and Peter stayed late into the evening, finally leaving just Tony and Paul, who stayed with Fuengsin throughout the entire night. The room became exceedingly still and every sound seemed to have a distant echo; regular sounds such as water flowing from the tap seemed etched in remarkable definition. Every moment was poignant.

Morning came and more visitors arrived to join the family. Fr Gerard Hughes visited and Peter was there again. He stayed on until the afternoon, but then had to depart for London. It was an emotional farewell. Then after 35 hours of constant vigil Tony and Paul decided they needed to get some rest, so late in the afternoon they returned to Hagley for a couple of hours rest. They were both exhausted.

Arriving back home, Paul sat on a sofa and reflected for a couple of minutes that he was losing a mother and a teacher. Wiping away a tear, he then proceeded to bed, first paying respects at the shrine in the back bedroom. Tony stayed downstairs and tiredness overcame him before he could make it upstairs. Paul likewise became submerged in a deep state of sleep, but he was woken up at 6.30 p.m. as his body was struck by cramp that seemed to come out of nowhere. He turned his body with some discomfort and then the pain subsided. He got up and had a bath, but remained in an aqueous dreamlike state as he felt a floating sensation; it was very strange. The cramp had completely disappeared.

Shortly after 7 p.m. Paul wandered downstairs and woke up his father, who had dozed off on the sofa. They had planned to leave at around 7.30 p.m. Meanwhile Peter was in London again and had arranged for evening Mass to be said for Fuengsin at the Monastery of Christ the King. In Hagley, at 7.20 p.m. Paul went to a shelf in the dining room to select a book to take to read. He saw one jutting out from the shelf and decided to pick a passage at random. It fell open at a page where Paul's eyes were drawn immediately to the following quote:

> A woman child, O Lord of men, may prove
> Even a better offspring than a male![2]

Just as Paul was pondering this quote, the phone rang. It was Ven. Ajahn Khemadhammo who broke the news: Fuengsin had just passed away. It was Thursday 23 February 1995.

* * *

On arriving at the hospice shortly before 8 p.m., Ven. Khemadhammo was there to greet Tony and Paul. Paul was keen to ask about how Fuengsin had passed away, about her state of mind. He was informed that it had been very peaceful. He was delighted as he was sure it meant an excellent transition, but as to why she had chosen to go when Paul and Tony were away remained a mystery, though it is said that a person will 'stay' whilst their loved ones are nearby, and pass on when they have gone out of the room. Sometimes it can help reduce the distress.

In the void of the following minutes and hours there was nothing to be done but reflect. It seemed that the passing was very quick, happening a little over a month after the diagnosis, though most of those who knew her reflected that the pain Fuengsin had experienced since the previous June was most likely coming from the cancer — she had been battling it for more than six months.

After a final regard of Fuengsin's body, arrangements were made to leave the body overnight at the hospice. Pranee, who was one of those who had been by Fuengsin at the passing, stayed to wash the body and she was joined by Ramona. Tony and Paul then went back home to get some proper rest.

They returned the next morning where the body was still *in situ*. Lama Lodro came and performed *phowa*, a Tibetan Buddhist practice to transfer consciousness so that Fuengsin could attain a better rebirth or even liberation in the after-death Bardo. During the course of the practice the lama seemed to channel some vocal sounds and then at its conclusion placed a special card on the body. All along in these final days a statue of Luang Phor Sodh in meditation had been by her side. This morning the figure of the Abbot seemed to Paul to be in a deep state of absorption.

The death was formally registered in the afternoon and funeral arrangements made with Porter & Sons in Stourbridge. At 6.20 p.m. Fuengsin's body was 'welcomed' at the Chapel of Rest, Porter & Sons, with chanting led by Ven. Dr Rewata Dhamma. Mass continued to be said in various churches, initiated by Tony. There were also ceremonies continuing at Buddhist temples and centres, including *dana* offerings and meditation practice at the Forest Hermitage (Wat Pah Santidhamma), the Birmingham Buddhist Vihara, Wat Sanghathan and at Karma Ling.

Fuengsin's passing was announced in the local papers. An article appeared in *The Birmingham Post*, on 28 February 1995. It was entitled 'Tributes to Buddhist Champion' and described Fuengsin as 'a Buddhist who greatly influenced dialogue between people of different faiths in the Midlands'. Meanwhile, news of the passing was shared and relayed abroad, reaching Thailand, where it caused enormous shock as it came unexpectedly.

An invitation was extended to those who knew Fuengsin to attend the cremation at Stourbridge Crematorium. It duly took place a week after her passing, on 2 March, which was again a Thursday; arriving just in time that morning from Thailand were Vasana and Ead. At 1.50 p.m. a hearse with Fuengsin's body arrived at the home in Hagley. Fifteen minutes later the cortege left for Stourbridge crematorium, with Tony and Paul in the funeral car following the hearse. Paul had been given instruction by Pranee to quietly provide a running commentary of familiar places — the intention being to inform Fuengsin's consciousness and enable her to know the way. Paul didn't question and did as instructed. The cortege made its measured way and arrived at the Crematorium, where there were already many people gathered; relatives and friends had taken days off work to pay their final respects and the chapel soon became full. On people's seats were copies of *Attachment*, the last book Fuengsin translated for Luang Phor Sanong.[3] Fuengsin had used it a lot. Among those in attendance was Peter Tyler, who had been born just round the corner and the last time he had been there was to attend his grandmother's cremation.

At 2.30 p.m. the cremation ceremony started; two consecutive 15-minute slots had been booked. This was a Buddhist ceremony and for many the first time that they had attended such a service. There were seven monks in attendance. They started by formally instituting a temporary Buddhist site, beginning with a tribute to the Triple Gem. The ceremony included the offering of new robes for making merit and ritual chanting, which were common traditions in Thailand, but unusual in Britain. However, for many an especially touching aspect was the forgiveness meditation, in which all attendees forgave Fuengsin of any wrongdoings against them and asked Fuengsin to similarly forgive them.

Midway through the service were tributes from Reverend Andrew and Sister Mary, who described Fuengsin's contributions to interfaith — embodied so much in Fuengsin's being. There was also a Dhamma talk from Ven. Dr Rewata Dhamma. Burmese Bhante explained the purpose of dedicating merits through analogy: it was like cultivating soil in which a good seed could bear much fruit, for without the soil no fruition could arise. Then there was the final blessing, offering a final chance for people to bid farewell. The body lay inside the coffin with incense sticks and flowers on top, and then to symbolise the merits from the ceremony, blessing water was slowly poured on a tree outside.

Afterwards a reception was held at the family home. At the reception Tony's sister, Liz, related that on the night of the 22 February, Fuengsin had appeared in a vivid dream to her and to one of her children, Patrick. She was standing calmly, not saying a word, dressed in a red dress, beside a paved path, near a square-shaped monument. Vasana was listening nearby and a tear came to her eye — for she had the same vision that night in Thailand. Unknown to them Fuengsin had been put in a red dress in the coffin. The family was joined also by Bhante, who sat in a wicker chair in the sun lounge; he seemed in a reflective mood.

Fig. 95: Ven. Dr Rewata Dhamma at the Trafford family home following Fuengsin's cremation.

The next afternoon Tony collected the ashes from the Chapel of Rest, Porter & Sons, and brought them home, placing them in the dining room. That moment seemed to bring a lull in activity, a little time to let everything sink in. Tony and Paul received continual support from friends locally, much of it practical to help keep their feet on the ground and maintain an even keel. They also visited Chepstow, drawing strength from family roots whilst further sharing the news.

Then on the morning of the 6 March the ashes were taken to the Forest Hermitage in Lower Fulbrook. The first monk to greet them as they came in was Ven. Ajahn Suthep, who smiled and received the ashes, placing them carefully in the shrine room. The ashes were kept there until after lunch. Then they were collected and carried down the garden path where they were interred at the foot of an apple tree, well irrigated by an underground stream. Present were Phra Ajahn Khemadhammo, Phra Ajahn Suthep, a monk from the Netherlands, Ajahn Kit, Namjal, Aunts Pranee and Preeya, Ramona and a friend, Rosemary, Tony and Paul. It was then evident that the image that had been perceived in the vision could be identified as this garden, with the path leading down from a miniature Shwe Dagon monument to the site of the ashes. One Thai lady suggested trying to open the casket to look for relics, but the seal on the casket was too strong and so the ashes remained intact. Fuengsin did not want her ashes to be separated and had really wanted them to be placed inside a pagoda at the Birmingham Buddhist Vihara, but they hadn't completed it. Even so, Wat Pah Santidhamma was true to its name as she had proposed — a peaceful spot, an ideal resting place for the Dhamma-farer.

Fig. 96: The site of Fuengsin's ashes at the Forest Hermitage, Lower Fulbrook.

Notes

1. The unusual storm of hailstones was noted in Pedgley, D. E. (1996). *A remarkable winter cold front hailstorm, 22 February 1995. Weather*, 51, pp. 330-341.

2. Quote from 'King Khosala's daughter' (*Book of Kindred Sayings* (Saṃyutta-nikāya), Sagatha Vagga 3 (Kosala-samyutta) Verse 16. This had been quoted in Narada's *The Teachings of the Buddha*.

3. *Attachment* by Ven. Ajahn Sanong Katapunyo may be accessed online at: http://fuengsin.org/translate/sanong/attachment/

15

Fuengsin's Legacies

There was emptiness after the cremation. Not just in terms of the dispersal of well-wishers and the ceasing of related activities, but somehow there was something lost in the atmosphere. In this emptiness there was pause for reflection. Many questions remained, some not yet expressed, but in the absence there was still some continuity.

According to Thai Buddhist belief, after a person passes away, unless that person attains to the state of *nirvana*, then in accordance with the Law of Karma, dependent upon various factors, there will be rebirth of consciousness, and so on, giving rise to a new life.[1] It is said that this arising of the next 'destination' often occurs within seven days, further key periods being within 50 days and 100 days of the passing. Up until that time, there are activities involving happy and respectful remembrance to transmit positive energies to the deceased. This is characterised by merit-making, which are acts of generosity, moral virtue and meditation. Fuengsin had remarked that on these occasions retaining a calm and positive state of mind was important since unbridled sorrowfulness reverberates beyond the physical realm: she related that when people were mourning with tears it was like they created a heavy shower for the departed, making it harder for them on their onward journey.

Fuengsin was fortunate in that she had chosen many friends who understood much about life and death, so that the practices that she had taught — especially of meditation — were continued. They also retained a bright outlook and a number of people remarked to Paul, 'She'll be supporting you now.' It seemed that the calmness she displayed radiated to those around her, not just to those in the immediate vicinity, and it was not confined to those who had met her. Shortly after Paul had returned to Kingston upon Thames, he was invited for Sunday lunch with Georgina's family in their large rambling house. Paul hadn't known the family for long and they had never met Fuengsin in person, yet at the meal table Georgina seemed to intuit what had happened at the hospice. Although she was Christian and Fuengsin was Buddhist, she gently expressed no concerns at Fuengsin's transition, sensing the passing was peaceful and adding that she felt a deep purity.

Fuengsin was certainly not forgotten. When Vasana returned to Thailand, she got together with a group of 22 of their liberal arts friends, who knew Fuengsin from their days in the Faculty. Under the direction of Khunying Orachorn, who took Vasana to view a marble shop, they arranged for a commemorative headstone to be engraved, inscribed with Fuengsin's name in English and Thai. They then presented it as a gift for Tony to place at the foot of the apple tree at the site of her ashes.

Fig. 97: Memorial Stone for Fuengsin, Forest Hermitage.

Vasana later gave a tribute in the *Chulalongkorn University Faculty of Arts 50 Years Anniversary Annual*. In the article she related the shock at her passing and then the response of the group of her friends to make a gift of the memorial stone. She described Fuengsin's character at Chula and her contribution to Buddhism in the UK.

Phra Ajahn Khemadhammo, who had kindly made himself available for much of Fuengsin's final weeks, continued his caring pastoral role towards Tony and Paul. In early April he sent a card to them. Inside was enclosed a short note in which he asked about their welfare and also a letter from Westhill College, written by Margaret Breiner, in which the College had made a donation in memory of Fuengsin. The Abbot also mentioned Fuengsin and family in the latest issue of the monastery's newsletter.

A few days after my return I was shocked to hear that Fuengsin Trafford, or Daeng as she was better known to her Thai friends, was suffering from a particularly nasty and virulent form of cancer and was not expected to live long. I had got to know Fuengsin, who had come to this country from Thailand as a student more than thirty years ago, long before there were many Thais here, and married and settled in the Midlands, when I spent some time in Birmingham in the late seventies. When we started ANGULIMALA she was one of the first to join and accepted appointments as Buddhist chaplain to a couple of establishments. As a devout Buddhist, serious meditator and the daughter of a prison governor this was nothing out of the ordinary for her. Then, when we felt it was time for this wat to have a Thai name it was she who told me that I should call it Wat Pah Santidhamma. During her last week, as she rapidly deteriorated, we watched with her and it was a patient and peaceful passing. For years she had been active in Buddhist and interfaith circles in the Midlands and at her funeral the crematorium was crowded with the many friends she'd made over the years. She will be much missed. Her ashes have been interred at the foot of a small apple tree planted by her devoted husband and son in the grounds here at Wat Pah Santidhamma. May Fuengsin know the secure peace of Nibbana.[2]

Fuengsin's passing was a loss to quite a few monastics and meant some related projects were put on hold. Luang Phor Sanong reflected that now there was no-one to do the translation work, though Wat Sanghathan gained the services of one of Fuengsin's friends, Preccha, who became a maechi on a permanent basis and later Pranee also served in this capacity for a while.[3] It seemed that Fuengsin wished that her causes should continue to receive help by whatever means available. Although she left behind relatively few material possessions, there were a few notable items: in her will she indicated that her Thai edition of the Pali canon should be given to Phramaha Somboon at the Wolverhampton vihara. Of the remaining works relating to religion, Paul was granted first look; he decided to keep these initially in the house and later took some volumes with him when he had his own flat. Fuengsin also left some savings for Paul, which were to support the completion of his PhD. The fact that there was not much in the way of physical goods in some ways made her absence more pronounced, because of the many services she had rendered.

Vasana indicated how the news had come as a complete surprise in Thailand and without any family member to explain in person the hiatus was pronounced. Tony and Paul were conscious of this awkward situation and resolved that at least one of them should go to visit Fuengsin's family, but they needed first to be sure of receiving a proper invitation. An invitation duly arrived from Fuengsin's sisters and in late October 1995 Tony made a trip to Bangkok. His presence was greatly appreciated as he could at least convey to the household that Fuengsin's passing was peaceful.

Whilst in Thonburi, Tony also visited the Potikanok family where Ajahn Gaew had been teacher to Fuengsin. He went with Darunee, Ajahn Gaew's daughter, to make an offering at Wat Paknam. At that time Paul, who had been staying in Surrey to continue with his PhD, came up to the family home in Hagley. *En route* to the house he decided to buy some flowers at the florist, to place in front of the shrine. It was a very unusual thing for Paul to do. On return from Thailand, Tony showed a photograph from Wat Paknam, which had the same date as Paul's return and in the photo were purple orchids, the same kind as Paul had bought and placed in the shrine at home. Coincidentally, that year Assistant Professor Prakhong, Fuengsin's long-time *kalyanamitta* at Wat Paknam, passed away soon after. On returning to Thailand from abroad she was found having hardly unpacked, giving the appearance that she had become exhausted.

News spread even to Northeast Thailand. During a visit to Wat Pah Baan Taad, Jane presented *dana* to Luang Ta Maha Boowa on Fuengsin's behalf. As she made the offering, Ven. Paññavaddho was on hand to interpret and shared the news with the Abbot. A look of sadness came over his face; even though they had only met once 23 years ago he evidently still remembered her. It was a period in which several chapters were closing, but new ones were about to begin.

* * *

Within weeks of Fuengsin's passing, Paul had already made a resolution to write her biography. It was a useful goal that motivated him to keep in touch with some of Fuengsin's friends and accordingly he made a list of a few people in particular whom he ought to thank and thence retain contact. In Hagley he continued family conversations with the Crabtrees. Alfred encouraged him: 'But you are in a unique position, aren't you? Here you are brought up with your father as a Catholic and there, having got the Catholic attitudes and teaching and all the rest of it, but you've also been taught by your mother. And from what I can gather, your mother put into you quite a lot one way or another!'

A key contact was The Reverend Andrew Wingate, who kept in touch with Tony and Paul, reiterating the significance of Fuengsin's life and work, offering touching reflections on how he had been personally affected in his mission. He also kept them informed about interfaith events in Selly Oak Colleges and gave Paul considerable incentive to share his mother's life story. On 21 April 1995, he wrote:

> I would certainly encourage your thought of writing a biography of Fuengsin if you find the time. It would certainly be very interesting to know about her Thai roots from within Thailand within her early years as well as what she contributed here. I have talked with your father, and have written a small piece about my involvement with her over the last few weeks in particular, and some reflections as a Christian on the Buddhist way of death that I experienced and admitted. This is a way of showing to others how interreligious differences can be transcended in these situations.

Soon after, he came to visit Tony and Paul to inform them that he was hoping to write a paper for an academic journal and asked how they felt about it. They readily agreed and eventually, two years later, an article was published in *Theology* with the grand title, 'A Woman of Faith Dies: Death of a Champion of Buddhism.'[4] It was unusual subject matter for a journal devoted to Christian theology, albeit one that had a broad outlook in its treatment of ministry and theological education. However, as director of an Anglican college, Andrew Wingate was able to offer much for reflection on pastoral and theological levels. He was struck especially by the personal qualities of Fuengsin, the calmness in facing up realistically to the situation, and the support that was offered to her by the Buddhist community.

> I saw the strong sense of unity and support from the Buddhist community. There are various strands in local Buddhism, but all owned Fuengsin as their concern. Distinctions between Theravada, Mahayana and other schools seem to fall away in face of such a situation. I saw also the strength of friends across cultures, Europeans through where she lived, through her husband's church, through her interfaith work and, above all, Thai friends who live around. There was no sense of illness and grief being privatized, around the close family. It was shared in the community. Nor were details of the illness kept hushed; it was on the basis of realities that care could be shown, with Fuengsin in some ways the rock of strength in the midst of it all.

Theologically, he found significant differences, but still much of value.

> The Christian talks of salvation, the Buddhist of Nirvana, and they are clearly very different. But both provide a framework for approaching death constructively. I learnt that the Buddhists do not leave the person alone to face death. The teaching of the Buddha, the power of meditation, and the support of the monks are all there. The above book [*Attachment*] says, "Monks chant to

help us develop a meritorious state of mind. When we listen to them chanting and giving the discourses of the Dhamma, all the merit will concentrate in the mind alone." For a Christian, it is to Jesus we look: "Come unto me all that labour and are heavy laden, and I will give you rest." The Buddhist talks of 'taking refuge'.

Whatever one's world views, the conclusion was that Fuengsin set an example, centred on loving-kindness and compassion. It led to a peaceful passing that seemed completely fitting.

* * *

The whole episode raised searching questions about what could be offered between Buddhists and Christians, questions that were taken up elsewhere, in an emerging forum to which Fuengsin had contributed significant foundations. Less than a year after Fuengsin's passing there was the first meeting of the European Network of Buddhist-Christian Studies, which took place in a snowy Hamburg between 9 and 11 February 1996.[5] It was hosted by Dr Gerhard Köberlin, at the Academy of Mission at the University of Hamburg, with the assistance of Prof. Aasulv Lande from Lund University and Dr Perry Schmidt-Leukel from Munich.

At this inaugural meeting, a keynote speech was given by Ven. Dr Rewata Dhamma, on the topic of what as a Buddhist he expected from friendship with Christians. True to the approach established by the Multi-Faith Centre in Birmingham, he opened with a few comments on what a Buddhist expects from another Buddhist. He started by relating the diversity of the various schools, noting that in the West there was the distinction of free access to so many of them. Given this context, Bhante stressed how important it is that we learn respect, quoting an edict on one of Emperor Ashoka's pillars:

The one who does not respect another's religion does not respect his own.
The one who respects another's religion respects his own.

The initial Network meeting included a large Birmingham contingent that had already been developing an internal coherence, providing a solid launchpad for further gatherings. The desire to maintain the dialogue was thus readily apparent and the next meeting took place at the Benedictine Monastery of St Ottilien, on the outskirts of Munich. The participants widened, involving more lay and monastics and the Network has since continued with this broad approach, notable for being academic but with community representation.

Paul had been invited initially as Fuengsin's representative and on the plane to Germany he met up with one of her colleagues at Ascension College, Elizabeth Harris. There was another traveller who was also involved in interfaith, Sandy Martin [now Bharat], who was a follower of Paramahansa Yogananda. It was by coincidence that she was *en route* to somewhere else and Paul made a connection that was to lead to his eventually becoming involved with the International Interfaith Centre in Oxford. Whilst he was not formally an academic or faith representative in this area, he naturally continued with engagement on a personal level. He returned from Hamburg to Surbiton in the evening and was met with a warm welcome of Iftar offered by the resident landlord, Thaer Sabri, a Muslim originally from Jordan.

Back in Birmingham, a few months later, under the guidance of Andrew Wingate, the College of Ascension, now formally the United College of the Ascension, also furthered the Christian–Buddhist dialogue, organising courses and conferences. One conference, held on 4–6 June 1996, was partly in honour of Fuengsin and explored the theme of 'love meets wisdom'.[6] Its introductory notes remarked:

> At one level Buddhism seems further away from Christianity than any of the major world faiths. At another level, the Christian/Buddhist encounter can yield great fruit, when people of integrity from the two faiths grow to understand what each has to offer.

Among its speakers was Ramona Kauth, whom Fuengsin had designated as the person to carry on the work that she had undertaken at the College, which was symbolised by Ramona inheriting a shawl. Fuengsin's memory was cherished: Paul attended the gathering and noticed that on display in the main conference room was a framed photograph of Fuengsin flanked by four colleagues in interfaith.

Interfaith in Birmingham reconfigured in the late 1990s. The Birmingham Council of Faiths became more prominent, with Ramona much involved. However, in 1999 Selly Oak Colleges became absorbed into the University of Birmingham, as the Selly Oak Campus. By this time the Multi-Faith Centre had vanished, but arguably much of the pioneering work had been already absorbed in the public sector. For some of the interfaith pioneers, opportunities presented themselves elsewhere. Andrew Wingate moved to the Diocese of Leicester in 2000 and subsequently became Director of Interfaith Relations and was a founding director of the St Philip's Centre for Study and Engagement in a Multi-Faith Society. He was then appointed as Royal Chaplain to Her Majesty the Queen in 2008.

Fig. 98: USPG College of Ascension lecturers in interfaith (from left to right):
Sharada Sugirtharajah, Dr Elizabeth Harris, Fuengsin, Canon Andrew
Wingate, and Canon Jemima Prasadam.

From his base in Surrey, Paul was starting to make more frequent use of his word processor as he jotted notes and typed letters relating to spirituality and interfaith. Among Fuengsin's friends in Birmingham he identified 'Senior Ada' (Ada Pask) as someone with whom he should particularly make an effort to retain contact. She responded and wrote back; like many of Fuengsin's friends, she was kind-hearted, with some forthright views and she wouldn't say anything that she didn't firmly believe. So in asserting that Fuengsin was 'very high up' she really meant it. Paul mentioned this on the phone to Peter Tyler, who remarked in a follow-up letter:

I laughed because of the story you have heard — that is she "very high up" =is= exactly right — this has been exactly my experience too.

Peter went on to describe an episode.

The day after she died I . . . spent a great deal of the day in prayer + meditation. In the late afternoon I decided I should really go for a walk, so I went around the local streets. As I set off it was a bright clear February day – half way through my walk there was the most stupendous thunderstorm - quite unreal in the middle of winter in England! As I walked I had no protection and got completely soaked — then suddenly there was the most phenomenal thunder-clap // and lightning simultaneously over my head — in which instant I had an insight into what I can only describe as "enlightenment". It only lasted a few seconds yet it completely changed my outlook — and even today — 5 months later — I can recall it — in fact it is not something I recall but live.

The "vision" was connected with Fuengsin's form + voice and a great out-pouring of compassion + wisdom.

Yes — I have no doubt that she has achieved rebirth in a very enlightened realm and will continue to help all of us by radiating spiritual energy.

Fuengsin's enduring influence was evident in his further reflection:

> I often feel her benign presence through meditation — although I didn't seek it or cling to it (as we were told at the Funeral) — she brings it gratuitously![7]

Peter returned to [the Benedictine Monastery of Christ the King in] Cockfosters at a time when the monastery was starting to enter into dialogue with the Dalai Lama. This led Peter and monastic confrères to visit His Holiness in Bodh Gaya, where they could practise meditation together. They have since shared further retreats in Florence and Northern Ireland. He thus expanded his encounter with Buddhism to include Tibetan and other traditions, consolidating what he received from Fuengsin, whom he acknowledges as important in providing his first encounter with Buddhism — not just the theory, but also the practice.

As per Fuengsin's advice, Peter remained Christian, a view that was rein-forced for him when the Dalai Lama came to Cockfosters and responded to a question about Buddhists becoming Christians and Christians becoming Buddhists with: 'You can't put a yak's head on a sheep's body.' However, such was his commitment to exploring contemplation and meditation that Paul invited him to Surrey to give an introductory talk at the KUGOS Meditation Society in October, to which he agreed.[8]

* * *

Paul was keen to disseminate his mother's work and identified the Internet as having great potential. In September 1995 he wrote to Ven. Ajahn Piboon, the Abbot of Wat Sanghathan in Birmingham, seeking permission for Fueng-sin's translations of Luang Phor Sanong's teachings to be published on the World Wide Web. This was gladly granted and Paul was given complete liberty to do this as he saw fit. It resulted in all four projects (A Taste of Dhamma, Oneness, Attachment and the Calendar on Dependent Origination) being prepared as a series of Web pages available to networked computers. Paul scanned the books' images with the help of a colleague in machine vision, resulting in the first books going online a few months later. He also received permission from Dr Rewata Dhamma to publish online a leaflet with details of the Dhamma-Talaka Peace Pagoda in Edgbaston, and helped set up the first website for the Samatha Association.

He continued with his meditation practice and exploration of the burgeoning online resources, reflecting that whilst his mother had been alive, she had never formally taught him her method of meditation. What Fuengsin held most dear she did not teach directly, but she would talk about it informally and sometimes communicate non-verbally, so gradually Paul received Dhamma by way of transmission. A few months after she had passed away, whilst browsing topics on a Buddhism forum, Paul saw a post from Thailand inviting people to donate towards Buddha images in the Dhammakaya tradition. The message came from a supporter of Wat Phra Dhammakaya, located in Pathum Thani, some 30 miles from the centre of Bangkok. Paul hadn't heard of this temple, but sent a reply and subsequently learnt about the project and the temple. He was informed of its connection with Wat Paknam. It had been founded in 1970 by a nun, Khun Yay Chan, a disciple of Luang Phor Sodh who excelled in meditation. He then subscribed to *The Light of Peace*, an international publication, and eventually became involved with the main branch in the UK.

Paul retained contact with Senior Ada and they sent each other winter greetings. However, he still hadn't met her and a year after Fuengsin's passing, he confessed in a letter that he still wasn't sure who she was. Having suffered chronic weariness he felt he could benefit from healing himself and asked whether she would be available. He commented, 'I have had a major difficulty in finding someone who is supportive of my spiritual background, especially that which has come through Fuengsin via her Buddhist lineage.'

Senior Ada agreed and Paul went to visit her at her home a couple of months later, on 4 April. Even though she lived in Birmingham and there were maps available showing the precise location in Erdington, he struggled to get there, almost catching the wrong train, but eventually he reached his destination at around 4 p.m. Ada thought he wouldn't make it; shortly before she had a vision of Fuengsin pacing up and down the length of her lounge wringing her hands, worried. When Paul arrived she remarked how worn out he looked, but he stayed quite a while and the situation became more relaxed. Later Ada had another vision of Fuengsin, this time it was in the bathroom. She perceived Fuengsin in an altogether different mood, dancing with joy. It was a complete transformation and Ada wasn't sure why. However, during the course of the afternoon she tried to 'read' Paul and had further visions, one of which related to Paul providing instruction in the Buddhist path. On hearing about Paul's work on the Internet, she was keen to encourage him there. Ada was in the process of accreditation and needed testimonials about healing sessions, so Paul willingly provided one in a letter he sent in May.

At Ada's recommendation, Paul later visited a healing practitioner in Stourbridge, where he shared his mother's background and passing. The practitioner was formally qualified as a medical doctor, but preferred to embrace a more holistic approach. She didn't appear keen on Fuengsin's interfaith work and on being told about Fuengsin's cancer of the pancreas, commented that such a condition is often a reflection of someone who has a low opinion of themselves. Paul was a bit taken aback, but the remark about Fuengsin's emotional state though strange seemed credible, especially in view of her difficulties in childhood.

Some years later Paul and Tony visited the Forest Hermitage and found that, along with two Thai ladies, Pranee was staying in the grounds, practising as *maechi*. When they arrived, one of these ladies glanced at Paul and then connected him with a vision she had during meditation. As she was sitting there in meditation, she felt someone sitting beside her — it was a young lady dressed all in white — and when she saw Paul she immediately saw the connection. Later she talked about healing and she said that she herself had some problems with her stomach, which might have been related to cancer, but she could cure it through meditation. She informed Paul that Fuengsin didn't quite reach that level where she could heal herself.

* * *

Paul completed his PhD in 1997 and then did some voluntary work at the International Interfaith Centre in Oxford in February and March 1998. He maintained contact with only a few of Fuengsin's many friends, including some in Hagley such as Mollie Pauli, who related how she drew comfort when dipping into the booklets produced by Wat Sanghathan. However, later that year he started his first full-time job at the University of Derby, as Internet Resource Developer (MultiFaithNet). As it became clear that he would undertake interfaith work also, he came to regard himself as a 'second generation interfaith worker'.

Since then there has been an occasional trickle of fresh insights or the jogging of memories almost lost, some of which have come during several visits that Paul has since made to Thailand. During one of them, in 2005, he met up with Vasana and Songsee and was presented with a copy of the 50th anniversary annual for alumni of the Faculty of Arts at Chulalongkorn University, who studied there between 2497 and 2501. They showed him the entry for his mother:

- 148 -

59. เฟื่องศิลป์ แทรพฟอร์ด (ศรายุทธพิทักษ์)

เกิด   24 ธันวาคม 2479

            Mr. Tony Trafford

บุตร   ดร.เฟื่องศักดิ์ Trafford

การศึกษา

‣ ร ร เตรียมอุดมศึกษา

‣ อบ. (จุฬาฯ)

ถึงแก่กรรม 25 กุมภาพันธ์ 2518

Fig. 99: Fuengsin's entry in the *Faculty of Arts 50th Anniversary* volume.

Vasana explained that the entry gives her name as Fuengsin Trafford (Sarayutpitag) and then gives some bio data: her date of birth followed by her husband's name and then her son, 'Dr Fuengsak Trafford'. Paul was mystified. Then Vasana explained that this was the Thai name that Fuengsin had given Paul. Songsee knew also, but for Paul it was the rediscovery of a forgotten identity.

* * *

This biography has taken a long time to complete — I was contacting people within weeks of my mother's passing about the project. Now more than 20 years later it has finally been achieved, with the hope that her life story, like a lotus blossom, may continue to inspire the spiritual path.

Notes

1. Buddhist teachings on people 'passing away' are subtle and difficult to express in words. This is colloquial language in case there are objects on 'person' and 'passing away'. Among Buddhists there is quite some variance in view. Some would say that 'Who or what passes away?' is already a misconceived question.

2. *Santidhamma: Buddhist Teaching and Practice in the Heart of England.*
   Newsletter Sources: Yann Lovelock, a fellow member of Angulimala, and Forest Hermitage Newsletter Spring 1995.

3. A *maechi* is a female renunciant follower of the Buddha, who observes the Eight Precepts. They retain the legal status of a lay person, but because of their practice we can respectfully call them 'nuns'.

4. Andrew Wingate, 1997. 'A Woman of Faith Dies: Death of a Champion of Buddhism', *Theology*, Volume 100, No. 75, pp 170–9. Reproduced online with permission: http://fuengsin.org/tributes/theology/

5. European Network of Buddhist-Christian Studies, website: http://www.buddhist-christian-studies.net/
   Ven Dr Rewata Dhamma's text at the meeting in February 1996 is reproduced at: http://chezpaul.org.uk/interfth/cbfriend.htm

6. A copy of the notice for the USPG conference in June 1996 is at: http://chezpaul.org.uk/interfth/uspg.htm

7. About 20 years later, Peter described the episode in which Fuengsin advised him to deepen his Catholic practice, quoting her on a BBC Radio 4 programme called *Beyond Belief*. Several guests on the programme had converted from Christianity to Buddhism, whilst Peter had studied Buddhism and remained Christian. http://www.bbc.co.uk/programmes/b006s6p6/episodes

8. Peter Tyler was appointed Professor of Pastoral Theology and Spirituality in 2014. He is also Programme Director, MA Theology at St Mary's University College, Twickenham, where he has many students undertaking projects in Buddhist-Christian dialogue.

A Synopsis of Buddhism

The word 'Buddhism' refers to a record of canonical teachings of the one we know as the Buddha, or, more respectfully, the Lord Buddha. He is regarded as a Fully Enlightened One, who followed a path in meditation to supreme realisation and further was able to transmit the path to others so that they too might become Enlightened and continue the transmission. Those who follow his path are called 'Buddhist' and today Buddhists live predominantly in Asia: the 'Northern Schools' that cover Nepal, Tibet and Mongolia; the 'Eastern Schools' that include Korea and Japan; and the 'Southern Schools' that range from Sri Lanka through to Thailand and Cambodia. However, in recent decades there have been growing numbers of organisations in Europe and America, which may be denoted 'Western Schools'.

There are Buddhists in almost every country of the world. Their expressions vary considerably, but most Buddhists constantly recollect and pay homage to the 'Triple Gem', namely: the Buddha, born some 2500 years ago in India as Siddhartha Gotama, and all the Buddhas since time immemorial; the Dhamma (both his teachings and supramundane reality); and the Sangha (both the monastic community who practice and continue the transmission and the noble followers who tread the path beyond our place and time).

Buddhist practice may be summed up in three Pali words: *dāna*, *sīla* and *samādhi*, which can be translated as generosity, virtue (or ethical conduct) and meditation. Generosity is practised at many levels, material and immaterial — hence, for example, one may give time as well as money. Advanced forms of generosity may involve considerable sacrifice, as exemplified by the Jataka story of the Bodhisattva Vessantara, who through compassion was prepared to give up everything, even his family.

In one verse of the Dhammapada, a concise anthology of teachings given by the Buddha, sīla is summarised by:

> Cease to do evil, cultivate good and purify the mind.
>
> Dhammapada, verses 183

Buddhists train themselves to know how their intentional actions (*karma*) are linked to particular results or outcomes (*vipaka*). Hence the importance of cultivating purity of mind for:

1. Mind precedes all mental states. Mind is their chief; they are all mind-made. If with an impure mind a person speaks or acts then suffering follows him like the wheel that follows the foot of the ox.

2. Mind precedes all mental states. Mind is their chief; they are all mind-made. If with a pure mind a person speaks or acts then happiness follows him like his never-departing shadow.

Dhammapada, Canto 1 verses 1,2

In order to avoid impure or unskilful actions there is a basic formulation of rules for lay followers: the *pañca-sikkhāpada* or five virtues (*pañca-sīla*), commonly referred to as the Five Precepts. They are traditionally recited in the presence of bhikkhus, a practice with which Fuengsin became familiar as a child, brought up in a traditional Thai family. Nowadays, especially for practitioners abroad, they are often conducted at home, perhaps in front of a shrine containing a Buddha image. The precepts are rendered in English and Pāli as follows:

1. I undertake the precept to abstain from the taking of life.
   Pāṇātipātā veramaṇī sikkhāpadaṃ samādiyāmi.
2. I undertake the precept not to take that which is not given.
   Adinnādānā veramaṇī sikkhāpadaṃ samādiyāmi.
3. I undertake the precept to abstain from misconduct in sensual actions.
   Kāmesu micchācāra veramaṇī sikkhāpadaṃ samādiyāmi.
4. I undertake the precept to abstain from false speech.
   Musāvāda veramaṇī sikkhāpadaṃ samādiyāmi.
5. I undertake the precept to abstain from liquors that cause intoxication and indolence.
   Surā-meraya-majja-pamādaṭṭhānā veramaṇī sikkhāpadaṃ samādiyāmi.

These precepts may be treated as principles that an individual should apply intelligently according to their specific situation. Whilst these are formulated in terms of refraining from, they have a positive counterpart as pure or skilful performance, which is the cultivation of worthy and meritorious actions, actions of which the wise are said to approve. These are respectively: the cultivation of loving kindness, generosity, contentment, truthfulness and heedfulness.

The continual practice of virtuous conduct, particularly through observance of the precepts, has a gradual impact on one's behaviour. A further practice, which has a longer-term view, is to practise perfections until they are intrinsic. In the Pali canon these are referred to as the Ten *pāramī* (Perfections), namely: *dāna* (generosity), *sīla* (moral virtue), *nekhamma* (renunciation), *paññā* (wisdom), *viriya* (vigour), *khanti* (patience), *sacca* (truthfulness), *adhiṭṭhāna* (determination), *mettā* (loving kindness), and *upekkhā* (equanimity). These are special qualities of a noble being that must be cultivated for Bodhisattvas, those beings who, out of compassion, resolve to attain to Buddhahood for the welfare of others. The Jataka, part of the canonical literature, provide hundreds of accounts describing at a level accessible to followers generally how these perfections are gradually obtained through wonderful accounts of heroic efforts.

Whilst there are opportunities for spiritual growth in every thought, deed and word, the main engine for practice is meditation, described in varying levels of detail elsewhere in the canon, which is a huge subject that cannot be exhausted. When we say 'meditation', we mean the cultivation of mind, particularly expressed through the Pali word *bhāvanā* in its most encompassing sense: to see and know, know and see at deeper and deeper levels. One who is thus consummate in their practice of the precepts and ennobled through Perfections is able to turn their mind to the highest goals, to understand and realize them. Perhaps the most famous formulation in Buddhism of these goals is the Four Noble Truths (*āriya sacca*): the reality of *dukkha* (unsatisfactoriness or suffering), its origin, its cessation, and the path to cessation. This path is characterised by the Buddha as the Middle Way, namely an Eightfold Noble Path (*atthangika-magga*), which means undertaking a virtuous path of the right practice in the right way: right view, right intention, right effort, right speech, right action, right livelihood, right mindfulness and right concentration. Fuengsin practised Middle Way meditation — Dhammakaya — which is described in the next section.

Practitioners tread this path until it leads to the supremely happy and peaceful state in which there is permanent release from the spectres of birth, old age, sickness and death. By practising diligently, one may gradually see three characteristics about our normal existence: it's inherently unsatisfactory, is ever-changing and what we thought of as 'self' is not what it seemed. So we strive for transcendence. This is a universal path open to all "sentient beings", but it is exceedingly subtle in nature, so hard to find and difficult to tread because we have three deep-rooted fires to overcome: greed, hatred and delusion. Nevertheless the Buddha gives encouragement to keep practising indicating many times a succession of benefits "to be realized in the here and now."

Acknowledgement

This article draws on the author's contribution to *A Global Guide to Interfaith* by Sandy and Jael Bharat, published by O Books, and on his Master's dissertation on the Fifth Precept, *Avoiding pamāda: An analysis of the Fifth Precept as Social Protection in Contemporary Contexts with reference to the early Buddhist teachings.*

A Short Introduction to Meditation

We provide here basic instructions on the practice of Dhammakaya meditation, also known as the Middle Way. This simple technique is suitable for beginners and is widely taught at Dhammakaya temples and meditation centres around the world. Further details may be found online at: http://www.mdwmeditation.org/.

1. The sitting posture, which has been found to be the most conducive for meditation, is the half-lotus position. Sit upright with your back and spine straight — cross-legged with your right leg over the left one. You can sit on a cushion or pillow to make your position more comfortable. Nothing should impede your breathing or circulation. Your hands should rest palms-up on your lap, and the tip of your right index finger should touch your left thumb. Feel as if you are one with the ground on which you sit. If you are unable to sit cross-legged then that's okay — just try to find a similar posture where you can remain relaxed and alert. Feel that you could sit happily for as long as you like.

2. Softly close your eyes as if you were falling asleep. Relax every part of your body, beginning with the muscles of your face, then relax your face, neck, shoulders, arms, chest, trunk and legs. Make sure there are no signs of tension on your forehead or across your shoulders.

3. Close your eyes and stop thinking about the things of the world. Feel as if you are sitting alone — around you is nothing and no-one. Create a feeling of happiness and spaciousness in your mind.

    Before starting, it is necessary to acquaint yourself with the various resting points or bases of the mind inside the body.

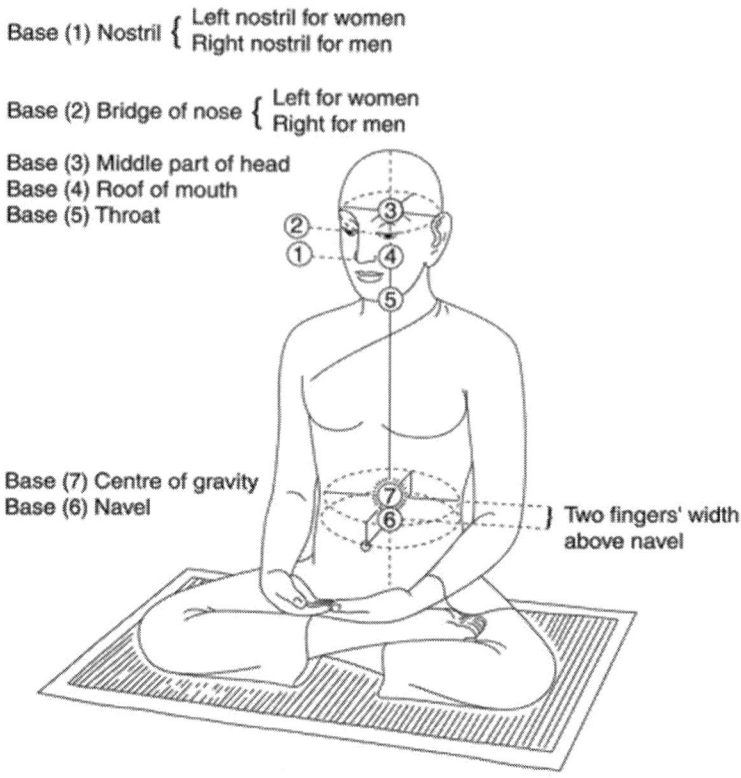

Base (1) Nostril { Left nostril for women / Right nostril for men

Base (2) Bridge of nose { Left for women / Right for men

Base (3) Middle part of head
Base (4) Roof of mouth
Base (5) Throat

Base (7) Centre of gravity
Base (6) Navel

} Two fingers' width above navel

Fig. 100: The seven bases of the mind.

- The first base is at the rim of the nostril, on the right side for men and on the left side for women.
- The second base is at the bridge of the nose at the corner of the eye — on the right side for men and on the left side for women.
- The third base is at the centre of the head.
- The fourth is at the roof of the mouth.
- The fifth is at the centre of the throat above the Adam's apple.
- The sixth base is at a point in the centre of the body at the meeting point of an imaginary line between the navel through the back and the line between the two sides.
- The seventh base of the mind is two fingers' breadth above the sixth base.
- This base is the most important point in the body. It is the very centre of the body and the point where the mind can come to a standstill.

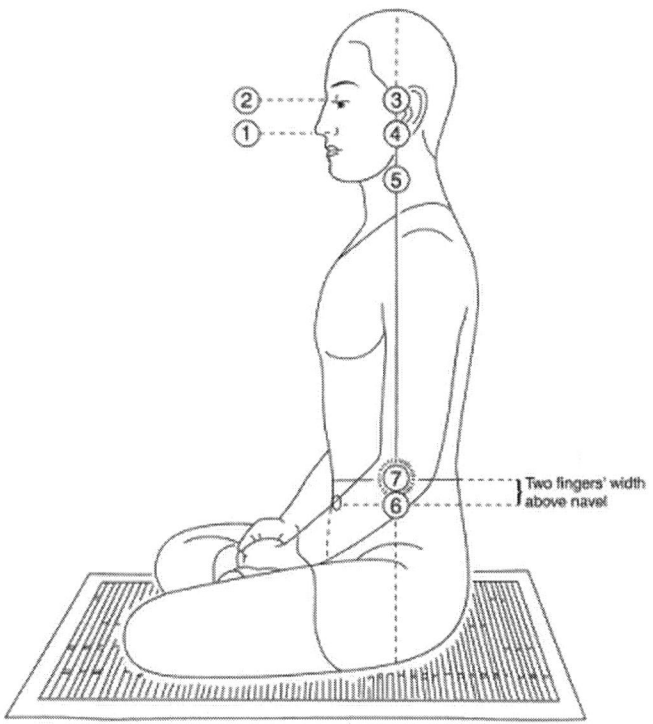

Fig. 101: The seven bases of the mind (side view).

4. Feel that your body is empty space, without organs, muscles or tissues. Gently and contentedly rest you attention at a point near to the seventh base of the mind — at the centre of the body. Whatever experience arises in the mind, simply observe without attempting to interfere. In this way your mind will become gradually purer and inner experience will unfold.

5. If you find that you cannot dissuade the mind from wandering, then your mind needs an inner object as a focus for attention. Gently imagine that a bright, clear, crystal ball, the size of the tip of your little finger, is located inside at the centre of the body. Perhaps you'll find you can imagine nothing, but later you'll be able to see a crystal ball of increasing clarity. Allow your mind to come to rest at the very centre of the crystal ball. Use the subtlest of effort and you'll find that

the crystal ball becomes brighter and clearer. If you use too much effort you will find that it gives you a headache.

6. If you find that your mind still wanders from the crystal ball, you can bring the mind back to a standstill by repeating the mantra, 'Samma-araham', silently, as if the sound of the mantra is coming from the centre of the crystal ball. Repeat the mantra over and over again without counting.

7. Don't entertain thoughts in your mind. Don't analyze what's going on in the meditation. Allow the mind to come to the standstill — that's all you need to do. If you find that you can imagine nothing, then repeat the mantra, 'Samma-araham', silently and continuously in the mind. If you find that you're not sure about the location of the centre of the body, anywhere in the area of the stomach will do. Persevere because today's day-dream is tomorrow's still mind, today's darkness is tomorrow's inner brightness, today's perseverance is tomorrow's fulfilment. Don't be disappointed if you find your mind wandering. It is only natural for beginners. Make effort continuously, keep your mind bright, clear and pure, and in the end, you will achieve your goal.

8. Keep repeating the mantra and eventually the sound of the words will die away. At that point a new bright, clear, crystal ball will arise in the mind of its own accord. The crystal ball will sparkle like a diamond.

9. This stage is called *pathama magga* (primary path). At this stage the shining crystal ball is connected firmly to the mind, and is seated at the centre of the body. You will experience happiness. With continuous observation at the centre of this crystal ball, it will give way to a succession of increasingly purer bodily sheaths until it reaches the ultimate one called 'Dhammakaya', the highest level of attainment of supreme happiness.

Glossary

This glossary provides a list of mainly Thai and Pali terms plus the names of some Buddhist practitioners, particularly monks, and places that were significant for Fuengsin. A chapter number where each term occurs is also provided.

Phra **Abhidhamma** (Thai: พระอภิธรรม, Pali: *abhidhamma*) [Ch. 10]
> Higher Buddhist teachings, exploring in depth especially how the mind functions

Ajahn (also spelt *Acharn*, Thai: อาจารย์, Pali: *ācariya*) [Ch. 3]
> Professional teacher; monks who have been in robes at least five years may be formally addressed as Phra Ajahn

Ambedkar [Ch. 10]
> A legal expert who drafted the Indian Constitution when India became independent in 1947, a Dalit who converted to Buddhism and inspired millions to follow suit.

Phra **Ananda Bodhi** (Thai: พระอานนท์โพธิ) [Ch. 6]
> A Canadian who learnt meditation originally in the Mahasi Saydaw method, subsequently ordained as a Theravada bhikkhu and later was recognised by the 14th Karmapa as an incarnate lama. He learnt some Dhammakaya meditation after the passing of Luang Phor Wat Paknam. It is not known by the author who were his teachers.

anapanasati (Thai: อานาปานสติ, Pali: *ānāpānasati*) [Ch. 12]
> Mindfulness of in-and-out breathing or, simply, mindfulness of breathing

anattā (Thai: อนัตตา, Pali: *anattā*) [Ch. 12]
> [are] not-self. All conditioned phenomena are said to have no intrinsic self, none of this is to be regarded as 'me' or 'mine'

Angthong (Thai: อ่างทอง) [Ch. 1]
> Lit. 'Golden Bowl', a central Thai province

Angulimala (Thai: องคุลิมาล) [Ch. 10]
> Angulimala was formerly a mass murderer, but reformed and became a disciple of the Buddha and then attained Arahantship; eponymously named Buddhist chaplaincy service established at the Forest Hermitage under spiritual direction of Ven. Khemadhammo.

Aniccang (Thai: อนิจจัง), Pali: *aniccaŋ*) [Ch. 12]
> Of impermanence. [adj.] All conditioned phenomena are said to be impermanent. Note the adjectival form is used because these qualities are used in reference to something

Ao Manao (Thai: อ่าวมะนาว) [Ch. 11]
> Lemon Bay, a bay with a popular beach, lying to the south of Hua Hin

Ar (Thai: อา) [Ch. 1]
>Aunt (or uncle) considered to be younger or junior to one's father. [These terms can apply more generally to cousins in different generations.]

Phra Arahan (Thai: พระอรหันต์, Pali: *arahat*) [Ch. 15]
>Enlightened One (lit. 'worthy one'). One who has attained to nibbana, permanently freed from dukkha

Aranyaprathet (Thai: อรัญประเทศ) [Ch. 8]
>Thai Border town with Cambodia

Ariya magga mee ong 8 (Thai: อริยมรรคมีองค์8, Pali: *ariyo aṭṭhaṅgiko maggo*) [Ch. 2, 10]
>Eightfold Noble Path. Fundamental Buddhist teaching about the path to the cessation of unsatisfactoriness: Right View, Right Intention, Right Speech, Right Action, Right Livelihood, Right Effort, Right Mindfulness, Right Concentration.

Ariya sacca see (Thai: อริยสัจสี่) [Ch. 2]
>Four Noble Truths. Fundamental Buddhist teaching that states there is an unsatisfactory nature to life or existence, that it has a root cause (craving based on ignorance), that the unsatisfactoriness may be brought to an end and how to this may be achieved.

Phra Chao Asok Maharaj (Thai: พระเจ้าอโศกมหาราช) [Ch. 15]
>Emperor Ashoka. Celebrated South Asian Emperor who lived around 200 years after the Buddha. He abandoned rule by force to rule by Dharma, proclaimed through edicts written on pillars set up throughout his kingdom.

Ayutthaya (Thai: อยุธยา) [Ch. 1]
>Central Thai province, former capital of Thailand from fourteenth to eighteenth century CE

baan meuang (Thai: บ้านเมือง) [Ch. 8]
>home land, homeland, country; using 'home' makes this term nostalgic.

Baht (Thai: บาท) [Ch. 1]
>The currency of Thailand. 1 baht = 100 satang

Ban Phe (Thai: บ้านเพ) [Ch. 3]
>Lit. 'Phe Home', a subdistrict of Rayong

Phra Rajawang Bang Pa-In (Thai: พระราชวังบางปะอิน) [Ch. 8]
>Bang Pa-In Royal Palace. An eighteenth-century palace on the Chao Phraya river in Phra Nakhon Sri Ayutthaya, which predates the current Bangkok era

Bangmod (Thai: บางมด) [Ch. 4]
>Lit. 'Ant district', the district where Thonburi Technical College was established, the name becoming synonymous with the college

Bhante (Thai: ภันเต, Pali: *bhante*) [Ch. 9]
>Venerable Sir. 'Bhante' is a respectful term of address for a bhikkhu,

more common in Burmese communities, typically given to a monk with the main responsibility for a temple.

Phra **Bhavanakosol (Veera Kanuttamo)** (Thai: พระภาวนาโกศล (วีระคณุตตโม)) [Ch. 11]

Advanced meditation instructor at Wat Paknam, now with official title Phra Phrarajbrahmathera, long-time director of meditation at Wat Paknam

Chao Khun **Bhavanavithet (Phra Ajahn Khemadhammo)** OBE (Thai: เจ้าคุณ ภาวนาวิเทศ (พระเขมธัมโม)) [Ch. 10]

English bhikkhu trained in the Thai Forest Tradition, disciple of Ven. Ajahn Chah, Founder Abbot of Forest Hermitage. In 2003 he was appointed an Officer of the Most Excellent Order of the British Empire (OBE) for services to prisoners.

Phra **Bhikṣu** [Skt] (Thai: พระภิกษุ, Pali: *bhikkhu*) [Ch. 2]

Monk. A bhikkhu is a male renunciant who chooses to maintain the Patimokka discipline to train the mind in the direction of nirvana

Phra **Bhikṣuṇī** [Skt] (Thai: พระภิกษุณี, Pali: *bhikkhunī*) [Ch. 2]

Nun. A bhikkhuni is a female renunciant who chooses to maintain a discipline, formally observed by maintaining 227 rules, to train the mind in the direction of nirvana

Bhumibol Adulyadej (Thai: ภูมิพลอดุลยเดช) [Ch. 1]

King Bhumibol Adulyadej (Rama IX), King of Thailand, 1946–

Ajahn John **Blofeld** (Thai: อาจารย์ จอร์น โบลเฟลต์) [Ch. 3]

John Blofeld was a Sinophile, student and teacher of Chinese Buddhism during the 1920s to 1940s, and then settled in Thailand. He was one of Fuengsin's teachers of English language, and authored several books on Norhern traditions of Buddhism, including *The Wheel of Life.*

Phra **Bodhisattva** (Thai: พระโพธิสัตว์, Pali: *Bodhisatta*) [Ch. 10]

One who, motivated by compassion for living beings, spends many lifetimes accumulating paramis in order to attain Buddhahood

boon (Thai: บุญ, Pali: *puñña*) [Ch. 2]

Merit. It is like an energy store arising from good deeds, which yields fruits in terms of positive circumstances. It has for many centuries been cultivated diligently (as in 'making merit') by Thais, especially when the going gets tough.

Boowa (or **Bua**) (Thai: บัว) [Ch. 6]

Lotus

Bot (Thai: โบสถ์, from Pali: *uposatha*) [Ch. 12]

Chapel, where ordinations and other official acts of the Order take place. They usually contain important Buddha images.

Brahmavihāra (Thai: พรหมวิหา 4, Pali: *Brahmavihāra*) [Ch. 2]

Four Brahmaviharas (lit. 'Brahma abidings'). These are the four primary kinds of love in Buddhism: *mettā* (loving kindness), karuṇā (compassion), muditā (sympathetic joy) and upekkhā (equanimity).

Jane **Browne** [Ch. 6]

Secretary of the Hampshire Buddhist Society in the mid-1960s and close friend of Fuengsin from that time onwards

Phra **Buddha Chao** (Thai: พระพุทธเจ้า) [Ch. 1]

Lord Buddha. 'Buddha' is a title, which means 'one who is Fully Enlightened or Awakened'. Particular reference is made to the Buddha Gotama, the one who lived in India around the sixth century BCE. Thais are usually show respect to the Buddha by prefixing with 'Phra' and appending with 'Chao', a term used for a prince.

Phra **Buddha Roop** (Thai: พระพุทธรูป, Pali: *Buddha rūpa*) [Ch. 6]

Buddha form or image Buddha rupa is most accurate, Buddha statue is okay. A physical form or semblance of the Buddha, which in Buddhist societies are accorded great respect and reverance.

Buddha Sakaraj (Thai: พุทธศักราช) [Ch. 1]

Buddha era

Phra **Buddha Sasana** (Thai: พระพุทธศาสนา) [Ch. 1]

This is how Thais refer to the teachings of the Buddha, referred to academically in the West as 'Buddhism'.

Buddha vihara (Thai: วิหารพระพุทธ) [Ch. 6]

Lit. 'Dwelling place of the Buddha' (Pali), formally the space in which monastics undertake ceremonies and special functions, hence can be equated with monastery and Thai temples are often called 'Buddha vihara'. More loosely any centre devoted to Buddhist practice.

Buddhadasa bhikkhu (Thai: พุทธทาสภิกขุ) [Ch. 6]

Lit. 'Buddha slave' (Pali), a Thai bhikkhu admired, especially by social activists, for his philosophical and intellectual approach, and simple mode of practice. He was unusual for his open dialogue with other world views. He passed away in 1993.

Buddhist Era; abbreviated as พ.ศ. (BE) [Ch. 1]

The Buddhist calendar was introduced in Thailand in 1912 CE to replace the previous Rattanakosin Era convention. There are different views on precisely what occasion is marked — one view is that it gives the number of years since the Buddha's paranibbana, i.e. passing into final Enlightenment without remainder.

Chalerm Suttirak (Thai: เฉลิม สุทธิรักษ์) [Ch. 1]

Fuengsin's first cousin, later to become Lt Gen. Suttirak, the longest serving Director of Thailand's Military Communications (1966–74).

Chander Bodhi [Ch. 10]

Ven. Chander Bodhi. Indian bhikkhu, President of the Punjab Buddhist Society, contributor to Buddhism courses at the Multi-Faith Centre in Birmingham

Khun Yay Ajahn Maharattana Upasika **Chandra Khonnokyoong** (Thai: คุณยาย
อาจารย์มหารัตนอุบาสิกาจันทร์ขนนกยูง) [Ch. 15]

>   Khun Yay Chan was a disciple of Luang Phor Sodh, who declared her 'sec-
>   ond to none' for her meditation practice. She went on to found Wat Phra
>   Dhammakaya at the age of 60.

Changwat (Thai: จังหวัด) [Ch. 1]

>   Province. Thailand is divided into 76 provinces; a province is divided into
>   **mueang** (subdistricts), of which **amphoe mueang** is the capital district;
>   meuang are subdivided into **tambol**s and further subdivided in **muban**s
>   (villages).

Chen / Chan / Ch'an / Zen (Thai: เซน) [Ch. 12]

>   A school of Mahayana Buddhism that developed in China during the sixth
>   century and spread generally in the Far East. The term derives from San-
>   skrit *dhyana*, which means 'meditative absorption'.

Chieng Mai (or Chiang Mai) (Thai: เชียงใหม่) [Ch. 11]

>   Lit. 'New city', Chieng Mai was founded in the thirteenth century CE,
>   originally as capital of old Kingdom of Lanna

choie choei (Thai: เฉยๆ or เฉย เฉย) [Ch. 4]

>   (In meditation), silently, passively, just letting it be

choie laek (Thai: เชยแหลก) [Ch. 4]

>   Unfashionable, out-of-date (slang)

chompoo (Thai: ชมพู) [Ch. 3]

>   Rose apple, colour of rose apple (pink)

Chonburi (Thai: ชลบุรี) [Ch. 3]

>   Province located to south-east of Bangkok

Chulalongkorn (Thai: จุฬาลงกรณ์) [Ch. 1]

>   King of Thailand, King Rama V, name of the first University to be estab-
>   lished in Thailand (often shortened to *Chula*)

Damnoen Saduak (Thai: ดำเนินสะดวก) [Ch. 11]

>   Lit. 'comfortable avenue' (or 'way to proceed/navigate'), this amphoe
>   (district) is famous for its floating market

dāna (Thai: ทาน, Pali: *dāna*) [Ch. 2]

>   Giving, generosity, charity — a basic quality that Buddhists practise

Dhamma (Thai: พระธรรม, Pali: *dhamma*) [Ch. 4]

>   Truth, reality, norm. A key word that has meanings at ordinary and
>   supramundane levels; it can mean the Buddha's teachings, and also the
>   attainment of those teachings in seeing as it really is; as a sacred word it
>   should have the 'Phra' prefix when speaking in Thai. More common for
>   the former meaning is the equivalent, Phra Buddha Sāsanā (Thai:
>   พระพุทธศาสนา).

Phra **Dhammadhiraraj Mahamuni** (Thai: พระธรรมธีรราชมหามุนี) [Ch. 5]

>   A senior monk from Wat Mahathat who was instrumental in establishing
>   Wat Buddhapadipa

Dhammaduta   (Thai: ธรรมทูต) [Ch. 10]

A Dhamma Ambassador, one trained in being a messenger wherever there is a need

Phra **Dhammapada** (Thai: พระธรรมบท) [Ch. 6]

Lit. 'Holy Way of Dhamma' (Pali), a treasury of concise statements attributed to the Buddha with regard to the path to Enlightenment.

Dhammakaya (Thai: ธรรมกาย, Pali: *dhammakāya*, Skt.: *dharmakāya*) [Ch. 4]

Taken directly from the Pali it means 'body of Dhamma' or 'Truth body', i.e. the unconditioned reality and essence of Buddhahood

Dhammaprasit (Thai: ธรรมประสิทธิ์) [Ch. 8]

Lit. 'Dhamma success' (derived from the Pali *siddhi*). Dhammaprasit House was founded in 1970 with the aim of establishing a monastery in Pathum Thani (later to become Wat Phra Dhammakaya).

Dharmachari [Skt] (Thai: ธรรมจารี, Pali: *Dhammacāri*) [Ch. 12]

Dharmachāri (lit. 'one who lives/experiences Dharma'). In FWBO specifically denotes someone who has taken ordination in the order.

Doen pai sù khwam sùk (Thai: เดินไปสู่ความสุข) [Ch. 8]

Lit. 'Walk towards happiness', a magazine published by Dhammaprasit House

kwam **duk** (Thai: ความทุกข์, Pali: *dukkhaŋ*) [Ch. 12]

Of unsatisfactoriness, suffering [adj.] The problem of life, the reality of the First Noble Truth, is that it's not satisfactory

Dusit Thani (Thai: ดุสิตธานี, from the Pali *tusita*, rendered in Thai: ธูษิฏา) [Ch. 8]

Tusita heaven. The fourth heaven realm in Buddhist cosmology, in which Bodhisattvas reside before their final rebirth where they attain to Buddhahood. The name is particularly auspicious for Thais, so it has been given to many secular places such as a 1:20 scale model town designed by King Rama VI.

Brian **Dyas** [Ch. 6]

President of the Hampshire Buddhist Society in the mid-1960s

Farang (Thai: ฝรั่ง) [Ch. 3]

Farang, Guava. The Thai word for the guava fruit, introduced by Portuguese traders in the sixteenth century.

Farang (kon) (Thai: ฝรั่ง (คน)) [Ch. 3]

Westerner (people). Foreigner, generally associated with white Caucasians. Its etymology is unclear; a popular theory is that it is derived from the Persian word that refers to Western Europeans, perhaps the Franks.

Feun (Thai: ฟื้น) [Ch. 1]

Capt. Luang Sarayutpitag's given name, means 'recovery' or 'renaissance'

Friends of the Western Buddhist Order [Ch. 12]

Buddhist organisation founded by Sangharakshita in the UK in the late 1960s

Fuengsak[da] (Thai: เฟื่องศักดิ์ from Pali: *sakkata*, pp. of *sakkaroti*=vb. honour, esteem, treat with respect, receive hospitably) [Ch. 15]

The Thai name Fuengsin gave to Paul.

Fuengsilapa (Thai: เฟื่องศิลป์) [Ch. 1]

Lit. 'She who flourishes in the Liberal Arts', Fuengsin's given name, but seldom used in full.

Ajahn **Gaew Potikanok** (Thai: อาจารย์แก้ว โพธิกนก, Pali: *Bodhi kanaka*) [Ch. 4]

Lit. 'Crystal [of] golden Buddha-nature', Ajahn Gaew was Fuengsin's first teacher of Dhammakaya meditation; Potikanok is a Thai-style Romanised phoneticisation of Bodhikanok used by the family.

Phra **George Anāvilo** (Thai: พระจอร์จอนาวิโล, Pali: *anāvilo*) [Ch. 12]

Lit. 'Pure, clean, unstained'. Senior English bhikkhu (lay name George D. Bickell), long-time resident at Wat Mahathat, practitioner and teacher of Vipassana meditation

Himapan (Thai: หิมพานต์, Pali: *Himavanta*) [Ch. 12]

A forest which surrounds the base of Mount Meru in Indic religious traditions of South and Southeast Asians. In Thai culture it is often depicted in art as home to many creatures not ordinary visible, including nagas.

Hinayāna (or more commonly, Hinayana) (Thai: หีนยาน, Pali: *Hinayāna*) [Ch. 6]

Low vehicle. A term, generally considered as derogatory, referring to Buddhist traditions in Sri Lanka and Southeast Asia that focus primarily on individual Enlightenment. It has often been [mis]applied as synonymous with practice according to Theravada traditions. The alternative of 'Southern Schools' is generally preferred.

Hua Hin (Thai: หัวหิน) [Ch. 11]

Lit. 'rock head', a coastal district with a fine beach resort, often used as a residence of King Bhumibol — increasingly so in his later years.

Hua Lamphong (Thai: หัวลำโพง) [Ch. 11]

Main railway station in Bangkok, a central hub with lines to the north, south, east and west

Huajook (Thai: หัวจุก) [Ch. 9]

Topknot. A traditional Thai style in which hair is bunched in shape of a topknot.

Na **Ing** (Thai: น้าอิง) [Ch. 2]

Aunt Ing, a close friend of Fuengsin who taught her how to compile scrapbooks

jai yen (Thai: ใจเย็น) [Ch. 2]

Lit. 'cool mind/heart'. Calm, composed — an essential quality for Thais to maintain or otherwise they will at least lose face.

Jambu tawipa [Skt] (Thai: ชมพูทวีป, Pali: *Jambudīpa*) [Ch. 12]

A continent in Buddhist cosmology, roughly in the area of India, sometimes used as the old name for India

Jamikorn (Umpan) (Thai: จามิกร (อำพันธ์)) [Ch. 1]
Fuengsin's fourth eldest sister

Jamras Kamkoon (Thai: จำรัส) [Ch. 8]
Husband of Vasana, flight captain for Thai International Airways

Jātaka (Thai: ชาดก, Pali: *Jātaka*) [Ch. 12]
A series of more than 500 accounts of previous lives of the Buddha illustrating how as a Bodhisattva he gradually developed paramis.

jong kraben (Thai: โจงกระเบน) [Ch. 1]
Traditional Thai-style trousers, a piece of cloth wrapped around the waist with two ends pulled in and tucked at the back. They are similar in length to breeches.

Kamma (Thai: กรรม — *kham*, Skt.: *karma*) [Ch. 4]
Intentional action (or deed) in body, speech and mind

Kammatthana (Thai: กรรมฐาน, Pali: *kammaṭṭhāna*) [Ch. 4]
Lit. 'the place of *kamma*', being particularly the subject of meditation, which includes a traditional list of 40 meditation objects

Kanchanaburi (Thai: กาญจนบุรี) [Ch. 8]
Province in the West of Thailand, directly to the West of Bangkok beyond Nakorn Pathom, with the infamous Death Railway and the Bridge over the river Khwae

Phra **Kapilavaddho** (Thai: พระกบิลวัฑโฒ, Pali: *Kapilavaḍḍho*) [Ch. 8]
Ven. Kapilavaddho (named after the birthplace of the Buddha, hence the implied meaning of 'He who spreads Dhamma'), the ordained name of William Purfurst, later Richard Randall, when he became bhikkhu at Wat Paknam, Bhasicharoen in 1954.

Kaya (Thai: กาย, Pali: *kāya*) [Ch. 4]
Body, relating to material, immaterial and transcendent bodies

kesa, loma, nakka, danta, tako (Thai: เกศา, โลมา, นะขา, ทันตา, ตะโจ, Pali: *kesā, lomā, nakhā, dantā, taco*) [Ch. 15]
The five dermatic constituents of the body (i.e. outer coverings of the body), to be contemplated continually by a practitioner. This *kammatthana* practice is popular in Thai forest traditions.

kham wai-alai (Thai: คำไว้อาลัย) [Ch. 1]
Lit. 'words of mourning', i.e. mourners' tributes.

khao mun gai (Thai: ข้าวมันไก่) [Ch. 11]
Hainanese chicken and rice — steamed rice with chicken cooked in oily coconut sauce

khao tom (Thai: ข้าวต้ม) [Ch. 11]
Rice gruel. Staple dish, often served at breakfast, to which may be added bits of fish, meat, leaves and spices.

Khuddaka Nikāya (Thai: ขุททกนิกาย, Pali: *Khuddaka Nikāya*) [Ch. 10]
Collection of little texts

Khun (Thai: คุณ) [Ch. 1]
    Mister, Ms., you (polite)
Khun Da (Thai: คุณตา) [Ch. 6]
    grandfather
Khun Yay (Thai: คุณยาย) [Ch. 1]
    A term of respect for an elder woman
Ko Samet (Thai: เกาะเสม็ด) [Ch. 3]
    Samet island. An island located in the Gulf of Thailand off the coastline of
    Rayong, approximately 220 km southeast of Bangkok, part of Ban Phe.
Ko Samui (Thai: เกาะสมุย) [Ch. 11]
    Island off the east coast of the Kra Isthmus in Thailand, located close to
    Surat Thani town.
Kong phan thá-hǎn puen yài ti neung raksa Phra Ong (Thai: กองพันทหารปืนใหญ่ ที่
๑ รักษาพระองค์ ฯ) [Ch. 1]
    His Majesty's 1st artillery battalion
Kris Sakaraj (Thai: คริสต์ศักราช) [Ch. 1]
    Lit. 'Christ era'. Common Era, abbreviated as CE (aka AD)
Krung Thep Mahanakorn (Thai: กรุงเทพมหานคร) [Ch. 1]
    Bangkok. The capital of Thailand (the full title is much longer). Its origi-
    nal name from which we get the phonetics was บางกอก
kusalakamma 10 (Thai: กุศลกรรมบถ ๑๐, Pali: *dasakusalakamma*) [Ch. 12]
    Ten wholesome actions: three in body (not taking life, not taking that
    which is not given, not engaging in sexual misconduct), four in speech
    (refraining from false speech, from malicious speech, from harsh speech,
    and from gossip), and three in mind (refraining from covetousness, from
    ill will, and from wrong view).
Kuti (Thai: กุฏิ, Pali: *kuti*) [Ch. 12]
    A hut, especially used for solitary meditation practice. It is usually
    associated with forests, where it is commonly the residence of a monk,
    but the term may also apply to a monastic's quarters in urban areas.
Chao Mae **Kwan Im** (Thai: เจ้าแม่กวนอิม) [Ch. 15]
    Guanyin, Kuan Yin, Kannon [Japanese] and other variants. Bodhisattva of
    Compassion, especially revered in East Asia.
Laṅkāvatāra Sūtra (Thai: ลังกาวตารสูตร, Pali: *Laṅkāvatāra Sūtra*) [Ch. 10]
    A sutra of Mahāyāna Buddhism recounting a teaching primarily between
    the Buddha and a bodhisattva named Mahāmati ('Great Wisdom'). It is
    significant in the development of Buddhism, especially in China and the
    Far East.
Likay (Thai: ลิเก) [Ch. 2]
    Likay is a form of traditional Thai folk theatre — earthy tales of good
    triumphing over bad.
Lama **Lödrö** [Ch. 9]
    Resident Lama at the Tibetan Buddhist centre, Karma Ling, Birmingham

Lookseua (Thai: ลูกเสือ) [Ch. 9]

Boy Scout (lit. 'Tiger cub'). The Thai Scout movement was founded by King Rama VI.

Lopburi (Thai: ลพบุรี) [Ch. 3]

Lopburi (lit. 'Lop city'), is the name given to a province and capital city about 150km NE of Bangkok; derives from 'Lava pura'.

Luang (Thai: หลวง) [Ch. 1]

Great, superior, royal. In the context of ranks of the nobility that existed until 1932, the second lowest rank, below Phra and above Khun

Lung (Thai: ลุง) [Ch. 1]

Uncle — mother or father's elder brother

Mae Kha (Thai: แม่ค้า) [Ch. 2]

Lit. 'Mothers who trade', i.e. female traders

Maechi (Thai: แม่ชี) [Ch. 3]

Nun. A Thai term for a female practitioner who is a renunciant follower of the Buddha and observes the Eight Precepts. She usually resides at a temple, leaving behind household life to devote herself more fully to intense Buddhist practice, symbolised by wearing the white robe and shaving her head. She is technically an upasika in that she retains the legal status of a lay person, but because of their practice we can respectfully call her a 'nun'.

Magruk Thai (Thai: หมากรุกไทย) [Ch. 11]

Thai chess. Similar to standard chess, but with some different and not so powerful pieces.

Maha (Thai: มหา, Pali: *mahā*) [Ch. 1]

Great. A very common prefix in compound words found in Buddhist and royal language. It comes from *mahant*, but the 'nt' gets dropped in compounds.

Phra Ajahn **Maha Boowa Ñanasampanno** (Thai: พระอาจารย์มหาบัว ญาณสมปนฺโน) [Ch. 6]

Famous monk and abbot in the Thai Forest tradition, disciple of Luang Pu Mun, who established his monastery in Udon Thani, Northeast Thailand, and played an important role in helping to establish the tradition in the West.

Maha Wittyalai Silapakorn (Thai: มหาวิทยาลัยศิลปากร) [Ch. 3]

Silpakorn University (lit. 'University of the fine arts'), Thailand's most distinguished university of Fine Arts

Mahachai (Thai: มหาชัย) [Ch. 11]

Fishing town with railway terminus in Samut Sakhon province, line leading into Bangkok

Mahasi Sayadaw (Thai: มหาสี สยาดอ) [Ch. 5]

Burmese monk and meditation master after whom a meditation system was named and popularised as the 'Mahasi method' based on mindfulness on the rising and falling of the abdomen

Mahāyāna (or Mahayana) (Thai: มหายาน, Pali: *Mahāyāna*) [Ch. 6]

Great vehicle. A term referring to Buddhist traditions that focus primarily on Enlightenment of all beings with some sacrifice regarding an individual's own attainment

mai pen 'rai (Thai: ไม่เป็นอะไร) [Ch. 15]

It's nothing / never mind / it doesn't matter. A very common Thai saying in response to an apology or something not going as intended.

Māra (Thai: มาร) [Ch. 6]

Death, The Evil One. The general meaning is death, but in the Buddhist context, capitalised, it is not physical death, but refers to a force of obscuration preventing beings from Enlightenment.

Mathayom suksa (Thai: มัธยมศึกษา) [Ch. 2]

Secondary study, i.e. Secondary Education in Thailand

metta (Thai: เมตตา, Pali: *mettā*) [Ch. 6]

Loving kindness. One of the four *Brahmaviharas* (divine abidings), qualities of love according to the Buddha's teachings. The others being *karunā* (compassion), *muditā* (sympathetic joy) and *upekkha* (equanimity).

metta bhavana (Thai: เมตตาภาวนา, Pali: *mettā bhāvanā*) [Ch. 12]

Meditation practise to cultivate states of loving kindness

Phra Sri Ariyamettan (Thai: พระศรีอริยเมตไตรย์, Pali: *Buddha Metteyya*) [Ch. 15]

Maitreya Buddha. The last of the five Buddhas said to appear on Earth some time in the future, during the present world cycle (*kappa*), characterised especially by *metta*. The Buddha-to-be is said to be residing in Tusita heaven.

Mitrapab (Thai: มิตรภาพ) [Ch. 8]

Lit. 'Friendship', a joint US–Thai educational foundation that was founded in the late 1960s with the specific aim of establishing in every province a school with at least four classrooms for deprived children.

Mongkol chiwit 38 (Thai: มงคลชีวิต 38, Pali: *Mangala Sutta*) [Ch. 2]

Sutta on the 38 Blessings of Life

Mongkut (Thai: มงกุฎ) [Ch. 1]

With reference to King Mongkut of Thailand (Rama IV), full title, Phra Bat Somdet Phra Poramenthra Maha Mongkut Phra Chom Klao Chao Yu Hua (Thai: พระบาทสมเด็จพระปรเมนทรมหามงกุฎฯ พระจอมเกล้าเจ้าอยู่หัว). He served as a monk for 20 years before assuming the throne.

Mor-Sor-Jor (Thai: ม.ส.จ.) [Ch. 11]

Abbreviation of the museum dedicated to the practice and teaching of the late Abbot of Wat Paknam; 'Mor' is short for his title, [Chao Khun] Phramongkolthepmuni; 'Sor-Seua' denotes his given name of Sodh [= 'fresh']; 'Jor' is short for his ordained name of Candasaro.

Morradok (Thai: มรดก) [Ch. 4]
> Cultural heritage or inheritance; hence *morradok dhamma* is 'dhamma heritage' or 'dhamma inheritance'

Muang (or Meuang) Thai (Thai: เมืองไทย) [Ch. 1]
> Thailand, the place of the Thai people

Phra Ajahn **Mun Bhuridatto** (Thai: พระอาจารย์มั่น ภูริทตฺโต) [Ch. 8]
> Lit. 'blessed with wisdom', forest monk of the early twentieth century, widely claimed as a meditation master who attained to Arahatship.

Na (Thai: น้า) [Ch. 1]
> Aunt (or uncle) considered to be younger or junior to one's mother

Nāga (Thai: นาค) [Ch. 3]
> A being described in the Buddhist cosmology as being a kind of protector, somewhat like a dragon or serpent

Nai Boonman Poonyathiro (Thai: นายบุญมั่น ปุญญาธีโร) [Ch. 15]
> Thai meditation teacher, former bhikkhu, who came to the UK in 1962, where he settled for a number of years. He laid foundations for lay practice, resulting in the establishment of the Samatha Trust. He subsequently returned to Thailand, but still visits the UK to teach on retreats.

Nakorn Ratchasima (or Rajasima) (Thai: นครราชสีมา, Pali: *rājāsimā*) [Ch. 3]
> Nakorn Ratchasima (lit. 'royal boundary'), a province (changwat) and city in the North East of Thailand, part of Isaan region, shortened to Korat.

namdarn peeb (Thai: น้ำตาลปีบ) [Ch. 2]
> Sugar tin

Ñanasampanno (Thai: ญาณสมฺปนฺโน) [Ch. 6]
> Lit. 'One fully accomplished in seeing' (Pali)

Nangsao (Thai: นางสาว) [Ch. 1]
> Miss

nangsu anuson ngaansop (Thai: หนังสืออนุสรณ์งานศพ, Pali: *anussaraṇa*) [Ch. 1]
> Lit. 'book of funeral remembrance'. A cremation volume, being a life record of the deceased highlighting their virtuous activities, prepared as a book and distributed at their cremation.

Napakadol Posanacharoern (Thai: ณภคดล โปษรณจริญ) [Ch. 1]
> Fuengsin's nephew, taught various school subjects by Fuengsin when she was at Thonburi Technical College.

Nareepol (Thai: นารีผล, Pali: *phala*) [Ch. 12]
> Lit. 'Fruit girl'. Fruit that resemble young maidens referred to in the Thai version of the Vessantara Jataka

Nibbana (Thai: นิพพาน, Pali: *nibbāna*) [Ch. 8]
> Enlightenment, lit. 'extinguishing' (Pali). More commonly known in English by its Sanskrit equivalent, *nirvana*, it refers to the blowing out of that which sustains Samsaric existence (symbolised as three fires of greed, hatred and delusion). In Thai, reference to an arahat who still lives and breathes is อนุปาทิเสส, Pali: *anupādiseso* (one without clinging).

Nikāya (Thai: นิกาย, Pali: *Nikāya*) [Ch. 10]
> Group or collection. Collection of Buddhist texts; also a division within formal Thai Sangha

Nikāya Theravāda (Thai: นิกายเถรวาท, Pali: Nikāya Theravāda) [Ch. 5]
> Theravadin. Practitioner of Theravada (defined primarily in terms of the Sangha)

paathung (Thai: ผ้าถุง) [Ch. 8]
> batik — traditional silk brocade, probably to be made as a skirt or sarong

Padmasambhava (Thai: ปัทมสัมภวะ) [Ch. 12]
> Meaning 'lotus-born', regarded as a Guru Rinpoche, 'Precious Master' and the one who firmly established Tibetan Buddhism

Pah (Thai: ป้า) [Ch. 1]
> Aunt — mother or father's elder sister, as referred by a nephew or niece

Pali (Thai: บาลี) [Ch. 2]
> Pali is the 'language of the text', a written approximation of what was considered to be the colloquial language used by the Buddha in his teachings (approximates to Magadhi).

pañña (Thai: ปัญญา, Pali: *pañña*) [Ch. 11]
> wisdom

Phra Ajahn **Paññavaddho** (Thai: พระอาจารย์ปัญญาวัฑโฒ, Pali: *Paññavaddho*) [Ch. 8]
> He who spreads wisdom. A disciple of Ven. Kapilavaddho, also ordained at Wat Paknam, later emigrated to Thailand in the early 1960s to spend the rest of his life with Luang Ta Maha Boowa at Wat Pah Baan Taad.

Paôy Pêt (or **Poipet**) (Thai: ปอยเปต) [Ch. 8]
> Border town in Cambodia, near Aranyaprathet

Pārāmī (Thai: บารมี, Pali: *pārāmī*) [Ch. 2]
> Perfections. Specific qualities, such as generosity and wisdom, whose perfection are required to become fully Enlightened. In Theravada Buddhism there are 10 specified.

Paticcasamuppada (Thai: ปฏิจจสมุปบาท, Pali: *paṭiccasamuppāda*) [Ch. 10]
> Dependent Origination. Fundamental Buddhist teaching about conditions arising in dependence on other conditions, the engine for the unsatisfactory wheel of existence.

Phra **Patimokh** (Thai: พระปาฏิโมกข์, Pali: *Pāṭimokkha*) [Ch. 2]
> Patimokkha. A set of rules of training formally instituted by the Buddha to support practice. It gradually evolved during his lifetime until it consisted of 227 rules for bhikkhus and 311 for bhikkhunis and was incorporated in the Vinaya.

Phi (or simply **P'**) (Thai: พี่) [Ch. 1]
> (Prefix for) Elder brother or sister. For addressing monastics, this is often prefixed by 'Luang', hence 'Luang Phi'.

Phirapnong (Thai: พี่รับน้อง) [Ch. 3]

Lit. 'elder brothers and sisters welcome junior brothers and sisters'. Organising group to welcome newcomers [at university].

Phra (Thai: พระ, Pali: bara (for vara)) [Ch. 1]

Excellent, noble, holy, revered, venerable. A very frequently used prefix for anything or anyone holy. When used alone it can be shorthand for a Buddha image or monk. A term of respect principally applied with religious conotation, meaning holy or revered, but also applied to members of royalty in their formal titles.

Phra Pathom Chedi (Thai: พระปฐมเจดีย์) [Ch. 3]

Lit. 'the primary holy stupa', an ancient historical site with archaeological evidence relating to Buddhist practice dating back more than 2,000 years

Phra Prang Sam Yod (Thai: พระปรางค์สามยอด) [Ch. 3]

Lit. 'Three Holy Towers'. Khmer religious site, of early Hindu significance

Chao Khun **Phramongkolthepmuni** (Thai: เจ้าคุณพระมงคลเทพมุนี) [Ch. 4]

The last royal title to be conferred on Bhikkhu Sodh Candasaro, according to the formal system administered by the Supreme Sangha Council of Thailand. Often the ordained name would be appended to provide the full name.

Phra Bhikhsu [Pesala] Luang **Pichit Chaloton (Lam Kanitatham piti)** (Thai: พระภิกษุหลวง พิชิต ชโลธร (หลำ กนิฏฐภิติ)) [Ch. 3]

Most Ven. Pichit Chaloton was a highly revered monk who taught advanced meditation in Wat Sanghachai, in a soi off Phet Kasem road in the Bangkok Yai district in Thonburi, about 1.5 miles from Fuengsin's family home in Wongwien Yai. He published a series of discourses with the title 'Discourse on the knowledge of Dhamma according to the practice of samatha and Vipassana kamatthana'.

Pii tii Wai Kru nai longrien (Thai: พิธีไหว้ครูในโรงเรียน) [Ch. 2]

Ceremony of performing wai to schoolteacher, i.e. Teachers' Day Ceremony

Poltho (Thai: พลตรี) [Ch. 1]

Lieutenant General

Prachā (Thai: ประชา) [Ch. 10]

People, citizens

Prajnaparamita [Skt] (Thai: ปรัชญาปารมิตา) [Ch. 12]

Perfection of Wisdom

Ajahn **Prakhong** (Thai: อาจารย์ประคอง) [Ch. 4]

Lit. 'supports or helps', Fuengsin's close friend in meditation in Thailand, who was the one who first took her to Wat Paknam

Prathom suksa (Thai: ประถมศึกษา) [Ch. 2]

Primary study, i.e. primary education in Thailand, which consists of six years of study

Preta (Thai: เปรต, Pali: *peta*) [Ch. 11]

Departed spirit, hungry ghost. Thais generally believe that there is a realm of petas, an unfortunate realm, where there are unsatiated desires for food, hence the term 'hungry ghost'

Puja (Thai: บูชา, Pali: *pūjā*) [Ch. 8]

Devotional practice, including bowing, making offerings and chanting

Rai chue phubanchakan ruean chamklang Ratburi (Thai: รายชื่อ ผู้บัญชาการ เรือนจำกลางราชบุรี) [Ch. 2]

List of Commanders of Ratchaburi Central Prison

Pho Khun **Ram Khamhaeng** (Thai: พ่อขุนรามคำแหงมหาราช) [Ch. 2]

The third king of the Phra Ruang dynasty, ruling the Sukhothai Kingdom (a forerunner of the modern kingdom of Thailand) from 1278–98.

ranard ek (Thai: ระนาดเอก) [Ch. 11]

Thai percussion instrument — a kind of xylophone where wooden bars are struck with small mallets.

Ratanakosin Sok (Thai: รัตนโกสินทร์ศก) [Ch. 1]

Ratanakosin Era, abbreviated as ร.ศ. (RE) A system of counting dating to the start of the reign of King Rama I in 1782.

Ratchaburi (or Rajburi) (Thai: ราชบุรี) [Ch. 2]

Lit. 'the royal land', a central province in Thailand to the West of Bangkok, in Thai pronounced 'Rardburi'

Ratchadamnoen (or Raj[a]damnoen) (Thai: ราชดำเนิน) [Ch. 1]

Lit. 'royal avenue', an avenue in central Bangkok, perhaps best known for including the Democracy Monument

Ratchadamnoen Klang (Thai: ราชดำเนิน กลาง) [Ch. 11]

Central royal avenue. The main section of Ratchadamnoen, an avenue in central Bangkok.

Rayong (Thai: ระยอง) [Ch. 3]

An Eastern Seaboard province, roughly 200–300 km to the southeast of Bangkok

Rewata Dhamma, Ven. Dr [Ch. 9]

Burmese bhikkhu, who came to England in 1975 to establish a Buddhist vihara in Birmingham. He was abbot of that vihara until his passing in May 2004.

Roshi Jiyu-Kennett [Ch. 9]

Trained in Japan and founder of the Order of Buddhist Contemplatives, in the Soto Zen tradition. She was Vajira's teacher.

Samatha (Thai: สมถะ) [Ch. 4]

Pali term for calm abiding and quietude necessary to sustain meditation insight

samathi (Thai: สมาธิ, Pali: *samādhi*) [Ch. 2]

Meditative concentration. A calm and collected state of mind in which a practitioner can investigate further the mind and the nature of things

samma araham (Thai: สัมมา อะระหัง, Pali: *samma arahaŋ*) [Ch. 15]
>A mantra used in the Dhammakaya tradition; it is a reference to the highest state a human can achieve

San Phrabhumi (Thai: ศาลพระภูมิ) [Ch. 2]
>Spirit house

Luang Na **San Tippasanto** (Thai: หลวงน้าสันต์ ทิพพสนุโต, Pali: *sandhi*) [Ch. 11]
>Lit. 'one who breaks [wheel of Samsara]', Fuengsin's main teacher of Dhammakaya meditation from 1988, following the passing of Ajahn Gaew

Phra **Sangha** (Thai: พระสงฆ์) [Ch. 1]
>The Sangha monastic community, one of the Triple Gem, refers to those who have formally undertaken to observe rules of training as instituted by the Buddha. In Western literature we may refer to them as 'monks'.

Maha Sthavira **Sangharakshita** (Thai: มหาสถวีระ สังฆรักษิต) [Ch. 9]
>Usually known as Sangharakshita (lay name Dennis Lingwood), founder and long-time spiritual guide of the Friends of the Western Buddhist Order, established in the UK in 1967.

Sanghathan (Thai: สังฆทาน, Pali: *Sanghadāna*) [Ch. 2]
>Gifts for the [monastic] community. Charitable offerings to Sangha members, which may include food and requisites; *dāna*, a central concept in Buddhist practice, means 'giving' in a complete sense; it is the first of 10 *pārāmī* (Perfections).

Sangwal or Sangwan (Thai: สังวาลย์) [Ch. 1]
>The given name of the Princess Mother

Phra Ajahn **Sanong Katapunyo** (Thai: พระอาจารย์สนอง กตปุญฺโญ) (1944-2012) [Ch. 12]
>Long-time abbot of Wat Sanghathan (from the 1970s), who set up several temples overseas including one in Birmingham, under the same name (but later name changed for legal reasons).

Roy Ek Luang **Sarayutpitag** (Thai: ร้อยเอก หลวงศรายุทธพิทักษ์) [Ch. 1]
>Capt. Luang Sarayutpitag. Fuengsin's father (formal title, as a member of the Thai nobility)

sati (Thai: สติ, Pali: *sati*) [Ch. 11]
>mindfulness

satipañña (Thai: สติปัญญา, Pali: *satipaññā*) [Ch. 11]
>Mindfulness endowed with wisdom, an approach emphasised in the Thai Forest Tradition, especially promoted by Luang Ta Maha Boowa.

Rongrien **Satri Witthaya** (Thai: โรงเรียนสตรีวิทยา) [Ch. 1]
>Satri Witthaya School (lit. 'A School for Ladies Knowledge-learning')

Sawasdee (Thai: สวัสดี) [Ch. 2]
>Hello, goodbye. A standard greeting, with polite form having suffix 'khrub' for men and 'ka' for women.

Siam (Thai: สยาม) [Ch. 1]
>An exonym for Thailand used as far back as the early European explorers

and traders, possibly before. It became associated with indigenous ethnic peoples in what is now central and southern Thailand.

Siddhattha Gotama (Thai: สิทธัตถะ โคตะมะ, Pali: *Siddhattha Gotama* [Skt. *Siddhārtha Gautama*]) [Ch. 1]

Siddhattha Gotama. The Buddha's family name was Gotama and his given name was Siddhattha.

sila (Thai: ศีล, Pali: *sīla*) [Ch. 2]

Actually pronounced 'sin' in Thai, *sila* means 'moral virtue' and is the basis of Buddhist ethical practice

Sima (Thai: สีมา, Pali: *sīmā*) [Ch. 3]

Boundary

Sin ha (Thai: ศีลห้า, Pali: *pañca-sīlāni*) [Ch. 6]

Five Precepts (or moral virtues). The rules of training undertaken by lay Buddhists: refraining from taking life, from that which is not given, from sexual misconduct, from false speech and from taking intoxicants, which lead to heedlessness.

Sing[k]alovadasutra [Skt.] (Thai: สิงคาโลวาทสูตร, Pali: *Sigalovada Sutta*) [Ch. 10]

Sutta of the Speech to Sigala. Teaching given to a householder, Sigala, on how to conduct wholesome relationships, characterised in terms of six directions, each representing a relationship type, such as parent–child.

Sodh Candasaro (Thai: สดจนฺทสโร) [Ch. 4]

The given first name (Sodh, meaning 'fresh') and ordained name (*Candasaro*, from the Pali, means 'radiant like the moon') of the late Abbot of Wat Paknam, the one who rediscovered the Dhammakaya tradition in 1917 and taught the method at the Wat until he passed away in 1959; the teacher of Ajahn Gaew, Fuengsin's meditation teacher. See *Life and Times of Luang Phaw Wat Paknam*.

Soi (Thai: ซอย) [Ch. 2]

Lane or side street. A side-street of a main road and its branches, forming a small community area.

Phra Maha **Somboon** (Thai: พระมหาสมบูรณ์) [Ch. 10]

A Thai Dhammaduta monk, serving in the UK since 1968 (the longest for any Thai monk), Abbot of Wolverhampton Buddha Vihara since 1982.

Somboon Rukyati (Thai: สมบุญ รักญาติ) [Ch. 1]

Miss Somboon Rukyati (lit. 'well-matched in virtue' + 'loves relations'). Fuengsin's mother, later Mrs Somboon Sarayutpitag

Somdet (Thai: สมเด็จ) [Ch. 1]

His/Her Majesty, can be applied in lay and religious context for the most senior clergy.

Somdet Phrajao Taksin Maharaj (Thai: สมเด็จพระเจ้าตากสินมหาราช) [Ch. 1]

King Taksin, the ruler of Thonburi Kingdom, 1767–82, during which Burmese were repulsed and Thailand was unified

Somdet Phra Srinagarindra Boromarajajonani (Thai: สมเด็จพระศรีนครินทราบ
รมราชชนนี) [Ch. 1]

Her Majesty Srinagarindra Boromarajajonani, the royal title for the
Princes Mother, the mother to H.M. King Bhumibol

Phra Bat **Somdet Phra Poramentharamaha Vajiravudh Phra Mongkut Klao
Chao Yu Hua** (Thai: พระบาทสมเด็จพระปรเมนทรมหาวชิราวุธฯ พระมงกุฎเกล้า
เจ้าอยู่หัว) [Ch. 1]

King Vajiravudh of Thailand (King Rama VI), ruled 1920-1935, was educated at Eton and Christ Church, Oxford. He established Chulalongkorn
University as the first university in Thailand.

Phra Bat **Somdet Phra Poramintharamaha Prajadhipok Phra Pok Klao Chao Yu
Hua** (Thai: พระบาทสมเด็จพระปรมินทรมหาประชาธิปกฯ พระปกเกล้าเจ้าอยู่หัว)

King Prajadhipok (Rama VII), the last king to serve as an absolute mon-
arch of Thailand

Songkran (Thai: สงกรานต์) [Ch. 2]

The Thai (lunar) New Year, usually fixed in the calendar for 13 April and
running for three days

Sri Racha (or Siracha, becoming Silacha) (Thai: ศรีราชา) [Ch. 3]

A subdistrict of Chonburi, known for its eponymous hot sauce

Kruba **Srivichai** (Thai: ครูบาศรีวิชัย) [Ch. 10]

Teacher Srivichai. A famous Thai monk (1878–1938), known for his virtuous conduct and coordination of many temple projects in Northern Thailand, particularly around Wat Phrathat Doi Suthep.

Suan nung kong chao Budh Nai Angrit (Thai: ส่วนหนึ่งของชาวพุทธในอังกฤษ)
[Ch. 6]

Some Buddhists in England. The title given to Fuengsin's survey of Buddhists, mainly in Hampshire, carried out in the late 1960s and submitted
as a contribution to her father's cremation volume.

Phra **Sunthorn Vohara (Sunthorn Phu)** (Thai: พระสุนทรโวหาร (สุนทรภู่)) [Ch.
11]

Royal Thai poet who served in the courts of King Rama II and King Rama
III, during the Rattanakosin era, in the first half of the nineteenth century CE, and was famous for epic verse.

Surapan (Thai: สุรพันธ์) [Ch. 1]

Fuengsin's brother, nickname 'Lek'

Surat Thani (Thai: สุราษฎร์ธานี) [Ch. 11]

The largest of the southern provinces of Thailand, on the western shore
of the Gulf of Thailand. The main town has the same name.

Phra **Sutra** (Thai: พระสูตร, Pali: *sutta*) [Ch. 10]

Suttas — general teachinsg of the Buddha given to lay and ordained alike

Tak-roh (Thai: ตะกร้อ) [Ch. 11]

Rattan ball. Usually played bare-foot, this is the traditional Thai football
and still very popular.

Tan Ajahn (Thai: ท่านอาจารย์) [Ch. 6]

A respectful way of referring to a monastic teacher

Tewee Bodhiphala (Thai: เทวี โพธิพละ) [Ch. 2]

Lit. 'Queen/Princess' Bodhiphala, Fuengsin's childhood friend/neighbour

Tha akaatyan Don Muang (Thai: ท่าอากาศยานดอนเมือง) [Ch. 5]

Don Muang International Airport. Thailand's principal international airport until the opening of Suvarnabhumi in 2006, when it became a domestic airport only. It lies in the northern suburbs of Bangkok.

That (Thai: ธาตุ, Pali: *dhātu*) [Ch. 10]

Element, property. This term can be variably used to refer to conditioned and unconditioned elements

Phra **That** (Thai: พระธาตุ, Pali: *vara dhātu*) [Ch. 10]

Holy relics, normally in reference to those of the Buddha and his disciples

Thate (Thai: เทศน์, Pali: *desanā*) [Ch. 6]

Discourse, collection of teachings. In this context it means 'a discourse from the collection of teachings of the Buddha'. Note the Thai symbol makes the last syllable silent, so you can't actually tell how to spell just from the way it is spoken.

Thengatha (Thai: เถรคาถา, Pali: *Theragāthā*) [Ch. 12]

Verses of the Elder bhikkhus (monks). The eighth book of the Khuddaka Nikaya, consisting of poems in which the bhikkhus relate key episodes and experiences on their individual path to arahantship.

Thera (Thai: เถระ, Pali: *Thera*) [Ch. 5]

Elder. Title for a senior monastic, usually one who has been in robes at least 10 years.

Theravāda (Thai: เถรวาท, Pali: *Theravāda*) [Ch. 5]

[Of] the original doctrine of the Elders. The oldest surviving branch of Buddhism, considered by many practitioners in Southeast Asia and Pali scholars, at least, to be fairly close to what was practised at the time of the Buddha

Therigatha (Thai: เถรีคาถา, Pali: Therigāthā) [Ch. 12]

Verses of the Elder bhikkhunis (nuns). The eighth book of the Khuddaka Nikaya, consisting of poems in which the bhikkhunis relate their experiences on the path to nibbāna.

Thonburi (Thai: ธนบุรี) [Ch. 1]

An urbanised area, formerly a town and then city before becoming part of Bangkok in 1970

Lama **Thubten** [Ch. 9]

Resident Lama at the Tibetan Buddhist centre, Karma Ling, Birmingham, until his passing in 1989.

Thudong (Thai: ธุดงค์, Pali: *dhutanga*) [Ch. 2]

Wandering ascetic. Dhutanga practices involve a particularly scrupulous way of living and practising the Buddhist path, characterised by wandering from place to place to avoid attachments.

Trilakkh (Thai: ไตรลักษณ์, Pali: *tilakkhaṇa*) [Ch. 12]

Three characteristics of existence: *anicca*, *dukkha* and *anatta* (see individual entries)

Phra **Tripidok** (Thai: พระไตรปิฎก, Pali: *Tripitaka*) [Ch. 10]

Lit. 'three baskets', the Pali Buddhist canon for the Southern Schools, nominally Theravada. It comprises the *vinaya*, *suttas* and *abhidhamma*.

Tuk Vised Dhammakaya (Thai: ตึกวิเศษธรรมกาย) [Ch. 11]

Lit. 'Splendid Dhammakaya Building', completed in 1979 in the grounds of Wat Paknam, comprises a library, museum and monks' accommodation

Umpai (Thai: อำไพ) [Ch. 1]

Fuengsin's third eldest sister

Upasok, Upasika (Thai: อุบาสก, อุบาสิกา, Pali: *upāsaka*, *upāsikā*) [Ch. 3]

Upasaka (masculine) or upasika (feminine) are formerly committed lay followers of the Buddha who undertake to keep a discipline of minimally five precepts or rules of training, more commonly eight precepts. This derives from the Buddha, who formally classified his followers in four categories: bhikkhus, bhikkhunis, upasakas and upasikas. In Thailand they typically dress simply and wear white at the temple, but when outside the temple they may wear clothes more conventional in society.

Vajira (Thai: วชิชิร, Pali: vajira) [Ch. 9]

thunderbolt; diamond. A pioneer of Buddhism in the Midlands, Vajira (lay name Dorothy Bailey) has practised in Theravada, received her ordained name in FWBO, and then went on to ordain in Soto Zen tradition.

Vasana Kamkoon (Thai: วาสนาค้ำคูณ) [Ch. 3]

Vasana Kamkoon (Mrs.). Close friend of Fuengsin from Chula and remained so for rest of her life

vata-songsarn (Thai: วัฏสงสาร, Pali: *Saṃsāra*) [Ch. 6]

Wheel of Samsara (lit. an eternal going round and round). The perpetual cycle of existence, a phrase when used in Buddhist context is associated with a state of unsatisfactoriness; Buddhist Englightenment leads to release from Saṃsāra; if something is pitiable, Thais say 'na songsarn' (Thai: น่าสงสาร).

Vesak[h] Puja (Thai: วิสาขบูชา) [Ch. 8]

Vesak. Commemoration of the Buddha's birth, Enlightenment, and passing, usually in May for Thai calendar

Maha **Vessantara Jataka** (Thai: มหาเวสสันดรชาดก, Pali: *Mahā Vessantara Jātaka*) [Ch. 12]

The account of the Bodhisattva Vesantara who was later to become Buddha Gotama

Phra Maha **Vichitr Tissadatto** (Thai: พระมหาวิจิตร ติสสทตฺโต) [Ch. 5]

The first abbot of Wat Buddhapadipa, 1965–69, during which time he received the royal title of Chao Khun Sobhana Dhammasudhi. He later disrobed, but continued to teach meditation under the name Dhiravaṃsa.

Vijja (Thai: วิชชา, Pali: *vijjā*) [Ch. 4]

In the Buddhist context, it means 'advanced seeing and knowledge relating to Dhamma'

Vijja Dhammakaya (Thai: วิชชาธรรมกาย, Pali: *vijjā dhammakāya*) [Ch. 4]

The method of meditation associated with the direct attainment of Enlightenment and Buddhahood according to the Middle Way (as practised by Fuengsin)

Vijja Horasat (Thai: วิชชาโหราศาสตร์) [Ch. 4]

Advanced astrology. Astrology has long been widely practised in Thailand and was often learnt in conjunction with traditional medicine.

vijja mogpol pitsadaan (Thai: วิชชามรรคผลพิสดาร, Pali: *vijja magga phala*) [Ch. 11]

'Special insights of the Path and its fruits'. Two volumes on advanced meditation published by Wat Paknam in 1974 with contents similar to the Blue Book dictated by Ajahn Gaew to nuns for presentation to Fuengsin in 1972, with some variations in content.

Phra **Vinay Pidok** (Thai: พระวินัยปิฎก, Pali: *vara vinaya pitaka*)

The Vinaya rules of training for monastics

Vipassana (Thai: วิปัสสนา, Pali: *vipassanā*) [Ch. 4]

Insight (based on seeing) into the supramundane

Wah (Thai: วา, abbreviated ว.) [Ch. 1]

Wah is a unit of length equal to 2 metres

Wai (Thai: ไหว้) [Ch. 2]

Standard Thai greeting and paying respects. It involves bowing slightly with palms together, the position of the hands raised according to the respect being conveyed (touching forehead for monks and elders).

Wat (Thai: วัด) [Ch. 1]

Monastery or temple. Thailand has officially about 30,000 monasteries, which are the residences of the monastic community

Wat Anongkaram (Thai: วัดอนงคาราม) [Ch. 1]

Temple in Thonburi with family associations for the Sarayutpitag household

Wat Bot Bon Bangkuwien (Thai: วัดโบสถ์บนบางคูเวียง) [Ch. 12]

The temple in Nonthaburi where Luang Phor Sodh first attained to Dhammakaya.

Wat Buddhapadīpa (Thai: วัดพุทธปทีป) [Ch. 5]

Lit. 'Monastery of the Buddha lamp', the official Thai temple in the UK under royal sponsorship

Wat Khao Mai Daeng (Thai: วัดเขาไม้แดง) [Ch. 6]

Lit. 'Red Wood Hill Monastery', A small monastery on a hill in Chon Buri province, sponsored by Khun Yay Somboon Sarayutpitag.

Wat Mahathat (Thai: วัดมหาธาตุ, Pali: *mahā dhatu*) [Ch. 5]
Lit. 'Great Elements (relics)', a royal monastery known for its education and training. It has long had an international outlook, with many students from the West.

Wat Pah Baan Taad (Thai: วัดป่าบ้านตาด) [Ch. 6]
The monastery established by Phra Maha Boowa in Udon Thani province, Northeast Thailand

Wat Pah Santidhamma (Thai: วัดป่าสันติธรรม) [Ch. 10]
Lit. 'Forest Monastery of Peaceful Dhamma'. The Forest Hermitage is the more commonly known name in the UK

Wat Paknam Bhasicharoen (Thai: วัดปากน้ำภาษีเจริญ) [Ch. 4]
Lit. 'Water gate monastery, at the place of superior development', the temple is named after its location, which is near to a lock on a canal named Bhasicharoen

Wat Phra Dhammakaya (Thai: วัดพระธรรมกาย) [Ch. 15]
Lit. 'Temple of the Holy Dhammakaya', a very large temple in the Dhammakaya tradition, located in Pathum Thani, some 30 miles from the centre of Bangkok. It was established by Khun Yay Ajahn Maharattana Upasika Chandra Khonnokyoong after she ran out of space to teach all her students at Wat Paknam.

Wat Phra That Doi Suthep (Thai: วัดพระธาตุดอยสุเทพ) [Ch. 10]
A temple named after the mountain on which it is situated, a popular pilgrimage site containing Buddha relics.

Wat Sanghathan (Thai: วัดสังฆทาน) [Ch. 12]
Temple in Nonthaburi, reinvigorated by Ven. Ajahn Sanong Katapunnyo

Wat Santidhammaram, Tambol Samre (Thai: วัดสนติธรรมาราม ตำบล สำเหร่) [Ch. 3]
Temple near to Fuengsin's home, where she was taught by Phra Luang Pichit.

Wat Thepsirin (Thai: วัดเทพศิรินทร์) [Ch. 1]
A royal Thai temple of the Second Class

Rongrien **Wattana Suksa** (Thai: โรงเรียนวัฒนะศึกษา) [Ch. 2]
Wattana Suksa School

Wayam'ra (Thai: วะยามระ) [Ch. 1]
The first title given to Fuengsin's father, received during the reign of King Rama VI

Wijit (Thai: วิจิตรา) [Ch. 1]
Fuengsin's eldest sister

Wilai (Thai: วิไล) [Ch. 1]
Fuengsin's second eldest sister

Witiyalai Technik Thonburi (Thai: วิทยาลัยเทคนิคธนบุรี) [Ch. 4]
Thonburi Technical College. The College was established on 4 Feburary

1960. It was where Fuengsin started full-time work on graduating with a BEd from Chula. It eventually became KMUTT.

Wolverhampton Buddha Vihara [Ch. 10]

A vihara in the West Midlands established in 1976 by followers of Dr Ambedkar. The abbot has since the early 1980s been Ven. Phra Maha Somboon.

Wongwien Yai (Thai: วงเวียนใหญ่) [Ch. 1]

An area of Thonburi, named after a large roundabout, a major traffic intersection that lies in central Bangkok, close to the Memorial Bridge

Yoga (Thai: โยคะ) [Ch. 6]

Lit. 'connection, relation, bond' (Pali). Yoga has many meanings in a Buddhist context: as a general path of practice, to specific meditative exercises. In the Dhammakaya tradition it is used mainly conventionally, as physical exercise to attune mind and body.

Phra Ajahn **Yongyuth** (Thai: ยงยุทธ) [Ch. 6]

Founder and Abbot of Wat Khao Mai Daeng; a cousin of Fuengsin, who passed away in 2545 (2002)

Bibliography

This section contains a small collection of books that Fuengsin used in her teaching plus a few other related titles, a few shown with more recent editions. Also included are some journal publications.

Blofeld, John 1972. *The Wheel of Life: The Autobiography of a Western Buddhist*, 2nd edition, Rider & Company

Blofeld, John 1977. *Compassion Yoga: The Mystical Cult of Kuan Yin*, Unwin Paperbacks

Conze, Edward 1988. *Buddhist Wisdom Books: The Diamond and the Heart Sutra*, Mandala, Unwin Paperbacks

Dhammakaya Foundation 2010. *Life and Times of Luang Phaw Wat Paknam*, 4th edition, Pathum Thani: Dhammakaya Foundation
http://en.dhammakayapost.org/book/?p=25

Dhammakaya Foundation 2005. *Second to None: The Biography of Khun Yay Maharatana Upasika Chandra Khon-nok-yoong*, Pathum Thani: Dhammakaya Foundation
http://en.dhammakayapost.org/book/?p=19

Goldstein, Joseph 1976. *The Experience of Insight: A Natural Unfolding*, Unity Press

Hart, William 1987. *The Art of Living — Vipassana Meditation as Taught by S. N. Goenka*, San Francisco: Harper & Row

Hume, David 1777 and 1751. *Enquiries concerning Human Understanding and concerning the Principles of Morals*, P. H. N. (ed.), 3rd. ed. (1975), Oxford: Clarendon Press

Khema, Ayya 1991. *When the Iron Eagle Flies: Buddhism for the West*, Penguin Arkana

Kornfield, Jack 1977. *Living Buddhist Masters*, Unity Press

Nārada, 1980. *The Buddha and His Teachings*, 4th edition, Colombo: Vajirarama

Olson, Grant A. 1992. *Thai Cremation Volumes: A Brief History of a Unique Genre of Literature*, Asian Folklore Studies, Volume 51, pp. 279-294
http://nirc.nanzan-u.ac.jp/publications/afs/pdf/a917.pdf

Phramongkolthepmuni (1949, 1951, 1953-1955), Phrapalad Sudham Sudhammo (ed.) 2006. *Visuddhivācā, Translation of Morradok Dhamma (Dhamma Heritage) of Luang Phaw Wat Pak Nam Phramongkolthepmuni*, 60th Dhammachai Education Foundation, Dhammakaya Foundation, Thailand

Phramongkolthepmuni (1953, 1954), Phrapalad Sudham Sudhammo (ed.) 2008. *Visuddhivācā, Translation of Morradok Dhamma (Dhamma Heritage) of Luang Phaw*

Wat Pak Nam Phramongkolthepmuni, Volumes I and II, 60th Dhammachai Education Foundation, Dhammakaya Foundation, Thailand
http://en.dhammakayapost.org/book/?p=33

Rahula, Walpola Sri 1967. *What the Buddha Taught*, 2nd edition, Gordon Fraser

Randall, Richard 1990. *Life as a Siamese Monk*, Aukana

Rowlands, Mark (ed.) 1982. *Abhidhamma Papers*, Samatha Trust

Sangharakshita 1987. *A Survey of Buddhism: Its Doctrines and Methods through the Ages*, 6th edition, Tharpa Publications

Sangharakshita 1996. *The Three Jewels: An Introduction to Buddhism*, 3rd edition, Windhorse

Siddhiyanvidesh, Ven. Phrakhru [Phramaha Somboon Siddhiyano] 2009. *Odds and Ends*, Wolverhampton Buddha Vihara

Sogyal Rinpoche 1992. *The Tibetan Book of Living and Dying*, Harper Collins (HarperOne)

Sumedho, Ven. Ajahn 1992. *The Way It Is*, Amaravati Publications; reprint edition
http://www.amaravati.org/documents/the_way_it_is/index.html

Suzuki, Shunryu 1970. *Zen Mind, Beginner's Mind*, Weatherhill

Tate, Ven. Ajahn (Ed. Ariyesako Bhikkhu) 1993. *The Autobiography of a Forest Monk*, Wat Hin Mark Peng, Nong Khai

Thich Nhat Hanh (trans. Mobi Quynh Hoa) 1976. *The Miracle of Being Awake: A Manual on Meditation for the use of young activists*, Kandy: Buddhist Publication Society

Trafford, Fuengsin 1993. *Buddhist students in the United Kingdom* In: The Journal of International Education, Vol. 4, No. 1, UK Council for International Education

Various authors 1977. *Crystal Mirror V*, Emeryville: Dharma Press

Wingate, Andrew 1997. *A Woman of Faith Dies: Death of a Champion of Buddhism*, Volume 100, No. 75, pp 170-179. Reproduced online with permission:
http://fuengsin.org/tributes/theology/

Wingate, Andrew 2005. *Celebrating Difference, Staying Faithful: How to Live in a Multi-Faith World*, Darton, Longman and Todd

Illustration Credits

The author acknowledges the following sources for images used in this biography.

Rear cover: flowers from a vector graphic created by Lee Namwook and Kim Haejin of Creyong

Figure 1: Royal Thai Household — Princess Mother Museum of Satri Withaya School, Bangkok

Figures 20 and 99: Chulalongkorn University Faculty of Arts Alumni Association

Figure 43: KMUTT Archive

Figure 46: Potikanok family

Figure 56: *Y Cymro*

Figures 58 and 59: Judith Weyland

Figure 86: Phil Loach for the County Express

Figure 98: USPG College of the Ascension, Birmingham

Figures 100 and 101: Middle Way Meditation Institute, Pathum Thani, Thailand.

Index

About the Author

Paul Trafford, Fuengsin's son, lives in Oxford, where he works at the Museum of the History of Science. He holds postgraduate degrees in mathematics, computer science and the study of religion, and has spent most of his working life in higher education. His career has been mainly in the field of I.T., where he has created bespoke Web applications such as multimedia language-learning tools. He has also conducted research in e-learning and mobile technologies, including collaboration with Gakushuin University in Tokyo on teaching mathematics to business students. In the heritage and culture sector, he has developed Web interfaces to museum collection management systems, particularly for the Qatar Museums Authority, living in Doha between the summers of 2012 and 2014. He thereby gained new insights into cultural factors affecting large organisations with diverse employee backgrounds and the Middle East more generally.

Following a little in his mother's footsteps as a 'second-generation' inter-faith worker, Paul has offered his services, mainly as a volunteer, in Buddhism and interfaith. He served as a member of the fundraising team for the University of Derby's Multi-Faith Centre, where he was also Buddhist Faith Advisor, and went on to act as a Trustee of the International Interfaith Centre in Oxford. These organisations have supported him in many activities at home and abroad, enabling him to give presentations on the use of technology to support online communities, to encourage young people to explore interfaith, through to sharing reflections on aspects of palliative care. He is also a founding Director of the Dhammakaya International Society of the UK, which promotes meditation for inner peace as a means to world peace. Presently he is conducting interdisciplinary research in the application of Buddhist ethics, particularly to the design of social networking sites.

55966302R00199

Made in the USA
Charleston, SC
12 May 2016